# RITES OF RETALIATION

# THE STEVEN AND JANICE BROSE LECTURES IN THE CIVIL WAR ERA

*Rachel Shelden, editor*

*William A. Blair, founding editor*

The Steven and Janice Brose Lectures in the Civil War Era are published by the University of North Carolina Press in association with the George and Ann Richards Civil War Era Center at Penn State University. The series features books based on public lectures by a distinguished scholar, delivered over a three-day period each fall, as well as edited volumes developed from public symposia. These books chart new directions for research in the field and offer scholars and general readers fresh perspectives on the Civil War era.

LORIEN FOOTE

# RITES OF RETALIATION

## CIVILIZATION, SOLDIERS, AND CAMPAIGNS in the American Civil War

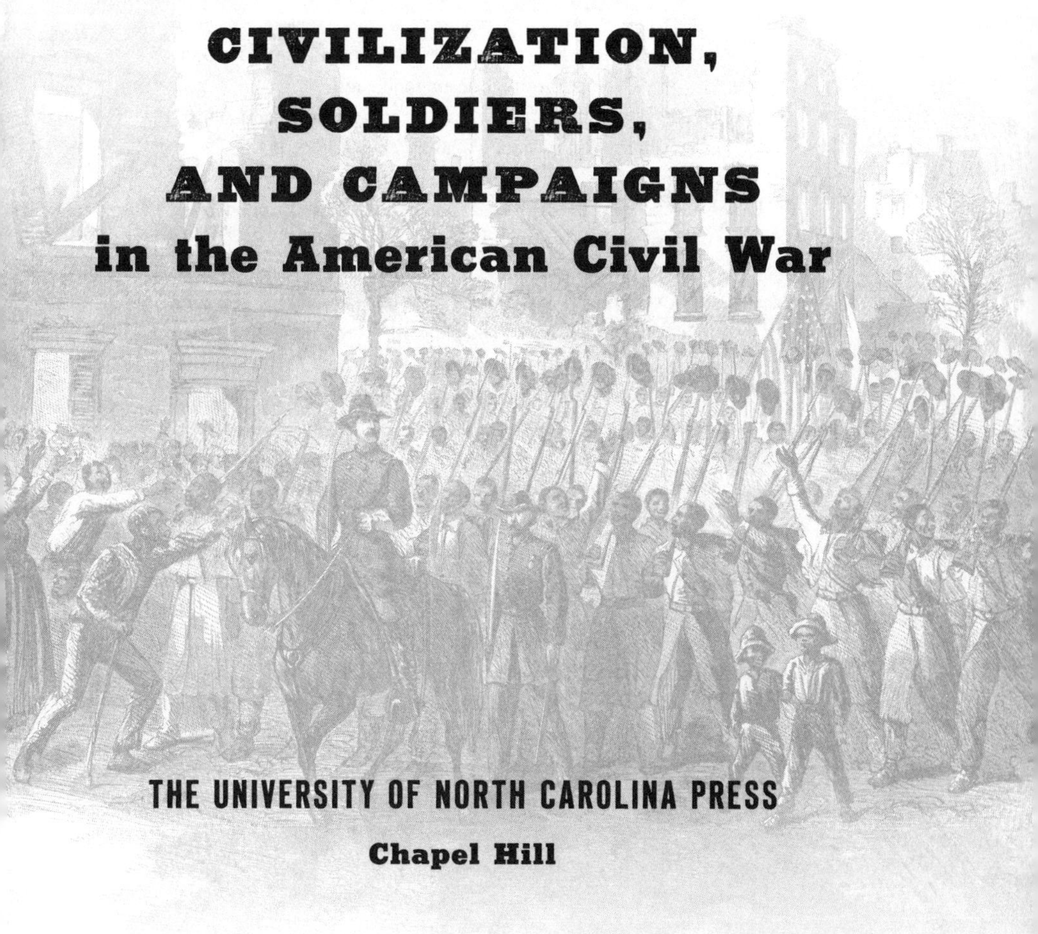

THE UNIVERSITY OF NORTH CAROLINA PRESS

Chapel Hill

This book was published with the assistance of the George and Ann Richards Civil War Era Center at Penn State University.



Designed by Jamison Cockerham
Set in Arno, Scala Sans, Irby, Gatlin Bold, and Cutright Bold
by Tseng Information Systems, Inc.

*Manufactured in the United States of America*

The University of North Carolina Press has been a member of the Green Press Initiative since 2003.

Cover illustration: From *Harper's Weekly*, March 18, 1865. Courtesy Library of Congress

LIBRARY OF CONGRESS CATALOGING-IN-PUBLICATION DATA
Names: Foote, Lorien, 1969– author.
Title: Rites of retaliation : civilization, soldiers, and campaigns in the American Civil War / Lorien Foote.
Other titles: Steven and Janice Brose lectures in the Civil War era.
Description: Chapel Hill : The University of North Carolina Press, 2021. | Series: The Steven and Janice Brose lectures in the Civil War era | Includes bibliographical references and index.
Identifiers: LCCN 2021015344 | ISBN 9781469665269 (cloth ; alk. paper) | ISBN 9781469665276 (paperback ; alk. paper) | ISBN 9781469665283 (ebook)
Subjects: LCSH: United States. Army. Department of the South—History. | Lex talionis. | Punishment—Philosophy. | Reciprocity (Psychology) | United States—History—Civil War, 1861–1865—Prisoners and prisons. | United States—Civilization—19th century.
Classification: LCC E611 .F655 2021 | DDC 973.7/1—dc23
LC record available at https://lccn.loc.gov/2021015344

Portions of this work also appear, in somewhat different form, in Lorien Foote, "Campaign for Charleston: Military Science, Emancipation, and Social Collapse," in *The Oxford Handbook of the Civil War*, ed. Lorien Foote and Earl J. Hess (New York: Oxford University Press, 2021); Lorien Foote, "'The Sternest Feature of War': Prisoners of War and the Practice of Retaliation," in *Crossing the Deadlines: Civil War Prisons Reconsidered*, ed. Michael P. Gray (Kent, Ohio: Kent State University Press, 2018), 81–100; and Lorien Foote, "Civilization and Savagery in the American Civil War," *South Central Review: The Journal of the South Central Modern Language Association* 33, no. 1 (Spring 2016): 21–36.

*To the prisoners of the*

*54th Massachusetts, 8th USCT,*

*and 1st North Carolina*

# CONTENTS

*Acknowledgments* *xi*

*Introduction* The Ritual of Retaliation *1*

1 FELONS AND OUTLAWS *17*

2 SERVILE INSURRECTION *49*

3 PRISONERS *81*

4 MASSACRE *113*

5 HUMAN SHIELDS *141*

6 PILLAGERS AND ASSASSINS *175*

*Conclusion* The Crisis of Civilization *207*

*Notes* *213*

*Bibliography* *257*

*Index* *281*

# FIGURES & MAPS

## FIGURES

Maj. Gen. Ethan Allen Hitchcock *12*

Maj. Gen. David Hunter and Lt. Robert Gould Shaw, 2nd Massachusetts *19*

Capt. Charles T. Trowbridge, 1st South Carolina *22*

Susie King Taylor, 1st South Carolina *37*

Confederate secretary of war James A. Seddon *46*

"Flag Presented by Citizens of New York to the First S.C. Volunteers" *51*

Sgt. William Bronson, Sgt. Henry McIntrye, and Sgt. Harry Wilkins, 1st South Carolina *54*

Col. Thomas Wentworth Higginson, 1st South Carolina, and Col. James Montgomery, 2nd South Carolina *59*

"Raid of the Second South Carolina Volunteers (Col. Montgomery) among the Rice Plantations of the Combahee, S.C." *69*

Capt. John W. M. Appleton, 54th Massachusetts, and his sketch of Darien, Georgia *76*

Gen. P. G. T. Beauregard *79*

Appleton's sketches of picket fight and battle lines on Sol Legare Island, July 16, 1863 *83*

Maj. Gen. Quincy A. Gillmore *86*

Charge of the 54th Massachusetts at Fort Wagner, July 18, 1863 *89*

Appleton's sketch of officer deaths at Fort Wagner, July 18, 1863 *90*

Sap roller, siege of Fort Wagner, Morris Island *101*

"Retribution" *105*

"British Civilization. How the English Treat Prisoners of War—Sepoys to Guns" *108*

Appleton's sketch of Baldwin, Florida, and location of the 54th Massachusetts camp *115*

Brig. Gen. Truman Seymour *118*

Charles W. Fribley and Kate Ault Fribley *129*

Pvt. Thomas O'Dea's drawing of Andersonville Prison as it appeared on August 1, 1864 *131*

"Bursting of a Shell in the Streets of Charleston, South Carolina" *142*

Maj. Gen. John G. Foster and Maj. Gen. Samuel Jones *144*

Michael P. O'Connor house *149*

Sojourner Truth with a photograph of grandson James Caldwell, 54th Massachusetts *154*

"Quarters of the Union Officers Exposed to Federal Fire in Charleston" *166*

Maj. Gen. William Tecumseh Sherman and his staff in May 1865 *180*

Provost buildings, Hilton Head *187*

Brig. Gen. Judson Kilpatrick *193*

Lt. Gen. Wade Hampton III *196*

"Marching On: the 55th Massachusetts Colored Regiment Singing 'John Brown's March' in the Streets of Charleston" *205*

"The Last of the First Negro Soldiers: The First South Carolina Volunteers" *209*

MAPS

South Carolina Sea Islands *20*

Charleston Harbor *25*

Georgia Sea Islands *35*

Florida Raids, 1st and 2nd South Carolina *53*

Battle of Olustee Prisoners *116*

Sherman and Retaliation *178*

# ACKNOWLEDGMENTS

This book marks what I hope to be the midpoint of my career as an academic historian, and it has been a joy to reflect on those who have supported me in the research and writing of a book that feels like a milestone in my journey. Part of that feeling stems from the fact that this is a Brose Lecture book. I was deeply honored when Bill Blair called and asked me to present the Brose Distinguished Lecture Series at the George and Ann Richards Civil War Era Center at Penn State University. I thank him for giving me this amazing experience. My deep gratitude goes to Steven and Janice Brose for their generous endowment of the lectures and of the study of Civil War history and for their personal kindness during my visit. Matthew Isham and Barby Singer were their usual wonderful, competent selves and made sure I had a great experience. The faculty, administrators, graduate students, fellows, and members of the public audience who attended my three talks asked great questions and helped me refine my thinking. I would like to thank Lois, Pete, and Peter Agnew for driving up from New York and providing friendly family faces during the lectures.

*Rites of Retaliation* would not be the book that it is without Rachel Shelden, who took over as director of the Richards Center when I gave my lectures in 2019. Her brilliant report afterward helped me see what the book should really be about. During the revision process in 2020, amid the stress of the pandemic, she took the time to answer paragraph-level questions.

I was able to travel the country to conduct research for this book because of the Patricia and Bookman Peters Chair in History at Texas A&M University. I thank Bookman Peters for his generous support of historical research. I am also grateful for the faculty development leave that I received from my university, which supported the final phases of writing. My colleagues in the history department at Texas A&M have supported and encouraged me in immeasurable ways. I would like to thank David Vaught and Carlos Blanton, who had succeeding terms as department head during the research and writing of this book and who made sure I had resources, time, and headspace. Kate Unterman and Adam Seipp told me it was OK that I had to let some things go. Walter Kamphoefner and David Hudson stepped up so that I could step down and write this book.

Several people took photographs for me of primary source material in archives or looked something up for me in an archive they were visiting. Thanks go to Shane Makowicki, John Wendt, and Zac Cowsert. Peggy Ann Brown did some research in newspapers for me. Angela Riotto shared with me some sources she found in her research on Confederate former prisoners of war. Because he seems to know everything, I asked Chris Barr a lot of questions about Civil War prisoners, prisons, and the Sea Islands. He always knew the answer or knew someone who did.

Greg and Sarah Eastman might as well designate the guest bedroom of their house in Arlington, Virginia, as The Lorien Foote Research Room. They even let me come when they are not home. Their hospitality has extended across several of my book projects. Holly and Kevin Fletcher also opened their home to me for weeks at a time during the research for previous books and continue to welcome me with open arms when I need a place to stay. I don't know what I would do without the Eastmans and the Fletchers.

In my research experience, archivists have always been knowledgeable and helpful. I found material I would not have otherwise and received scans of materials because of the assistance of these historians and experts. I would like to particularly thank the following individuals: at the South Caroliniana Library (one of my favorite archives), Edward W. Blessing, Graham Duncan, and McKenzie Lemhouse. At the South Carolina Historical Society, Karen Stokes, who has also published many helpful books on the history of the Civil War in South Carolina. At the U.S. Military Academy Library Special Collections, Susan Lintelmann. At the Library of Congress Manuscript Division, Michelle Krowl. At the U.S. Army Heritage and Education Center, Rich Baker and Lori Wheeler. At the Wisconsin Veterans Museum, Samantha Wolf. At the Wisconsin Historical Society, Lee Grady. At the Massachusetts Historical Society, Sabina Beauchard, Anna Clutterbuck-Cook, and Peter Drummey. At the Boston Public Library, Kimberly Reynolds. At the Clarke Historical Library, John Fierst and Mariah Billington-Rives. At the Virginia Historical Society, Jennifer M. Huff. At the West Virginia and Regional History Center, John Cuthbert and Mary Mullett.

A trip to Charleston made the history written in this book come alive for me. Adam Domby gave me a tour of the military and prison sites around Charleston Harbor. We had a great day and a fabulous dinner and provided a model to the rest of America about how two people can have a political discussion, disagree, truly listen to each other, and remain great friends. Ernest Parks gave us a tour of the Seashore Farmers' Lodge Museum on Sol Legare Island. He is an incredible steward of the history of his community and one of the friendliest men you'll ever meet.

I was able to try out some very early ideas about retaliation before presenting the Brose Lectures. I would like to thank Andy Lang and Anne Marshall for inviting me to participate in the symposium "New Approaches to Civilian Military Relations in the American Civil War" at Mississippi State University in February 2017. There I hesitantly suggested that retaliation was a ritual. I am grateful for the conversations with Andy, Anne, and Aaron Sheehan-Dean, D. H. Dilbeck, and Drew Bledsoe that encouraged me that I was on the right track. Thanks go to Mike Gray for seeing the potential of my project and including me in his edited collection on new directions in the study of Civil War POWs. Writing the chapter on retaliation for that volume helped me see a broader picture. He and Sandi also sent me scones during a difficult time, and I will always remember that.

I benefited from the comments and feedback of Civil War historians I deeply admire and respect who read the entire manuscript. I sent my work to them because I love the work they do. I am more grateful than I can express to Aaron Sheehan-Dean, Steve Berry, Megan Kate Nelson, Jason Phillips, Rachel Shelden, Earl J. Hess, and David Silkenat. Military historian, rigorous critic, and generous colleague Brian Linn made sure that the book has something to say to those outside the Civil War bubble. Historian and educator Bill Collopy and English professor Ira Dworkin also read the entire manuscript and proffered useful thoughts. Mark Bauman and Eric Bauman gave me comments from a public audience perspective and reminded me that not everyone would know who all these generals were. I am also grateful to Jonathan White and the anonymous reader for the University of North Carolina Press who provided many helpful suggestions.

I love the illustrations for this book. Thanks go to Hal Jespersen for making the incredible maps. Steve Wise helped me find locations and images and used his vast knowledge of the Department of the South's military history to keep me from making errors. Thomas R. Fasulo runs an incredible website about the Battle of Olustee, filled with primary sources, and assisted me with tracking down an image. Mary L. Sieminski put me in touch with David L. Richards, who provided the wonderful photograph of Charles and Kate Fribley. Lisa Keys at the Kansas Historical Society was professional and friendly. Annette Sumpter at the Penn Center moved quickly on a last-minute request so I could use the image of the veterans of the 1st South Carolina.

This is my second book with UNC Press, and both times have been great experiences. I cannot say enough about Mark Simpson-Vos: he is helpful in every way, he gives detailed attention to my books, he answers a lot of emails in a timely fashion, and he has made the path so smooth for me. The entire editorial, production, and marketing team at the press is expert, professional, and outstanding. Thanks go to Dominique Moore, Erin Granville, Cate Hodorowicz, Jay Mazzocchi, Mary Caviness, Dino Battista, and Julie Bush.

I have suffered a stupid health crisis during the research and writing of every book I have published. For this one, it was cancer, surgery, and a traumatic allergic reaction to the surgical glue. I would be disloyal and ungrateful if I did not acknowledge how the presence of the risen Lord Jesus Christ sustained me during the long, painful, sleepless nights and the exhausting recovery. Because I know that nothing in my life or my death will separate me from his love, I had the physical, emotional, and mental strength to work on this book.

Thinking about how far I've come has made me think back to where I started. I would like to acknowledge some special friends who were with me at the beginning of my academic career at the University of Central Arkansas. We taught four classes a semester, graded thousands of tests and papers, attended uncountable department meetings, served on a ridiculous number of hiring committees, and laughed together through it all. My journey has taken me to a different place, but I will always be grateful I started it with them. Thanks go to Wendy, Don, Roger, David, and David.

Finally, I would like to thank Col. Robert Gould Shaw, Col. Charles W. Fribley, Maj. Archibald Bogle, Corp. James Henry Gooding, and all the prisoners from the 54th Massachusetts, 8th USCT, and 1st North Carolina. They suffered to save the country that I love, and no one took their honor. They will always be remembered.

# RITES OF RETALIATION

# INTRODUCTION

# THE RITUAL OF RETALIATION

The Union naval steamer *Crescent* approached Morris Island, South Carolina, located in the outer entrance of Charleston's harbor, with 600 Confederate officers—prisoners of war—enclosed in its filthy and vomit-encrusted hull. It was 11:00 A.M. on September 7, 1864. Four companies of the 54th Massachusetts (Colored) Infantry and five companies of the 21st United States Colored Infantry waited on the beach. The ever-present red sand flies swarmed around the Black men in blue uniforms, tormenting the soldiers with bites worse than a mosquito's. The vessel landed, the Confederate prisoners disembarked, and the Union soldiers formed an escort around them.[1]

The calm and quiet demeanor of the Confederate officers as they moved north up the narrow beach masked a consuming inner rage at the humiliation of being under the control of armed Black men. They marched three miles, the entire length of the island, passing camps filled with Black soldiers. Underneath the dry quartz sand, and sometimes poking out of it, were the bones of Union soldiers who had died the year before in the failed assaults and successful siege operations that had captured Morris Island. Somewhere nearby were the remains of the first colonel of the 54th Massachusetts, Robert Gould Shaw, the white son of prominent abolitionists, whom Confederates had buried in a mass, unmarked grave to dishonor him. The Confederate president, Jefferson Davis, had declared Shaw to be a felon and an outlaw rather than a legitimate combatant.[2]

The soldiers of the 54th escorted their prisoners to a one-acre stockade placed between two earthwork fortifications, Fort Strong (formerly Fort Wagner) and Fort Gregg. Inside were four streets, with a row of nineteen tents on both sides of each street. The tents held four men each. Outside, a platform ran the length of the palisade fence to support the guards of the 54th as they observed the Confederate officers. Artillery from these earthworks continually bombarded nearby Confederate positions and fired into the business and residential areas of Charleston. Confederate batteries returned fire and shelled Strong, Gregg, and the camps of Union soldiers on Morris Island. Mortar and shell from the Confederate batteries fell all around the Confederate officers inside the stockade. That night, the prisoners lay on the sand in front of their tents, watching and listening to an awe-inspiring fireworks display. Red balls of iron and bright streaks of fire filled the sky as whining shells passed over their heads in two directions. Most prisoners developed headaches from the concussion of the explosions.[3]

They had no protection from the fragments of shell that fell inside the stockade. That was the point. The U.S. War Department had sent them to Morris Island to expose them to artillery fire. It was an act of retaliation. Across the harbor, 600 Union officers—prisoners of war—watched shells from the Federal bombardment fall around the buildings that had confined them in the city of Charleston for the past forty-one days.

Retaliation was consistent with the code that governed the conduct of U.S. armies in the field during the Civil War, General Orders No. 100, issued on April 24, 1863. Article 27 proclaimed that "civilized nations acknowledge retaliation as the sternest feature of war. A reckless enemy often leaves to his opponent no other means of securing himself against the repetition of a barbarous outrage." The next article cautioned that retaliation was not revenge but rather a means of "protective retribution." Retaliation was legitimate only if it was done "cautiously and unavoidably" and only after "careful inquiry into the real occurrence." The author of the code, Francis Lieber, an expert on the international laws of war, warned that "unjust or inconsiderate retaliation removes the belligerents farther and farther from the mitigating rules of regular war, and by rapid steps leads them nearer to the internecine wars of savages."[4]

Retaliation against prisoners of war was a ubiquitous feature of the American Civil War. Field commanders used retaliation during almost every military campaign, and civilian leaders frequently turned to the practice when they confronted contentious policy issues. Union and Confederate officials shared a ritual of retaliation that played an important role in determining how each side fought the war. Through this ritual, the combatants staked broad claims about what civilized war should look like in practice and negotiated details about how to interpret the laws of war and conduct campaigns. Retaliation determined how Abraham Lincoln and Jefferson Davis implemented policy, what orders generals in the field enforced upon their commands, and how soldiers behaved when they interacted with the citizens they encountered. Retaliation changed the behavior of key actors in the war and swerved the Union and the Confederate leadership off their preferred policy paths.[5]

This book will explore events in the Federal campaigns against Charleston and the states of South Carolina, Georgia, and Florida that exemplify how retaliation functioned during the American Civil War. It immerses readers in a narrative that follows Union and Confederate civilian administrators, field and line officers, soldiers, and prisoners of war. Rather than offer a broad, superficial survey of every retaliation incident that occurred during the war, this study delves deeply into particulars because personalities, national and local circumstances, and contingencies shaped how retaliation worked in each instance that officials used it.

The Department of the South makes an ideal location for study because three contentious issues between the Union and the Confederacy converged in this theater of operations: the Federal recruitment and deployment of Black troops, the Confederate treatment of Union prisoners of war, and the Federal treatment of noncombatants who lived within the zones of active military operations. Partly because of the character and policies of the Federal military officials who fought here, including the abolitionist Maj. Gen. David Hunter, the technologist Maj. Gen. Quincy A. Gillmore, the hard-war practitioner Maj. Gen. William Tecumseh Sherman, and the well-connected Col. Robert Gould Shaw, retaliation incidents in the Department of the South were regular, prolonged, and unusually well documented.

Because Federal armies were not able to sustain invasions into the interior or conduct lengthy occupations of white communities in the Department of the South until 1864, this region lacked the retaliation rituals against Confederate partisans and guerrillas that were characteristic of the border states and the western theater. Union military commanders treated guerrillas as bandits and pirates rather than as legitimate combatants, often summarily executed them, and refused to alter this policy. The Confederate government, although it sought to protect its officially sanctioned partisans who employed irregular tactics, was ambivalent about unaffiliated guerrillas, and the Confederate Congress never authorized retaliation on their behalf. Instead, the Confederate leadership focused legislative attention on the armed Black men in the Union army, particularly those fighting in the Department of the South in 1862–63.[6]

Zooming our historical lens onto this region alters our picture of national policy. When we follow across time the process of retaliation incidents that originated in this location, for the first time we see what the Lincoln administration did to protect freeborn Black men who fought under the United States flag and why it worked. One of the most important contributions of this book is that it lays out for the first time the sequence regarding retaliation over the Federal use of freeborn Black troops in combat. Connecting dots that historians have not connected before shows that the Confederate government changed one of its policies because of this retaliation. It has become a truism in the scholarly literature on the American Civil War that although the United States resumed prisoner exchanges with the Confederacy in February 1865, Black soldiers were not included in the exchange. As we will see, this is not true.

Retaliation in the Department of the South was part of a broader negotiation between the Union and the Confederacy about the very nature of war. The portrait of war presented here will help us better understand modern warfare. In all wars throughout time, combatants enter a conflict with a set of assumptions about the right way and the wrong way to fight. They hold their enemies to these assumptions, justify their own behaviors, and try to enforce their views of combat on their enemies. The retaliation rituals of the American Civil War were foundational for establishing the norms that Western nations codified in the twentieth century and that shaped the rules the United States uses in its conflicts today.

This book will also help scholars of the Civil War more accurately depict its violence. Historians debate whether the fighting in the Civil War was relatively restrained or atrociously violent. The perspective here is that the war contained elements of both, and local patterns varied across time and space. Rather than make broad generalizations, this book illuminates how retaliation shaped a dynamic of violence that was unique to each military campaign.[7] It considers how officers on the ground used retaliation, in the midst of military campaigns, to interpret, debate, and apply the laws of war to complex local circumstances.[8]

While the topic is retaliation, the book's overarching purpose is to help readers understand that Americans experienced the Civil War as a crisis of civilization, not just as a crisis of republicanism and nationhood. Students and scholars who have spent time with nineteenth-century primary sources will recognize the ubiquity of the term "civilization" in public and private conversation. Americans in the Civil War era considered themselves part of a transatlantic set of civilized nations that represented the pinnacle of social evolution to that point in history. Civilization was a worldview that framed how people saw themselves and others within the natural world. It ordered humans along a sliding scale. At the bottom were "savages," those who lived and acted similarly to wild animals and thus could be treated as less than fully human. At the top were the "civilized," those who exemplified the characteristics and achievements that differentiated humans from beasts. White Americans entered the war confident of their civilized status and took for granted that what it meant to fight a civilized war was obvious and shared.[9]

It turned out, however, that Americans fought over the meaning of civilization and who could be included in the civilized world. The war also heightened their fears of the "savages" and "barbarians" who lurked beneath the civilized veneer of American society—the Black, white, and Indian men who had no control over their animal nature. Northerners and Southerners incessantly accused the other side of savage behavior. This was more than just hyperbolic rhetoric.[10] When white soldiers plundered Southern farms and former slaves burned plantation houses, this was a potential threat to Americans' very civilization. This book, then, is about one of the things that mattered most to Americans in the Civil War era: whether they could fight a civil war and maintain their essential identity as civilized people. We will explore the crisis through the eyes of those tasked by their societies with implementing a civilized war: administrators in the War Department, military commanders, and commissioned officers.

The purpose of retaliation was to enforce the international laws of war among civilized nations, and the practice during the Civil War highlighted three essential elements to civilization and civilized war as the majority of Americans understood them. Northerners and Southerners agreed that one mark of a civilized nation was that its people and its government restrained and channeled human passion and violence to constructive ends. Self-control, order, and deliberation underlay the violence of a civilized war, which was most easily defined through contrast with its opposite. Animal-like anger, uncontrolled passion, and unlimited and indiscriminate violence marked a "savage" conflict.[11] Civilized nations fought with uniformed combatants who represented the state and were under the discipline and control of gentlemen officers. Gentlemen officers ensured that the effects of violence on noncombatants were minimized.

The second indispensable aspect of civilized war was that combatants participated in the accumulated wisdom of civilized people stretching back to ancient times. Americans perceived themselves as part of a shared history and took care to contextualize every action taken in warfare as a consistent outgrowth of that history. As most educated Americans knew, their lineage included Saint Augustine in the fourth century, who articulated conditions that must be met for a war to be morally justified, and the eleventh-century church councils in France that proclaimed the Peace of God to protect clergy, women, children, and the poor from violence. In the seventeenth and eighteenth centuries, European philosophers, lawyers, and statesmen wrote thick books explaining the customs of war, rules of conduct for troops, and how civilized nations imposed restraints on violence. Americans mined these books and used their own examples from Western history to justify their policies or accuse their enemies. They constantly cited precedents for actions they took. Official and private correspondence during the Civil War was filled with historical references.[12]

Finally, civilized war was honorable, not in the modern sense of just or virtuous but in its classical definition. Nations had a reputation to uphold before a peer audience. The Union and the Confederacy had to convince other civilized nations, who observed and judged them, of the righteousness of their conduct. Civilized war was a performance where mastery of rhetoric, protocols, and etiquette were vitally important to establishing a nation's claim to civilized status.[13] These three elements—restraint of violence, historical precedent, and honor—were present to some degree in each ritual of retaliation that occurred during the war and were particularly significant to the incidents that occurred in the Department of the South.

In order to understand the story that this book tells, it is important to establish that military leaders on both sides in the Civil War agreed upon the basic rules and established rituals of retaliation. Retaliation was different from revenge by both purpose and procedure. Its intent was to prevent the enemy from continuing specific acts of "barbarous outrage" and to enforce the "civilized usages of war." Maj. Gen. Henry W. Halleck, who served as general-in-chief of Union armies for nearly two years and was an acknowledged authority on the subject, wrote that its object was deterrence and prevention. Lincoln instructed one of his generals, "I wish you to do nothing merely for revenge, but that what you may do, shall be solely done with reference to the security of the future." Confederate secretary of war James A. Seddon believed the point was to "produce a thorough reformation of the offending nation." The head of the Confederate Bureau of War thought "a little *real* shooting of prisoners" would "do good, prevent suffering, and save life."[14]

A combatant considering retaliation wrote a letter to his opponent that contained several elements placed in sequence. First was a statement of the desire to fight the war on civilized principles. Then the writer named a specific barbarous act the enemy had committed that supposedly violated the international laws of war. He offered an opportunity for the recipient to disavow the incident in three acceptable ways: (1) indicate that perhaps the writer of the letter was misinformed as to the facts, (2) suggest that perhaps the guilty parties had acted without the sanction of higher authority, or (3) submit evidence that the perpetrators would be punished. The writer concluded with a timeline to receive a response before he implemented a named measure of retaliation against a named individual or group of people.

Before implementing retaliation, a combatant was obligated to conduct his own careful investigation. Confederate secretary of war George W. Randolph, Seddon's predecessor, instructed his subordinates to be "certain of the facts before proceeding to measures of retaliation." Retaliation was a legitimate resort only in cases where enemy authorities sanctioned the barbarity and not in cases where an individual committed an unauthorized act. "Without clearest evidence of malicious purpose on their part, it would be hideous to retaliate," Ralph Waldo Emerson wrote to Maj. Gen. Ethan Allen Hitchcock, the Union commissioner for exchange of prisoners. "Individual instances of cruelty and crime occur in all wars which no authority can entirely prevent," Halleck informed Union officials. "Complaints are not made where the proper authorities employ all legitimate means to rebuke and punish the offenders." As we will see, when an official failed to follow the proper decorum in writing the letter, investigating the facts, or determining responsibility, the ritual malfunctioned and did not fulfill its purpose.[15]

There was also broad agreement that retaliation had limits. In his 1861 treatise on international law and in subsequent general orders issued to Union armies in the field, Halleck commented that the rules did not permit a combatant to commit a savage act under any circumstances. A nation could not reciprocate in kind if its enemy massacred prisoners of war or poisoned food, for example. During his term as commander of the Department of the Missouri, Halleck was presented with an opportunity to practice what he preached. When Confederate forces evacuated Mudtown, Arkansas, they poisoned the abandoned provisions they left behind. Forty-two officers and enlisted men of the 5th Missouri Cavalry (Union) became ill and a captain died after eating the food. In General Orders No. 49, issued February 27, 1862, Halleck wrote, "We cannot retaliate by adopting the same barbarous mode of warfare." He proclaimed that any Confederate soldier guilty of the act would not be treated as a prisoner of war if captured but would be hanged as a felon. Officers who commanded guilty troops were responsible for the behavior of their men, even if they had not ordered the poisoning, and thus would be ironed as criminals upon capture.[16]

Another limit was that retaliation had to be proportional to the offense. Francis Lieber frequently corresponded with Halleck regarding how to implement retaliation properly. The "elementary principle" was "*Tit for Tat,* or Eye for Eye," he instructed the general in June 1863. "If one belligerent hangs ten men for one; the other will hang then times ten over the ten, and what a geometrical progression of skulls and crossbones we would have!" Retaliation must never cross a boundary beyond "simple death." "If one of our officers was nailed to a board and roasted," Lieber wrote, "we could never retaliate by roasting." Execution would be an appropriate response in this instance.[17]

An important purpose of the ritual of retaliation was to provide a framework for responding when an enemy violated the rules of civilized warfare, but to do so in a way that measured and controlled violence. Proper instances of retaliation meted out an exact response. For example, when Confederates put Federal prisoners of war to work in their trenches on the front lines near Fort Gilmer during the siege of Petersburg, Virginia, in October 1864, U.S. authorities questioned refugees and deserters from the Confederate lines to determine the exact treatment of the prisoners. The retaliation was precise to the circumstances of the Federal prisoners; officials put Confederate prisoners to work in trenches ten hours a day and served them one pound of flour and a third of a pound of bacon daily. In response, Confederates removed their prisoners from the trenches, and the Union immediately did likewise.[18]

Belligerents were careful when they chose the subject of retaliation. Ideally, a combatant would not have to retaliate when the enemy committed a barbarous act but could instead capture the perpetrators and punish them. Since that was rarely a realistic option, the next best choice was to retaliate upon prisoners of the same rank and from the same command as the person(s) who violated the laws of war, or if the guilty party were a civilian, upon a civilian of equal status in society. If an officer committed an atrocity, an officer of the same rank should suffer the retaliation, not an enlisted soldier. In a discussion over appropriate targets for retaliation, Confederate general Robert E. Lee suggested that in cases where a body of Union troops were guilty of "outrages," Confederates should not accept surrenders from that command during battle. He believed this would incentivize civilized soldiers to restrain their barbaric comrades.[19]

Important Union and Confederate officials ultimately agreed that proper retaliation allowed for the execution of prisoners of war who were innocent of the original atrocity. Although Halleck proclaimed early in the war that the United States would retaliate upon offenders and not upon innocent prisoners, he outlined two important exceptions to the rule. If an enemy targeted innocent prisoners of war, responding in kind was appropriate if there was a reasonable expectation that retaliation would effect a change in policy and if the response did not include the savage cruelty of torture or indiscriminate massacre. The other exception was in cases of corporate guilt, where an entire army, city, or other community of people could be held responsible for the acts of its rulers or representatives because the majority had encouraged and acquiesced in the conduct.[20]

Authorities in the American Civil War decided over time that military officers made the best targets for retaliation. A general officer was responsible for the conduct of enlisted men in his command and was therefore guilty of any crimes that his soldiers committed. Jefferson Davis held all commissioned officers culpable for policies their civil governments announced. He explained that commissioned officers, unlike enlisted men, had the option to resign, and if they remained in an army charged with implementing barbaric orders, then they were guilty of all that army's atrocities and were appropriate subjects for execution. U.S. secretary of war Edwin Stanton suggested to President Lincoln another reason that the "whole weight of retaliatory punishment . . . should be made to fall upon the officers of the rebel army." Besides the fact that privates were conscripted and held to service against their will, officers were men of higher social status and influence with their governments. Threats against them would carry weight with the opposing government because prominent friends would bring pressure on their behalf.[21]

When an official in the Union or the Confederacy initiated a retaliation ritual, he knew that his government might publish, and always preserved, the resulting correspondence for contemporaries and later historians to evaluate. National honor was at stake. The language and formal, standard structure used in communication with the enemy during the process of retaliation assured the writer of his own place within civilization (a particularly important goal for the Confederate project of seeking international legitimacy) and allowed him to put in the record explicit statements avowing an intention to restrain war. "It is my desire as far as lies in my power to mitigate the horror of this war as much as possible," was one of several stock phrases that officials drew from when they composed retaliation correspondence. An exchange between Union lieutenant general Ulysses S. Grant and Robert E. Lee exemplifies the rhetoric that negotiators used to uphold their reputation. "It is not my desire to retaliate for acts which I must believe are unauthorized by commanders of troops in arms against the authority of the United States," Grant wrote Lee during a retaliation ritual involving the alleged murder of two Federal officers. "But I would ask that those barbarous practices be prohibited as far as they can be controlled." Lee responded that murder was "at variance with the rules by which the Confederate Government endeavors to conduct hostilities." He called the incident "one of those acts of unauthorized violence proceeding from individual passions, which it is difficult to prevent, but which are not the less to be lamented." Lee reminded Grant that Federal soldiers likewise committed outrages and assured his enemy that he endeavored "by every means in my power to prevent such violations of the rules of civilized warfare, which only tend to inflame feelings already unfortunately too much embittered, and which unavoidably reflects upon the party of which the perpetrators belong."[22] Grant and Lee agreed that civilized warfare attempted to remove the individual passions and feelings that escalated violence. Each knew how to use the pattern of negotiation to defuse such passion; each assured the other that he was committed to the rules and proclaimed that atrocities were abnormalities that enjoyed no official sanction. This common negotiating tactic allowed both sides to claim civilization in the face of acts that suggested otherwise and to uphold their honor in the court of civilized world opinion.

Because maintaining honor was an essential component of retaliation, civil officials generally gauged opinion of a proposed retaliatory measure before implementing it. Field commanders with a military background rarely consulted anyone outside military channels when conducting a retaliation ritual during active military operations. Officers were confident in their knowledge of the relevant texts on the customs of war and in the shared military culture of West Point–trained officers. For civil officials, on the other hand, it was important to get a sense of whether the general public would affirm their actions. Newspaper editorials were one way for officials to measure opinion, because editorials frequently called for retaliation or proffered opinions about what constituted appropriate retaliation for enemy atrocities. Another was listening to or reading congressional debates over retaliatory measures. Citizens also wrote to government officials to point out enemy atrocities, call for retaliation, and suggest retaliatory measures. Jefferson Davis regularly received letters from state officials and ordinary citizens across the Confederacy that allowed him to assess how his constituents would respond to retaliatory measures that he initiated. For example, an 1862 letter from an attorney in Jacksonville, Alabama, suggested that the Confederacy should hold one white enemy prisoner for each slave "abducted" from a plantation. Kenneth Raynor, a former Whig congressman, wrote Davis from Raleigh, North Carolina, in December 1862 with reports that the U.S. Army and Unionist citizens were plundering property and stealing slaves. He requested retaliation and referenced the British reaction to the Sepoy Mutiny of 1857–59 as a historical precedent. A farmer in Balcony Falls, Virginia, wrote Davis in February 1865 to suggest that the Confederate president send two columns of 100,000 Blacks into "Yankeedom" to burn, pillage, and destroy in retaliation. "Away then with all squeamishness," he recommended.[23]

The U.S. War Department was careful to sample key constituencies when officials considered a retaliatory measure that fell in gray areas of the customs of war or that would result in the suffering or death of people who had not perpetrated the atrocity. The task often fell to Ethan Allen Hitchcock, the U.S. commissioner for exchange of prisoners from 1862 to 1865. He is a more important figure in the story of prisoners of war and retaliation than historians have previously realized. His correspondence with a wide range of people and his ability to bluntly confront Secretary of War Stanton were critical in shaping the process of retaliation. Hitchcock was an elderly officer—a good friend called him "a relic of the last century"—whose antebellum career was marked by a concern with the laws of war and protecting Indians from fraud. He was obsessed with hermetic philosophy and believed that some of the major authors writing since A.D. 1000 were members of a secret sect that criticized the Catholic Church through a coded double meaning in their literary works. Hitchcock wrote eight books about the secret meaning he uncovered in famous books, including the plays and poems of Shakespeare. His interest in metaphysics, philosophy, literature, and spirituality and his rejection of orthodox Christianity brought him into the circle of New England transcendentalists.[24]

Hitchcock utilized his friendships with men and women of the literary world while evaluating retaliatory measures. In November 1863, for example, U.S. War Department officials believed they had evidence that Confederate prison officials were deliberately withholding rations and supplies from Union prisoners of war in order to cause them unnecessary suffering. On November 7, Hitchcock instructed the U.S. agent for exchange to ask his Confederate counterpart for an official statement of the ration issued to Union prisoners and to inform him that this statement would be considered as evidence when U.S. authorities considered retaliation. If no state-

Maj. Gen. Ethan Allen Hitchcock, the U.S. commissioner for exchange of prisoners, 1862–65. His correspondence and advice was central to retaliation rituals during the Civil War. (Library of Congress Prints and Photographs Division, Daguerreotype Collection)

ment was forthcoming, U.S. authorities would act on their best information. On November 9, Stanton instructed Hitchcock to ascertain the exact treatment of Union prisoners held in Richmond and to mete out a precisely similar measure of food, clothing, and medical treatment to Confederate prisoners in Northern prisons. Stanton's order prompted a thorough discussion of the proposed retaliation. Hitchcock first cautioned Stanton that mistreating prisoners might lead to an uprising of Confederate prisoners in the more loosely guarded Northern prisons. Halleck believed that Confederate treatment of Union prisoners was more barbarous than a list of examples from history, including at the hands of the pirates of Tripoli, within the British hulks of the American Revolution, and inside the Black Hole of Calcutta. Because the public press in the Confederacy and ordinary people in the South applauded the maltreatment of Union prisoners, Halleck believed that the proposed retaliation was compatible with the laws and usages of war. "Nevertheless," he cautioned, "it is revolting to our sense of humanity to be forced to so cruel an alternative."[25]

Hitchcock then sent feelers to New England reformers and transcendentalists. He wrote to Mary Peabody Mann, the wife of educational reformer Horace Mann and the sister of Sophia Peabody Hawthorne, the painter and wife of Nathaniel Hawthorne. Mary Mann was an enthusiastic admirer of Hitchcock. "I am very anxious to know how such a measure strikes you and would be very glad if you could, without too much trouble, learn the opinions of some of your thinking (and feeling) friends, and give me a hint of them," he asked. "Can we deliberately reduce to starvation a body of helpless prisoners of war, in retaliation for the inhumanities practiced by ruffians and barbarians in Richmond upon our unhappy POWs? Is there a middle course by selecting *some* of the number, say a few conspicuous officers in our hands, and make them practically feel the horrors of scant food—nearly nude at the same time? What do you think is for our dignity in the eyes of history?" Mann replied immediately. "Your letter shakes my very soul," she said. "My feeling is this—it would be wholly derogatory to the dignity of our government and the spirit of humanity . . . to retaliate in kind." Mann believed that some retaliation was necessary to protect Union prisoners. "As I do not believe human souls can be killed, but only bodies," she said, "I have hoped that our government would call out from our prisoners of war the most valuable officers, man for man if necessary, a lesser number if this would answer the purpose, and shoot or hang them." Mann shared Hitchcock's letter with Ebenezer R. Hoar, the anti-slavery associate justice of the Massachusetts Supreme Court. "It would be utterly abhorrent to everyone to attempt to retaliate by starvation or torture of any kind," Hoar wrote in a separate letter. "Civilized society repudiates such a course in dealing with the most cruel and atrocious criminals. We have never allowed it in our visitation of justice upon Indians, pirates, or other savages." Hoar's idea was to select some prisoners for long imprisonment or execution. Sophia Hawthorne provided a letter that reflected a common perception of retaliation among faithful Christians. "No retaliation of any kind!" she said. The only true course was "perfect Christian forbearance." A professedly Christian nation could not return to "the old Jewish rule of an eye for an eye." "To do evil with the idea that good may come of it, is the basest form of action. It takes out of God's hands his Providence and pushes Him aside that we may follow our own narrow views." The noble course was to treat all prisoners with care and humanity without reference to the actions of the Confederacy. Her husband and Ralph Waldo Emerson agreed with her, she wrote.[26]

Hitchcock used these and other letters to determine that public opinion was "strong against harsh measures." His investigations into the facts revealed that the returned Union prisoners who looked starving were those who came from the hospitals and whose sickness was not wholly the result of bad treatment. Armed with this information, he persuaded Secretary Stanton to suspend the question of retaliation for the time being. "No act of positive violence on our part will be permitted to damage us in the eyes of civilization," he told Mann. Over the next few months the War Department revisited the question of ration retaliation and in May 1864 ultimately ordered a 20 percent reduction in rations for Confederate prisoners. This was not a retaliation in kind, and it still provided the prisoners with a larger ration than British or French soldiers received at the time. Investigation of new facts and vetting the opinion of key constituencies again marked the decision-making process.[27]

The rhetoric, rituals, and process associated with retaliation were part of being civilized. They were intended to uphold honor, ensure that both sides conformed to the laws of war, serve as a forum to negotiate the practicalities of laws that were open to interpretation, provide a method for combatants to disavow unauthorized actions on the part of rogue individuals, and de-escalate the violence of war when it threatened to spin out of control. They were ubiquitous. Indeed, only one high-ranking official on either side learned to question retaliation as an effective measure to ensure conformity to the usages of civilized war. In the summer of 1863, Hitchcock, faced with voluminous retaliation correspondence over multiple issues in his role in the War Department, had an epiphany. The only way to stop rebel atrocities was to prosecute the war vigorously, end the rebellion, and seize the persons who committed them. "If we cannot do this, we cannot do anything," he decided. For the next two years, Hitchcock endorsed every letter he received about retaliation with some variation of the following phrase: "Measures of mere retaliation cannot determine this question; it can only be settled on the battlefield." His was a lonely voice among the military and civil leadership of the Civil War. The rest were convinced that retaliation served a critical purpose.[28]

With this background and context in mind, it is time to turn to the Department of the South, where combatants fought over the meaning of civilization and used retaliation to shape particular policies and practices. The story follows David Hunter, an abolitionist general of the Union army, and his decision to recruit Black troops and use them in a raiding strategy against coastal South Carolina, Georgia, and Florida. Former slaves who enlisted in the 1st and 2nd South Carolina (Union) Infantry, men like John Sutton and Prince Rivers, liberated slaves, burned plantations, and killed Confederate soldiers. Hunter believed he could civilize the barbarians he recruited, but to his Confederate counterpart, Gen. P. G. T. Beauregard, the war had unleashed savage Blacks in a servile insurrection that threatened the existence of Southern civilization. The narrative contrasts the perspective of Col. Robert Gould Shaw, Col. Thomas Wentworth Higginson, and Col. James Montgomery, commanders of Black regiments who reflected broader disagreements within the Union military about controlling the animal passions of soldiers in civilized war. We will go inside the Confederate War Department, where its secretary, James A. Seddon, worried about the judgment of the civilized world and debated his subordinates over the appropriate legal response to Federal actions.

The story involves combat, an assault and siege at Fort Wagner in Charleston Harbor and a set-piece battle at Olustee, Florida, and the consequences for national policy on both sides when Confederates captured Black prisoners, dishonored the bodies of Shaw and Col. Charles W. Fribley, and massacred wounded men. We will follow the prisoners of the 54th Massachusetts, men like Daniel States, as he endured in the Charleston Jail waiting for retaliation to work, and James Henry Gooding, when he entered the gates of Andersonville prison after Confederates conceded he was a legitimate combatant. The battle narrative involves a technologist, General Gillmore, whose big guns fired into the heart of Charleston, turned the jewel of Southern civilization into a lawless ruin, and prompted Confederate major general Samuel Jones to use Union prisoners as human shields.

The treatment of prisoners of war exemplified the American crisis of civilization. This book follows the story of the 1,200 commissioned officers brought to the Department of the South for retaliation and observes what happened when they crossed the boundary that supposedly separated civilized man from natural animal. We will meet Union major general John G. Foster, who was convinced the Confederate treatment of Union prisoners was savage, and uncover his decision to give 600 Confederate officers a ration that deprived them of health, an action that academic historians have completely missed in their political and military narratives of the war. We will investigate William Tecumseh Sherman's execution of forty-three Confederate prisoners of war near Cheraw, South Carolina, and witness his subordinates' fears that civilization was failing to constrain the savage passions of revenge and license. Events in the Department of the South threatened the identity of Americans as civilized people and tested their willingness to employ civilized war's sternest feature.

# 1

# FELONS AND OUTLAWS

Maj. Gen. David Hunter was an oddity. He was a regular officer from the old army with a West Point education, *and* he was an abolitionist. The two usually did not go together. In 1856, the army had posted Hunter to Fort Leavenworth in Kansas, where free-soil settlers were at war with the radical pro-slavery expansionists of Missouri. What he saw there convinced him that slavery caused the Civil War and that emancipation was necessary to defeat rebels against the U.S. government. If given a major command, he wrote Republican senator Lyman Trumbull on December 9, 1861, "I would advance south, proclaiming the negro free and arming him as I go. The Great God of the Universe has determined that this is the only way in which this war is to be ended, and the sooner it is done the better." In March 1862, the U.S. War Department sent the sixty-year-old to command the Department of the South at Hilton Head, South Carolina, where the Union navy and army in November 1861 had captured a set of coastal islands and the 10,000 slaves who lived there. U.S. Treasury Department agents and Northern philanthropists controlled the plantations and organized free labor and educational experiments there. Hunter had a grand strategic vision for victory in his department: arm slaves on the islands; send them on raids using the rivers of South Carolina, Georgia, and Florida; use the raids to liberate slaves and destroy the resources of slaveholding rebels; and arm the liberated slaves to conduct more raids.[1]

Robert Gould Shaw, on the other hand, fit the mold of young men from his Boston Brahmin social class. His parents were wealthy radical abolitionists with kinship ties to New England's mercantile and industrial elites. Like his multitude of cousins, he had traveled extensively in Europe, attended

Harvard, pursued parties and pleasure more than his studies, questioned whether he shared his parents' commitment to reform, and fought depression as he struggled to find a profession. Four days after Abraham Lincoln called for troops to suppress the rebellion, the twenty-four-year-old volunteered to serve. He wanted to do his duty to defend the honor of the United States. After a brief stint as a private in a New York militia unit, he received a commission, as a second lieutenant, in the 2nd Massachusetts Infantry. Shaw's attitudes mirrored those of the other gentleman officers in his regiment. He believed slavery was bad, rebellion was even worse, educated men should lead, and lower-class soldiers needed the hard hand of discipline to keep them in line. He wrote lengthy letters to his parents from the 2nd's camp in northern Virginia.[2]

Despite their differences, Shaw and Hunter had something important in common. By the end of the summer of 1862, the Confederacy declared Shaw to be a felon and outlawed Hunter in a sweeping retaliation proclamation designed to enforce President Jefferson Davis's interpretation of civilized war on the Union armies operating in South Carolina and Virginia. The wartime military actions of Hunter and Shaw uncovered the deepest fears that white Americans on both sides of the battle lines shared. Being a civilized person in a civilized nation was an important part of their identities. The wartime behavior of white enlisted men in Virginia and the decision of a rogue Union commander to recruit Black men to fight in South Carolina defied many white Americans' understanding of themselves as civilized people. Retaliation against Shaw and Hunter would determine whether Americans were what they claimed, able to control the darkest passions of men and to civilize the "barbarians" in their midst.

Hunter acted on his strategic vision within two months of arriving at Hilton Head. The Union had early momentum in the symbolically important campaign against Charleston, the city that birthed the secession movement. Confederate forces fired the opening shots of the war from Charleston on April 12, 1861, when their artillery forced the surrender of the United States garrison at Fort Sumter in Charleston Harbor. Three weeks later, the USS *Niagara* inaugurated a naval blockade. The presence of this screw steamer was a symbolic gesture, since the single vessel could not hope to close the three different channels that gave ships access to the port of Charleston. Military action began in earnest on November 7, 1861, when a Union fleet of seventy ships under the command of Samuel DuPont attacked Port Royal, located fifty-two miles southwest of Charleston and thirty-two miles northeast of Savannah. It was one of the best natural harbors along the south Atlantic coast, and the

Maj. Gen. David Hunter, outlaw, and 2nd Lt. Robert Gould Shaw, felon, according to Jefferson Davis's August 1862 retaliation proclamation. Hunter and Shaw actually had very different interpretations of civilized conduct in war and of the role of Black troops. (Library of Congress Prints and Photographs Division)

Union hoped to gain a coaling and supply station for a legitimate blockade of Charleston. The Union vessels moved in an elliptical pattern as their guns took turns pounding the defending forts. Confederate forces evacuated and Union troops under Brig. Gen. Thomas W. Sherman took possession of the island. DuPont achieved the Union's first major victory of the war. The U.S. Navy possessed a base for the South Atlantic Blockading Squadron and for army incursions along the coastline of three Southern states.[3]

The Union victory at Port Royal had drastic social consequences disproportionate to the minor number of troops involved. White families fled the surrounding islands, abandoning plantations and 10,000 slaves to the occupying Federal forces. Plantation owners in the South Carolina low country as far inland as thirty miles from the coast evacuated thousands of slaves to the central and up-country regions of the Carolinas. The Union occupiers transformed the Sea Islands into experimental communities with no parallel in the history of the antebellum South. Two days after entering Port Royal,

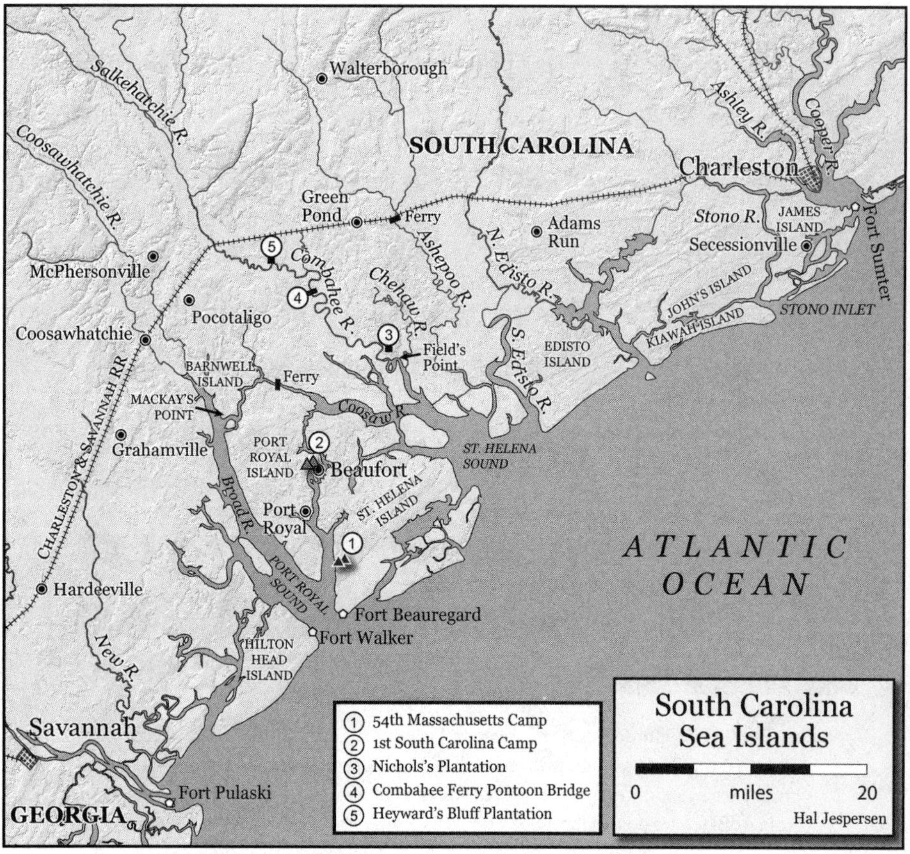


Sherman appointed a superintendent of contrabands who organized local African Americans into a workforce that unloaded supplies and navigated naval vessels. Through the First Confiscation Act of August 1861, Congress had authorized agents of the Federal government to seize property, including slaves, which had been used to support insurrection. The luxury cotton grown in the Sea Islands offered an opportunity for the government to make a profit, so Secretary of the Treasury Salmon P. Chase sent a Treasury agent to collect the cotton crop and plan for production on the abandoned plantations in 1862. He also sent Edward L. Pierce, a young anti-slavery Massachusetts attorney, to investigate the condition of the Black people and develop a plan for them. Robert Gould Shaw's father, Francis George Shaw, helped form the National Freedmen's Relief Association in order to fund and recruit labor superintendents and teachers for the plantations.[4]

When Hunter arrived on the scene, he saw the Black men in his department as a pool of soldiers rather than a source of labor. This revolutionary view challenged most white Northerners' assumptions about the place of Black people in civilization. They believed that enslaved men and women were not fully civilized, because they lacked the historical traditions, formal education, and higher culture necessary to participate in republican government. Hunter's predecessor held this perspective. In his general orders organizing Black labor on the abandoned plantations, Sherman appealed to Northern philanthropists to come to his department. He wanted teachers "until the blacks become capable themselves of thinking and acting judiciously." New England volunteers would teach Black people on the islands "the rudiments of civilization . . . their amenability to the laws of both God and man, their relations to each other as social beings." Northerners like Sherman thought it would take decades at minimum to incorporate Blacks fully into civilization.[5]

Hunter agreed that formerly enslaved Black people were ignorant and degraded. He differed in his belief that the military itself was an effective training tool of civilization. "The discipline of military life will be the very safest and quickest school in which these enfranchised bondsmen can be elevated to the level of our higher intelligence and cultivation," he publicly announced. "Their enrollment in regular military organizations, and the giving them in this manner a legitimate vent to their natural desire to prove themselves worthy of freedom, cannot fail to have the further good effect of rendering less likely mere servile insurrection, unrestrained by the comities and usages of civilized warfare."[6]

When he arrived at Port Royal, Hunter moved quickly. One of his critics within the army remarked that Hunter was "dreamy by habit & efficient in spasms." If so, then Hunter had one of his spasms in May 1862. On May 6, he began organizing military companies of Black men from the islands. He sent James Cashman, a local Black man, to enlist 100 men from St. Helena Island. He appointed Brooklyn bricklayer, firefighter, and Methodist class leader Charles T. Trowbridge to captain the first company of recruits. And he sent a message to the Treasury's labor superintendents in charge of the abandoned plantations asking them to tell the former slaves about military service and taking down the names of any volunteers.[7]

Three days later, Hunter issued an order emancipating all the enslaved men and women in the Department of the South, comprising South Carolina, Georgia, and Florida. Because those three states had "taken up arms against the United States," he had declared martial law on April 25. "Slavery and martial law in a free country are altogether incompatible," General Orders No. 11 proclaimed on May 9. "The persons in these three states, here-

Charles T. Trowbridge, 1st South Carolina. Trowbridge captained the first company of recruits in Hunter's Regiment and in the 1st South Carolina. He was in constant command of armed Black soldiers from May 9, 1862, to February 9, 1866. (From S. Taylor, *Black Woman's Civil War Memoirs*, 46)

tofore held as slaves, are therefore declared forever free." When the number of volunteers for the military companies failed to meet Hunter's expectations, he ordered all able-bodied Black males between the ages of eighteen and forty-five to Hilton Head. On May 12, what one New England teacher on Port Royal called "the black day," he sent to the plantations squads of Union soldiers who rounded up terrified Black men at gunpoint and shot a handful who resisted. The Hunter companies went into camp at Hilton Head and began to drill.[8]

Hunter's conscription ran roughshod over the goals and desires of the Black men and women living on the coastal islands, who wanted the freedom to determine their own futures. He also alienated Treasury officials and Northern philanthropists, who wanted to produce a lucrative cotton crop and prove the capabilities of Black people to work under a free labor system and who had invested time and Federal resources organizing work on the plantations. Hunter assumed that Black men wanted to fight for their freedom; indeed, he believed that only by fighting for their freedom would they deserve it. However, attorney Pierce wrote Hunter that the Black men on the plantations did not want to be soldiers. They did not yet know whether they could trust Union officials, and their main goal was to preserve and protect their families in a time of chaos and flux.[9]

When the white Union soldiers arrived on Mrs. Jenkins's plantation on St. Helena Island to take away the able-bodied men, several Black women gathered with axes in their hands but eventually set them aside and said goodbye to their husbands and sons with the "wildest expressions of grief." The Northern superintendent of the plantation wrote Hunter that one woman said that "she had lost all of her children and friends, and now her husband was taken and she must die uncared for." All expressed their belief that this was a "final separation" of their families. The Black leader of the people on another plantation reminded Union officials that their master had told them that the Union army would sell them to Cuba and suggested that this forced conscription was similar enough to the master's threats. "This rude separation of husband and wife, children and parents, must needs remind them of what we have always stigmatized as the worst feature of slavery," one Treasury official on St. Helena Island lamented.[10]

Hunter acted without the permission or sanction of the Lincoln administration and without consulting its other representatives in the Department of the South. After Hunter issued the conscription order, Pierce told him that he was "thwarting a plan of the Government." Hunter replied, "He could not help it if two plans of the Government conflicted." The major general was being disingenuous, since the War Department was not aware of his orders until after he issued them.[11]

Lincoln publicly disavowed Hunter's actions, issuing a proclamation on May 19 voiding General Orders No. 11. "Government of the United States had no knowledge, information, or belief of an intention on the part of General Hunter to issue such a proclamation," Lincoln declared, "nor has it yet any authentic information that the document is genuine." The president carefully worded the rest of the proclamation. He hinted that as commander in chief of the army and navy he might have the power to declare slaves in a state free if it were a "necessity indispensable to the maintenance of the government" but that any such power belonged to the president and not to the "decision of commanders in the field." Lincoln reiterated the official policy of his administration, a promise of federal financial aid to any state that adopted a plan to abolish slavery gradually, and appealed to the people of the slaveholding states to accept the offer.[12]

Although Lincoln retracted the order and publicly chastised Hunter, his administration was shifting its policy regarding slavery in the spring of 1862.

The desire to suppress the rebellion was trumping fears that Blacks did not belong in a civilized war, especially among Republicans who believed that all human beings shared equal natural rights to liberty. Republicans in Congress and Northern governors who advocated emancipation as a moral imperative or as a weapon of war increased their pressure on the president after Hunter's order. When Secretary of War Edwin Stanton wrote Massachusetts governor John A. Andrew asking the state to supply three or four more infantry regiments, Andrew responded on May 19 that his people would be reluctant to step forward under current administration policy. "But if the President will sustain Hunter, recognize all men, even black men, as legally capable of that loyalty the blacks are willing to manifest, and let them fight, with God and human nature on their side, the roads will swarm, if need be, with multitudes whom New England would pour out to obey your call," he wrote.[13]

Hunter, for his part, ignored Lincoln's rebuke and moved forward with his plans. He wrote Stanton on May 31 to request steamers and additional troops for operations against Charleston, Savannah, and Jacksonville, Florida. He intended to occupy the entire south Atlantic coast. "The slaves would flock into our posts, and the enemy be thus injured as much as in any other way," he wrote. "According to my experience they would rather lose one of their children than a good negro." Stanton authorized Hunter on June 9 to move against Charleston with the troops already under his command.[14] Operations against the city were already underway when Hunter received Stanton's telegram.

Hunter and Admiral DuPont made this first serious attempt to capture Charleston after Robert Smalls, a Black pilot on a Confederate steamer, brought the vessel to the Union fleet on May 13 and conveyed important intelligence. Confederate troops had abandoned a fort at the mouth of the Stono River, which offered the Union a beachhead on James Island, where Confederates had amassed infantry and built significant fortifications to defend both the land and water approaches to the city. On May 21, DuPont sent gunboats up the Stono that fired on Confederate cavalry who were helping panicked planters remove their slaves. This action opened the way for hundreds of slaves to cross into Union lines. On June 2, two divisions of Union soldiers landed on James Island and built a fortified camp at Grimball's Plantation.[15]

The Confederate position on James Island contained five miles of earthworks and the superbly constructed Tower Battery, located near the village of Secessionville. The battery had four faces configured in a giant *M*

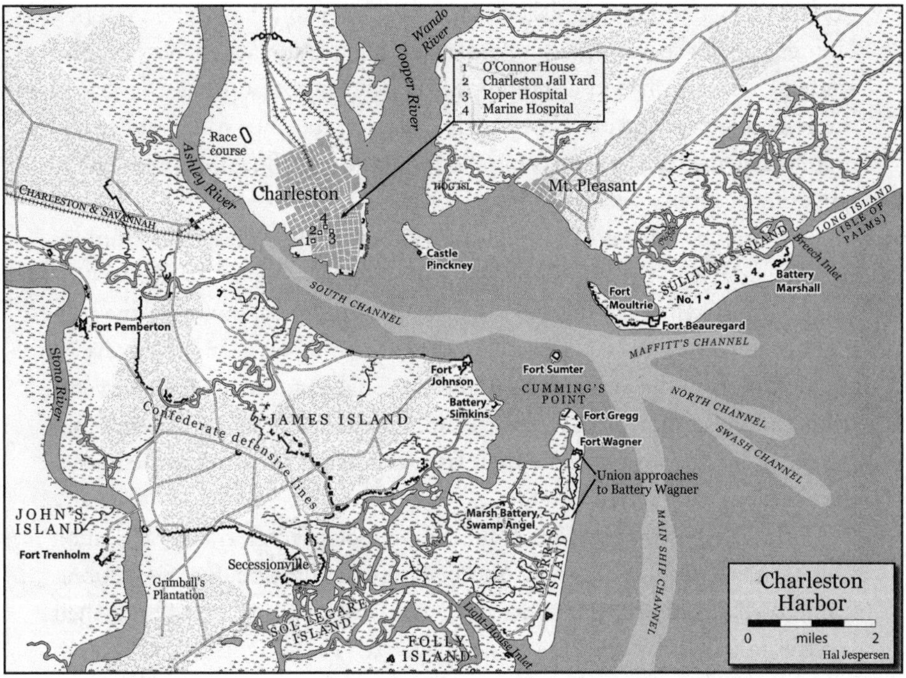


shape and seven guns mounted on parapets up to sixteen feet high. Marshes surrounded the works so that the only approach for attacking troops was a stretch of land 200 yards wide directly in the front. When Confederate troops probed the Union position at Grimball's Plantation on June 10, they were repulsed in an open field engagement in front of the Union works. Hunter returned to Hilton Head and ordered his subordinates on James Island to abort active operations but to maintain their toehold on the island. Instead, they took the offensive. On June 16, 6,000 Union soldiers attacked the Tower Battery, but its defenders repulsed them. Although 500 assailants gained the parapets, there was no steady flow of supporting reinforcements because of the constricted approach to the earthworks and the inexperience of Union regimental commanders. Hunter ordered Union troops to withdraw on July 1.[16]

During the operations on James Island, the U.S. House of Representatives launched an investigation of Hunter at the instigation of border state Democrats. These opponents of emancipation wanted to know whether there was an armed Black regiment in South Carolina. Stanton responded on June 14 that the War Department had "no official information" on the organization of a Black regiment and had not authorized such an organization nor armed it. He then asked Hunter to report on the House's queries. Hunter's response was a mixture of sarcasm and passionate advocacy for his strategic vision. A friend of Hunter's from the antebellum army described the general's "piercing black eyes." "He had a countenance so expressive and mobile that any feeling was visible at once in the sparkling of his eye and the quivering of his lip," he recalled.[17]

The sparkle and quiver of emotion came through clearly in Hunter's June 23 letter to Stanton. "No regiment of 'fugitive slaves' has been or is being organized in this department," he wrote. "There is, however, a fine regiment of persons whose late masters are 'fugitive rebels'—men who everywhere fly before the appearance of the National flag, leaving their servants behind them to shift, as best they can, for themselves." The loyal men of his regiment did not wish to avoid their late masters but were rather anxious to pursue them, he claimed.[18]

Hunter cited instructions from the previous secretary of war, Simon Cameron, to his predecessor Sherman as justification for his actions. Cameron had authorized Sherman to "employ all loyal persons offering their services in defense of the Union" and neglected to specify any "character or color" or "nature of the employment." Hunter had not received authority to issue uniforms or arms, but he sarcastically reminded Stanton that he had no specific authority to issue shovels or spades to laborers, either. "To me it seemed that liberty to employ men in any particular capacity implied with it liberty also to supply them with the necessary tools, and acting upon this faith I have clothed, equipped, and armed the only loyal regiment yet raised in South Carolina." Hunter concluded with a reminder that historical precedent was on his side, necessary for officers' actions within the traditions of civilized war: the British had employed former slaves as valuable auxiliary troops in the West Indies.[19]

Republicans in Congress loved Hunter's response. "The clerk could scarcely read it with decorum; nor could half his words be heard amidst the universal peals of laughter," Hunter noted proudly. A Democrat in the House wrote that Republican members heard the letter "with loud applause and boisterous manifestations of approbation."[20] Hunter was proving to be a handful for the Lincoln administration.

Meanwhile, the conscripted Black men continued to drill at Hilton Head but were not paid for their services and deserted in droves, undermining Hunter's extravagant claims to Stanton that he would have 50,000 Black soldiers by the end of the fall. Stanton did not order Hunter to disband the companies, but he did not give permission for Hunter to muster them into the Union army, either. The Lincoln administration also put the occupation of Port Royal squarely under War Department rather than Treasury Department control. On June 16, the secretary of war sent Brig. Gen. Rufus Saxton to the Department of the South and ordered him to take charge of the plantations and their inhabitants. Saxton had permission to operate independent of any military official in the department except Hunter. The Massachusetts-born and West Point–trained general came from a family populated with reformers, abolitionists, and transcendentalists.[21]

Hunter had set the stage for a Confederate response to his policies, but the War Department neglected the military situation in the Department of the South for the next month. There were more pressing matters taking place closer to the capital, and these consumed the administration's time and attention during June and July. The story of retaliation requires a brief foray to another scene of action, where military events prompted Confederate president Jefferson Davis to address Hunter's activities in South Carolina.

Stanton's and Lincoln's eyes were on the events taking place in Virginia, where the secretary and the president created a new army that represented a new direction for the Union war effort, one that suggested more support for Hunter's actions than he had so far publicly received from the administration. This new army raised another specter. War always threatened to unleash dark passions of revenge and license, carefully controlled in a civilized man and in a civilized war, and it began to seem that the white men of the Union army were not as civilized as they claimed to be.

The context for the Lincoln administration's change in policy was the poisonous distrust and disagreement between the War Department and its ranking general in Virginia, Maj. Gen. George B. McClellan. McClellan believed that professional army officers were best prepared to conduct war "upon the highest principles known to Christian civilization." Officers must maintain order over troops, protect noncombatants and their property, act from scientific military principles rather than political motives, and restrain the worst passions of men, who had the potential as soldiers to "degenerate into a mob of thieves." He insisted that "revenge" and "useless effusion of blood" had no part in warfare. He fought to preserve the Constitution (as he interpreted it), including its protections of slavery in the Southern states. McClellan took his time organizing and disciplining his field army, the Army of the Potomac. He was disinclined to explain his military plans in full to Lincoln, whom he viewed as a frontier buffoon who should trust his expertise, and had come to hate Stanton, whom he saw as his enemy. "Had [Stanton] lived in the time of the Savior, Judas Iscariot would have remained a respected member of the fraternity of the apostles," McClellan wrote his wife, "and the magnificent treachery & rascality of E. M. Stanton would have caused Judas to have raised his arms in holy horror & unaffected wonder."[22]

Stanton loved power and schemes; he was vindictive and duplicitous. The secretary of war manipulated truth when he reported on McClellan to Lincoln and other members of the cabinet in order to make McClellan appear more insubordinate and incompetent than he was. Secretary of the Navy Gideon Welles remarked, "I doubt his sincerity always." Although Stanton seems to have genuinely believed that emancipation was necessary to win the war and acted consistently in that respect, Maj. Gen. Ethan Allen Hitchcock, who viewed Stanton more kindly than most, said that he was not "a man of reason." "He has no general principles of action," he wrote. "He decides a point one way one day, and a week later, forgetting his decision, and having no definite principle to go by, he decides the same point another way."[23]

In mid-June 1862, McClellan's Army of the Potomac was advancing toward the Confederate capital at Richmond from its base on the Chesapeake peninsula, moving at a pace that caused congressional Republicans to question his loyalty. The army operated under its commander's orders to protect the private property of Virginia citizens and treat them "with courtesy and kindness." On June 26, the War Department created the 50,000-man Army of Virginia, formed from three corps occupying northern Virginia, and placed it under Maj. Gen. John Pope, a braggadocio and gregarious regular army officer from Illinois who was an outspoken supporter of Republican policies. Earlier in the war, he had fined citizens in Missouri who did not actively resist Confederate guerrillas and had acted inventively and decisively in the capture of the Confederate Island No. 10 on the Mississippi River. Pope's army would protect Washington, defend the Shenandoah Valley, and disrupt the railroads around Charlottesville and Gordonville, Virginia. A significant percentage of its leadership and rank and file were Midwestern or German immigrant in origin, anti-slavery Republican in politics, and advocates of punishing the rebel citizens who displayed their hostility to the occupying Union forces.[24]

Pope spent July in Washington directing his army from a distance. He courted Republican politicians and met with Stanton regularly at the War Department. On July 4, he mentioned Hunter's actions in South Carolina to a group of officers who gathered in his room, one of whom recorded Pope's "clear and strong" ideas: "He thinks [Black men] ought to be taken and used remorselessly wherever needed." Unlike Hunter, Pope did not envision

Blacks as soldiers but rather as laborers, but he thought Congress should "let the commanders in the field use Negroes as circumstances require." At a dinner with Secretary Chase, Pope "expressed himself freely and decidedly in favor of the most vigorous measures in the prosecution of the war."[25]

Pope knew that those in Republican leadership in Washington had turned the corner on emancipation. They acted from a combination of long-held anti-slavery sentiment, the reluctance of border state slaveholders to accept Lincoln's proposals for gradual, compensated emancipation, and the significant labor contribution that refugees from slavery made to the Union war effort. The immediate catalyst, however, was a reversal of Union war fortunes in Virginia. Confederate general Robert E. Lee gained command of the Army of Northern Virginia and went on the offensive. In a series of battles that took place June 26 through July 1, McClellan inflicted heavy casualties on Lee but surrendered the initiative and retreated from the outskirts of Richmond back down the Chesapeake peninsula. The Confederate military resurgence gave credence to those who claimed that vigorous measures were needed in order to destroy the rebellion, especially since newspapers widely reported that impressed slaves labored to build the fortifications that shielded Confederate armies. On July 14 and 17, Congress passed bills that provided freedom to slaves whose masters were in rebellion and authorized the recruitment of Black soldiers for segregated regiments with white officers. On July 22, Lincoln read his cabinet a draft of an emancipation proclamation.[26]

One of the junior line officers in Pope's army was Robert Gould Shaw. At his rank, he could not shape policy on a wide scale, as Hunter and Pope attempted to do. Within the more limited sphere of his company and regiment, however, he was no less ardent about the best way to defeat the rebellion. Like McClellan, he believed civilized warfare controlled and disciplined soldiers to minimize the violence of war and its effects on noncombatants. He was proud of how his regiment imposed order on its enlisted men. "We marched through Martinsburg and Winchester in close order, and band playing, so that there should be no chance of the men's falling out and committing any outrages," he wrote his mother. "A house on the other side of Martinsburg was set on fire by some soldier, but, on the whole, our men show very little of the vices common in armies that have been some time in the field."[27]

Shaw thought it was important to place guards over the property of citizens in the path of his army's march. "I have never seen guards placed except to prevent plundering," he informed his family. "If the soldiers were allowed to plunder indiscriminately, we should have an army of thieves and robbers that would be perfectly unmanageable." On July 28, 1862, Shaw learned that Pope had issued orders forbidding any commander to place a guard over private property. "The soldiers will speedily make away with all food within ten or fifteen miles of the camps," Shaw predicted. He did not object to soldiers living off the land, however. He abhorred pillage and plunder, but he believed a combatant was justified in using the enemy's resources in order to win.[28]

Pope issued a series of orders in July, with the full approval of President Lincoln, which sought to balance the restraints of civilized war with a set of military policies that targeted the morale of Virginia's population and the resources as well as the armies of the Confederacy. Pope instructed the Army of Virginia to live off the countryside (General Orders No. 5), but consistent with the civilized principle of keeping men under discipline and restraint, only commanding officers could order confiscation. They had to give vouchers to citizens who could receive payment at the end of the war if they had remained loyal to the United States since the date of the vouchers. He ordered officers not to place guards over houses or other private property (General Orders No. 13) but reminded them that Articles of War empowered them to "restrain" troops to the full extent required for discipline and efficiency.[29]

Pope also held rebel civilians responsible for any attacks on Union supply lines by guerrillas (General Orders No. 7); his commanders would turn them out en masse to repair damage to railroads or telegraphs, and he would levy additional fines on them. A citizen who fired on army personnel would be summarily shot. Finally, he ordered commanders in the Army of Virginia to arrest all disloyal male citizens within their lines (General Orders No. 11). Any citizen who did not take an oath of allegiance to the United States would be turned out of his home and put outside Union army lines. Any citizen who took the oath and violated it would be shot. Citizens who communicated to people within Confederate lines would be treated as spies.[30]

Most of the officers and soldiers in the Army of Virginia supported these measures and the idea of confiscating rebel resources and punishing citizens who provided resources and information to rebel armies. Pope's corps commanders immediately issued orders to implement the new policies. On July 27, 1862, 1st Corps commander Maj. Gen. Franz Sigel required the provost marshals of all brigades and divisions to arrest all male inhabitants within the lines of the corps and to send a list of those who would not take the oath of allegiance. Rufus King, a division commander in the 3rd Corps, stationed his regiments around Fredericksburg so that they would be in position to stop citizens from communicating with people outside of Union lines. Orders went down the chain to follow Pope's instructions about how to procure supplies from the countryside. The chief of staff for the 3rd Corps instructed subordinates that there must be no "indiscriminate marauding." To keep the men from "strolling about the country," he told colonels of regiments to observe daily roll calls, keep the men busy in drill, and confine and punish absentees. Many officers at the regimental level, and the soldiers they commanded, exceeded the letter of Pope's orders. They took whatever they wanted, ransacked homes, and otherwise indulged in arbitrary destruction.[31]

Pope's orders and the subsequent behavior of Union soldiers in Virginia outraged Confederate authorities. President Jefferson Davis wrote, "Pope is trying to establish in Virginia the reign of terror with which he paralyzed Missouri." John B. Jones, a clerk in the Confederate War Department and the author of a bestselling novel about the western frontier, thought Pope was "brutal" and "savage" and that his army was "committing shocking devastations." Lee wrote Maj. Gen. Stonewall Jackson, "I want Pope to be suppressed. The course indicated in his orders, if the newspapers report them correctly, cannot be permitted and will lead to retaliation on our part. You had better notify him the first opportunity." Lee ordered cavalry commander Maj. Gen. J. E. B. Stuart to protect the families of those arrested and to assist those trying to get within Confederate lines.[32]

Davis was particularly angry at the timing of Pope's orders because the Confederacy had signed the Dix-Hill cartel on July 22 arranging for the general exchange of prisoners of war. It stipulated that both sides would exchange all prisoners of war currently held, private for private and officer for officer, with a sliding scale of equivalents derived from a table used during the War of 1812 that allowed prisoners of different military rank to be exchanged for each other. For example, a major general could be exchanged for forty privates. Each side was obligated to parole prisoners within ten days of their capture and deliver them to specified locations. The framers of the cartel expected that paroled men would return home on their own recognizance until notified that they had been formally exchanged. If one side held a surplus of prisoners compared to the other, the excess prisoners, who were paroled but not exchanged, could not "discharge any duty usually performed by soldiers," which included "field, garrison, police, guard, or constabulary duty." Exchange was not complete until the officer's or soldier's equivalent arrived within his own lines.[33]

Davis thought the Lincoln administration had played him. "Scarcely had [the cartel] been signed when the military authorities of the United States commenced a practice changing the character of the war from such as becomes civilized nations into a campaign of indiscriminate robbery and murder," he fumed to Lee. Davis had spent much of his life immersed in the professional military culture of the United States. He had attended West Point (starting at age sixteen), adopted a "lifelong military bearing," thought professional training was necessary for military success, was an effective combat commander and war hero of the Mexican War, and served as a reforming and micromanaging secretary of war for the United States from 1853 to 1857. During his term, he sent three officers to Europe to observe and report on European militaries and the Crimean War. As the president of the Confederate States of America, he essentially acted as his own secretary of war. He made all major decisions and interfered in trivial matters.[34]

Davis retaliated against the United States for the actions of Pope in Virginia and Hunter in South Carolina. He confronted Union officials about a cluster of incidents that in his view marked a deliberate swing on the part of the United States toward "merciless atrocities" and "savage war." Under instruction from Davis, Lee wrote two letters addressed to "General Commanding U.S. Army, Washington" on August 2. Lee followed the retaliation protocol in the composition and rhetoric of his letter. He proclaimed a desire to fight a civilized war and then named a series of offenses on the part of particular Union officers, including Hunter and Pope. "Hunter has armed slaves for the murder of their masters, and has done all in his power to inaugurate a servile war, which is worse than that of the savage, inasmuch as it superadds other horrors to the indiscriminate slaughter of all ages, sexes, and conditions," Lee wrote. Pope's orders "direct the murder of our peaceful citizens as spies if found quietly tilling their farms in his rear, even outside his lines." Included in the list of offenses were recent U.S. War Department orders that confiscated the property of those who actively sympathized with the rebellion. "Some of the military authorities seem to suppose that their end will be better attained by a savage war in which no quarter is to be given, and no age or sex to be spared, than by such hostilities as are alone recognized to be lawful in modern times," Lee summarized. "We find ourselves driven by our enemies by steady progress toward a practice which we abhor and which we are vainly struggling to avoid."[35]

Having established the high ground, as was necessary in all such correspondence, Lee gave the United States fifteen days to respond with a correction of the facts or a disavowal of the policies before Confederate authorities retaliated. Lee enclosed a sample order from the Confederate War Department (General Orders No. 54) that proclaimed the commissioned U.S. officers of Pope's and Hunter's commands—such as Robert Gould Shaw—to be felons rather than public enemies entitled to prisoner of war status. Prisoners already held from Pope's command were immediately placed in close confinement until the United States retracted the offending policies. They were also reserved for hanging in the event that troops from Pope's army carried out the execution of citizens.[36]

The Confederate president wanted the civilized world to notice the restraint of his chosen method of retaliation. In his original instructions to Lee, in the general orders eventually issued by the War Department, and in a message to the Confederate Congress, Davis explained that he could not retaliate in kind against the United States because the Confederate government refused to target unarmed men, women, and children. Nor could he retaliate on enlisted soldiers, who were innocent because they had no choice but to obey orders. Commissioned officers, however, had the option to resign, and if they had chosen to remain in the Union army and implement its barbaric orders, they were guilty of all its atrocities.[37]

U.S. War Department officials did not respond immediately. They were behind on correspondence because of changes in leadership in the command structure and continued controversy among Lincoln, the War Department, and McClellan. The latter issued orders intended to contradict those of Pope. "We are not engaged in a war of rapine, revenge, or subjugation," his August 9 General Orders No. 154 read. "This is not a contest against populations; but against armed forces and political organizations. . . . The idea that private property may be plundered is the worst idea that can pervade an army. Marauding degrades as men and demoralizes as soldiers all who engage in it and returns them to their homes unfitted for the pursuits of honest industry." McClellan wrote his wife that Pope "ought to bring defeat upon any cause that employs him."[38]

The new general-in-chief who was responsible for answering Lee's retaliation letter was Henry Wager Halleck, a scholarly, West Point–trained engineering officer who had published the most important and widely read books in the United States on military theory and international law. He had traveled to France in 1843 to study its military, and French authorities had given him full access. Successfully commanding Union armies in Missouri and Mississippi before Lincoln brought him east to rein in McClellan, Halleck was supposed to provide trustworthy military advice to Lincoln and lead Union armies to victory. On July 23, Halleck had arrived in Washington. But the politics in the capital and the fear of failure unnerved him, and he immediately abdicated his role of providing strategic direction. He refused to make hard decisions regarding operations in the field and instead defaulted to his talents, organization and administration. Those around him in the Lincoln administration quickly learned that he worried incessantly. Most thought that, like Stanton, he had a "nasty disposition."[39]

Halleck retained his confidence in his own expertise about the customs of war, however, bolstered by his regular correspondence with an intellectual kindred spirit, Francis Lieber, a veteran of the Battle of Waterloo and émigré from Germany. Lieber was a professor of history and political economy at Columbia University in New York City and an expert on republican government and international law. Lieber thought Halleck was an intellectual giant and envied his position in the center of public events. Halleck wanted to ensure military policy aligned with the civilized customs of war and asked for Lieber's legal counsel in cases that involved gray areas of the law.[40]

Halleck had to catch up on the Union retaliation correspondence after he arrived in Washington. He found that War Department clerks had misfiled a letter from Robert E. Lee, dating back to July 6, inquiring about Union major general Benjamin Butler's execution of a Confederate citizen in New Orleans. He responded to that letter on August 7. He assured Lee that the United States would fight the war "in strict accordance with the laws and usages of modern warfare." He promised to punish all excesses by subordinates and to investigate the facts about the alleged execution of citizens. He included a warning, however. "In regard to retaliation by taking the lives of innocent persons I know of no modern authority which justifies it, except in the extreme case of a war with an uncivilized foe which has himself first established such a barbarous rule," he said. "The United States will never countenance such a proceeding unless forced to do so by the barbarous conduct of an enemy who first applies such a rule to our own citizens."[41] He did not immediately respond to Lee's August 2 letter, which included the proclamation of felony against Pope's officers and Hunter.

The matter became urgent, however, when one of Hunter's Black companies engaged in a skirmish with rebel guerrillas on August 8 and when a corps of Pope's army clashed with Stonewall Jackson's troops at the Battle of Cedar Mountain on August 9. Hunter, failing to hear back from Stanton with authorization to muster his Black regiment, had actually disbanded it, except for one company under the command of Captain Trowbridge, sent on August 5 to garrison St. Simon's Island (off the coast of Georgia) and protect the 500 freed people, mostly women and children, living in settlements established by the Union navy. Freedmen John Brown and Edward Gould had already armed and organized twenty-five men to protect the clus-

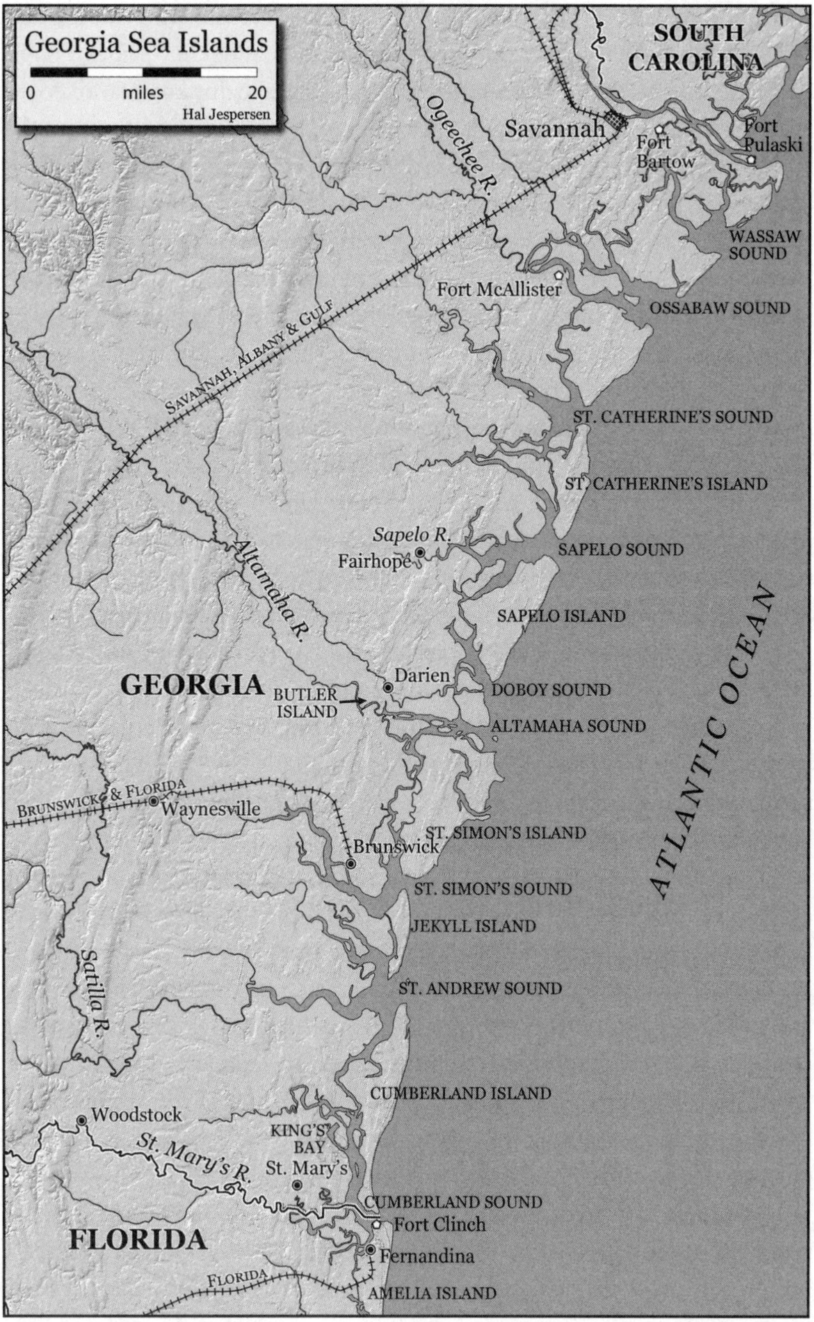

Georgia Sea Islands
0
miles
20
Hal Jespersen
SOUTH CAROLINA
Savannah
Ogeechee R.
Fort Bartow
Fort Pulaski
WASSAW SOUND
Fort McAllister
OSSABAW SOUND
SAVANNAH, ALBANY & GULF
ST. CATHERINE'S SOUND
ST. CATHERINE'S ISLAND
Sapelo R.
Fairhope
SAPELO SOUND
Altamaha R.
SAPELO ISLAND
ATLANTIC OCEAN
GEORGIA
Darien
BUTLER ISLAND
DOBOY SOUND
ALTAMAHA SOUND
BRUNSWICK & FLORIDA
Waynesville
ST. SIMON'S ISLAND
Brunswick
ST. SIMON'S SOUND
JEKYLL ISLAND
Satilla R.
ST. ANDREW SOUND
CUMBERLAND ISLAND
Woodstock
KING'S BAY
St. Mary's R.
St. Mary's
CUMBERLAND SOUND
Fort Clinch
FLORIDA
Fernandina
FLORIDA
AMELIA ISLAND

ter of settlements. Susie King Taylor, a fourteen-year-old who had learned to read while a slave in Savannah and escaped by boat to Union lines, taught forty children in the island's school during the day and any adults who could spare time at night. On August 8, the owner of one of the plantations on the island landed with a small party to kidnap any persons they found out alone and take them to the mainland. Two men who escaped this effort alerted the people. Brown and Gould led their men on a hunt for the rebels. When they entered a swamp, the rebels fired from behind a log and killed Brown. When Trowbridge and his men landed the next day, they joined a party of sailors and continued the chase for the next several days. The rebels escaped, and the leader wrote a friend, "If you wish to know hell before your time, go to St. Simon's Island and be hunted ten days by niggers." When white Union soldiers sang the popular song "John Brown's Body," the freed people thought the song referred to their local hero. Union officials in the department considered Brown to be the first Black man to fall under arms in combat with Confederates. Trowbridge's company remained on picket duty on St. Simon's for two months and regularly scouted on the mainland.[42]

The skirmish on St. Simon's precipitated General Saxton's mid-August decision to organize another Black regiment in order to protect the freed people better and ensure greater stability for the free labor operations on the Sea Islands plantations. The War Department had stripped the Department of the South of white troops to support military operations in Virginia. When Union troops evacuated Edisto Island, Saxton had to move 1,500 people from there to St. Helena Island and abandon hundreds of acres of cotton and food crops. Freed people living on St. Simon's could see rebel flags flying on the mainland and the smoke from the numerous Confederate salt manufacturing facilities that dotted the coast. They lived in constant fear of kidnapping raids. Saxton requested permission to arm 5,000 freed people to protect the settlements on the islands and enable a group to return to Edisto. He believed that more slaves would escape to Union lines, especially those manufacturing salt, greatly weakening the rebellion, if he could guarantee their safety.[43]

Stanton authorized Saxton to "arm, uniform, equip, and receive into the service of the United States" up to 5,000 volunteers "of African descent." They would receive the same pay and rations as white volunteers and, if their masters were rebels, be regarded and treated as free men. He ordered Saxton to reoccupy all of the Sea Islands and defend the freed people living there. Finally, Stanton put in writing his approbation of Hunter's proposed strategy in the Department of the South. "The population of African de-

Susie King Taylor. A valued member of the 1st South Carolina, she served the regiment as laundress, teacher, and nurse. (Library of Congress Prints and Photographs Division)

scent that cultivate the land and perform the labor of the Rebels constitute a large share of their military strength and enable the white masters to fill the armies and wage a cruel and murderous war against the people of the Northern States," he said. "By reducing the laboring strength of the Rebels their military power will be reduced. You are therefore authorized by using any means in your power to withdraw from the enemy their laboring force and population and to spare no effort consistent with civilized warfare to weaken harass and annoy them."[44]

Arming Black men and employing them in combat in the Department of the South was now the official policy of the United States government, in direct defiance of the just-issued Confederate retaliation proclamation. When fifteen days passed without a response from U.S. authorities, the Confederate War Department issued General Orders No. 60 on August 21, which declared General Hunter to be an outlaw. Such a declaration meant that the individual forfeited the whole of his legal rights. The declaration thus placed Hunter entirely outside the framework of the law. He had no standing in court and no security for his person, because anyone could assault or kill him without any legal ramifications. Declarations of outlawry were increasingly rare in the nineteenth century, and indeed, a few months later when the United States published its general orders that encapsulated the laws of war, the U.S. code claimed that declarations of outlawry were violations of the laws of war. The Confederate order also announced that any captured U.S. commissioned officer who drilled, organized, or instructed slaves, with a view to their armed service in the war, was not recognized as a prisoner of war but would be executed as a felon.[45]

The Confederacy was not yet in a position to act on its declaration against Hunter, but the Davis administration was in the process of implementing its order against Robert Gould Shaw and the other officers of Pope's army. On August 9, a corps of 9,000 men from the Army of Virginia under Maj. Gen. Nathaniel Banks clashed with Stonewall Jackson's 15,000 troops at the Battle of Cedar Mountain. During the initial phases of the battle, when the attack of three Union regiments caused the left flank of the Confederate line to collapse, Union soldiers expressed their outrage over the Confederate War Department's retaliation orders by killing Confederate soldiers after they had surrendered. Confederate reinforcements turned the tide, and in one of the last actions of the battle, four Confederate brigades bore down on three Union regiments, including the 2nd Massachusetts, which was taking position in some woods at the edge of a wheat field.[46]

Robert Gould Shaw, serving as an aide-de-camp to Brig. Gen. George H.

Gordon, was working with the colonel of the 2nd to position the regiment when Confederates appeared on its front and flank and unleashed intense musketry fire. Capt. Henry Sturgis Russell, Shaw's relative and dear friend, greeted his cousin and then, as the honor of an elite gentleman required, stood calmly in his place while bullets whizzed around him. The well-disciplined 2nd Massachusetts, the last organized Federal regiment on the field, took 35 percent casualties before withdrawing.[47]

The Battle of Cedar Mountain decimated the officer ranks of Banks's corps. In one brigade, every field officer and every adjutant was dead or wounded, as were every one of the line officers of the 28th New York. Only eight of the 2nd Massachusetts's twenty-two officers made it through the battle unscathed. Confederates captured a total of thirty-seven officers from the corps, including Brig. Gen. Henry Prince and Henry Sturgis Russell. As Confederate soldiers led Russell off the battlefield, they told him that he would hang because of their War Department's retaliation orders. The prisoners were put under guard, marched fifteen miles to Orange Court House, and then sent to Richmond on the train. Russell noted that the Confederate officers and soldiers who guarded him were kind and civil.[48]

Russell arrived at Libby Prison in Richmond on August 11, and the guards put all the captured officers from Pope's army in a separate room with deserters, thieves, and lunatics. This was an important symbolic move. The Confederacy thus proclaimed that Pope's officers were not legitimate combatants entitled to POW status but felons incarcerated with thieves. For officers who viewed themselves as honorable gentlemen, it was also a public shaming. On August 15, guards at Libby put a cart loaded with coffins under the window. Crowds threw stones at the window and yelled at the officers, calling them Pope's Sepoys, a reference to the 1857–59 Indian rebellion against the British that Americans on both sides used as a shorthand for uncivilized conduct in war.[49]

Robert Gould Shaw, with his brigade near Culpeper Court House, Virginia, was frantic when he thought of Russell. "It makes me choke to think of him, especially since that inhuman order of Davis' concerning Pope's officers," Shaw wrote his mother. "I don't think it will make a great deal of difference in the treatment of them; but it will be an excuse for neglect." Shaw was so "enraged" that he briefly considered letting himself be captured so he could help his beloved cousin but realized that would be "wrong and foolish." "I can never think of our poor dead fellows, and of Harry, without longing for another battle," he told his mother. "It gives us all a desire to fight them."[50]

The Confederacy now held its first significant contingent of officer prisoners from Pope's army, with one of them, Russell, a prominent New England scion whose relatives were Republican organizers in Massachusetts. Retaliation against officers brought influence to bear on civilian administrations. Secretary of the Treasury Chase noted in his diary, "This cannot be permitted without shameful disgrace." At the same time, Lincoln received a letter from an important Virginia Unionist stating that Pope's army was demoralizing loyal people as well as Confederates because soldiers were plundering without restraint.[51]

The Union War Department immediately adjusted its conduct of the war in Virginia. It is important to connect new orders that Pope issued on August 14 with the incarceration of his officers as felons. It is also important to connect them to the fact that the Union leadership agreed with the Confederate leadership about the behavior of soldiers who pillaged. The dominant Northern view was that self-control was the essence of civilized manhood. Men who acted without restraint were "unmanned" and "animal." The civilized customs of war allowed armies to forage, but Union officials were aware that the behavior of some troops in the Army of Virginia crossed the line. They could not publicly sanction it and because of the threat of retaliation had to clarify their position in official orders. Pope stated in General Orders No. 19 that his order to subsist on the country "has either been entirely misinterpreted or grossly abused." He wanted it distinctly understood that soldiers had no right to enter houses, molest persons, or disturb the property of any citizen. He said that acts of "pillage" and "outrage" were "disgraceful" and would receive devastating punishment. He reminded troops that only commanding officers could order the seizure of provisions and forage for subsistence.[52]

Pope gave teeth to his orders. He established mounted patrols to scour the countryside for five miles around the camps to bring in soldiers absent without authority. One brigade in General Sigel's 1st Corps was notorious for plundering local inhabitants under the direction of its provost marshal. Pope ordered Sigel to treat troops caught plundering the country as "common robbers," to shoot them on the spot, and to arrest the offending provost marshal. Pope empowered the most stringent brigade provost marshal in his army, Marsena Rudolph Patrick, to issue sweeping enforcement orders. "With this in my hand I can fight anything," Patrick commented gleefully. He lined up every regiment in his brigade and read them the new orders. "The officers and men were taken aback, but they could say nothing."[53]

The Union War Department leadership stood firm about arresting citizens and requiring oaths, however. Halleck issued War Department General Orders No. 107 on August 15, which asserted that the international laws of war allowed for oaths of allegiance. "This government claims and will exercise the right to arrest, imprison, or place beyond its military lines any persons suspected of giving aid and information to its enemies or of any other treasonable act," he instructed McClellan. "You will assure Lee that no unseemly threats of retaliation on his part will deter this Government from exercising its lawful rights over both persons and property of whatever name or character."[54]

In the meantime, the Davis administration faced an unintended consequence of its order declaring Pope's officers to be felons: it had created a potential legal nightmare. The governor of Virginia, John Letcher, requested that the Confederate military turn Pope's officers over to the state for prosecution for violating its local laws. He pointed out that Davis had called Pope's officers robbers and murderers rather than prisoners of war. If they were criminals rather than legitimate combatants, they were under the laws of Virginia. Confederate secretary of war George W. Randolph recognized the serious implications of a nation at war allowing the civil government to prosecute officers in the enemy army. Davis told Randolph to ask Letcher about specific cases in order to buy time.[55]

By the end of August, the Union and Confederacy were in a standoff over the question of arresting citizens and requiring oaths. Halleck, distracted and sleepless from dealing with emergency after emergency as he tried to manage conflict between Pope and McClellan and to follow complex troop movements when Lee sent more troops to attack Pope, neglected a vital element in the retaliation ritual: he had never informed Lee that soldier pillaging was indeed unsanctioned, and he did not send to the Confederates the Union's clarifying orders of August 14 and 15 that showed that pillaging would be harshly punished.

Because of this oversight, when Pope lost the Battle of Second Manassas during August 28–30, Confederate prison officials continued to treat his—and only his—captured officers as felons rather than as POWs. Units of McClellan's Army of the Potomac fought under Pope at Second Manassas. Confederates separated McClellan's officers from Pope's officers when the prisoners arrived in Richmond. Pope's officers joined their comrades from Cedar Mountain in a separate room. The Confederacy now held ninety-seven officers from Pope's command.[56]

Henry Sturgis Russell's initial fears of being hanged had worn off with time. "We felt very easy," he later wrote his parents, "knowing that not all would suffer, and each thinking himself safe." He paced up and down the 90′ × 50′ room, trying to walk the equivalent of nine miles every day. "Really, the only suffering I had was the idea of being a prisoner," he said. His cellmate Capt. William D. Wilkins was not so sanguine. He thought that Russell "with a nervous step walks the floor incessantly like a caged wild beast." For his own part, "thoughts of Wife, babies & home drive me almost frantic & I can scarce restrain myself from committing some crazy act of violence." Bitterness poured out in every line he wrote in his diary, especially after the officers of the Army of the Potomac left Libby Prison on September 11 to be exchanged. "They have been here 2 days; we for more than a month," he complained, "And our Gov't . . . *Acquiesces* with the rebels, makes no effort on our behalf, & endeavors to drive degradation into our souls by compelling us to submit to this degrading distinction."[57]

The retaliation correspondence regarding Russell, Wilkins, and the rest of Pope's officers languished while military events in Virginia and Maryland distracted both the Lincoln and the Davis administrations. Lincoln removed Pope from command in Virginia and sent him to Minnesota. Lee invaded Maryland and fought the Battle of Antietam on September 17, and the Union victory there prompted Lincoln to issue the preliminary emancipation proclamation on September 22. Robert Gould Shaw had not forgotten Pope's officers, however, and it colored his view of the proclamation. He knew his parents rejoiced, but he was more ambivalent. "Jeff Davis will soon issue a proclamation threatening to hang every prisoner they take, and will make this a war of extermination," he said. "I would give anything to have had Harry free before Lincoln issued that; I am so afraid it will go hard with him."[58]

Shaw did not need to worry about his cousin. Immediately after issuing the preliminary emancipation proclamation, the Lincoln administration turned its attention to Pope's officers languishing in Libby Prison. The U.S. War Department verbally, without putting it in writing, informed the Confederate government that Pope was removed from command and that his orders were not being enforced. This response was subtle because the Lincoln administration intended to keep arresting citizens and administering oaths of allegiance during active campaigns. The War Department did not, as it had with Confederate accusations of soldier plundering, admit any wrong or adjust any conduct. Pope's orders were not being enforced simply because the Army of Virginia did not exist anymore.[59]

Confederate officials took the opportunity, however, to publicly proclaim a victory and the righteousness of their conduct throughout the retaliation process. On September 24, the Confederate agent for exchange, Robert Ould, immediately released and delivered to Union authorities all ninety-seven of the imprisoned officers from Pope's command. He sent a note to his counterpart acknowledging the assurance of U.S. authorities that Pope's orders were inoperative. "I trust you will perceive by this action of the Confederate government . . . that there has been at no time any disposition on its part to be severe upon them personally," he wrote. He used stock rhetorical phrases in the rest of the letter: "highest obligations of duty," "just measures of retaliation to meet injustice," "earnest desire that the war shall be conducted in every respect in accordance with the usages of civilized warfare." Four days later, Henry Russell visited Shaw's parents on Staten Island on his way home to Boston. "I thank God he is safe at last," Shaw said.[60]

Shaw was right to worry about the Confederate president issuing another retaliation proclamation, however. After the apparent victory regarding Pope's orders, Jefferson Davis was convinced he could shape Federal policies through the threat of retaliation. His administration would now turn its attention to the Department of the South, where Union officials defied his retaliation order against officers who commanded Black troops. Events there brought the Confederate military in South Carolina its first contingent of Black prisoners wearing the uniform of the United States.[61]

Operating under Stanton's order to Saxton, military authorities in the Department of the South organized the 1st South Carolina Volunteers in October 1862 and mustered its first companies into service in November. Charles T. Trowbridge was the senior captain in Company A, formed from the freedmen who had done service on St. Simon's. They called the Brooklyn bricklayer and firefighter "Captain Scroby," and he had their loyalty. He was large and brawny, "a prize fighter by nature & an abolitionist by grace." He had a splendid singing voice and loved to belt out Methodist hymns. He visited his men regularly in their tents and ensured they had time to learn to read and write with the help of Susie King Taylor, who had joined the regiment as a laundress and teacher. Recruiting for other companies proceeded more slowly than Saxton would have liked, however. The freed people were suspicious because the men in Hunter's original regiment were never paid. When recruiters visited the plantations, the men hid in the woods, worried about another forcible conscription. There were safer, and more lucrative, opportunities to work for the navy, the Quartermaster's Department, or the engineers or to be self-employed as a fisherman or boat pilot.[62]

Many of the men who did enlist in the 1st South Carolina already had experience serving as armed pickets guarding island plantations and settlements. In October, the Black pickets on St. Helena fired on two boats of rebels attempting to land and successfully drove them off. The regimental descriptive book of the 1st South Carolina Volunteers includes commendations for behavior under fire of several enlisted men for actions that occurred in October before they had enlisted in the regiment. Fortune Baker, a twenty-five-year-old boatman from Talbot Island, Florida, "honorably conducted himself on Barnwell Island on October 18, 1862, when attacked by the enemy," even though Baker did not enlist until November 20. His previous experience under fire and his bravery earned him an immediate appointment as a sergeant in Company H.[63]

Saxton, an activist anti-slavery commander, immediately implemented Stanton's orders to liberate slaves and destroy local resources. He deployed Trowbridge and Company A in a raid on the Georgia-Florida coast that made thirteen landings between November 3 and November 10 (the company was not yet officially mustered). The soldiers broke up Confederate picket stations, destroyed nine saltworks, took corn and rice, burned buildings, killed horses, and brought 155 slaves away from the mainland. Additionally, the sixty-two men of Company A successfully fought off an attack from eighty Confederate soldiers.[64]

The leader of the expedition, Col. Oliver T. Beard of the 48th New York, was careful to document the performance of the Black troops. The majority of white Americans believed that Blacks participated in civilization only because of their subjugation in slavery. In their natural state, they did not possess self-control and restraint, which were essential characteristics of civilized war, but instead instinctively followed their animal passions of sensuality and violence. Because the essence of courage was self-control over instinct, most white Americans assumed that Blacks would not endure the terrors of battle. A worse threat was that Blacks would go wild in an orgy of revenge and indiscriminate violence. Beard offered facts from the expedition to dispute those assumptions. He knew it was important to convince skeptical officers in the Department of the South and in the War Department that it was possible to incorporate uncivilized people into a civilized war. "On the last expedition the fact was developed that colored men would fight behind barricades," he reported. "This time they have proved, by their heroism, that they will fight in an open field." He described the men as "cool" under fire, which was the common phrase nineteenth-century Americans used to describe a restrained man's absolute control over his body and emotions. Saxton agreed. "There was no excitement, no flinching, no attempt at cruelty when successful," Saxton told Stanton. "They seemed like men who were fighting to vindicate their manhood and they did it well." The raids "will carry terror to the hearts of the rebels."[65]

The same day that Company A returned from its expedition, a Confederate captain with a few of his men from the Lamar Rangers landed on St. Catherine's Island for a raid and encountered six Black men in Federal uniforms carrying muskets. The rebels killed two of the soldiers and captured four. Brig. Gen. Hugh W. Mercer, the Confederate district commander in Georgia, wrote his superior, Gen. P. G. T. Beauregard, for instruction. He asked permission to execute the captives. "They are slaves taken with arms in hand against their masters and wearing the abolition uniform," he said. "Some swift and terrible punishment should be inflicted that their fellows may be deterred from following their example. This is by no means the first case that has arisen and I much fear that unless something be done to prevent similar outrages it will not be the last." Beauregard, in turn, asked the War Department for guidance, with the endorsement that he agreed with Mercer. The new Confederate secretary of war, appointed on November 19, was James A. Seddon, a Virginia lawyer and planter with no military experience. He was a well-educated orator and influential Democratic politician. He was also very sick. "He looks like a dead man galvanized into muscular animation," the department clerk John B. Jones said. "His eyes are sunken and his features have the hue of a man who had been in his grave a full month."[66]

Seddon wrote back with the policy that would remain his preference for his entire tenure as secretary of war. "Slaves in flagrant rebellion are subject to death by the laws of every slave-holding state," he wrote. "They cannot be recognized in any way as soldiers subject to the rules of war and to trial by military courts; yet for example and to suppress any spirit of insubordination it is deemed essential that slaves in armed insurrection should meet condign punishment." Seddon instructed Beauregard to summarily execute the prisoners and others captured in the future under similar circumstances. He cautioned that only commanding generals of a locality should order executions in order to prevent abuse of "this grave power under the immediate excitement of capture." He also sent a copy of this letter to the Confederate commander in Mobile, Alabama, "for his guidance."[67]

Although the War Department had authorized local commanding generals to execute Black prisoners summarily, Davis preferred state officials to handle Black soldiers and their white officers according to state laws. In his eyes, if the Black men from the Carolina and Georgia Sea Islands were slaves engaged in insurrection rather than legitimate combatants, states should

James A. Seddon, Confederate secretary of war, November 21, 1862–February 5, 1865. His preferred policy was summary execution of Black U.S. soldiers, but U.S. retaliation and internal debate within his own War Department caused him to issue inconsistent and conflicting orders during his tenure. (National Archives Catalog, Record Group 111, Records of the Office of the Chief Signal Officer, Series, Civil War–Era Photographs)

prosecute them and implement the mandated death penalties. On December 23, 1862, he issued a proclamation that the War Department incorporated the next day into General Orders No. 111. Most of this order dealt with an ongoing retaliation incident in New Orleans, but its final sections turned to the U.S. decision to arm former slaves in Louisiana and South Carolina. Lincoln's preliminary emancipation proclamation proved that the United States cared nothing for "the laws of nations, the dictates of reason and the instincts of humanity," and therefore deterrence required "the terms of just retribution." The order included the retaliation ritual's necessary disclaimer: Davis appealed to God to witness that he "was not guided by the passion of revenge" but instead "reluctantly yield[ed] to the solemn duty." Section 3 instructed military authorities to deliver slaves captured in arms to state governors for trial according to the law of each state. Section 4 gave identical instructions for commissioned officers "found serving in company with armed slaves in insurrection."[68]

Davis expected this retaliation order to have the same effect as his proclamation against Pope's officers: the Federals would adjust their policy. In this case, however, both Stanton and Lincoln believed that liberating and arming former slaves was essential to suppressing the rebellion. There was ample historical precedent of other civilized nations enlisting former slaves as soldiers. Great Britain had done so during the American Revolution, as did the Spanish in the Caribbean. In his official end-of-the-year report, Stanton argued that the South's population of four million slaves were loyal to the Union and could hold territory that Union armies liberated from the rebellion. They needed protection and employment where they lived. Stanton pointed out that in the history of warfare, "no great territory has been permanently reduced without depriving the leaders of its people of their lands and property." "By striking down this system of compulsory labor, which enables the leaders of the rebellion to control the resources of the people," Stanton wrote, "the rebellion would die of itself." Slavery made the Confederacy weak. "No enemy was ever so vulnerable," Stanton thought, "if the means at hand are employed against them." Stanton signaled on December 28 the Lincoln administration's commitment to its policy regarding Black troops and its determination to protect its commissioned officers from retaliation. He instructed his subordinates to hold all captive Confederate commissioned officers and not to exchange them.[69]

Jefferson Davis was about to be reminded that retaliation worked both ways.

# 2

# SERVILE INSURRECTION

On November 25, 1862, a published expert on the accomplishments of civilized man took command of the 1st South Carolina Volunteers. Thomas Wentworth Higginson was a Harvard-educated transcendentalist and abolitionist. He had distributed hand axes to a crowd who tried to rescue the fugitive slave Anthony Burns from the courthouse in Boston in 1854 and had openly admitted his financial backing of John Brown's raid on Harpers Ferry in 1859. He believed that race and religion had nothing to do with a people's capacity to reach a civilized condition, which produced the highest cultivation of mind, manners, morals, and body, but he did believe that Anglo-Saxons were farthest along on the scale of progress. Higginson considered Black people "childlike" and "undeveloped," physically weaker than Northern whites were, but he expected them to grow quickly into full adulthood with the proper training.[1]

Colonel Higginson thought the men of his regiment were bright and valiant. They had performed courageous deeds escaping slavery and had faced more danger than their white officers had. His first order to them expressed pride. "Many of the bravest actions in the history of the world have been done by black troops," General Orders No. 1 read. "No white man in the nation has so much to fight for as the black men who compose this regiment. You are fighting for your own liberty and the liberty of your children. Nobody can make you free unless you have the courage to fight for your own freedom, and if you resolve to be free, nobody can make you slaves. All the white citizens of South Carolina cannot put you back into slavery once you have learned the use of arms."[2]

From January to June 1863, the 1st South Carolina escalated the size and scope of its raids on the mainland, and the 2nd South Carolina, commanded by Col. James Montgomery, and the 54th Massachusetts, commanded by Col. Robert Gould Shaw, joined the ranks of Black troops active in the Department of the South. The raiding expeditions of these three regiments exposed deep divisions among Union officers over the policy of employing Black troops in a strategy of destruction. Some Union officers believed that Blacks were still a barbaric race rather than a civilized one and needed more control and discipline than white soldiers. Using such troops to destroy property was dangerous because it unleashed passion and destruction, characteristics of savage war, rather than restraint, characteristic of civilized war.

The contrast between Higginson, Montgomery, and Shaw reflected broader disagreements over who could be included in civilization and broader fears that the war was undermining, rather than salvaging, American civilization. The raids convinced Confederates, on the other hand, that the United States had unleashed savage Blacks in a servile insurrection that would destroy American civilization. The retaliation ritual in the Department of the South exposed internal debates over law and federalism within the Confederate government that hampered a unified response to what the leadership viewed as an existential threat.[3]

To prepare for the 1st South Carolina's first action as a regiment, Higginson implemented daily drills and required his men to conform to every aspect of military etiquette, learning proper salutes and polishing their accoutrements. He expected his men to exemplify the highest standard of morals and manners, but his main object was to "develop self-respect." "I allow no man to stand with his cap off, talking to me out of doors," he said. "I explain that slaves do that—*soldiers* give a military salute, which the officer is as absolutely required to return as the soldier to offer." The colonel avoided typical army punishments that were reminiscent of slavery, such as a ball and chain.[4]

The white officers of the 1st South Carolina looked for evidence that their men, though not fully civilized, were ready to fight in a civilized war. Higginson and Dr. Seth Rogers, the abolitionist surgeon of the regiment, commented that the soldiers of the 1st were more religious and moral as a group than the typical white regiment. They sang and prayed continually and spoke of "a Gospel army." The adjutant and quartermaster of the regiment had their young wives in camp, and both women frequently went to the men's tents to teach them to read. They never saw or heard anything improper. "They both declared that they would not have moved about with anything like the same freedom in any white camp they had ever entered,"

“Flag Presented by Citizens of New York to the First S.C. Volunteers.” This engraving for an 1863 publication by the Reformed Protestant Dutch Church depicts the manly qualities of Sgt. Prince Rivers. (Higginson, “First Black Regiment,” 521; courtesy of the South Caroliniana Library, University of South Carolina, Columbia)

Higginson noted, "and it always roused their indignation to hear the negro race called brutal or depraved." The colonel and his surgeon were convinced that Blacks possessed the restraint necessary to be included in a civilized war. "I should not fear any wanton outrage from them," Higginson said. "After all their wrongs, they are not really revengeful." They were "kind hearted, forgiving and as truth loving as the average of whites," Rogers thought, "more so than the Irish of the lowest rank."[5]

In a twist on the usual perspective, the advocates for the 1st thought the white soldiers in the Department of the South posed the greatest threat to civilized war. New York and New Jersey soldiers who arrived in February beat up Black men on the islands, stole personal property from the freed people, and burned down all the houses on a plantation. "They behaved like marauders in an enemy's country," one witness wrote, "and disgraced the name of man, American, or soldier." Simon Bolivar Hulbert, a private in the 100th New York, commented, "It is the opinion of most of the soldiers that they are fighting for negroes & so they abuse the negroe where ever they meet him. . . . The men will kill them if they ever cross their path." Prince Rivers, the provost sergeant for the 1st, fought off a contingent of Philadelphia soldiers who tried to tear the sergeant stripes off his uniform. In contrast to the uncontrolled, barbaric behavior of these white soldiers, Seth Rogers proudly noted the restraint of the 1st. The first time the regiment marched to its brigade headquarters in Beaufort, South Carolina, "we were greeted with such language as pertains to vulgar negro haters." The enlisted men, however, were "manly" in their response. "Not a head was turned to the right or left, not a word spoken."[6]

Secure in the conviction that the 1st was ready to participate in civilized war, Brig. Gen. Rufus Saxton sent a portion of the regiment, 462 officers and enlisted men, on a raid up the St. Mary's River, which forms part of the Georgia-Florida border, on January 23. Capt. Charles Trowbridge took Company A, veterans of this type of action, and Company F on the steamer *Planter* and destroyed a major salt manufacturing facility on the coast. Higginson took a detachment of 250 men on the steamers *John Adams* and *Ben De Ford* up the narrow, crooked, and winding river. Corp. Robert Sutton, who had escaped from a plantation on the river, piloted the vessels and picked the points to shell the banks. Sutton had a quiet charisma and dignity that made him a natural leader of men. "He seems to me kingly, and oh! I wish he could read and write," Rogers said. "He ought to be a leader, a general, instead of a corporal." Confederate cavalry fired on them from positions in the woods, and one cavalryman actually jumped from the bank

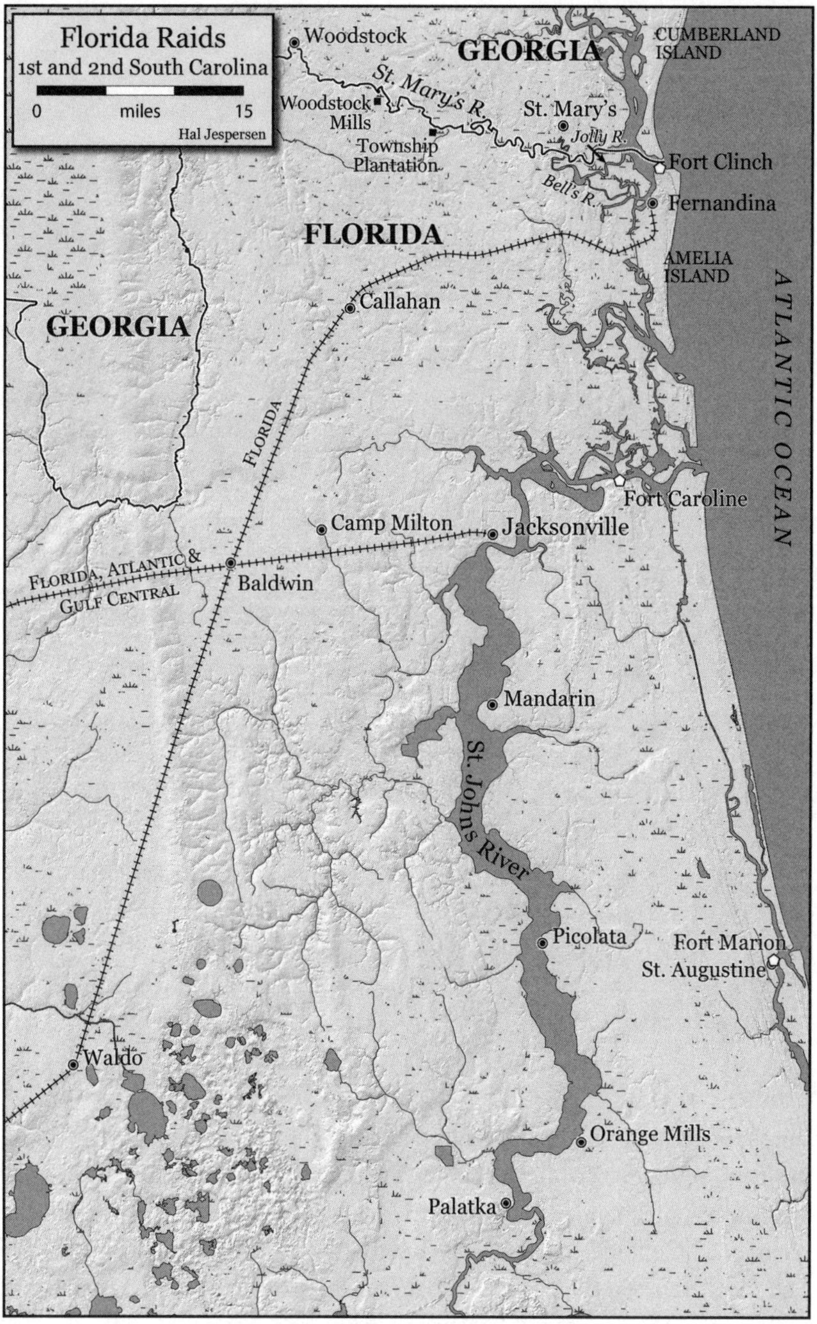

Florida Raids
1st and 2nd South Carolina
0 miles 15
Hal Jespersen
Woodstock
GEORGIA
CUMBERLAND ISLAND
St. Mary's R.
Woodstock Mills
Township Plantation
St. Mary's
Jolly R.
Fort Clinch
Bell's R.
Fernandina
FLORIDA
AMELIA ISLAND
Callahan
GEORGIA
ATLANTIC OCEAN
FLORIDA
Fort Caroline
Camp Milton
Jacksonville
FLORIDA, ATLANTIC & GULF CENTRAL
Baldwin
Mandarin
St. Johns River
Picolata
Fort Marion
St. Augustine
Waldo
Orange Mills
Palatka

Sgt. William Bronson, Sgt. Henry McIntyre, and Sgt. Harry Wilkins, 1st South Carolina. Bronson was the first sergeant in the first company of recruits. The noncommissioned officers of the 1st were men experienced in protecting Black settlements on the Sea Islands from Confederate raiders and whose knowledge of rivers and plantations in South Carolina, Georgia, and Florida led to the 1st's successful raiding activities. (Higginson, "First Black Regiment," 526, 529; courtesy of the South Caroliniana Library, University of South Carolina, Columbia)

onto a boat, but a sergeant killed him. Higginson kept the men, except the gunners, below deck while the boats were in motion. On January 26, Higginson and 175 men landed at Township Plantation, Florida, and defeated the charge of a Confederate cavalry company. The heroes of the skirmish were Sgt. Jacob Jones, a thirty-year-old laborer from Beaufort, and Sgt. Thomas Fields, an eighteen-year-old carpenter from St. Charles, Florida. The detachment burned the plantation house and outbuildings to keep the cavalry pickets from using them as a screen. They also took a piano for use in the regiment's school.[7]

The expedition met its first test, in terms of its commitment to the restraints and processes of civilized war, on January 27, when the detachment arrived at the nearly abandoned village of St. Mary's. Confederate pickets often operated out of it, and a Union gunboat that patrolled the river had partially burned it sometime before. Only three elderly women remained, and they waved white handkerchiefs as the steamers pulled into the wharf. Because the location was known as a rendezvous for rebels, Higginson searched their house. When the Federals returned to the wharf, rebels fired at them from behind the houses in the village. Higginson's skirmishers returned fire while gunners from the steamers threw shot and shell among the houses. Higginson fired the town, except for the houses of the women, because the laws of war allowed him to burn buildings used as cover by enemy forces during an attack. A few soldiers from the 1st showed an inclination to vandalism once the town began to burn, but Higginson would not let them take anything for themselves.[8]

Another test was the detachment's January 30 interaction with the citizens of Woodstock Mills, Florida, a small village located about twenty miles up the river with a post office, school, church, store, and jail. A Northern-born widow, Ernestine Strong Alberti, owned the steam sawmill and fifty-two slaves, although most of them had already escaped to the Yankees. Higginson sent a landing party that put guards around every house. The detachment confiscated a flock of twenty-five sheep and other supplies for direct military use but did not touch the houses. "I did not injure anything except the feelings of the inhabitants, who did chafe at the complexion of my guards — blackguards — though the men behaved admirably — even one who threatened to throw an old termagant into the river took care to add the epithet 'Madam,'" Higginson said. There were only seven men in Woodstock Mills, and Higginson took them hostage as security for the lives of his men in case Confederates captured any of them on the return trip. He took Abraham Bessent out of bed while his daughter stood "with averted head in the background." "He is a very influential rebel," Rogers remarked, "and may become a very important hostage when Jeff Davis begins to hang us." Higginson removed the stocks and shackles from the slave jail as trophies. He introduced Corporal Sutton to Mrs. Alberti, his former owner, who said, "*We* called him *Bob*." When the hostages got on the steamers, Sutton and Prince Rivers searched them for concealed weapons. On the return trip, Confederates fired at the steamers from bluffs on the shore and shot the captain of the *John Adams* in the head. Sutton returned fire from the pilothouse.[9]

The white officers of the 1st were exultant at the end of the expedition.

They had returned with supplies: 40,000 bricks (taken from a brickyard on the river), 250 bars of railroad iron, eight sticks of lumber, rice, and sheep. Most of the slaves living along the St. Mary's River had already left before the expedition arrived, but the 1st brought away a few families. It was what the regiment did *not* do that most impressed its superiors. "Nothing was taken for public use save articles strictly contraband of war," Higginson told General Saxton. "No wanton destruction was permitted, nor were any buildings burned unless in retaliation for being fired upon, according to the usages of war. Of course no personal outrage was permitted or desired." The expedition proved Black men "could be trusted with the conquered foe," Rogers told his family. "Not a single unbecoming act have I seen or heard on the part of the guards, skirmishers, or pickets. It was not for want of temptation, and I am led to wonder at their self-control." Saxton forwarded the reports to Secretary of War Edwin Stanton with a request to "arm and discipline" every Black man that came into Union lines.[10]

Confederate authorities saw the activities of the 1st in Florida differently. Corp. Robert Sutton personified the threat that secessionists had feared since Republicans in the North first started winning elections on a platform of restricting the spread of slavery: race war and the destruction of civilization itself. From the beginning, secessionists spoke not only of the Constitution and of their rights but also of civilization and savagery.

This threat was a cornerstone of secessionist arguments for creating a new, separate nation. A Republican regime would abolish slavery and institute political equality between Blacks and whites. This outcome "destroys the property of the South," Stephen F. Hale, the Confederacy's commissioner to Kentucky, explained in December 1860, "lays waste her fields, and inaugurates all the horrors of a San Domingo servile insurrection . . . to gratify the lust of half-civilized Africans." Hale warned of "degradation," "ruin," and "an eternal war of the races." Southern slavery, he claimed, "has done more to civilize and Christianize the heathen than all human agencies beside." If the Confederate experiment failed, "the light of our civilization goes down in blood . . . [and] the dark pall of barbarism must soon gather over our sunny land, and the scenes of West India emancipation, with its attendant horrors and crimes (that monument of British fanaticism and folly), be re-enacted in our own land upon a more gigantic scale."[11]

Confederate president Jefferson Davis's response two years later to the Emancipation Proclamation sounded the same notes. "Several millions of human beings of an inferior race, peaceful and contented laborers in their sphere, are doomed to extermination," he told the Confederate Congress, "while at the same time they are encouraged to a general assassination of their masters." It was impossible for him to conceive of the 1st South Carolina as a regiment of legitimate soldiers; they were slave barbarians in servile insurrection overturning the foundation of Southern civilization. Davis had a retaliation proclamation in place, General Orders No. 111, to deal with Colonel Higginson and the 1st. Military authorities would deliver any of them captured in arms to state authorities for trial. The Emancipation Proclamation itself deserved an additional response. It was "the most execrable measure recorded in the history of guilty man."[12]

Davis dropped a bombshell on the Confederate Congress in mid-January 1863 that exposed important fissures among Confederate politicians about appropriate retaliation over the Federal deployment of Black troops. Davis proposed to deliver *all* commissioned officers of the U.S. Army (not just those who commanded Black troops) who were captured in states covered in the Emancipation Proclamation to state authorities to be tried as criminals for inciting servile insurrection. White enlisted soldiers who were captured, he explained, would be treated as "unwilling instruments in the commission of these crimes" and would be paroled. General P. G. T. Beauregard acted immediately on this proposition. On January 21, his chief of staff wrote a Federal lieutenant, captured in command of white troops in Florida and held in the Charleston Jail. "You are not subject to exchange and will probably be turned over to local authorities of the State of Florida for trial," the letter read. "It is needless for me to inform you that this course is a necessary consequence of the Proclamation of the President of the United States, by which the Army and Navy of the United States were instructed to aid Negroes against their masters."[13]

Although all Confederate civilian and military officials were united in their moral outrage over the U.S. recruitment of Black troops and the threat it posed to civilization, they were divided over the appropriate response. The Confederate Congress rejected Davis's dangerous and impractical idea after holding a series of secret sessions in February and March. They recognized that his proposed solution actually violated the international laws of war. Senator Thomas J. Semmes, a Louisiana lawyer and a member of the Committee of the Judiciary, wrote the report explaining that captured U.S. officers remained "public enemies" who were not subject to the municipal laws of the states. An invading army and all its members entered a territory openly under authority from a belligerent government. Under British and American precedents, an army was not obligated to obey any law of an invaded country, and its laws replaced local law in territories it temporarily controlled. Thus, local laws regarding servile insurrection were not binding on U.S. officers, and they could not be tried and punished for the crime, just as they could not be tried and punished for murder, arson, or robbery while acting as public enemies. Retaliation was a belligerent right that could be implemented only by Confederate authorities.[14]

The Senate then debated alternative procedures for the retaliation. Mississippi senator James Phelan argued that U.S. officers in command of Black troops were not entitled to the right of surrender and proposed to authorize officers and soldiers of the Confederate states to "take the life of such officer at any time and under any circumstances." His colleagues rejected this idea.[15] The final congressional resolution on retaliation, passed May 1, 1863, announced that a Confederate military court should try U.S. officers who commanded Black troops for inciting servile insurrection and put them to death or otherwise punish them. Black men taken in arms against the Confederacy, even if they were born free in a Northern state, would be delivered to state authorities in the states where they were captured.[16]

During the period that the Confederate Congress debated and passed its resolutions, Union general Rufus Saxton deployed another Black regiment, the 2nd South Carolina, to action in the Department of the South. However, its commander, Col. James Montgomery, threatened to undermine Saxton's claim that his white officers fought a civilized war. Montgomery was a frontier schoolteacher and clergyman who had learned to fight slaveholders with John Brown in Kansas during the 1850s. He was a religious zealot who fought a holy war against slavery and a war of vengeance against slaveholders. "He never drinks, smokes, or swears, & considers that praying, shooting, burning, and hanging are the true means to put down the Rebellion," Robert Gould Shaw wrote of him. Montgomery's experience on the Kansas-Missouri border taught him how to bushwhack and live off the enemy. "A guerrilla company, to be effective, must be self-sustaining—must subsist on the enemy," he said. "Therefore we feed ourselves at Pro-slavery larders and our horses at Pro-slavery corn-cribs." Montgomery arrived in the department on January 13 and recruited two companies from a refugee camp at Key West, Florida, by February 25. He fascinated and impressed Higginson and Rogers with tales of his exploits in Kansas. He bragged about shooting five Confederate prisoners of war in retaliation for the murder of five of his soldiers there. "This man seems to me one of the John Brown men of destiny," Rogers said.[17]

Montgomery did not share Higginson's paternal affection and admiration for his men. He thought Blacks were savages, rather than merely further

Col. Thomas Wentworth Higginson, 1st South Carolina, and Col. James Montgomery, 2nd South Carolina. Higginson thought Montgomery's policy of using Black troops to destroy slaveholders' property was uncivilized. (Higginson, "First Black Regiment," 523; courtesy of the South Caroliniana Library, University of South Carolina, Columbia; carte de visite of Montgomery used with permission of kansasmemory.org, Kansas State Historical Society)

back on the sliding scale of civilization, and that slavery kept them in that condition. "You are a race of slaves," he told some Black soldiers. "A few years ago your fathers worshiped snakes and crocodiles. Your features partake of a beastly character." He shared with Saxton, Higginson, and Maj. Gen. David Hunter the belief that military training was the best "school" to prepare Black people for "all the privileges and duties of social and civil life." Unlike Higginson, who merely observed his men's deep Christian faith, Montgomery believed "the religious element is the only foundation on which we can build, in making soldiers of these freedmen." His regimental chaplain, Homer H. Moore, another Kansan with a powerful personality, helped enforce a ban on drinking, card playing, and profanity. Because Montgomery categorized Black people as savages with little control over their animal nature, he thought they were incapable of true courage. "It is folly to suppose that a race, which has been in bondage for 200 years, can be as brave as freemen," he said, "and all our energies must be devoted to making the most of them." Montgomery used draconian measures to discipline his enlisted men. He shot a soldier whom he had warned twice to quit talking after taps and executed a deserter without a court-martial. "He doesn't like the red-tape way of doing things," another officer commented.[18]

Saxton sent Montgomery and the two companies of the 2nd with Higginson and the 1st on a mission to occupy Jacksonville, Florida, and "make it a base of operations for the arming of negroes." He expected slaves from Florida, Georgia, and South Carolina to flee to this outpost, receive arms, and capture and hold Florida as an asylum for freed people. Saxton thought the success of the Seminoles against the U.S. Army in Florida from 1835 to 1842 proved that the terrain of the state was ideal for defensive warfare. Confederates would not be able to drive the freed people out once they gathered in large numbers and possessed weapons. This was indeed a strategy to foment insurrection among the slave population of the South. The troops left South Carolina on March 6 and entered Jacksonville on March 10. This was the third time that Union troops had taken possession of it, and only about 500 of its residents remained. Higginson posted the raw recruits of the 2nd on the outskirts of town. On March 11, as the men of the 2nd were learning to march and use their weapons, 200 Confederate cavalrymen attacked the camp. The Black soldiers returned fire, fell back in disorder but without panic, rallied, marched forward, and engaged a line of infantry until artillery fire from Union gunboats scattered the rebels.[19]

Higginson issued orders from Jacksonville that publicly proclaimed his commitment to the customs of civilized war. General Orders No. 1 and No. 2 held all officers responsible for "restraining their commands from all violence & all plunder." The colonel prepared his soldiers to fight a conventional battle at Jacksonville. He fortified the town, built earthworks, destroyed buildings and trees in its vicinity that could shield approaching troops, and sent out mounted reconnaissance parties to patrol for enemy troops. His skirmishers regularly drove off companies of rebel soldiers under the command of Confederate brigadier general Joseph Finegan who were camped about eight miles away. Finegan was a forty-nine-year-old Irish immigrant who had made his fortune in Florida as a planter, lumberman, and railroad operator. His political connections secured him command in his state, but he had limited military experience. Five navy gunboats helped keep Finegan at bay.[20]

Consistent with national policy and the practice in other Union military departments, Higginson required all male citizens of Jacksonville to report to his headquarters and take an oath of allegiance to the United States. Those who refused he made hostages to secure the lives of his enlisted men, should any be captured. The men of Company K visited all the houses in town to demand that inhabitants give up their weapons. Higginson sent detachments of soldiers on foot and on gunboats to bring in slaves, cattle, cotton, and prisoners to use as hostages. White regiments, the 8th Maine and 6th Connecticut, arrived from Hilton Head to support the occupation and fought alongside the men of the 1st during reconnaissance missions and Confederate probes of the outer defenses of the town.[21]

Many of the Black soldiers of the 1st and 2nd were from Jacksonville and its surrounding counties. They occupied and patrolled a town where they knew the white inhabitants and had bitter memories of their experiences in bondage.[22] They now had power, manifested in street patrols and checking the passes given to white men, over their former masters. White officers had an unspoken test for these soldiers in order to decide if they truly belonged among civilized people: how would they treat the white women of the town?

White Americans of the middle and upper social classes considered the position and treatment of women to be essential measures of a nation's position on the progressive scale from barbarism to civilization. The most advanced societies, they believed, removed as many women as possible from mindless drudgery. Women became the ornaments, the proof, of civilization through their education, refinement, taste, and purity. Their modest dress and demeanor gave no hint of animal passion. Southern men of the plantation class believed they were civilization builders whose wives and daughters embodied and validated their accomplishments. A planter's wife was simultaneously his primary dependent and the heroine of his personal epic, and her love was his prize. Protecting women was thus an essential goal of civilized war.[23]

Savage warfare, according to the worldview, did not respect the bodies of women, and savages, who had no control over their appetites, raped and killed women as part of warfare. Confederate secessionists had overtly proclaimed that slavery was the best mechanism to protect white women from uncivilized Black men. When they depicted the end of slavery destroying their civilization, one of the most frequently invoked images was Black men ravaging white women.

Higginson's orders showed his concern for protecting the women of Jacksonville. He did not allow soldiers to "stray about the town," enter houses, or be out in the streets after 8:30 P.M. They had to be with an officer at all times, excepting the provost guard. The colonel cautioned his men "against unnecessary conversation with the inhabitants, especially women." Women and children had the freedom to pass in and out of the town. Higginson was confident in his men, and his actions reflected that when he dealt with women who professed to be in "perpetual fear" of his soldiers and accused his men of insulting them. Higginson conducted investigations that credited the testimony of his men. In one case, it turned out that an "insult" was merely a soldier sitting down on the steps in front of a house. Officers of the 1st did not expect Black soldiers to remain silent if white women insulted them. "When women taunt them with language most unbecoming, as they sometimes do, I should be very sorry if they did not return a silencer," Dr. Rogers said. One soldier of the 1st, Jake Reed, wanted revenge when he returned to Jacksonville, but his target was not women. His master had sold Reed's wife away to Georgia. Reed threatened publicly to burn his master's house, found the white man who had shot at him during his escape from slavery the year before, and put a loaded gun to the man's head. Higginson arrested and confined Reed.[24]

The 1st's treatment of persons and private property in the Jacksonville vicinity officially conformed to the customs of war, but the Southerners whose homes they burned and property they confiscated did not care about the niceties of the law. Some officers of the 1st pushed the boundaries. When one party burned houses occupied by women and children, whose men were in Confederate service, in order "to get rid of screens for the enemy," a legitimate action, the regimental chaplain divided the personal property. "What seems to belong to the woman, I yield to her," he told Rogers, "but what seems to belong to the man I have brought into camp." Even Higginson admitted to some internal struggles. "The distinction between legitimate and illegitimate plunder is naturally hard to enforce," he wrote. Taking furniture and sending it home, as white troops had done during an earlier occupation of Jacksonville, was clearly wrong. But Higginson's provost marshal collected furniture from abandoned houses for use in officers' quarters and to preserve it from destruction. The men of the regiment, who had not eaten fresh meat for a while, did what hungry Union soldiers were doing in Virginia, Tennessee, and Mississippi: took pigs and chickens to eat. Although sticklers for the laws of war called this stealing, officers looked the other way, as they did everywhere.[25]

Montgomery escalated the confiscation and destruction of private property when he took his companies of the 2nd on foraging raids up the St. Johns River on March 14 and 17. They embarked on the armed transport *General Burnside*. "Boys I don't want you to interfere with private property but if any pigs or turkeys attack you, you must defend yourselves," he told the men. Montgomery "carefully avoided taking anything but hard bread, for he religiously believes we ought to live on the rebels," Rogers said. The troops landed at the plantation of Col. Stephen Bryant, who owned eighty-seven slaves and had just returned from taking them farther away from Union lines. They took pork, poultry, horses, and Bryant. His wife followed them to the boat venting her rage, hoping all the Black soldiers "would go to hell" and excoriating Montgomery for separating her from her husband. One of the enlisted men said something about the separation of husbands and wives in slavery. "Your wives? What are your wives but nasty old black things?" Mrs. Bryant said. "It required a stern word of command to restrain the men," recalled one of Montgomery's officers.[26]

The 2nd visited several plantations on a more extended raid to Palatka on March 23–27. Confederates fired from concealed positions when the 2nd pulled into the wharf, but Montgomery did not burn anything in the town, although his officers thought the laws of war would have justified such a response because Higginson wanted to use the location as a headquarters. A detachment from the 2nd sent into the woods captured a rebel camp, fifteen soldiers, and nine bales of cotton. They also captured a rebel lieutenant. He escaped when the party passed his house and his wife and other women came outside crying. Montgomery allowed him a moment to say good-bye on his pledge of honor not to escape, but when the women crowded around him, he darted away. Montgomery did not fire after the retreating figure because of the women's presence. The 2nd moved from plantation to plantation along the river. They seized poultry, pork, horses, and cattle and this time took furniture and ransacked houses. They liberated a few slaves, but masters had already removed most of them farther into the interior of the state. Montgomery spoke with Thomas Russell, one of the residents, who reported the gist of the conversation to Finegan. "They had been acting in a mild way all along," Russell summarized, "but they intended now to let us feel what war actually was."[27]

Montgomery intended to recruit soldiers for his incomplete regiment from among the slaves in Florida, but instead he and Higginson were shocked to receive orders on March 27 to leave Jacksonville and return to Hilton Head. The Union headquarters of the Department of the South was engulfed in conflict among its top commanders and also between them and the War and Naval Departments in Washington.

Although the city of Charleston was of little strategic importance in the wider Union military effort, the Lincoln administration believed its symbolic power demanded that General Hunter and his naval counterpart, Adm. Samuel DuPont, make better progress toward its capture. Secretary of the Navy Gideon Welles wanted DuPont to run the gauntlet of Confederate defenses with his monitors, enter the harbor, and demand the city's surrender without assistance from the army. DuPont was skeptical but did not communicate his reasons effectively. And the War Department did not want the navy to get all the credit. Secretary of War Stanton had transferred 10,000 troops under the command of Maj. Gen. John G. Foster to the department in February so that the army could conduct a ground campaign or participate in joint operations, but antagonism between Hunter and Foster paralyzed the preparations. Foster left the department. As DuPont prepared to launch his purely naval assault against Charleston, Hunter recalled the troops from Jacksonville because he thought he might need them for his own operations against the city. DuPont's April 7 assault using a squadron of ironclad monitors against the outer fortifications of Charleston Harbor was a spectacular failure.[28]

The Federals' departure from Jacksonville on March 28 almost marred the honorable reputation of Black soldiers that Higginson was working so hard to establish. As the troops left their quarters and marched to the transports waiting on the wharf, a few soldiers from the 6th Connecticut and 8th Maine, and at least one soldier of the 2nd South Carolina, used straw and moss from their bedding to set three buildings on fire. A strong wind quickly spread the fire, which engulfed many private houses and commercial buildings in the city. Higginson and other officers of the 1st and 2nd were appalled and insisted that no Black soldiers were involved in the arson. Naval officers and Northern newspaper correspondents who were with the occupation forces supported this claim and saved the public reputation of the 1st. The Republican *New York Tribune* reported that Black soldiers "had nothing whatever to do with it and were simply silent spectators." The *New York Evening Post* blamed solely the white soldiers of the 8th Maine. The *New York Times* downplayed the fire as the act of a few ruffians and hoped people would not "twist and exaggerate an insignificant affair" into "one of the most shocking Union atrocities."[29]

The greatest credit to the Black soldiers in Florida, in a way, was that Confederate officials zeroed in on the burning of Jacksonville and the plundering of private property as the main offenses of the Union army in Florida. They did not accuse Black soldiers of "outrage" against white women and did not communicate to Union officials any such accusations about the occupation of Jacksonville. Thomas Russell reported that Black soldiers "abused and insulted women" on the St. Johns River, but in nineteenth-century parlance, this was not a charge of rapine or sexual misconduct. The Confederate commander of the Department of South Carolina, Georgia, and Florida,

General Beauregard, called the attention of the Confederate War Department only "to the wanton destruction of private property in Jacksonville."[30]

Confederates had not captured a single officer or soldier from the Black troops operating in Florida. With no bodies to work retaliation upon, Confederates moved to contain the ongoing insurrection of their slaves in Florida. Finegan posted troops in positions along rivers and roads to keep slaves from escaping to Federal gunboats. In addition, Capt. William E. Chambers took a detachment of twelve Confederate soldiers to investigate "conspiracies of the negroes . . . to leave their owners and go to the enemy." His superiors empowered Chambers to arrest Blacks and whites and gave him "much discretion . . . as to the measures necessary to arrive at the facts in this matter. He will however, act coolly and temperately, and not use unnecessary harshness not afterward to be justified."[31]

The men of the 1st and 2nd were heartsick when they left Florida, but they had accomplished more than they realized when they repulsed Confederate attacks, fought alongside white troops, and refrained from molesting women. They had changed the Lincoln administration's mind. Before the occupation, the War Department was not committed to the idea of employing Black troops on a wide scale, and its recruitment of Black men in other theaters was hesitant, limited, and ad hoc. But based upon reports of the 1st's activities in Florida, the moderate Republican newspapers that Lincoln used to gauge "the vital center of public opinion" withdrew their opposition to Black troops. The Black troopers had allayed the trio of fears regarding such regiments that haunted the Northern public. Higginson's men fought well, no racial conflict erupted between the Black and white regiments involved, and Black soldiers did not abuse white civilians. "I am glad to see the account of your colored force at Jacksonville," Lincoln wrote Hunter. "It is important to the enemy that such a force shall not take shape and grow and thrive in the South, and in precisely the same proportion it is important to us that it *shall*." Lincoln's cabinet now regarded "the question as settled, the policy avowed." The War Department subsequently launched a systematic and aggressive recruiting of Black regiments in all theaters of the war. Lincoln and his military advisors, however, true to the wording of the Emancipation Proclamation, still viewed the United States Colored Troops as a second-class auxiliary garrison force that would take over the occupation duties so unpopular with white soldiers.[32]

Hunter sought to capitalize on the momentum and to protect his Black troops from the threatened Confederate retaliation. On April 23, he wrote a letter to Jefferson Davis. "I have given you long enough to reflect on your folly," it read. "I now give you notice, that unless this order is immediately revoked, I will at once cause the execution of every rebel officer, and every rebel slaveholder in my possession." He also promised to execute a citizen or military prisoner for every Black soldier or employee of the U.S. government murdered or sold into slavery. For good measure, he equated Davis with Satan. He sent the letter to Secretary Stanton, who did not send it through official channels to Richmond. On May 27, Hunter wrote directly to Lincoln and asked the president to do something to protect Black Union soldiers. "I submit that the flag should protect and cover all its defenders," he said. "All prisoners captured and more particularly those of the aristocratic caste should be held as hostages to be hung man for man with any who may be executed by the rebels." Lincoln likewise did not act on the suggestion. Someone leaked Hunter's letter to the press, however, and several newspapers published it.[33]

Hunter had not accurately gauged the state of official or public opinion regarding the appropriate response to the Confederate retaliation resolutions. There was no popular support for the idea of executing citizens. Higginson thought the letter did more harm than good. "The threat to execute his prisoners unless Davis revokes, would only make the latter smile for he must know that it would never be carried out—because public sentiment would not sustain it," he said. "But public sentiment will sustain retaliatory acts & the threat of those carries a weight which the more extravagant threat only impairs." The *New York Herald* called it a "fanatical epistle." Confederate vice president Alexander Stephens thought the letter "may be a forgery."[34]

The Lincoln administration, for its part, was internally debating whether it would actually follow through on threats to execute military prisoners of war, and thus whether or not it should issue such threats as a way to protect its officers and soldiers. Because Confederates had not actually captured anyone from the Black troops in the Department of the South, the impetus for the discussion was an immediate crisis regarding events in Ohio. On May 15, Union major general Ambrose Burnside had executed two Confederate captains convicted of spying behind the Union lines in Kentucky. The Davis administration insisted the officers had been recruiting and gave official notice on May 22 that it would select two Union officers by lot from the prisoners held in Richmond and would execute them immediately. "I give you formal notice that for each officer so executed one of your officers in our hands will be immediately put to death and if this number be not sufficient it will be increased," the U.S. agent for exchange of prisoners responded. The two governments were standing on the brink of a potentially endless cycle of retaliatory executions.[35]

The heart of the problem was whether a combatant could execute someone who was innocent for the crimes of another. Maj. Gen. Ethan Allen Hitchcock, the U.S. commissioner for exchange of prisoners, had an epiphany during the sleepless nights that followed the Confederate notice. It guided all his future thinking and advice to Stanton about retaliation. "The more I think of this shocking state of things, the more I think we ought not to follow the barbarous example the rebels propose to set," he said. "We should meet it only by a more vigorous prosecution of the war, and by putting an end to the rebellion." U.S. authorities could then seize and punish the Confederate leadership who ordered the execution of the U.S. prisoners. The Union would gain advantage if it refused to retaliate. Its troops would "fight more desperately and not allow themselves to be taken." Foreign nations would sympathize with the United States, whereas "if we mutually go to murdering helpless POWs, foreign powers would undoubtedly interfere." Judge Advocate General Joseph Holt, alternately, thought the execution of prisoners was a "stern duty." "I would neither count officers nor measure rank in responding," he wrote Francis Lieber.[36]

Lincoln thought this particular case merited the actual execution of Confederate officers if necessary, but he also possessed leverage that made it unlikely he would have to perform the "stern duty": the United States had captured the son of Robert E. Lee. Lincoln ordered that Lee and another high-profile officer be reserved for execution if the Confederate government carried out its threat. General-in-Chief Henry W. Halleck gave standing orders to his subordinates to "hang" Lee "immediately" if they received "authentic" information that the two Federal prisoners selected by lot were executed. Lincoln certainly had the advantage in this particular retaliation ritual. Rumors swirled in the Confederate War Department that Robert E. Lee was opposed to Davis's actions in the case. "Our officers executed by Burnside were certainly recruiting in Kentucky within the lines of the enemy," a clerk noted, "and Lee may differ with the President in the equity of executing officers taken by us in battle." Jefferson Davis did not want to test the question of whether Lincoln would execute the son of his revered general. The confrontation turned into a hostage standoff, but it became clear as the weeks went by without the execution of the two Federal prisoners that the Davis administration had backed down. The Lincoln administration learned from this episode that it could intimidate Confederate leaders if retaliation threats were specific to individuals, credible, and involved socially prominent Confederates. It would take the actual capture of Black prisoners and their white officers to see if this lesson applied to the situation in the Department of the South.[37]

Hunter, meanwhile, looked to bring more Black troops to his department. On May 4, he sent a letter to John A. Andrew, the abolitionist governor of Massachusetts, who had been pivotal in organizing and recruiting the 54th Massachusetts (Colored) Infantry, currently drilling in its training camp in Readville, Massachusetts. Its enlisted men were mostly freeborn Northern Blacks, including two sons of Frederick Douglass, and its officers carefully chosen to represent educated anti-slavery sentiment and well-connected families. The colonel was Robert Gould Shaw. Shaw at first declined the offer of command but immediately reversed himself. "I felt ashamed of myself, as if I were cowardly," he said. Hunter asked Andrew to use his influence with Stanton to get the 54th sent to the Department of the South. He had plans "to make extensive incursions upon the mainland, through the most densely populated slave regions," and getting the 54th would put him in a position to implement them. Andrew obliged, and Stanton approved the assignment.[38]

Hunter also requested from Lincoln blanket authority to organize Black regiments, commission officers for them, and remove any officers from his department "who oppose vigorous prosecution of the war or any of its necessary measures." He challenged the president to change strategy. Rather than cooperate with the navy to attack Charleston, as Lincoln wanted, Hunter wanted to march a column of 10,000 soldiers through the counties in Georgia in which more than 75 percent of the population were enslaved. He claimed the Confederacy was a "mere hollow shell." "If we avoid their few strongholds, where they have prepared for and invited us to battle," he wrote of the rebels, "we shall meet no opposition in the total devastation of their resources, thus compelling them to break up their large armies . . . into scores of small fractions of armies for the protection of every threatened or assailable point." Slavery would disintegrate and panic would spread among the Confederate population.[39]

While he waited for the Lincoln administration to respond and for the 54th to arrive in theater, Hunter implemented his plans on a small scale. Harriet Tubman, the commander of the department's spy network, gathered intelligence on Confederate defenses, mapped the Carolina low country, and established contact with the enslaved population. On June 2, Montgomery and a detachment of 300 men of the 2nd South Carolina, guided by Tubman based on her advance work, ascended twenty-five miles up the Com-

"Raid of the Second South Carolina Volunteers (Col. Montgomery) among the Rice Plantations of the Combahee, S.C." The raid where soldiers burned plantation houses, liberated 725 slaves, and pillaged personal property was a significant departure from previous actions in the Department of the South. (*Harper's Weekly: A Journal of Civilization*, July 4, 1863)

bahee River on two steamers; confiscated cotton and horses; opened sluices to flood fields; burned four plantation houses, six mills, and thirty-four outbuildings; and brought away 725 slaves. More slaves tried to crowd onto the Union steamers, but there was not enough room for all of them.[40]

Hunter had assured Stanton that his Black troops "never disgraced their uniform by pillage" and that "even our enemies have not yet been able to allege against them a single violation of any of the rules of civilized warfare." The Combahee raid undermined this statement. The soldiers of the 2nd burned a private library with $15,000 worth of books, and officers took slaveholders' personal property—such as marble candlestands and furniture—and distributed it as trophies to their friends in other regiments. "Montgomery's raid was a most brilliant success," Higginson conceded, "though I don't believe in burning private houses, as he does."[41]

This raid was a significant departure from previous raids in the department because its objective was not recruiting and foraging but the destruction of slaveholder property that lined the river. Confederate military officials were in equal parts humiliated and outraged after the raid. Confederate pickets and stations along the river were confused, indecisive, and slow to respond when the 2nd disembarked. Some pickets left to get dogs to pursue the slaves running for the Federal gunboats rather than contest the landing. This was particularly annoying because Beauregard had instructed his subordinates to plan for just such a raid and to prepare to follow President Davis's December 1862 retaliation instructions. "Those taken prisoners will be closely guarded and watched night and day by a large detail, and turned over to state authorities as soon as practicable," a circular to the troops instructed. Instead, the Yankees got away without injury. "This raid by a mixed party of blacks and degraded whites seems to have been designed only for plunder, robbery, and the destruction of private property," Capt. John Lay wrote Beauregard's staff. "In carrying it out they have discarded all rules of civilized war, and have acted more as fiends than human beings."[42]

Hunter recognized that Montgomery's behavior during the Combahee raid had crossed a line. On June 9, he sent Montgomery a copy of General Orders No. 100, the U.S. War Department's encapsulation of how the customs of civilized war should govern troops in the field. The document was the product of the friendship between Lieber and Halleck and their mutual interest in international law. They were frustrated that no "systematic arrangement" of the laws of war existed in a form that was usable for Union army officers. Educated men accessed the laws of war through reading long, complex books in foreign languages, comparing writers that often disagreed with each other, and mining examples from history that offered contradictory interpretations about proper behavior in war. Lieber used his expertise to write a practical manual with short paragraphs. He got some research help, advice, and input from Generals Halleck, Hitchcock, and Holt. Halleck, because of his experience in the field dealing with women guerrillas, saboteurs, spies, smugglers, and informants, was responsible for the section of the code that included women in its categories of "war rebels" and "military traitors." No other civilized nation had produced such a document. "I had no guide, no ground work, no text book," Lieber said. "Usage, History, Reason . . . and a sincere love of truth and justice and of civilization have been my guide." He believed the code was a "contribution to the state of common civilization." Halleck had issued it to every command in the Union army on April 24.[43]

The principles enumerated in General Orders No. 100 spoke to the unfolding retaliation process in the Department of the South. "The more vigorously wars are pursued, the better it is for humanity," Article 29 stated. "Sharp wars are brief." The code gave commanders the principle of "military necessity" as the determining guide for action: "measures which are indispensable for securing the ends of the war, and which are lawful according to the modern law and usages of war." It provided specifics of behavior that was never lawful, including "revenge" and "wanton destruction."[44]

The code also proclaimed that captured and fugitive slaves were "immediately entitled to all the rights and privileges of a freeman" and were "under the shield of the law of nations." It asserted the legality of the 1st and 2nd South Carolina regiments (without mentioning them specifically). "No belligerent has the right to declare that enemies of a certain class, color, or condition, when properly organized as soldiers, will not be treated by him as public enemies." It also laid the groundwork for the United States to protect its Black soldiers. "The law of nations knows no distinction of color, and if an enemy of the United States should enslave or sell any captured persons of their army, it would be case for the severest retaliation," Article 58 read. "The United States cannot retaliate by enslavement; therefore death must be the retaliation for this crime against the law of nations."[45]

Contemporary legal scholars call Lieber's document a "legal masterpiece," and it formed the foundation for subsequent iterations of the laws of war in the twentieth century. It is important to keep in mind, however, that the professor did not merely distill a clear-cut and universally accepted body of laws. The code was a compound of Lieber's original contribution to legal theory and his interpretation of points disputed among previous writers and among previous nations at war. Although some civilian administrators and military officials referenced the "laws of war" as though they were unambiguous, they were instead a set of "philosophical disputes" in ponderous tomes. Precedents from European warfare and interpretations of law from European writers did not speak with a unified voice regarding the legality of emancipating slaves or serfs and arming them. Those who wanted to limit war to a conflict between professional armed forces argued that combatants should not touch local law and institutions, including slavery, although other voices affirmed that liberating slaves was a legitimate military necessity to defeat an enemy army.[46]

The Confederate War Department found ample legal precedent, including the claims and actions of the United States during the War for Independence and the War of 1812, for its perspective that nations could not use "servile insurrection as an instrument of war." Secretary of War James Seddon thought and spoke like the lawyer he was after he read General Orders No. 100. "The diplomatic correspondence, the solemn treaties of the United States, show reclamations for the value of escaping slaves and of slaves abducted by a military force in time of war, and the recognition of that claim by a foreign nation," he wrote. He denounced the code using legal terms such as "postliminium," invoking decisions in Great Britain, and referencing the "texts of the Roman Pandects." Accompanying the legal language was the consistent refrain about the existential threat to Southern civilization. "The savage passions and brutal appetites of a barbarous race are to be stimulated into fierce activity," he said. "The enemy who adopts such auxiliaries proclaims in advance his desire as well as design that the war shall be one for mutual extermination." Robert Garlick Hill Kean, head of the Confederate Bureau of War, thought the code was a "demoniac document."[47]

Hunter transmitted the code to Montgomery with a discourse on what it meant to be civilized. He reminded his subordinate that honor was an essential element of civilization. The United States must maintain its reputation before peer nations, and therefore it was a necessity that the Confederacy always appear at fault before the world. The Union and the Confederacy had to convince other civilized nations, who observed and judged them, of the righteousness of their conduct. This was especially important given that a retaliation order of the Confederate Congress was in place. Hunter told Montgomery that the Confederate government must not have any grounds to allege Union troops in the Department of the South violated the laws of war, which it would use as an excuse to implement the "atrocities" threatened against Black troops and white officers. If the war was to degenerate into a savage conflict, Hunter wrote, "it is of the first moment that the infamy of this deterioration should rest exclusively and without excuse upon the rebel Government."[48]

Hunter ordered Montgomery to comply strictly with General Orders No. 100 and "avoid any devastation which does not strike immediately at the resource or material of the armed insurrection which we are now engaged in the task of suppressing." Hunter instructed Montgomery to welcome fugitive slaves into the lines and to take horses, mules, and cattle. Because the rebels impressed grain and produce for their armies, Montgomery could take or destroy storehouses, but he should consider carefully before destroying crops in the ground, which might not be fit for use until the rebellion was over. "This right of war, though unquestionable in certain extreme cases," Hunter wrote, "is not to be lightly used, and if wantonly used might fall under the part of the instructions which prohibit devastation." Household furniture, libraries, churches, and hospitals were off limits. Hunter reminded Montgomery that so far, the Confederate retaliation orders were just words on a page, and until the Union had proof of actual actions, "it will be both right and wise to hold the troops under your command to the very strictest interpretation of the laws and usages of civilized warfare."[49]

Hunter made sure the historical record showed that his official instructions followed the laws of war. He also took steps to protect the troops under his command from the threatened Confederate retaliation. He ordered Montgomery to send any captured prisoners—soldier or citizen—in irons to Hilton Head to hold as hostages to ensure the proper treatment of any soldiers the Confederates might capture from the 2nd South Carolina. He also received permission from the War Department to not exchange prisoners in his theater of the war and to put those he held in "close custody." Commanders engaged in a retaliation ritual during the American Civil War usually took hostages, so Hunter's actions were typical.[50]

The U.S. War Department also made its first official statement to Confederate officials of its intention to protect Black Federal soldiers through retaliation. The U.S. agent for exchange of prisoners, William H. Ludlow, wrote his counterpart, Robert Ould, that the Dix-Hill exchange cartel made no mention of color. "It was unnecessary to make any such mention, for before the establishment of this cartel and before one single negro or mulatto was mustered into the U.S. service you had them organized in arms in Louisiana," he noted. "You had Indians and half-breed negroes and Indians organized under Albert Pike, in Arkansas." Ludlow was direct. "You have not a foot of ground to stand upon in making the proposed discrimination among our captured officers and men," he said. "I now give you formal notice that the United States Government will throw its protection around all its officers and men without regard to color, and will promptly retaliate for all cases violating the cartel or the laws and usages of war."[51]

The Department of the South gained a well-connected advocate for the laws of war when Robert Gould Shaw arrived at Hilton Head with the 54th Massachusetts the day after Montgomery's Combahee raid. Shaw brought with him the attitudes he had formed when he was one of "Pope's officers" in Virginia and had believed his commander to be in the wrong. He believed in the premise that civilized warfare controlled and disciplined soldiers to minimize the violence of war and its effects on noncombatants. Similar to other members of New England's interconnected network of elite families, he feared that his civilized society, with its high culture of art and letters, refined manners, and hierarchical order, in fact harbored ignorant, vulgar, and violent lower classes, particularly the semi-barbaric Irish. He distrusted the mass of enlisted men, white or Black, and employed strict discipline to ensure they did not degenerate into a bestial armed mob. While Colonel Higginson avoided punishments reminiscent of slavery, Shaw did not have that problem commanding a regiment of freeborn men. He used the same physical coercion, such as bucking and gagging, that he had learned as a line officer in the 2nd Massachusetts commanding Irish soldiers. His severe methods produced a volunteer regiment that was as professional as Shaw could make it. He differed from Higginson and Montgomery in an interesting way. Of the three, he was the only one who allowed his close association with Black men to change him. Although he, too, viewed Southern Blacks as "childlike" and "no more responsible for their actions than so many puppies," when he discussed his own Northern-born men his letters reflected a trajectory from thinking of them as "nigs" to thinking of them as men worthy of respect.[52]

Shaw and Montgomery represented diametrically opposed views about the role of uncivilized people in a civilized war. On June 10, Montgomery left for an expedition to Darien, Georgia, taking with him the 2nd South Carolina and eight companies of the 54th Massachusetts. Three gunboats, firing shells as they ascended the Altamaha River, delivered the troops. Most of the white inhabitants of Darien had abandoned the village some time before, and fewer than twenty people (slaves and two white women), all noncombatants, were there when the 2nd and 54th arrived. There were no shots fired at the Union troops from the town; it was not a shelter for Confederate guerrillas. The 54th "formed line of battle in the principal square of the town," but its captains received orders to "take twenty men from the right of your company, break into the houses on this street take out anything that can be made useful in camp." Montgomery ordered the soldiers to put all the movable property and furniture on the boats; they carried off sofas, pianos, chairs, mirrors, books, china sets, and personal letters. Then Montgomery said to Shaw, "I shall burn this town." Shaw replied, "I do not want the responsibility of it." Montgomery ordered one company of the 54th to assist in setting fire to the town. Darien burned to the ground, with only the church and three small buildings left standing. Montgomery fired one building with his own hand. "Southerners must be made to feel that this was a real war, and that they were to be swept away by the hand of God, like the Jews of old," Montgomery told Shaw. "We are outlawed, and therefore not bound by the rules of regular warfare."[53]

Most of the white officers of the 54th were revolted and ashamed. The burning of Darien violated General Orders No. 100 and dishonored them before the world. Shaw called it a "dirty piece of business." "Besides my own distaste for this barbarous sort of warfare, I am not sure that it will not harm very much the reputation of Black troops and those connected with them," he said. "I have gone through the war so far without dishonor, and I do not like to degenerate into a plunderer and robber. There was not a deed performed, from beginning to end, which required any pluck or courage." The burning of Darien was sheer "wanton destruction."[54] Two of Shaw's captains, who played a prominent role in the regiment's later history, were more ambivalent. John W. M. Appleton, of Company A, was a thirty-one-year-old Harvard-educated abolitionist with a poet's eye for landscape, a talent for drawing, and an intimate romance with his wife, Mary. He rarely punished his men. "I feel that our success in this war depends upon our single hearted advancement of the cause of Freedom, and the destruction of Slavery," he said. He liked Montgomery and thought that "he is one of our kind that believes in making the enemy pay the way." Although he told Mary that he was "glad that you have not got to see a town so treated," he had personally "made a bonfire" of the Darien jail with its slave whipping post and kept the keys as a trophy. Luis F. Emilio was the son of a Spanish immigrant to Salem, Massachusetts, who had lied about his age and enlisted in the 23rd Massachusetts in 1861 at age sixteen. He was matter-of-fact about what happened in Darien. He wrote his parents, "I took twenty men and ransacked houses as I went along getting many useful articles." Emilio's father thought Montgomery had done just right; his mother did not. "I hope you will never rejoice in doing what you know must give great pain to others," she wrote back.[55]

Shaw feared that using Black troops for this type of raid kept them in an uncivilized condition and wrote his family to register his protest. His brother-in-law Charles Russell Lowell echoed his sentiments: "Instead of improving the negro character and educating him for civilized independence, we are re-developing all his savage instincts." Capitalizing on the family's influence in the highest political circles, Lowell wrote the solicitor of the War Department. He argued that Montgomery's course would lead to indiscriminate pillaging and that Black troops operating under retaliation threats were demoralized. "Instead of finding ourselves at the end of the summer with an army of disciplined blacks," he wrote, "we shall have a horde of savages not fit to fight alongside our white troops, if fit to fight at all."[56]

Higginson broke with Montgomery over the events at Darien. "He will never rise above a brigand," Higginson thought. "His hatred of control makes it hard for him to believe that a regiment which is well drilled can be fit for action. Whereas I believe that want of self-control will demoralize our men and want of drill will unfit them for *regular* warfare when needed."[57]

For their part, the free enlisted soldiers from Northern states in the 54th

Capt. John W. M. Appleton, 54th Massachusetts, and his sketch of Darien, Georgia. Abolitionist Appleton made a bonfire out of Darien's slave whipping post. (Appleton Military Memoirs, pp. 2, 23, box 3A, APWV; West Virginia and Regional History Center, West Virginia University Libraries, Morgantown)

wanted to engage in honorable warfare to prove their courageous manhood and demand full inclusion in civilization. During the burning of the town, Emilio noticed that the men of the 2nd "went in for this course" but that his men "did not evince much desire to burn or destroy." The regiment, like all others in the Union army, had its share of soldiers who enlisted out of financial desperation. It also had highly literate men in its ranks who fought for the cause of freedom and racial equality. James Henry Gooding was born into slavery, but a benefactor who may have been his father purchased his freedom and sent him to New York City when he was eight years old, where Quaker women at the New York Colored Orphan Asylum gave him a classical education. As a young adult, when he moved to New Bedford, Massachusetts, he hid his past and told people he was born free. He had traveled the world and visited the Arctic on whaling and mercantile voyages. Gooding was a passionate reader of history, literature, and the classics and a prolific essay writer and poet. The Republican *New Bedford Mercury* published weekly letters from him about the activities of the 54th. He accurately reported what happened at Darien. "There was no chance to show what sort of fighting material the 54th is made of," he said. Gooding was frustrated that Darien played into the hands of Northern Democrats who opposed Black troops. The Democratic press, he wrote, have "wrought their followers up to that delightful point of commanding the Powers that be to stop enlisting the 'impediments to civilization' instanter." He was angry that many Northerners expressed more outrage over the "vandalism" at Darien than at the fact that Confederates intended to hang any Black soldiers they captured.[58]

The soldiers of the 2nd left no written record of their thoughts and feelings about Darien, but we can discern a likely variety of perspectives in the regiment based on statements made in other contexts. They were escaped slaves fighting where they lived for freedom from the men they were fighting. Former slaves in the region often articulated their belief that the products of their labor—land, crops, and buildings—were rightfully theirs. They did not view slaveholder property in the same way that their white officers did, and some soldiers in the regiment may have believed that the products of their labor were theirs to burn. Some soldiers may have rejoiced in the burning of Darien as an act of revenge—or of justice—against specific people who had mistreated them or their relatives. Others believed that military service offered the opportunity to prove their manhood and establish claims for racial equality and might have agreed with Gooding that Darien did not accomplish that purpose.[59]

Most soldiers of the 2nd had more pressing concerns than worrying about whether their actions were civilized. They were trying to survive in a regiment where death was a consequence for disobeying orders, to rescue relatives from slavery, and to feed their refugee families. Defeat of the Union army in their region meant re-enslavement and death. One of their officers, who had been born in Georgia, stated the situation bluntly. "This is not a friendly boxing match with gloves, where neither party wishes to really hurt the other," he said. "It is a struggle for life, and the quickest and surest conquest is the best."[60]

Shaw wrote Hunter to find out if Montgomery acted under official departmental orders; if not, Shaw was determined to refuse to obey Montgomery on future expeditions. Shaw never received a reply to his letters because the Union War Department relieved Hunter from command. Hunter had failed in his primary task: maintaining a credible threat against the city of Charleston.[61] His replacement was Maj. Gen. Quincy A. Gillmore, an expert engineer, who believed that an abolitionist agenda had dictated military operations in the Department of the South for too long. It was time for firepower and technology to take over.

General Beauregard took the opportunity of the change in command to demand a change in the future conduct of the war in South Carolina and Georgia. The Louisiana Creole, who spoke only French until he was twelve, cultivated a persona of knightly chivalry and a bearing reminiscent of Napoleon. He had attended a private school in New York City taught by two brothers who had been officers under that legendary Corsican. He graduated second in his class at West Point in 1838, challenged another lieutenant to a duel of honor in 1845, and proved to be an outstanding engineer during the Mexican War. He had arranged the defense of Charleston in 1861 and, after service in Virginia and Mississippi, was back in the city that loved his haughty demeanor. He had large, melancholy eyes and went for months without smiling at those around him. He and Jefferson Davis hated each other.[62]

On July 4, Beauregard wrote a letter to Gillmore that was a classic expression of Americans' sense that their war was an outgrowth of a shared civilized history. This was one of the indispensable characteristics of a civilized war: combatants participated in the accumulated wisdom of civilized people stretching back to ancient times. Beauregard's letter, as was typical, was a lengthy reference to historical precedents and European texts on the customs of war. First Beauregard named specific actions that violated the customs of war and provided dates and locations. He informed Gillmore that Union troops had the right to seize towns but not to ravage and destroy houses or other property of individual citizens. The Union could sack a town or city only if "aggravated by an improper defense." Throughout his exegesis of the laws of war, Beauregard quoted Vattel's *Law of Nations*, the book military officers considered the authoritative text. Burning the countryside without absolute necessity, Vattel wrote, was born of "hatred and fury" and was the warfare of the "furious barbarian." Beauregard compared the burning of Jacksonville and Darien to a list of burnings during the War of 1812 that were illegal. History proved, he noted, that atrocious warfare always followed when a combatant used a "merciless, servile race" as soldiers. For this reason, Napoleon did not receive or employ serfs when he invaded Russia. "In conclusion," he wrote, "it is my duty to inquire whether the acts which resulted in the burning of the defenseless villages of Darien and Bluffton, and

Gen. P. G. T. Beauregard. The Confederate commander of the Department of South Carolina, Georgia, and Florida participated in several retaliation rituals in 1862–64. His correspondence displayed knowledge of historical precedent and European texts on the customs of war. (National Archives Catalog, Record Group 111, Records of the Office of the Chief Signal Officer, Series, Matthew Brady Photographs of Civil War–Era Personalities)

the ravages on the Combahee, are regarded by you as legitimate measures of war, which you will feel authorized to resort to hereafter."[63]

Gillmore did not immediately respond. He was busy planning a major offensive against the Confederate fortifications in Charleston's outer harbor. That offensive would change the retaliation ritual in the Department of the South. Hunter's raiding strategy had exposed fissures among Union officers about the use of Black troops in a civilized war and provoked debates in the Confederate government about the relationship between federal military law and state civil laws. The divide among Union officers was not resolved, but the Confederate government had announced a policy of retaliation. When Gillmore decided to use the 54th Massachusetts in a conventional battle, the death of Robert Gould Shaw and the Confederate capture of prisoners who were free Blacks born in the North would force the Confederate War Department to decide if implementing its threatened retaliation was worth the cost.

# 3

# PRISONERS

"You don't know what a fortunate day this has been for me and for us all, excepting some poor fellows who were killed and wounded. We have at last fought alongside of white troops," Robert Gould Shaw wrote his wife on July 16, 1863. The colonel was elated that finally his men had participated in the type of conventional battle that gave them the opportunity to earn honor and prove their place in civilization. Corporal James Gooding was likewise exultant. "It is not for us to blow our own horn; but when a regiment of white men gave us three cheers as we were passing them, it shows that we did our duty as men should," he reported to the readers of the *New Bedford Mercury*.[1]

The new commander of the Department of the South, Maj. Gen. Quincy A. Gillmore, had assigned the 54th Massachusetts to combat duty as part of his plan to capture Morris Island, a narrow strip of land that guarded the approach to Charleston Harbor. From there, Union army engineers and artillerists could establish batteries whose fire would destroy Fort Sumter and enable the Union navy to enter the harbor and capture the city. Gillmore sent the 1st South Carolina on a diversionary raid thirty miles up the Edisto River. The 1st liberated 200 slaves, burned mills and barns, and cut dams to flood fields. The 54th and the 2nd South Carolina were assigned to another diversion, a landing on James Island with a division of 5,260 Union soldiers, while the main body of Union troops prepared to launch the attack against Morris Island.[2]

The 54th and the 2nd, along with white troops from Massachusetts, Connecticut, Pennsylvania, and New York, landed on James Island at dusk on July 9. The soldiers waded through deep mud to the shore, marched in column, and camped in the same place that Union soldiers had camped during their failed assault on the island the year before. They could see the impressive and extensive fortifications of the Confederate troops occupying James Island.

On July 16 at 3:00 A.M., four companies of the 54th were on picket on the extreme right of the Federal line when six companies of skirmishers from the Confederate 25th South Carolina began to probe for the Federal position. The officer in charge of the 54th's companies ordered his men to lie down behind a hedge. He wanted to disguise his location and numbers while the enemy skirmishers advanced by degrees. When the rebels were 600 yards away, the pickets of the 54th stood up and fired a volley. The pickets and the skirmishers exchanged fire for several minutes, and then the main body of Confederate infantry, about 1,400 men, and an artillery battery arrived on the scene. The pickets of the 54th conducted a fighting retreat. They gave the other soldiers of their division, especially those of the 10th Connecticut on their left, time to get into position and halt the Confederate advance. The men of the 10th later spread the word that the "stubborn resistance" of the 54th saved them from capture.[3]

As the pickets from Companies B and H of the 54th fell back, they passed through Solomon Legare's plantation and around its main house. A detachment from the Confederate 5th South Carolina cavalry rode after them and drove them toward a marsh. Near the house, the rebels captured thirteen men of the 54th. Sgt. James D. Wilson of Company H, who before the war had been a member of the famous Ellsworth Zouaves of Chicago, refused to surrender. He shot three rebels, kept others at bay with the bayonet of his musket, and died of multiple gunshot wounds. Confederate officers wanted to take prisoners in order to hang the Black men publicly later as an example to slaves in the area, but when the officers were not looking, Confederate soldiers shot a few men who tried to surrender. About thirty soldiers of the 54th ran into the marsh to avoid capture. The cavalry could not follow into the bog, but infantry from the 25th South Carolina stood around its edges and fired at the floundering Black soldiers. Several drowned, but others managed to escape the morass. After the pickets returned, the 54th stood in line of battle while shells flew overhead and landed in their rear. Capt. John Appleton, who joined the regiment "to prove that colored people could fight," scribbled a note to his beloved wife, Mary, during the action in order to brag. "The first shell or so my boys ducked but they now stand grandly—talking quietly."[4]

The white officers of the 54th were so overjoyed about the behavior of their men under fire that they initially glossed over the real significance of

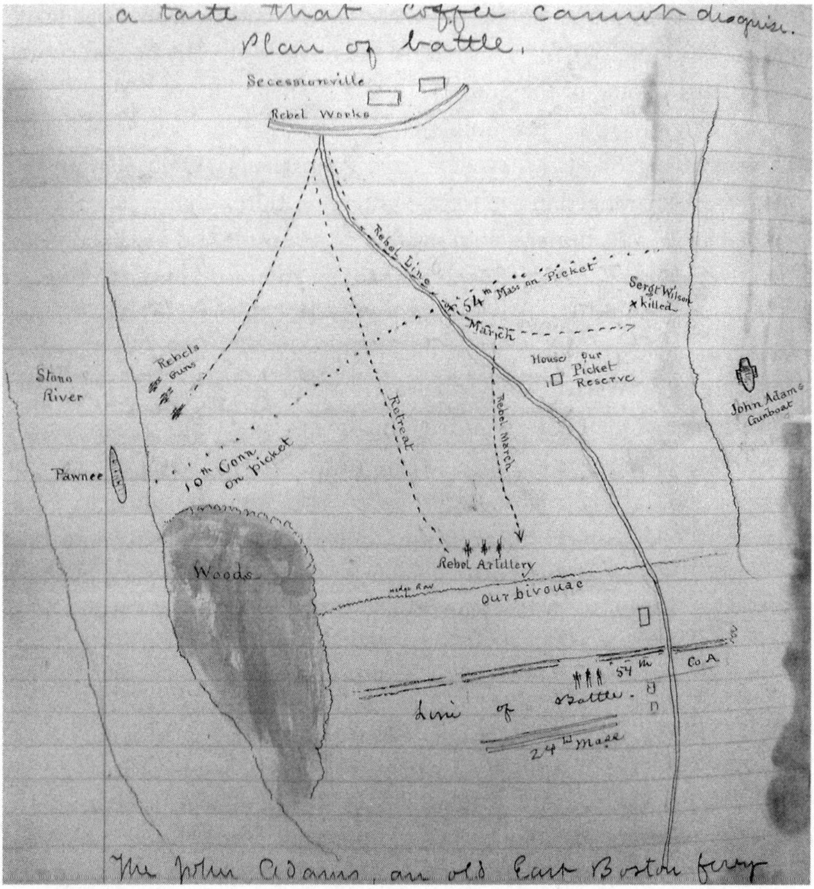

Capt. John Appleton's sketches of the 54th Massachusetts picket fight and battle lines on Sol Legare Island, July 16, 1863. Appleton marked the location where Sgt. James D. Wilson fought to the death rather than surrender. Still, Confederates took thirteen soldiers from the 54th prisoner. These prisoners were a legal and diplomatic predicament for the Confederate War Department. (Appleton Military Memoirs, pp. 49, 52–53, box 3A, APWV; West Virginia and Regional History Center, West Virginia University Libraries, Morgantown)

the regiment's action on Sol Legare Island—Confederate troops had taken thirteen Black men in Federal uniform prisoner. In the smoke and confusion of battle, some of the South Carolina soldiers did not realize whom they were fighting until the moments of surrender. None of the prisoners was from Massachusetts; they were from Pennsylvania, Ohio, Illinois, and Michigan. They ranged in age from eighteen to thirty-eight years old and included laborers, a farmer, a cook, a barber, a teamster, and a seaman. Confederate brigadier general Johnson Hagood, in command of the Confederate troops on James Island, wrote his superiors, "Thirteen prisoners Fifty-fourth Massachusetts, black. What shall I do with them?" He thought two of them were escaped slaves, the rest born free. After receiving instructions, he stripped them of their uniforms, tied them up in a gang (the same treatment runaway slaves received), and sent them to Charleston. Local officials put them in jail in Castle Pinckney, a small masonry fort on an island in Charleston Harbor. Their jailor, a captain in the Confederate army, asked permission to put them to work shoring up Confederate batteries.[5]

For the first time in the Department of the South, the Confederacy was in a position to implement its plan for retaliation. By this point, Gen. P. G. T. Beauregard's jet-black hair had turned white—from stress, as his friends said, or from the dearth of hair dye in the Confederacy because of the blockade, as his enemies said. His female admirers in Charleston still loved him, however, and filled his office with letters and bouquets. Beauregard immediately wrote to Richmond and informed his authorities he had Black prisoners. "Several," he said, "claim to be free, from Massachusetts." His subordinates had not given him specific reports, and he mistakenly conflated regiment designation with the residence of the volunteer soldiers from the 54th. Beauregard asked if he should turn over the free Blacks to South Carolina state authorities for trial. The gentlemen friends of Charleston diarist Emma Holmes thought this was a wrong step. "Many nice questions will now be involved," they told her. "If we hang them, will not the Yankees retaliate on our men?" Everyone knew that the Yankees held prisoners hostage on Hilton Head to prevent the Confederates from implementing their threatened retaliation against the Union's Black soldiers. According to the resolutions of the Confederate Congress, *any* Black men taken in arms against the Confederacy, even if they were born free in a Northern state, would be delivered to state authorities in the states where they were captured to be put on trial for inciting servile insurrection. Execution or other punishment prescribed by state laws would follow.[6]

Gillmore's operations on Sol Legare Island and Morris Island brought the retaliation ritual over the use of Black troops in the Department of the South to its apex and forced the Confederate government to decide whether it was willing to implement its threatened retaliation. As we will see, it was not. When Confederate military officials dishonored Robert Gould Shaw, a Union officer with prominent connections in the highest political and social circles, the United States announced a retaliatory policy that focused on Confederate treatment of Union soldiers born free in the North. Confederate officials were divided over the legality of their own policy. Believing that their reputation before the civilized world would suffer, the Davis administration and the Confederate Congress swerved off their intended course and in the end conceded the perspective of the Lincoln administration.

The story of the prisoners of the 54th Massachusetts reveals how the retaliation ritual worked to alter policy and practice during the American Civil War. It also demonstrates how important international honor was to the Confederate leadership during its crisis of civilization. Confederates believed in the superior status of their society, but their identity depended on other civilized nations including them in the roster of the civilized. They feared to take public action that threatened their claims to belong and instead turned to clandestine methods.

Before the Davis administration could react to the news of the free Black prisoners in South Carolina, Confederates captured more. While the 54th was in action on James Island, the Federal's main attack unfolded on Morris Island. Gillmore, who graduated at the top of his class at West Point in 1849, believed that war was a science and that new technology in heavy guns, rifled artillery, and engineering were the keys to victory. He was a technician, not an infantry commander. He had a good-natured face and a powerful frame. He excelled at designing trenches, building fortifications, and placing guns, but as one of his subordinates remarked, "He does not in the least understand how to manage men." He coordinated operations with the new Federal commander of the South Atlantic Blockading Squadron, Rear Adm. John A. Dahlgren, another "scientific warrior." Dahlgren spent fifteen years as an ordnance officer at the Washington Naval Yard, where he designed the cannon mounted on U.S. Navy ships during the war. He was a genius inventor and wrote what one British captain called "the best work on ordnance that has ever been written" but had logged little time at sea compared with other naval commanders. His manner was reserved and old-fashioned.[7]

The initial landing on the southern tip of Morris Island was a success. Union troops captured three-quarters of the narrow island on July 10 with the support of four navy monitors that advanced alongside the soldiers

Maj. Gen. Quincy A. Gillmore. An expert technologist, Gillmore had not mastered the etiquette of retaliation correspondence. He failed to conduct the ritual properly over the issues of Black prisoners from the 54th Massachusetts and the bombardment of Charleston. (Library of Congress Prints and Photographs Division)

marching up the sandy beach. Confederate defenders fled their entrenchments under the heavy shelling from the monitors and the infantry attacks against their batteries. Heatstroke caused more casualties for the Federals than enemy fire. Fort Wagner, an enormous sand earthwork with ample artillery, blocked any further infantry advance. On July 11, just before daylight, the overconfident Gillmore sent three regiments to attack Wagner. He used exhausted troops that had fought in the heat the day before, made no artillery bombardment of Wagner in preparation for the assault, and ordered a quick bayonet charge with no preparation for his troops. It was a disastrous failure. From July 12 to July 15, Gillmore's engineers, using twelve-hour shifts of Union soldiers, constructed four breaching batteries so that his artillery could pound Wagner to the ground in preparation for another infantry assault. On July 16, he gave an order that put in motion another retaliation ritual in the Department of the South: he sent Col. Edward W. Serrell, of the 1st New York Engineers, to find a place on the marsh between Morris and James Islands to construct a battery that could fire into the city of Charleston.[8]

Gillmore brought the 54th and 2nd South Carolina to Morris. Unlike Maj. Gen. David Hunter, who placed Black troops and the destruction of slavery at the heart of his strategy in the Department of the South, Gillmore viewed Black troops with indifference. He was willing to use them as a tool to support his firepower, but he thought Hunter's abolitionist agenda had hijacked the campaign for Charleston. "The fact of the matter is our General attends to military matters and lets niggers alone," a member of his staff said. Gillmore ordered all of his troops on James to evacuate during the night of July 16. The 54th marched in single file over narrow causeways and plank footbridges placed over the swamps. Driving rain made the footing slippery, and it took the regiment seven hours to make four miles. "I never had such an extraordinary walk," Shaw said. The 54th arrived on Morris Island the morning of July 18. Brig. Gen. George C. Strong wanted the Black soldiers to get their share of the action and honor, so Gillmore agreed to transfer the 54th to his brigade. "We have left Montgomery, I hope for good," Shaw said.[9]

Gillmore did not pay much attention to where he assigned his Black troops, because he expected technology to destroy Fort Wagner. On July 18 at noon, all the Federal land and sea artillery in range opened a massive bombardment of Wagner to prepare for a second infantry assault. Federals fired one projectile at the earthwork every two seconds. Exploding iron fragments created clouds of debris that disguised how effectively the sand earthwork absorbed this punishment. Its walls were disfigured but not destroyed, its garrison intact, its land-facing artillery undamaged. After witnessing the dazzling display of pyrotechnics, Gillmore, who had failed to orient regimental commanders to the lay of the land, ordered Strong's brigade forward for a frontal assault on Wagner at twilight. Strong believed that his troops would take Wagner easily and that this was an opportune moment to place a disciplined, effective, and well-led Black regiment in a major battle in the eastern theater. He put the 54th as his lead regiment.[10]

Wagner presented a major problem for attacking forces: a narrow approach, in this case a strip of land between the sea and wet marshes that would make it difficult for commanders to insert supporting units into the action. No more than 500 men at a time could pass through the defile leading to Wagner. The 54th formed in two lines and lay flat on the ground while the rest of the brigade got into position. The officers had orders to charge the earthwork without stopping to fire, and the soldiers fixed bayonets. Gillmore had not issued the assaulting columns scaling ladders or trenching tools, and the officers of the 54th had not seen a plan of Wagner. Shaw, the rigid disciplinarian, unbent before his men. He sat on the ground and spoke with them "familiarly" but with lips compressed and twitching from stress. "The eyes of thousands would look upon the night's work," he said. "Now boys I want you to be MEN!" One private yelled out, "Colonel, I will stay by you till I die." General Strong rode forward and addressed the regiment. "Don't fire a musket on your way up," he said, "but go in and bayonet them at their guns." He called the color-bearer forward. "If this man should fall, who will lift the flag and carry on?" Shaw removed a cigar from his mouth and said, "I will." The men cheered him loudly, and Strong gave the signal to advance.[11]

The 54th moved forward in its first combat action as an entire regiment. The men advanced in quick time and had to break formation to pass through a narrow defile. At 200 yards from Wagner, intense artillery and musket fire erupted from the earthwork. It became a "mound of fire" and a "sheet of flame." The men ran forward under severe crossfire. The 54th took enormous casualties on the approach. Shaw, Appleton, and other survivors of the charge crossed a line of shattered palisades, passed over some rifle pits, went into Wagner's ditch and up the slope of a parapet, and planted the regimental flags. Shaw stood for a moment at the top, waving his sword, shouting, "Forward, Fifty-Fourth!" Then he immediately died of multiple wounds. The other officers and men on the parapet engaged in desperate and fierce hand-to-hand fighting with the Confederate defenders, who used swords, muskets, handspikes, gun-rammers, and improvised hand grenades against the bodies of the attackers. A few men made a desperate effort to retrieve

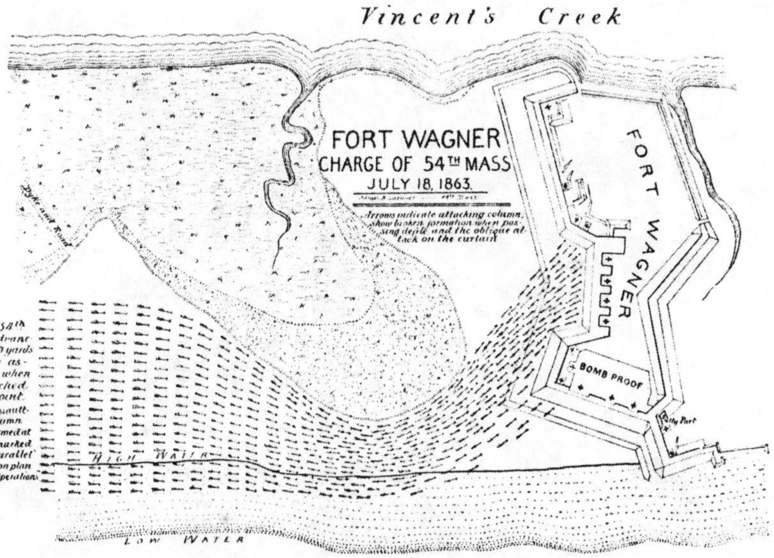


Charge of the 54th Massachusetts at Fort Wagner, July 18, 1863. Capt. Luis F. Emilio included this map in the official history of the 54th. It vividly illustrates the narrow approach that made it difficult for commanders to send supporting regiments and brigades into the action. (Emilio, *Brave Black Regiment*, 80)

Shaw's body but were shot during the attempt. "A wounded soldier of my company lay with his back against the fort, his broken arm across his body, he was taking cartridges from his box tearing them and laying them on his wounded arm for Lieut. Emerson, who was doing good work with a musket," Appleton said.[12]

Other regiments from Strong's brigade, including the 6th Connecticut and 48th New York, also gained a toehold on Wagner. They climbed the side facing the sea and discovered a gap in the Confederate lines at an angle of the earthwork because the 31st North Carolina had refused to leave the bombproof when ordered to take its position. About 100 men from a second Union brigade and some isolated men from the 54th, including Appleton, also gained the angle and seized two gun chambers but were trapped in a cul-de-sac inside the earthwork. They held on under heavy fire until they realized that no reinforcements were coming. Singly and in small squads, soldiers from the 54th and the other Union regiments on Wagner fell back. A shell broke Appleton's ribs, but he walked down the beach, through the file closers posted at the rear of the action (he rebuked them for firing on stragglers and wounded men alike), and to the hospital ship. Gillmore halted a third brigade before it entered the fray.[13]

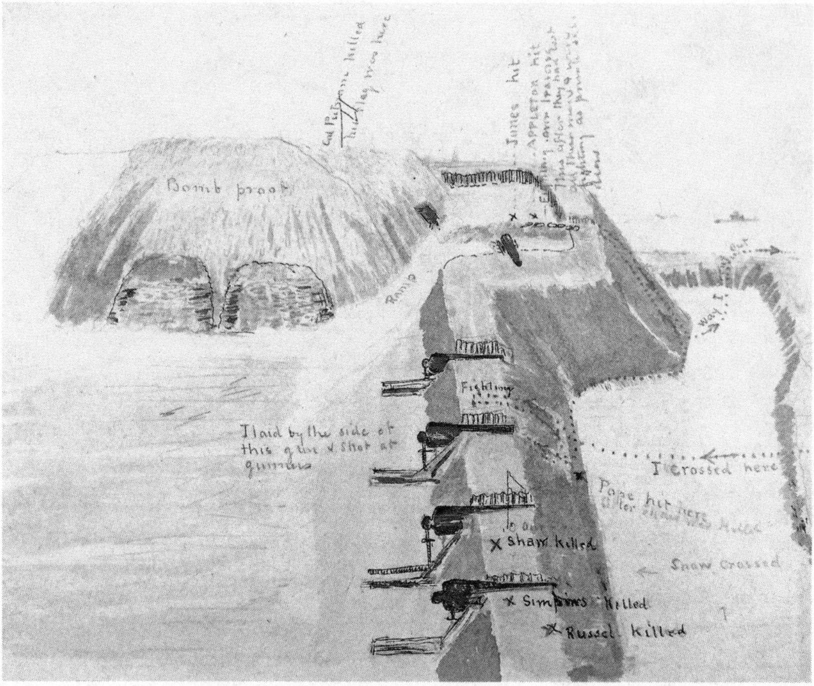


Capt. John Appleton's sketch of officer deaths at Fort Wagner, July 18, 1863. Appleton marked the location where he believed Col. Robert Gould Shaw was killed. Dots indicate where Appleton crossed Wagner's ditch, where he fought on the parapet, where he lay beside a gun and fired at the gunners, where he crossed over to the bombproof, where he was wounded, and where he left the battleground. (Appleton Military Memoirs, p. 61, box 3A, APWV; West Virginia and Regional History Center, West Virginia University Libraries, Morgantown)

The Federals suffered 30 percent casualties overall; the 54th Massachusetts, 42 percent; and the 48th New York, 50 percent. The 7th New Hampshire set a single battle record for Civil War regiments when it lost eighteen of its officers during the assault. Strong was mortally wounded. The 54th was the only regiment to reform after being repulsed. Eighteen-year-old Capt. Luis F. Emilio, the ninth-ranked captain in the line but the highest-ranking unwounded officer, put the men in battle line 700 yards from Wagner.[14]

What the Confederate defenders did after the battle proved to be of enormous significance at the national policy level, their actions prompting a decision point for the Lincoln administration regarding the Confederacy's retaliation resolutions. The battle ended at 1:00 A.M. on July 19. The immediate problem for Union and Confederate officers on Morris Island was to retrieve the wounded from the ground around Wagner and bury the dead. "In front of the fort, the scene of carnage is indescribable," Confederate brigadier general William Taliaferro told Beauregard. Union officers sent search parties toward Wagner with orders to prioritize the search for wounded men of the 54th. They worked all night. Confederate soldiers came out to the front of the earthwork and stripped the dead of valuables. At sunrise, there was an informal truce. General Hagood sent soldiers to bury the Federal dead in front of Wagner; they buried 600 bodies. One of them was Robert Gould Shaw.[15]

According to the customs of civilized war, and because officers were assumed to be honorable gentlemen whose deeds earned them glory, combatants returned the bodies of commissioned officers after a battle so that the dead officer could receive a burial with full military honors. If circumstances did not dictate the return of an enemy officer's body, then a civilized combatant buried the officer with the proper ceremonies. But at a council of Wagner's commanding officers, they decided not to treat Shaw according to military custom. They did not consider him a civilized or an honorable foe. One officer on the scene described the 54th as "unnatural." Just after daylight, the rebels stripped Shaw's uniform off, put his body in a burial trench in front of Wagner, and placed dead Black enlisted men on top of him. At 10:00 A.M., Gillmore requested permission to bury his dead, but Hagood responded that burials were already in process. Gillmore then requested the body of one of his brigade commanders, which Hagood sent to him.[16]

Confederates did not capture any white officers from the 54th during the assault on Wagner, but they captured at least seventy-three soldiers. One of them, Daniel States, an eighteen-year-old farmer from Philadelphia, lay wounded in the ditch surrounding Wagner. When Confederate soldiers brought him into Wagner, an officer ordered the guards not to kill him and took down the guards' names to ensure they did not do so. Confederates sent all of their prisoners to Charleston, where crowds of people on the streets jeered and taunted them. Some of the wounded men of the 54th lay all night on the wharf because Confederate soldiers refused to move them, and eventually officers sent Yankee prisoners to carry them. The white and Black wounded prisoners went to a makeshift hospital in a building on Queen Street. The surgeons there separated them and treated the whites first. States received good medical care and good food. General Beauregard sent instructions to the medical director to pay "due attention to the comfort of these men" and to provide clothes from the Quartermaster's Department for those who lacked them. The Catholic Sisters of Mercy made daily, and sometimes hourly, visits to the hospital with gifts of food and comfort. "They made no distinction between rank, color, or creed, but their efforts were directed to all alike," a grateful prisoner testified. Beauregard sent an inspector to the hospital on August 7 who reported that twenty-six men from the 54th were still alive there. One of them, Charles Stanton, a twenty-one-year-old boatman from Glenn Falls, New York, was well enough to serve as a nurse for the others.[17]

Confederates racially divided the unwounded prisoners. White prisoners went to a warehouse in Charleston. A few Black prisoners went to Castle Pinckney. One of them was Alfred Green, a twenty-six-year-old farmer from Hollidaysburg, Pennsylvania. Confederates locked him in a small room with about twenty men. They were "fed on mush." Others went to the Charleston Jail, a five-story octagonal brick building on an acre of ground enclosed by a high brick wall. Confining the men of the 54th in an iron-encased city jail with criminals, murderers, and prostitutes, as Confederate officials had done with Maj. Gen. John Pope's officers in Virginia, signaled that they were felons awaiting trial rather than soldiers confined as prisoners of war. They received cornmeal and water for rations and did repulsive menial labor.[18]

Back on Morris Island, Gillmore chose this moment to respond to the lengthy letter Beauregard had written him on July 4 inquiring whether he planned to conduct warfare according to civilized customs. For the first, but not the last, time, Gillmore failed to conduct retaliation correspondence using the standard format. His response on July 20 was terse. He did not comment on Beauregard's discussion of the raiding operations of Black troops under Hunter's regime, claiming that was "purely irrelevant." He wrote that he intended to conduct the war on civilized principles and expected from Beauregard "a full compliance with the same rules and maxims in their unrestricted application to all the forces under my command." Gillmore did not signify his agreement or disagreement with the specific principles Beauregard had listed. His own demand of Beauregard was vague; he did not specifically mention Black troops, nor did he inquire about the fate of the soldiers of the 54th Massachusetts. "I therefore submit that you should specify precisely to what you have referred," Beauregard replied.[19]

Gillmore also failed to do anything proactive to protect the Black prisoners of the 54th. On July 22, representatives of Gillmore and Beauregard met under flag of truce to negotiate the exchange of wounded prisoners. "Negroes mutually ignored in correspondence and conversation," Hagood reported to Beauregard. The only insinuation about the men of the 54th was a gross betrayal of them by Gillmore's emissary, who told Hagood that since Confederates had an excess of prisoners compared to the Federals, they "could select whom to exchange." On July 24, Confederate boats delivered 104 wounded Union prisoners to Charleston Harbor. None of them was from the 54th. During the delivery, one Union officer attempted to introduce the 54th into discussion, but as the Confederate officer in charge reported, "All information or conversation upon these troops was declined." He did reveal that Shaw was dead and buried in a trench with his men in front of Wagner.[20]

When the officers and men of the 54th learned what had happened to Colonel Shaw, they believed that Confederate officials had dishonored themselves before the civilized world. "We hope the *London Times* will make note of that fact," Corporal Gooding wrote in his column for the *Mercury*. "The men of the regiment are raising a sum to send the body of the Colonel home, as soon as Fort Wagner is reduced. They all declare they will dig for his body till they find it. They are determined this disgrace shall be counteracted by something noble." Captain Emilio spent two decades collecting material on the Confederate treatment of Shaw and the prisoners of the 54th in order to present a record of facts that would "convict" its leadership. "Not to cast aside passion and vindictiveness when dealing with a captive foe, especially during the prevalence of civil war, is, in modern times, a relapse into barbarism," he wrote. "Submitted to this crucial test of civilization, the conduct of the Confederate government . . . is an indelible stain."[21]

After the delivery of wounded prisoners, Gillmore answered Beauregard's request for specifics. "After having entered into a solemn agreement with me for mutually paroling and returning to their respective commands the wounded prisoners in our hands, you declined to return the wounded officers and men belonging to my colored regiments," he wrote, "and your subordinate in charge of the exchange asserted that the question had been left for after-consideration. I can but regard this transaction as a palpable breach of faith on your part, and a flagrant violation of your pledges as an officer."[22]

Gillmore still did not request specific information about where the men of the 54th were, nor did he notify Beauregard of his intention to protect the men of the 54th through retaliation against the hostages that General Hunter had collected in Hilton Head. Beauregard recognized that further conversation with his antagonist about civilized war would be fruitless. "I cannot bandy allegations with you," he wrote. The Confederacy did not recognize "armed negroes" as legitimate means of war, and Gillmore knew this. "You were surely bound to demand that negroes should be included in the proposed arrangement, but you did not demand it," Beauregard said. "You chose, sir, to ignore your negro ally after having given him the right or head of your storming column on the 18th of July. This, sir, will be the record of history."[23]

Gillmore's failure to use the ritual of retaliation properly put the protection of the Black troops in the Department of the South, and the fate of the prisoners of the 54th, in the hands of the Lincoln administration.[24] Influential voices within and without the government pressed for action. "If murdered, while prisoners of war, the retaliation should be instantaneous and unsparing," Judge Advocate General Joseph Holt wrote. "If we lead them into battle and then permit them to be butchered when captured and held as prisoners, the world will justly denounce our conduct as both criminal and cowardly." Francis George Shaw, the father of Robert Gould Shaw, wrote the War Department to demand a retaliation order to protect the Black soldiers captured at Wagner. Hannah Johnson, the daughter of an escaped slave and the mother of an enlisted soldier in the 54th, sent her letter directly to the president. She thought Confederates should "be compelled" to treat Black soldiers the same as white. "They have lived in idleness all their lives on stolen labor and made savages of the colored people, but they now are so furious because they are proving themselves to be men," she told Lincoln. "You must put the rebels to work in State prisons to making shoes and things, if they sell our colored soldiers, till they let them all go. And give their wounded the same treatment. it would seem cruel, but their no other way, and a just man must do hard things sometimes, that shew him to be a great man."[25]

U.S. War Department General Orders No. 100, the code that encapsulated the laws of war and how Union armies should implement them, provided a potential remedy for this situation. Section 58 said that if an enemy of the United States enslaved a soldier, it was a case for retaliation: "The United States cannot retaliate by enslavement; therefore death must be the retaliation for this crime against the law of nations." Francis Lieber, the author of the code, chose death, he explained to friend and correspondent Maj. Gen. Henry Halleck, the general-in-chief of Union armies, because "all modern codes of civilized nations declare personal freedom as the highest of earthly good, and depriving a man of liberty is like depriving him of life."[26]

Lincoln asked Halleck to draft the retaliatory order. Halleck modified the remedy of Section 58. He decided imprisonment with hard labor was the equivalent for selling men into slavery. He believed this threat against Confederate officers and soldiers was enough to stop Confederate president Jefferson Davis from executing Confederate policy. "It is possible the difficulty may be avoided without too much bloodshed," he explained to Lieber. On July 31, Secretary of War Edwin M. Stanton issued General Orders No.

252, which demanded that Confederates treat all U.S. soldiers as prisoners of war without distinction of color. "To sell or enslave any captured person, on account of his color, and for no offence against the laws of war, is a relapse into barbarism and a crime against the civilization of the age," it read. The order announced that the United States would put a Confederate prisoner of war to hard labor for every U.S. soldier sold into slavery and would execute a Confederate prisoner of war for every U.S. soldier put to death.[27]

The Lincoln administration took concrete actions to prepare to implement the retaliation order in South Carolina, a fact that historians neglect when they consider General Orders No. 252 from a national policy perspective. On August 8, Stanton wrote the abolitionist governor of Massachusetts, John A. Andrew. "If you have a list of the colored prisoners held in Charleston, and any details in regard to their mode of treatment, showing whether or not they are kept in close confinement, please communicate the same to this department in order that such measures as are justified by the laws of war may be taken for their protection," he said. "No official report has been received by this department on the subject."[28]

The success or failure of each retaliation incident in the Civil War depended on its own local dynamic. It is key that at this point, Union authorities had no official information about the fate of the prisoners of the 54th. Beauregard did not include any mention of them in a list of prisoners that he sent to Gillmore on August 16,[29] and the U.S. War Department had no official reports from the officers of the 54th. The customs of war demanded that a combatant have official information before implementing retaliation. It was particularly important to conduct this retaliation properly, because Union and Confederate officials feared that retaliation over the issue of Black troops had the most potential to escalate violence beyond control.

The U.S. War Department did have official information, however, including names and exact locations, about three Black sailors of the Union navy captured on the Stono River near Charleston on January 30. Orin H. Brown, William H. Johnson, and William Wilson were New Yorkers serving on the gunboat *Isaac Smith* when rebels took the entire crew. Confederate officials immediately paroled the white officers and men from the boat, but they put Brown, Johnson, and Wilson in a small cell in the Charleston Jail, where they languished in illness for months. They received only corn bread and water. Two weeks before the assault on Wagner, they managed to get a letter delivered to the U.S. consul in Nassau informing authorities about their situation. "We were born in New York and shipped from there. We have done no crime, and in the name of God, are we to be protected and aided or are we to be left here to die?" they petitioned. "We belong to the United States Navy and we ask for aid and protection."[30]

Secretary of the Navy Gideon Welles sent the letter to Stanton, who immediately ordered Ethan Allen Hitchcock, the U.S. commissioner for exchange, to confine in close custody three South Carolina prisoners as hostages in order to secure the lives of the three sailors, and to communicate this action to Confederate authorities in Richmond. Hitchcock, however, believed retaliation would not save the New Yorkers. "As a matter of fact the rebellion exists on a question connected with the right or power of the South to hold the colored race in slavery; and the South will only yield this right under military compulsion," he told Stanton. The only remedy was for the "loyal people of the United States to prosecute this war with all the energy that God has given them."[31]

The Lincoln administration used the fortuitous timing of the information about the Black sailors to give a signal to the Confederate government about its serious purpose to protect *free* Northern-born Black prisoners in South Carolina. Confederates received the message. A clerk in the Confederate War Department noted on August 13 that the United States held South Carolina soldiers as hostages for "free negroes."[32] The Lincoln administration drew its line in the sand for the Department of the South: it would protect Black men born free.

The Davis administration swerved off its intended course because of Lincoln's retaliation order, the South Carolina hostages, and internal divisions over the legality of executing Black men who were born free. South Carolina governor Milledge Bonham specifically requested that Beauregard turn over to him the "armed free Negroes from the Federal State of Massachusetts." Unaware of the Confederate congressional resolutions passed in May, he sent a lengthy justification to Secretary of War James A. Seddon explaining that the men of the 54th violated a South Carolina law of 1805 because they were "indirectly" "concerned" and "connected" with slaves in a state of insurrection. In addition, South Carolina law assumed all Black men were slaves. On July 29, Beauregard and Bonham received official copies of the congressional resolutions, and on August 1, Seddon directed Beauregard to turn the prisoners over because the resolutions clearly stated that free Blacks as well as former slaves were subject to state trials. Bonham received the men captured on James and Morris Islands and put them all in the Charleston Jail.[33]

The Confederate War Department was divided over the situation in South Carolina, however. Assistant Secretary of War John A. Campbell, a former justice of the U.S. Supreme Court, and Robert Garlick Hill Kean, head of the Confederate Bureau of War and a University of Virginia law graduate, believed that free Blacks born in Northern states were legitimate soldiers. Kean was blunt. "It is very clear the United States have the right to enlist any of their own citizens," he wrote. "They have long in those states regarded negroes as citizens, as in Massachusetts, allowing them the right of suffrage." Historical precedent, an essential element of defining civilized war, was on the side of the Lincoln administration: free Blacks served in the army during the War of 1812, and the French purchased Blacks to arm them during their occupation of Egypt in 1800–1801. Campbell told Seddon he doubted the legality of handing prisoners over to the state "when there is not testimony to show that these persons had been slaves in that State. The ground on which the claim of the State rests is not apprehended."[34]

Confederates were also deeply worried about the court of civilized world opinion. In the aftermath of Wagner, the Shaw family used their powerful financial, political, and literary connections in the North and in Europe to garner intense national and international publicity about the fate of Robert Gould Shaw and the heroism of the soldiers of the 54th Massachusetts. Francis George Shaw requested that his son's body remain where it was. "We can imagine no holier place than that in which he lies, among his brave and devoted followers, nor wish for him better company—what a body-guard he has!" The publication of this letter shamed the Confederacy. The *New York World,* not a proponent of Black troops, used the rhetoric of dueling in its editorial about the letter. "There can be no two opinions as to the high and magnanimous temper with which the father of Col. Shaw accepts what was intended as an insult to his dead son, as an honor not lightly to be tampered with. The brutality which sought to wreak its vengeance on the senseless clay of what had been a fearless foe, could not be more nobly chastised." Countless poems using the symbolism of Shaw's burial with his men appeared in Northern popular magazines such as *Harper's Weekly,* the *New York Tribune,* the *Christian Inquirer,* the *Evening Post,* the *Northern Christian Advocate,* and the *Atlantic Monthly.* Elizabeth Gaskell, the popular English author who was a correspondent of Sarah Blake Shaw, the colonel's mother, wrote an article for the British press that identified Shaw as the archetypical Northerner who gave up a life of luxury to die for the Black man. Harriet Martineau, the well-known English intellectual and essayist, wrote Sarah several months later: "I think you must have perceived that no one feature of this fearful war has interested people in Europe so much as the career and death of your son."[35]

The transatlantic sympathy for Shaw and the men of the 54th shook the Confederate leadership. Given the scrutiny of the international press, Davis and Seddon were worried about the diplomatic ramifications of executing any of these prisoners. Beauregard cautioned Bonham about "the grave international questions" involved. On August 10, Bonham promised Seddon that he would delay action regarding the men born free in the North until he heard back from the War Department. He instructed his attorney general to try prisoners who appeared to be slaves or free Blacks born in Confederate states. A commission interviewed the twenty-four Black captives who were not in the hospital, but only four appeared to be slaves. The rest were free men from states outside the Confederacy. "Under present circumstances the free negroes should be either promptly executed or the determination arrived at and announced not to execute them during the war," Seddon told Davis. "I do not think they should be regarded as regular prisoners of war, but dealt with in some exceptional way to mark our stern reprobation of the barbarous employment of such inciters to insurrection with all its attendant horrors in our slave-holding states."[36]

Seddon wanted to hold the prisoners of the 54th to hard labor during the war. Davis correctly pointed out that the congressional resolutions gave no discretion but required military authorities to hand all captured Blacks to the states, but he hinted to Seddon that it might be best not to bring any case to trial. Seddon accordingly asked Bonham not to try the captured Black soldiers of the 54th. "Or, if condemned, that your powers of executive clemency be exercised to suspend their execution," he wrote, "to allow the possibility of arrangement on this question, so fraught with present difficulty and future danger."[37]

Bonham disregarded the request of the Davis administration. On September 8, the Charleston District Police Court, a five-man tribunal, tried the four Black prisoners of the 54th who were alleged former slaves from Virginia and Missouri. The purported Virginians were George Counsel, a twenty-six-year-old laborer residing in West Chester, Pennsylvania, and Henry Worthington, an eighteen-year-old laborer appearing in the 1850 Ohio census at the age of three, both captured on Sol Legare Island. William Henry Harrison, also captured as one of the pickets on July 16, was a thirty-five-year-old teamster living in Chicago. Henry Kirk, a twenty-two-year-old laborer living in Galesburg, Illinois, was captured in the assault on Wagner.[38]

The prosecutors presented evidence that the prisoners had been in camp with Union regiments made up of slaves from South Carolina (the 1st and 2nd South Carolina) and were thus "connected" with slaves "in arms against the lawful authority of South Carolina." Bonham had appointed two prominent Charleston lawyers and former state legislators, Nelson Mitchell and Edward McCrady, as counsel for the defense, and they were well prepared with arguments that echoed the concerns that lawyers Thomas J. Semmes and Robert Kean had made during the Confederate policy debates. They questioned "the jurisdiction of the court, as a Civil Tribunal, to try offenses committed by persons engaged as soldiers in the act of war, and in the ranks of the enemy." The court unanimously decided it had no jurisdiction.[39]

The Lincoln administration's retaliation threats influenced Confederate military officers, who pressured South Carolina's local officials. Beauregard sent his chief of staff, Thomas Jordan, to remind Charleston's provost marshal that "should the prisoners be enslaved or executed, retaliation would fall alone upon the military forces of the Confederacy." Beauregard and Jordan openly expressed their opinion that South Carolina had no jurisdiction over their prisoners. Confederate officers in other departments were likewise reluctant to test Lincoln's resolve. On August 22, a military court in Mobile, Alabama, refused to try Union major general Neil Dow, who had Black soldiers under his command in Florida and Louisiana. Dow was a famous Northern temperance reformer whose supporters pressured the Lincoln administration to secure a prominent hostage for his life. Seddon ordered Dow sent to Richmond and treated as a regular prisoner of war.[40]

Confederate authorities decided to distinguish between Black Federal prisoners born in slavery and those born free in Northern states. They also decided they would not execute white officers. Although Davis worried the congressional resolutions tied his hands, he yielded to the pressure from officials in the War Department. He and Seddon agreed to hold white officers of Black troops indefinitely without bringing them to trial before military courts. On August 25, they tipped their hand regarding Black prisoners to the U.S. War Department during negotiations over prisoner exchanges. When U.S. agent Sullivan Meredith demanded that white officers and their Black troops be treated as prisoners of war and exchanged, his Confederate counterpart Robert Ould said his countrymen would "die in the last ditch" before giving up the right to return recaptured property to slavery, but "they were willing to make exceptions in the case of free blacks." "He could not exactly tell me how his authorities intended to distinguish between the two (free and slave)," Meredith reported, "but presumed that evidence as to the fact of freedom would be taken into consideration."[41]

Distractions were part of the rhythm of the more extended retaliation rituals during the Civil War. New threats to civilized war in the Department of the South and the crisis of events more pressing in other locations caused Federal officials to lose track of the Black prisoners in Charleston for three months. They seemingly ignored the situation of the men of the 54th, still held in jail but reprieved from immediate execution by the decision of the Charleston police court.

General Gillmore's ability to project artillery across space during his ongoing effort to reduce Fort Wagner and intimidate the city of Charleston took the spotlight temporarily from the problem of incorporating uncivilized people into civilized war and put it back on the problem of restraining violence. The assault on Wagner proved Gillmore to be an ineffectual infantry commander, but he was an expert engineer, and he was in his element during the next phase of the campaign for Morris Island. On July 19, he commenced a siege, digging his men into five parallels connected with a complex zigzag trench system. Batteries of artillery mounting thirty-eight guns protected each parallel and fired on Confederate targets. He used wire entanglements (a relatively new feature of war) and calcium lights to illuminate targets at night. Some of the batteries contained an experimental predecessor to the machine gun. As the army constructed the siege works, the navy's monitors were in action every day against Wagner, Sumter, and other targets of opportunity.[42]

Siege warfare was a well-developed science that required exhausting and dangerous manual labor from soldiers. Black enlisted men from the 54th, the 2nd South Carolina, and the 3rd USCT (newly arrived from Philadelphia), brigaded together under the command of Col. James Montgomery, did just over half of the fatigue duty required for the siege. They worked in eight-hour shifts to consolidate trenches with sandbags and lumber, mostly at night, under the fire of Confederate artillery from James Island and sharpshooters in Wagner. With the transition away from using Black troops to liberate slaves to using them as manual labor to support technology, Montgomery was not able to complete the recruiting and organization of the 2nd. It remained a "fraction" of a regiment, so its men usually had to work double shifts. "As might be expected, this kind of service filled our hospital with broken down men," Montgomery told his superiors. Engineers often put men from the 54th in the most advanced trenches working side by side with white soldiers and included them in the formation of a company of sharpshooters. A corporal from the 3rd USCT was proud of the work he did during the siege. "In those trenches our men distinguished themselves for bravery and coolness, which required more nerve than the exciting bayonet charge." Gillmore

Sap roller, siege of Fort Wagner, Morris Island. Black troops brigaded under Col. James Montgomery—the 54th Massachusetts, the 2nd South Carolina, and the 3rd USCT—did half of the fatigue duty required for the siege. General Gillmore awarded honor medals for bravery to two men in every company of Black troops that worked in the trenches under fire on Morris Island. (Library of Congress Prints and Photographs Division)

awarded honor medals for bravery to two men in every company of Black troops that worked in the trenches under fire on Morris.[43]

The engineers who dominated Gillmore's staff used the rhetoric of science rather than of civilization in their assessment of the use and capabilities of Black troops, but nineteenth-century assumptions about racial differences still permeated the conversation. Gillmore sent a circular to all the engineers on Morris about the "experiment" underway on the island to "test the fitness of the American negro for the duties of a soldier." He asked them to "observe and record" facts to prepare an "impartial and careful" answer to five questions comparing the performance of Black and white troops in the trenches. Gillmore wanted information about courage, skill, perseverance, and efficiency. He also requested an assessment of the difference between Black soldiers from free and slave states. Six engineering officers replied.[44]

Gillmore's aide-de-camp, Maj. T. B. Brooks, also his assistant engineer, summarized the responses. "We found the black soldier more timorous than the white, but in a corresponding degree more docile and obedient, doing just what he was told, to the best of his ability, but without enthusiasm," he reported. "The efficiency and health of a battalion depends so much upon its officers, that in order to institute a fair comparison, when so small a number of troops are considered, this element should be eliminated. This has not, however, been attempted in this paper." All agreed that Black troops from free states were superior to those from slave states.[45]

In addition to his experiment with Black soldiers in "important and hazardous" duty, Gillmore made the siege a test of artillery distance and experimental explosives. He and Admiral Dahlgren unleashed their combined firepower during a weeklong artillery bombardment of Wagner and Sumter that began August 17. On that same date, Gillmore received word that the "Swamp Angel" was ready. Colonel Serrell and fatigue parties from the 7th New Hampshire had constructed a battery whose platform and parapet floated on a sixteen-foot-deep mucky marsh between Morris and James Islands, located 7,900 yards from the city of Charleston. The engineering marvel supported 13,000 sandbags and a 16,300-pound, eight-inch Parrott rifle. As Gillmore had instructed, Serrell had positioned the Swamp Angel so that it could fire into the city.[46]

Gillmore's decision to use the Swamp Angel commenced another retaliation correspondence in the Department of the South that provided Beauregard with an opportunity to bring Gillmore before civilized world opinion and shame him. On August 21, Gillmore wrote Beauregard a short note. "I have the honor to demand of you the immediate evacuation of Morris Island and Fort Sumter by Confederate forces," it read. "All my heaviest guns have not yet opened. Should you refuse compliance with this demand, or should I receive no reply thereto within four hours. . . . I shall open fire on the city of Charleston from batteries already established within easy and effective range of the city." Gillmore forgot to sign the note.[47]

It arrived at Beauregard's headquarters in Charleston at 10:45 P.M. Beauregard was not there. Thomas Jordan, his chief of staff, returned the note for a signature. At 1:30 A.M. on August 22, the Swamp Angel fired a shell into the city using a compass reading from the steeple of St. Michael's church in downtown Charleston. A gun had never fired at a target at such a distance in the history of warfare to that point. The Swamp Angel's crew from the 11th Maine then launched sixteen more shells. Twelve of them were filled with incendiary liquid made at West Point's foundry, and four of them were filled with the experimental "Short's Solidified Greek Fire," but these latter exploded prematurely and did not reach the city. Only one shell hit a building, and Charleston fire companies quickly put out the resulting flames. No one was hurt.[48]

The firing of the Swamp Angel was the third time during the Civil War that the Union army deliberately bombarded the residential areas of a major city (the first was Fredericksburg, Virginia, on December 11, 1862, and the second was Vicksburg, Mississippi, on May 18, 1863). President Lincoln had a long-standing interest in such a tactic. He had encouraged Lt. Gen. Winfield Scott and Maj. Gen. George B. McClellan to bombard cities in April 1861 and May 1862, although they did not do so, and he personally promoted the testing and distribution of the experimental Greek fire to his commanders.[49]

Gillmore never doubted that his desire to shell Charleston was compatible with civilized war. The city was a legitimate military target because a Confederate army was camped there and it possessed fortifications, arsenals, and foundries that produced ironclads and torpedoes. Gillmore believed that the customs of Western warfare sanctioned his actions, because Confederate defenders had the responsibility to remove noncombatants when Union operations against the outer fortifications began. Forty days of continuous Federal attack served as sufficient warning of an imminent shelling of the city. The bombardment also reflected a special hatred for Charleston, the instigator of secession, and deep frustration over repeated military failures. Gillmore hoped that the bombardment would destroy the commercial value of the city for investors in Great Britain and the branches of Charleston-based firms in England that ran supplies through the blockade. Union engineers and artillerists also fired into the city just to see if they could. "As an experiment with heavy guns to test their endurance under the severest trial to which they could possibly be subjected in service, the results were not only highly interesting and novel, but very instructive," Gillmore reported.[50]

Beauregard seized on Gillmore's failure to sign his note and his four-hour notice of the firing to accuse his adversary of violating the customs of war. To understand Beauregard's goals in his correspondence with Gillmore, it is important to remember that retaliation rituals were in part an honor performance. Writers were self-conscious that representatives of civilized nations would read and judge their correspondence and historians would later evaluate it. Mastery of elaborate rules of etiquette were important in dueling rituals—as Beauregard knew from his experience in that line—and were similarly important in communication between combatants in honorable warfare. Ceremonies attended the deliveries of letters under flags of truce, and standard phrases in letters signaled that the writer belonged to the club of the honorable. The performance itself brought honor and allowed a participant to present before his peers a construction of events that he hoped would shame his enemy if the audience accepted the construction. A combatant's presentation of events was particularly important in situations such as the bombardment of Charleston, when each side could point to historical precedents and passages from Vattel's *Law of Nations* to support its position. The Union was performing well before the world in regard to its concern for the prisoners of the 54th; now Beauregard had an opportunity to draw attention to a different performance.

Beauregard had assumed for months that Federals would eventually bombard the city and had been trying to get local and state officials to remove women and children. "I understand it the wish of all, people and Government, that the city shall be defended to the last extremity," he had told the governor in October 1862, "hence I desire to be in all respects ready to make its defense equal to that of Saragossa." He asked the state to provide "depots" to receive people "in the event of a bombardment." After Gillmore's forces landed on Morris Island, newspapers printed orders from Charleston's mayor, at the general's insistence, for all women and children to leave the city. Confederate officers sent their families away. The state's Commission for the Removal of Non-combatants held a meeting the week before the Swamp Angel opened fire to discuss evacuation plans and the "campgrounds" established near Charleston, while Beauregard and Governor Bonham debated whether the time had come to implement a forced removal of the remaining noncombatant population. On August 19, Beauregard had sent an emissary to call on elite women who remained in the city with a personal request from the general to leave. Despite these efforts, many women stayed, and some who had left were already back by the time the bombardment started. No one dreamed the Yankees had the ability to send shells into the city from five miles away, and Beauregard and Bonham had wasted time trying to force the other to take charge of evacuation plans.[51]

Beauregard was matter-of-fact in his correspondence with Governor Bonham about the potential bombardment of Charleston, and his letters indicate that he knew it was the Confederacy's responsibility to remove women and children if the military intended to defend the city. His tone when he wrote Gillmore on August 22, however, was surprise and outrage. He did not reply to Gillmore's initial note until Gillmore returned it with a proper signature at 9:00 A.M. "It can now be noticed as your deliberate, official act," he wrote. "Among nations not barbarous the usages of war prescribe that when a city is about to be attacked timely notice shall be given by the attacking commander, in order that non-combatants may have an

"Retribution." Supporters of General Gillmore and General Beauregard debated the bombardment of Charleston in print. The court of civilized world opinion was the intended audience. This cartoon mocks Beauregard's outraged rhetoric. The artist undermines his own cause, however, for bombarding a city for motives of retribution violated the customs of civilized war. (*Harper's Weekly: A Journal of Civilization*, September 12, 1863, 592)

opportunity for withdrawing beyond its limits." Beauregard lectured that one to three days' notice was customary, and that the four hours Gillmore had given barely provided time for the delivery of the letter and a response. Beauregard claimed that Gillmore could not fire on a city to force the surrender of defensive works located several miles away (Sumter and Wagner). "Your omission to attach your signature to such a grave paper must show the recklessness of the course upon which you have adventured," he said. "I now solemnly warn you that if you fire again on this city from your Morris Island batteries without granting a somewhat more reasonable time to remove non-combatants, I shall feel impelled to employ such stringent means of retaliation as may be available during the continuance of this attack," he concluded. Throughout the letter, Beauregard dropped references to "sleeping women and children."[52]

Beauregard had a local international audience for his performance, the Spanish and British consuls in Charleston. He sent each of them a copy of Gillmore's original note and his response. He also notified Confederate authorities in Richmond that Gillmore had fired into Charleston with "no previous notice of intention" and that he had threatened retaliation if Gillmore fired again "without due notice." The Spanish consul immediately wrote Gillmore. "The short termination of your notification is not sufficient," he said. "I request a suspension of twenty-four hours to depart." The British consul requested an interview with Gillmore "on behalf of the great number of Her Britannic Majesty's subjects now in the city, of whom the greater number are women and children."[53]

Gillmore recognized that his failure to conform properly to the points of etiquette that honorable combat required had opened him to international criticism. He believed that he had not needed to give a notice, yet he had sent one. Once he did that, his official letter was open to scrutiny. His lack of signature and the four-hour time limit turned out to be public embarrassments. He thus suspended the bombardment for twenty-four hours. "The commencement of the attack on the defenses of Charleston, some forty days ago, is regarded as having given plain and emphatic warning that the city might be fired on at any time," he wrote the Spanish consul. "Nothing, however, is further from my wish than to endanger the lives or property of subjects of the Government which you represent." Gillmore informed Beauregard that he would resume firing at 11:00 P.M. on August 23. His letter defended the bombardment of the city. He admitted that the "inadvertent omission of my signature doubtless affords ground for special pleading" but was emphatic that he had not violated any premise of civilized war. It was a "well-established principle," he said, that "the commander of a place attacked, but not invested, having its avenues of escape open and practicable, has no right to expect any notice of any intended bombardment, other than that which is given by the threatening attitude of his adversary." If any noncombatant lives were in danger, Gillmore insisted, "the responsibility rests with those who have first failed to remove the non-combatants."[54]

The Swamp Angel resumed its fire on Charleston at 11:45 P.M. on August 23. Artillerists launched nineteen shells, and once again, those that were filled with Greek fire prematurely exploded almost immediately after leaving the gun. The extreme elevation of the gun that was needed to send its projectiles such a long distance weakened it, and it burst when trying to fire the twentieth shot of the evening at about 1:30 A.M. on August 24. The elevation and distance also weakened the effect of the shells when they landed, and once again, they did little damage to the city. Most of them did not explode on impact. No one was hurt. "All the Yankees did was scare the citizens dreadfully," Emma Holmes said.[55]

In the aftermath of the bombardment, the supporters of Beauregard and Gillmore continued the rhetorical battle in print, as newspapers were a forum that civilized combatants used to publicize their construction of events and appeal to the verdict of history. The *Charleston Mercury* ran an article, "Can a City Be Shelled, When a Fortress Not Contiguous to It Will Not Surrender?," that praised the "unanswerable power of reason" in Beauregard's letter, quoted Vattel's maxim that "all damage done to an enemy *unnecessarily* . . . is licentiousness," and compared the bombardment of Charleston to the English bombardment of French towns in 1694. The *London Times*, often sympathetic to the Confederacy, printed Beauregard's entire letter and excerpts from the Charleston papers.[56]

Corporal Gooding of the 54th wanted the world to consider a different perspective. "I can't help thinking, as a great many others think, that if the government exhibits so much needless humanity in deference to Mons. Vattel's played out theories, compiled two centuries since, as to restrain Gen. Gillmore from laying the nest of treason in her unhallowed dust now that we have the opportunity, we deserve to be beaten," he wrote to the *New Bedford Mercury*. "What if the London *Times* does work itself into a fume, and call on the 'whole civilized world to witness the inhuman barbarity of the Americans.'" Gooding rejected Britain's right to judge civilized behavior, considering its own record of barbarities. "We have never lashed a rebel to a gun and

"British Civilization. How the English Treat Prisoners of War—Sepoys to Guns." Literate Americans used the Indian Mutiny of 1857–59 as the standard example of a barbaric conflict. Corp. James Henry Gooding (54th Massachusetts), a well-read world traveler, invoked this British method of execution in his newspaper column to claim that Great Britain had no right to judge the actions of the United States. (*Harper's Weekly: A Journal of Civilization*, February 15, 1862, 109)

blown him to pieces, however richly some of them deserved it," he noted in a reference to Britain's method of execution during the 1857–59 Sepoy Rebellion in India.[57]

While Beauregard waged the rhetorical battle, Gillmore's siege of Charleston's outer defenses in the harbor was steadily progressing. The seven-day bombardment of Fort Sumter pounded its walls to rubble and silenced its big guns from a range of two miles. Army artillerists threw 4,804 projectiles at Sumter, and half of them struck the target. Since the fort was no longer a threat to navy operations by August 23, Gillmore believed that Dahlgren and his squadron should have entered the inner harbor. "Every shot I have fired and every foot of trench that I have dug, have looked to that result," he told the admiral. Dahlgren dreaded the torpedoes (underwater explosives) that Confederates had placed there and rightfully believed that the firepower of his ships was no match for the formidable Confederate batteries in the inner ring of fortifications protecting the city. Relations between the two men drastically deteriorated. Sumter was neutralized for harbor defense against a fleet and was reduced to an infantry outpost, but its garrison remained defiant.[58]

The garrison at Wagner, however, could not stop the construction of the siege works that doomed the earthwork. Its Confederate defenders—South Carolina, North Carolina, and Georgia troops—suffered a physical and emotional hell. On September 4, Beauregard held a meeting with his subordinates and determined to save the garrison at the expense of the fort. He sent a telegram to Richmond. "Repairs impossible. Approaches of enemy within forty yards. . . . Garrison much exhausted. . . . Nearly all guns disabled. . . . Communications with city extremely difficult and dangerous, Sumter being silenced." Two days later, Federal sappers reached Wagner's ditch. They had to dig through the decaying bodies of the men of the 54th who were buried in mass graves in front of the earthwork. That evening, Confederate forces evacuated Morris Island.[59]

Gillmore and his science-minded staff had pulled off numerous technical feats in the realms of artillery and engineering, but his possession of Morris did not change much in the campaign for Charleston. It did allow the ships of the Federal blockading fleet to take position in channels inside the bar of the harbor and effectively close the city to blockade-runners. Union artillerists were in position from Morris, and a new gun was placed in the marsh battery to open a persistent bombardment of the city that lasted from November 17, 1863, until February 14, 1865. However, Confederates still possessed James Island, the true pathway to an infantry assault on Charleston, and other harbor defenses. The robust Gillmore had reason to celebrate, though, and he enjoyed smoking a cigar in front of headquarters, sitting next to the gift presented to him by the 47th New York, a caged three-month-old American eagle, captured on an island off the coast of Georgia.[60]

The resulting stalemate in Charleston Harbor, with action centered on artillery duels and boat patrols, returned attention to the fate of Black troops in the Department of the South. Gillmore's reliance on them for fatigue duty during the siege of Wagner had aroused the ire of prominent Northern politicians, who wrote Stanton to protest in mid-November. The 3rd USCT, like the 54th, had well-connected officers. Stanton reminded them that "the spade is quite as much an instrument of war as the musket" but sent a special investigator to Hilton Head. It turned out that some officers took Black soldiers detailed for fatigue duty and used them to "prepare camps and perform menial duty for white troops." Gillmore had forbidden this when it came to his attention in September but had not done enough to enforce it.

He issued General Orders No. 105 on November 25: "Colored troops will not be required to perform any labor which is not shared by the white troops, but will receive, in all respects, the same treatment and be allowed the same opportunities for drill and instruction." The special investigator made sure it was enforced. For the 3rd USCT, fatigue duty reduced from 420 to 70 details per day, and guard duty increased from thirty-three to eighty-three details. "We have all of us been so long accustomed to oppress that race, that the mere habit will, in many cases, lead us to continue the practice, when policy, no less than duty, requires us to show them absolute justice," a Philadelphia friend of the regiment told Stanton. "There must for a long time be incessant vigilance in order to ensure their fair treatment."[61]

The protest from important Northern Republicans coincided with an attempt by the prisoners of the 54th in Charleston to communicate with Gillmore. On November 16, thirty of them petitioned Beauregard to forward a message that requested Gillmore to "send us a few things that we need." Although the prisoners were still in the hands of the state of South Carolina, because Governor Bonham had not returned them to Confederate custody despite the decision of the court he had convened, Charleston's provost marshal told them they could write Beauregard and "receive things" from Union forces. The provost marshal was granting them some rights that belonged to military prisoners of war. The record indicates that Beauregard did not forward their petition to Gillmore.[62]

With no official word regarding the fate of the prisoners in Charleston, the U.S. War Department made an effort in December to obtain information that would enable it to retaliate on behalf of the 54th. General Hitchcock had already begun gathering facts from various theaters of the conflict regarding the fate of Black prisoners. Every time his agent for exchange inquired about captured Black troops, the Confederate agent responded that he "had no troops of that class in his possession." Hitchcock wrote Gillmore asking for a report from each commander of Black troops in the Department of the South. He wanted to know the number of the missing and the "probable disposition" of the missing according to the best opinion of the officers. He also requested that officers enumerate the killed and wounded and, for each, "state whether they were either killed or wounded in fair fight, under the usages of war, or were subjected to any barbarous treatment whatever." Hitchcock wanted there to be no mistake about the purpose of his inquiry: to discover if the Confederates in the Department of the South had done anything that required "special action" under Lincoln's retaliation proclamation.[63]

The response Hitchcock received precluded any immediate action. On December 29, Gillmore submitted the report of Col. Edward Needles Hallowell, Col. Robert Gould Shaw's successor. Hallowell was a twenty-seven-year-old Philadelphia-born merchant and stockbroker whose abolitionism overcame his Quaker pacifism. His body took three months to recover from the wounds he received on July 18. Capt. John Appleton, who was awaiting his commission as major of the 54th through the intervention of the Massachusetts governor, had a complicated relationship with his superior, who had wanted to promote someone else. Appleton did not like the tenor or language of Hallowell's conversation regarding women, and he worried about his ability to lead. "I think Ned feels the magnitude of our undertaking to raise the colored man as far as we can in the Army, and by the means of it," Appleton said. "We meet so many checks and rebuffs, that it takes all the enduring courage a man can get, and all the strength the Lord gives him, to enable him to keep on. I do not mean that he is at all faint hearted, but he is not strong and he feels his cares."[64]

Hallowell and Appleton knew about the decision of the Charleston police court, although their understanding of the details was erroneous. Appleton had written his wife, Mary, on December 7 that she should no longer worry about what would happen if Confederates took him prisoner. He told her that the soldiers captured at Wagner were fine. "The State of S.C. saw that they had an elephant on their hands and they gave the men a regular trial and had them defended by both council and that state," he wrote. "The court agreed that the men had 'committed' insurrection but they must be tried upon the spot where the act was committed and . . . they turned the men back to the Government of the C[onfederate] S[tates] and they keep them imprisoned." The bottom line was clear to him: "they will return to their masters any fugitive slaves captured from us but will hold on to the Northern negroes as prisoners."[65]

This understanding influenced Hallowell's report to Gillmore. He estimated that Confederates took 50–100 enlisted men prisoner during the assault on Wagner. "I have no evidence that any officer or enlisted man of this regiment has been treated by the rebels in a barbarous manner," he stated. "The killed, wounded, and missing were killed, wounded, and taken prisoners, as far as I am able to ascertain, in fair fight." This answer explains why U.S. authorities did not retaliate for the treatment of the men of the 54th in the Department of the South at the end of 1863.[66]

Although it was not yet clear to the Lincoln administration what the Confederacy intended to do with the Black prisoners from the 54th, it was clear that on the Union side in the Department of the South, the debate over whether Black men belonged in a civilized war was over. Gillmore told Halleck on December 13, "The value and general efficiency of that class of soldiers has had a fair trial and a successful issue upon the field of battle and in the trenches." He requested that the War Department pay Black and white troops equally. "All distinctions calculated to raise in the mind of the colored man a suspicion that he is regarded as an inferior being, should be scrupulously avoided." He thought the U.S. government should give the families of Black soldiers land on the Sea Islands. "This is important as a military measure by making the soldier contented with his lot, by securing to him a home for his family during the war and for himself when the war is over." He asked permission to go to Florida, liberate more slaves, and organize more Black regiments for service in his department. Stanton authorized the operations. "Somehow the blood dances in my veins a little at the idea of an open country and a run among the rich planters of the North of Florida under Jim Montgomery," Appleton told Mary. "I am just wicked enough."[67]

Gillmore's move into Florida, and his continued bombardment of Charleston, produced the next stage of the retaliation ritual. Confederates had not changed their minds about the barbarity of their enemy, but their plans to implement a public and uniform measure of retaliation against free and enslaved Black men were falling apart under the scrutiny of civilized Europe, Lincoln's retaliation order, and the Federal possession of hostages from South Carolina. When a full brigade of Black troops, including the 54th Massachusetts, marched into a set-piece field battle on the Confederacy's southern edge, while Federal shells turned portions of the city that represented Southern civilization into a lawless wasteland, Confederate officials sought new ways to secure themselves from their barbarous foe.

# 4

# MASSACRE

On February 7, 1864, two regiments comprising mostly freeborn Black men from Northern states, the 54th Massachusetts and the 8th USCT, and a regiment filled mostly with escaped slaves from the coastal regions of North Carolina and Virginia, the 1st North Carolina, landed at Jacksonville as part of Maj. Gen. Quincy A. Gillmore's expeditionary force to Florida. The 8th was a brand-new regiment just arrived in the Department of the South from Camp William Penn near Philadelphia. The majority of its men were volunteers and draftees from Pennsylvania, Maryland, and Delaware, but there were some from Indiana and the Southern states and one from Jamaica. Its colonel, Charles W. Fribley, was a schoolteacher in Williamsport, Pennsylvania, with a degree from Dickinson Seminary. He had enlisted in the Union army as a private and risen to the rank of captain in the 84th Pennsylvania before the U.S. War Department appointed him to command the 8th. His young wife, Kate, accompanied him south and remained at Hilton Head when the 8th left for Florida. The regiment drilled regularly for dress parade but rarely for the field. Very few of the men had much training in firing their weapons quickly and effectively, and the commandant at Camp William Penn denied Fribley's repeated requests to give his regiment target practice.[1]

The 1st North Carolina, organized in the summer of 1863, was likewise untried in combat. During the siege operations on Morris Island, it had contributed more than its fair share of fatigue duty in the trenches. Its commander in Florida, Lt. Col. William Nikolaus Reed, was Black, according to the Confederacy's definition of race. He was born on St. Croix Island to an enslaved woman with African ancestry; his white father was originally from Schleswig-Holstein. Reed was raised by a ship captain, trained at a European military academy, served as an officer in the First Prussian-Danish War, and emigrated to New York in 1853. His skin and features were "white" enough not to draw attention to his ancestry, but a medical inspector for the Department of the South alerted Gillmore that Reed was a "mulatto." The major of the 1st, Archibald Bogle, was a twenty-two-year-old druggist from Melrose, Massachusetts. His father made the famous beauty product "Bogle's Magic Hair Dye," and Bogle used it liberally on his hair and moustache. He enjoyed studying military texts.[2]

When the Federal troops approached Jacksonville loaded in twenty armed transports accompanied by supply schooners and gunboats, Confederate cavalry in the city fired a few shots. Brig. Gen. Truman Seymour ordered John Appleton of the 54th, now the regiment's major, to "catch them." As the troops disembarked, the men of the 54th skirmished through the streets of Jacksonville. The Confederates quickly evacuated. "The town has many women and children in it they receive us well but are terribly afraid of our men," Appleton wrote Mary. "They come up to me and appeal for protection with tears in their eyes." Unlike the men of the 1st and 2nd South Carolina, who had occupied the city a year before, these Black men were Northerners and strangers. The 54th took some military and civilian prisoners and camped on the outskirts of town that night alongside the 8th USCT.[3]

The rest of the Federal troops took three days to land, but Union cavalry and the lead regiments advanced in three columns along the railroad track, captured five guns as Confederate forces fell back, and occupied the small village of Baldwin, located twenty-one miles west of Jacksonville, on February 9. It consisted of a hotel, a post office, two depots, and several sheds. The 54th arrived there on February 12. Union troops built a stockade, dug entrenchments, and foraged the countryside for food.[4]

Federal troops were back in Florida for both military and political reasons. Gillmore wanted access to the state's supply of cotton, lumber, and turpentine, and he wanted to cut off the supply of beef from Florida that fed Confederate forces farther north. Because an important goal of the expedition was to register voters loyal to the United States so that Florida would return to the Union before the fall U.S. presidential elections, Gillmore and Seymour ordered their troops to leave private property alone and to treat all inhabitants of Florida "courteously and kindly." "Generally the fact will be taught that we are here to bring back the sentiment of the people by kindness and protection, and not to exasperate by improper and barbarous irregularities unbecoming to discipline," Seymour enjoined. Gillmore threatened summary dismissal of any officer who allowed his men to pillage.[5]

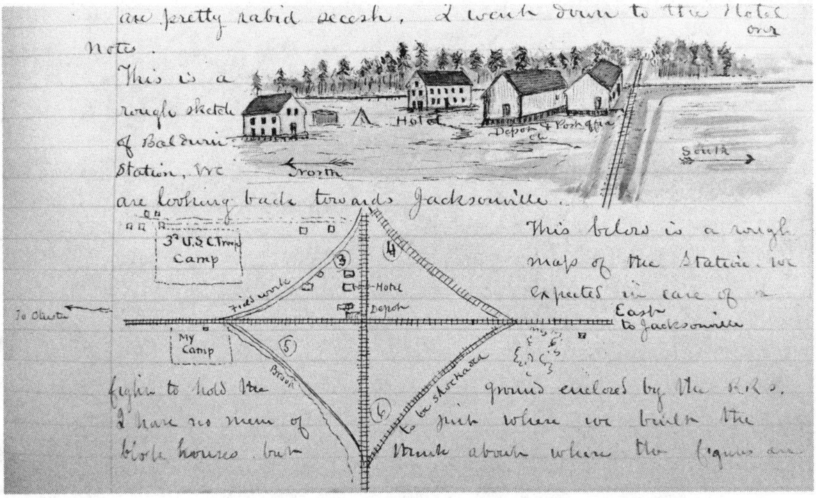


Capt. John Appleton's sketch of Baldwin, Florida, and the location of the 54th Massachusetts camp. In the area around Baldwin, the men of the 54th had their first opportunity to act as direct liberators of enslaved people. (Appleton Military Memoirs, p. 167, box 3A, APWV; West Virginia and Regional History Center, West Virginia University Libraries, Morgantown)

Promulgating the Emancipation Proclamation and recruiting Black soldiers was also an important goal of the expedition, and in carrying out this mission with Black troops, the Union army generated a deep rage among the Confederate citizens in the area surrounding Baldwin. The men of the 54th rescued some enslaved people locked in a smokehouse. This was the regiment's first opportunity to act as direct liberators. Slaves left surrounding plantations and came into Baldwin for protection. "It makes my mens eyes snap and twinkle," Appleton said, "and they beg me to allow them to go scouting for slaves." Men from the 54th and the 8th foraged liberally on the land and took equipment that Confederate soldiers had abandoned. Scouts returned to Baldwin with chickens, hogs, cattle, horses, swords, Arkansas toothpicks (the slang for heavy daggers), and a guitar. "I may say roasting all this has to be done on the sly as Seymour is fussy," Appleton said. He still preferred Col. James Montgomery's approach to rebels and their property. During the next few days, several white locals expressed to him their fear and hatred. "All the folks here are rabid secesh," he noted. "One woman with whom I had a talk told me plainly that I would be hung if taken. . . . How the people here hate the colored soldiers they tell me they 'aint used to seein niggers tote guns en it skeers them.'"[6]

With the situation in Florida between the Black occupation forces and

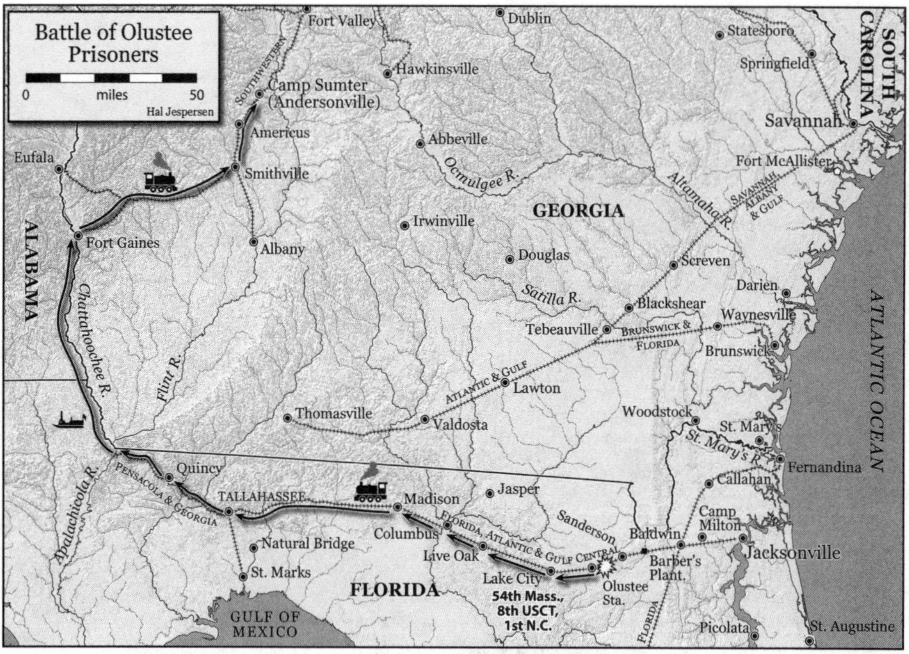


the white citizens emotionally charged and volatile, the scenario happened that both Union and Confederate officers dreaded the most. Confederates had proclaimed throughout the secession crisis and the ensuing years of war that Black men were savages who threatened the existence of Southern civilization and the purity of white Southern womanhood unless contained in the institution of slavery. Their worst fear was rape. On February 18, after a drumhead court-martial, General Seymour executed three Black soldiers from the 55th Massachusetts, which had arrived in Florida five days earlier, for raping an impoverished white woman near an abandoned Confederate military camp. Two were hung in the camp and one in Jacksonville. Appleton and the other officers of the 54th were "mortified." "I feel very badly about it as so much depends upon the behavior of our colored troops," he told his wife.[7]

The Confederate army in Florida, in the process of entrenching at Olustee Station on the railroad line thirty miles west of Baldwin, had scouts and spies throughout the countryside who reported in regularly. It is probable, although not recorded in the sparse remaining written records, that some Confederate officers and soldiers heard reports of this instance of rape and the subsequent executions.[8]

When Black soldiers of the 54th Massachusetts, the 8th USCT, and the 1st North Carolina clashed with Confederate soldiers at the Battle of Olustee two days later, violence in the Department of the South escalated beyond the boundaries of civilized warfare. Events in Florida revealed that the U.S. War Department's retaliatory measures had indeed forced the Confederate government to alter its original plans regarding Black troops. Confederate military officials implemented on a wider scale their decision to differentiate between freeborn Black soldiers and former slaves and gave evidence of that in their treatment of the men of the 54th, the 8th, and the 1st. Their handling of the white officers left dead and wounded on the battlefield also departed from the treatment that Robert Gould Shaw had received at Fort Wagner. Confederate officers and soldiers fighting on the ground and handling Yankee prisoners, however, did not always accept the official policy of the Confederate War Department and committed war crimes that challenged the ability of military leaders on both sides to restrain war through retaliation. Hatred and rage, rather than honor and restraint, marked events in Florida. As revenge, lawlessness, and violence escalated, many soldiers and officers in the region feared that Americans were losing their claim to a place in the civilized world.

Before the executions, Gillmore had already returned to Hilton Head, leaving Seymour in charge of the Florida expedition with instructions not to advance beyond Baldwin and to build fortifications at Jacksonville, Baldwin, and Palatka. The youthful-looking and full-bearded Seymour was a thirty-nine-year-old West Point graduate with antebellum war experience as an artillery officer and Civil War experience with brigade and division command at Malvern Hill, Second Manassas, and Antietam. He was in charge of the attack on Fort Wagner in July 1863, was seriously wounded, and returned to duty in December 1863. Neither his contemporaries nor historians can explain his bizarre behavior in Florida. He changed his mind and his mood rapidly. He sent Gillmore dispatches that starkly contradicted each other from one day to the next. On February 17, he announced that he planned to advance forty miles from Baldwin "without supplies" to Lake City and then farther west to destroy the railroad bridge over the Suwannee River. He ignored reports from locals that there was a substantial Confederate force between him and Lake City and gathered no intelligence. He had a corps of 5,500 infantry and cavalry and sixteen guns placed in field artillery batteries. On February 19, he put his lead units in motion from Baldwin.[9]

In the interim between the Federal landing at Jacksonville on February 7 and the advance from Baldwin on February 19, Confederate forces in Florida concentrated at Olustee Station, thirteen miles east of Lake City, and built fieldworks. They were under the command of Brig. Gen. Joseph Finegan,

Brig. Gen. Truman Seymour. His incompetence at the Battle of Olustee set up the 8th USCT, the 54th Massachusetts, and the 1st North Carolina for disaster. After the battle, he did nothing to investigate Confederate treatment of the Black prisoners from his command. (Library of Congress Prints and Photographs Division)

the militarily inexperienced Irish slaveholder with investments in the lumber and railroad industry. Gen. P. G. T. Beauregard, who thought the Federal presence in Florida was a serious threat to his ability to feed his armies, reinforced Finegan with troops from South Carolina and Georgia, including a brigade of battle-hardened veterans of campaigns in Virginia, Maryland, and the Carolinas under the command of Brig. Gen. Alfred Holt Colquitt. The Princeton-educated Colquitt was a former U.S. congressman who had served in the command of the venerated Gen. Thomas J. "Stonewall" Jackson. Like Seymour, he had endured criticism for his past performances, and his judgment was in question. Beauregard instructed Finegan to "prevent the capture of slaves" and to "hold the enemy at bay." He reminded his subordinates, correctly, that Union regiments in Florida were "composed largely of newly drafted men and recruits."[10]

By the morning of February 20, Finegan had even numbers with the Federals, who were marching in three columns along a sandy road that ran through an "exceedingly low and flat" landscape. The open pine forest, with minimal underbrush, was interspersed with shallow swamps. The 8th USCT was in the first infantry brigade with the 7th New Hampshire and the 7th Connecticut, marching behind a lead mounted brigade. New Yorkers comprised the second infantry brigade. The 54th Massachusetts and 1st North Carolina were in the "colored" brigade under the command of Col. James Montgomery and marched last. Appleton and two companies of the 54th, along with a detachment of men from the 1st North Carolina, were left at Barber's Plantation as the rear guard. Seymour marched his troops through the countryside with no thought to security. He did not expect to meet the enemy until he reached Lake City. There were no scouts and no flankers. The commanders of Black troops feared that Seymour did not know what he was doing. Before Fribley parted from Appleton, he remarked that "it seemed to him that we were commencing just as we first commenced in Virginia [in 1861], knowing nothing, with everything to learn."[11]

At noon, the Federal columns were within three miles of Olustee Station. Shortly thereafter, skirmishers from the Yankee cavalry and the 7th Connecticut encountered the advance pickets of Finegan's army. The 7th Connecticut possessed new weapons technology, seven-shot Spencer repeating rifles, and the rapid fire of its skirmishers confused the rebels. Finegan ordered the 2nd Florida Cavalry, the 64th Georgia, and two companies of the 32nd Georgia forward "to skirmish with the enemy and draw them to our works." The 64th Georgia was a new regiment that was untried in combat, and it formed a square to protect itself from Federal cavalry. Finegan decided not to wait for Federal forces to approach his defensive position. He ordered Colquitt and three regiments of his veterans, with a section of artillery, to march to the scene of action, which was now two miles from the Confederate works at Olustee Station. Once there, Colquitt formed a line of battle and ordered his men to advance. The 7th Connecticut—nearly out of ammunition, its line bent into a semicircle, and now taking flanking fire from an extended Confederate battle line—withdrew.[12]

Seymour's utter incompetence in the next phases of the battle, and the inexperience and confusion among his brigade commanders, set up the Black troops who fought at Olustee for disaster. He decided to mass his artillery in the center front, supported on either side by an infantry regiment. He positioned the artillery too far forward, a surprising mistake for a regular artillery officer, and Confederate riflemen had easy range of the men and horses who worked his guns. He sent the 7th New Hampshire to the right of the artillery and the 8th USCT to the left. The brigade commander, Col. Joseph Hawley, went right with the 7th. More than half of this regiment were new recruits and drafted men who had never practiced firing the damaged hand-me-down weapons they possessed. Hawley ordered the regiment to execute a complex deployment maneuver. Its officers misheard the order in the noise of battle and began to deploy the regiment differently than Hawley intended. Hawley halted the regiment and attempted a correction, but this caused its companies to become tangled and confused. One company "faced the enemy and opened fire." For the rest, "all semblance of organization was lost." The 7th broke, leaving its color-bearer, Sgt. Thomas H. Simington, who "faced the enemy alone."[13]

With the breaking of the 7th, Colquitt's line of battle, now reinforced and extended by additional troops coming up from Olustee Station, concentrated its fire on the 8th USCT, fighting for a brief time alone because Seymour was inserting regiments piecemeal into the battle, just as he had done at Wagner seven months before. Before coming to the front, the 8th had been advancing along railroad tracks when one of Seymour's aides galloped up and ordered the regiment to move at the double quick. They ran for half a mile and reached the Federal artillery position. "Put your regiment in, Colonel Fribley," Seymour said and left. The men still had on their heavy knapsacks, and their weapons were unloaded. Lt. Oliver Willcox Norton, who was a veteran of Fredericksburg, Second Manassas, Chancellorsville, Antietam, and Gettysburg, said the regiment tried to form a line "under the most destructive fire I ever knew." Confederate soldiers were only 200 yards away, and many of them were firing from behind the trunks of the big pine trees. The Confederate battle line extended past and fired upon the front and the flank of the 8th as it tried to deploy. Men were shot down before they could even load their weapons. "They were stunned, bewildered, and knew not what to do," Norton said afterward. "They curled to the ground, and as men fell around them they seemed terribly scared, but gradually they recovered their senses and commenced firing. And here was the great trouble — they could not use their arms to advantage. We have had very little practice in firing, and, though they could stand and be killed, they could not kill a concealed enemy fast enough to satisfy my feelings."[14]

The 8th sustained enormous casualties while the untrained men struggled to load and fire their weapons. The color company, which carried the regimental and national flags, suffered 70 percent casualties, and the regiment as a whole 63 percent. "After seeing his men murdered as long as flesh and blood could stand it, Colonel Fribley ordered the regiment to fall back slowly, firing as they went," Norton said. "As the men fell back they gathered in groups like frightened sheep, and it was almost impossible to keep them from doing so. Into these groups the rebels poured the deadliest fire, almost every bullet hitting someone." A bullet hit Fribley in the heart. "Take me out," he gasped, and died. A captain placed his body on a nearby artillery caisson. The major of the regiment went down with two broken legs. "We were without a commander, and every officer was doing the best he could with his squad independent of any one else," Norton said.[15] Individual soldiers of the 8th fired from behind the trees. Lt. Elijah Lewis grabbed the national colors and planted them on an artillery battery. Men rallied around it, but at this moment some of the artillery horses, whose controllers were dead, stampeded through the men and scattered them. "The fire from the enemy now became so destructive we could not keep our men in line," Lewis reported. "We were in disorder." Capt. Romanzo C. Bailey learned that he was in command of the regiment and ordered all the remaining officers to bring off their companies. In the chaos, and with all the color-bearers dead, Lewis forgot to bring the national flag with them, but a sergeant saved the regimental battle flag. The 8th brought off 204 of its wounded but left 64 wounded men and a wounded officer on the field. As the artillerymen retreated, leaving behind five guns, officers carried Fribley's body for some little distance away from the front but eventually threw it off the caisson where it had rested and left it lying on the ground.[16]

The 8th had been on the field for at least an hour, and during that time the brigade of New Yorkers arrived and moved into the position the 7th New Hampshire had abandoned. Colquitt was advancing his troops when the 47th, 48th, and 115th New York deployed and opened fire. The Confederate and Union lines of battle stood at close range and fired at each other through an open pine forest for the next hour. Many soldiers used the trees. "The fight was now conducted in Indian style," an officer in the 23rd Georgia said, "both sides availing themselves of the protection of the pine trees of which kind there was plenty." Because of this, wounds were usually in a soldier's arms or legs rather than his torso. The artillery on both sides fired too high and the infantrymen aimed their rifles too low. The Confederate lines extended beyond the Union lines on both sides, so the New Yorkers took fire from the front and flanks, suffering 824 casualties. At one point, several Confederate regiments ran out of ammunition but remained standing on the field for twenty minutes until the ordnance wagons and more reinforcements from Olustee finally arrived. The New York brigade was likewise low on ammunition and Seymour remained on the defensive, giving Colquitt time to resupply and resume the advance.[17]

The first sign that Confederates fighting on the ground at Olustee would not treat their opponents as civilized combatants who had the right to claim protection of the laws of war occurred as the 8th retreated. The regiment's surgeon, Alex P. Heichhold, set up his field hospital just to the rear of the fighting. He flew the large white flag that indicated its status. Yet twelve Confederate cavalrymen rode up and fired into the wounded men lying on the ground and were preparing to charge when the 54th Massachusetts advanced out of the woods and scattered them.[18]

The men of Colonel Montgomery's brigade were running toward the front under orders sent to them from Seymour, who wanted the 54th Massachusetts and the 1st North Carolina to check Colquitt's forward movement so the New York brigade could withdraw and form a new line in the rear. The men ran for two miles, throwing aside heavy coats, knapsacks, and excess equipment in order to maintain the pace. Stragglers and wounded men leaving the battlefield shouted at them, "We're badly whipped!" and "You'll all get killed!" When the 54th arrived, Seymour told Colonel Hallowell, "The day is lost you must go in and save us." The New Yorkers cheered the Black troopers, who deployed quickly and steadily on the Union left while enduring steady fire. They advanced 200 yards, firing effective volleys that halted the Confederate advance as the New Yorkers retired.[19]

The 54th and 1st—and a resupplied 7th Connecticut positioned just behind them—now bore the brunt of the fire of the entire Confederate line, which extended around their flanks. "Under such conditions after a while the men began to chafe, and exhibit a desire for aggressive action," Capt. Luis F.

Emilio wrote in the 54th's official history. Men crept out of line to act as sharpshooters. Sgt. James A. Wilkins, the color-bearer of the U.S. flag, moved forward without orders, followed by his company. Hallowell ordered them to return to the line. Jarring their rifles on the ground to reload rather than using ramrods, the men of the 54th rapidly fired 20,000 cartridges. The 1st likewise stood its ground and fought well, but as casualties mounted, including Lieutenant Colonel Reed, it withdrew, leaving seventy-seven wounded and dead bodies behind, including Major Bogle, alive but shot in the chest and leg. "Why the Fifty-Fourth was left thus exposed is inexplicable," Emilio wrote. "No orders were received to retire. No measures taken for its safe withdrawal. It would seem either that the position of the regiment was forgotten, or its sacrifice considered necessary."[20]

Throughout the Battle of Olustee, the field and line officers of the 54th maintained their commitment to the order and discipline that civilized warfare required, as opposed to the outlaw style of Montgomery. It became clear that the regiment was alone on the field. Montgomery, who was with them, said, "Now, men, you have done well. I love you all. Each man take care of himself." His subordinates were shocked at this "bushwhacking way." The soldiers started to do as Montgomery suggested, but Lt. Col. Henry Hooper ordered Color Sergeant Wilkins to "stand fast." He shouted, "Rally!" and the men again formed in line around Wilkins. Hooper gave the men a speech, ordered them to fix bayonets, and "exercised the regiment in the manual of arms to bring it completely under control." The 54th gave nine cheers to give the impression that reinforcements were coming and marched off the field in good order, eventually catching up with the rest of Seymour's retreating corps. The regiment left Corp. James Gooding mortally wounded on the field, along with nine other men. "The Yankees . . . pitched three negro regiments against us, and all acknowledged they fought well," Corp. Henry Shackleford of the 19th Georgia wrote his mother that night. "We walked over many a wooly head as we drove them back."[21]

The magnitude of the Union defeat, and the misfortunes of battle that caused the retreating Union regiments to leave behind a large number of Black and white wounded men on the field, created an opportunity for Confederate soldiers to inflict atrocities on the bodies of their helpless enemy. Massacres in the Civil War committed by uniformed soldiers were physical expressions of powerful emotions of hatred and rage, but they also reflected deeply embedded fears of social groups in their midst perceived to be barbarians or savages who threatened civilization itself, such as Black and Indigenous people. Anglo-Americans had a long tradition, extending back to the early colonial period, of applying different rules in their warfare against "barbaric" as opposed to "civilized" combatants. Americans in the eighteenth and early nineteenth centuries practiced irregular and unlimited warfare against Indians. They destroyed villages and agricultural resources, killed enemy women and children, brutalized noncombatants, and massacred wounded men after battle. The U.S. Army, especially its volunteer components, and state militias continued these practices in warfare against Native communities west of the Mississippi River during the Civil War. Military commanders there advocated total extermination if necessary.[22]

The categories of savagery, barbarism, and civilization loosened restraints on violence in the Department of the South because Confederates were convinced that Black people were incapable of fully joining civilization. One important restraint on violence in war is the goal of eventual reconciliation with the enemy or the goal of eventually incorporating the enemy as a citizen. When white Americans fought Indians, they demanded that the "barbarians" entirely remake the nature of their society in order to become civilized and recognized as citizens. Such an all-encompassing goal for the outcome of war created conditions that escalated violence. In their war to create an independent slaveholding nation, Confederates had no investment in reunion or reconciliation with the United States and were unwilling to envision Black men as citizens. On numerous occasions, Confederate officers and soldiers treated Black Union soldiers as they treated the "Indian barbarians" who lived outside the boundaries of civilization. The Battle of Olustee was one of them.[23]

Confederate forces did not pursue the retreating Federals—the rebel cavalry conducted such a desultory chase that Beauregard launched an investigation after the battle. Instead, soldiers roamed the battlefield, collecting abandoned rifles, equipment, and food; taking valuables; stripping the dead of all clothing; and killing wounded Black men. "The negroes were badly cut up and killed Our men killed some of them after they had fell in our hands wounded," Pvt. James Jordan, a conscript in the 27th Georgia, wrote the next day. Some of the Georgia soldiers bludgeoned men in the head with "lightwood knots." A white Federal soldier from the 48th New York with an ankle wound witnessed executions from his hiding place in a bush. Soldiers bayoneted men "without mercy," he said. A rebel officer dismounted next to Orderly Sergeant Brown of the 8th USCT, "placed his revolver close to the negro's head, and blew his brains out."[24]

It is impossible to reconstruct accurately the exact number of murders on the Olustee battlefield, and estimates range from 25 to 75 of the 158 Black soldiers listed as missing in Union casualty reports. Many Confederate soldiers did not participate in the post-battle massacre of wounded, and officers relatively quickly stopped those who did. "I tell you our men slayed the Negrows & if it had not been for the officers their would not one of them been spaired," Edwin Tuttle of the 26th Virginia told his parents.[25]

After the wave of atrocities was over, Confederate officials on the field at Olustee implemented the new policy of treating captured free Blacks as prisoners of war, but they also modified its implementation because they could not bring themselves to put white and Black men on a truly equal basis. Only three of their Black prisoners were not wounded, a statistic that tells its own story, and Finegan forwarded them with the 147 unwounded white prisoners to his superiors for processing. Confederates left the 418 wounded of both races on the field overnight, and then took the white wounded in wagons and ambulances to Olustee Station, where they remained lying on corn husks on the side of the road until the next afternoon. Confederate surgeons administered chloroform and performed amputations on this spot. Officials brought Black wounded soldiers off the field last, refused some of them medical treatment, and purposely performed unnecessary amputations on others. Black and white captives were loaded into boxcars, forty to a car, and taken by train to Lake City. Many Black captives died on the street as they waited for medical attention, some from their wounds and others from blows to the head from Lake City citizens. Officials distributed the most severely wounded prisoners, both white and Black, to hospitals, houses, and a stable near the depot and placed white prisoners with minor wounds in churches. The captives of both races in the best condition went 105 miles farther west to the Masonic Hall and the Odd-Fellows' Hall in Tallahassee. "Whites and negroes were laid side by side, in order to give the whites a taste of the equality they were fighting for," the *Tallahassee Floridian* reported.[26]

Confederate officers in the field at Olustee, as had their counterparts on Morris Island, dishonored the white officers who commanded Black troops and refused to treat them as gentlemen under the conventions of civilized war. The alteration in national policy meant that they could not form military courts and execute Union officers, but they could heap pointed indignities on their savage enemy. They found Colonel Fribley's body among the nearly 400 Union dead and buried it on the field underneath bodies of Black men, just as they had done with Robert Gould Shaw at Wagner. A correspondent for the *Savannah Daily Morning News* witnessed the burial, and newspapers as far west as Memphis reprinted his suggestion that the Yankee colonel had been treated too well: "Yes! the black-hearted Frieble [*sic*] had a dog's burial.

A leader of a horde of infuriated negroes, on a mission of murder, robbery, and rape, ought not to have been left to rot on the plain, for the obscene birds to fatten on his vitals, and the gaunt wolves to gnaw at his bones?" The article played on the worst fears of Confederate supporters about the threat Yankee abolitionists posed to the purity of white civilized Southern womanhood. Its author questioned whether Fribley's wife was white or Black and described the "trophies" from the battlefield. "Daguerreotypes taken from negro knapsacks, were of finely dressed white females! Showing that the Yankee theory of 'miscegenation' is in practice." Confederates found Major Bogle on the field with a chest wound and two bones broken in his right leg. As he lay on the corn husks at Olustee Depot in his full military regalia, with sword, sash, and belt, clearly indicating his status as an officer, soldiers taunted him. "They seemed to delight in the torture they inflicted on him; telling him hanging was too good; that he ought to be buried alive, with one of his negroes beneath him, and one above him," a witness recalled. At Lake City, Bogle enjoyed a brief respite. Authorities and civilians there treated him, in his own words, "kindly," and put him in a Presbyterian church.[27]

With wounded Black prisoners spread out in makeshift hospitals in local communities, General Beauregard and his subordinates tried to sort out how many and which Black regiments they had faced on the field. They wanted to know if they had any former slaves on their hands. Finegan and Colquitt initially reported to Beauregard, who hurried to Florida from Charleston once he heard of the engagement, that they faced 10,000 Federal troops (twice the actual number). Their initial questioning of Black prisoners led them to believe that seven Black regiments fought at Olustee, all of them numbering 1,000 men. The Confederate working list was the 54th Massachusetts, 55th Massachusetts, 56th Massachusetts, 58th Massachusetts, 66th Massachusetts, 8th Pennsylvania, and 1st North Carolina. After the battle, Confederate soldiers had picked up ammunition boxes marked "New Berne, N.C." "I will add that among the captured negroes there have been recognized by intelligent and reliable gentleman negroes known to have been the property of friends in North Carolina, and who are reported to belong to a North Carolina regiment now upon this coast," Brig. Gen. William Gardner told Beauregard.[28]

While Confederates investigated the background of their Black Union prisoners, Seymour's corps backtracked. It had retreated in some disorder back to Barber's Plantation the night of the battle, covered by an effective rear guard made up of the 54th Massachusetts, the 7th Connecticut, and the mounted brigade. Wounded men, 1,152 of them, tried to keep up.

There were not enough ambulances, wagons, and artillery caissons for all of them, so hundreds walked, crawled, and dragged themselves on the ground. "Along the side of the road, exhausted or bleeding men were lying, unable to proceed, resigned, or thoughtless of inevitable captivity," Captain Emilio recalled. After getting a few hours' rest, the Union troops in three parallel columns pushed on to Baldwin. "The men are pretty well tired out. Things go well," Seymour reported to Gillmore. Soldiers loaded the wounded on a train bound for Jacksonville. When the locomotive broke down, the 54th used ropes to drag the cars by hand the rest of the way into the city. Seymour's entire command was back in Jacksonville and building fortifications under the protection of naval gunboats by February 22. "In ninety hours we have marched one hundred and ten miles, fought a battle of three hours' duration, got badly whipped, and what there is left of our little army is back where we started from," one of Seymour's officers summarized. The lead elements of Finegan's force had advanced only six miles from the battlefield.[29]

Seymour proved at Olustee that he had not learned many lessons from his disastrous command at Fort Wagner, but he had learned at least one thing from the Northern furor over the Confederate disposition of Robert Gould Shaw: he needed to find out what had happened to the body of the colonel who led Black troops in battle. One of Seymour's staff officers accompanied by six cavalrymen, carrying a flag of truce and a message addressed to the "the general commanding Confederate Forces, Florida" found Finegan's advance pickets at Baldwin on February 23. Seymour asked Finegan to parole all of the wounded prisoners and to deliver them to the Union lines at Jacksonville. "The body of Col. C. W. Fribley was left upon the field at Olustee," he wrote. "If there have been any means of identifying his person, I request that his grave may be so marked that at some future day his family may be able to remove his remains." Finegan initially dismissed both requests. "The wounded prisoners have been sent forward and properly taken care of," he responded. "I regret to say that the body of Colonel Fribley has not been identified."[30]

Seymour could not let the matter drop, however, because Fribley's widow, who had accompanied her husband to Hilton Head when the regiment moved south, came to Jacksonville immediately and requested permission to retrieve some personal items Fribley carried into the battle, including an ambrotype, a letter from her, a watch, and his diary. The intervention of a woman whom Seymour classified as a "lady" into the process of negotiation changed the equation for both parties. Convention required a civilized combatant to treat a civilized woman with chivalry and courtesy. Seymour wrote Finegan again and asked his enemy to "mitigate the sorrow" of a "deserving and greatly suffering lady." He offered to pay anyone who possessed Fribley's personal effects for their return, a request that subtly indicated that Seymour suspected that Confederates had already identified and stripped the colonel's body, and asked permission for Mrs. Fribley to pass through to Confederate lines in company of the adjutant of the 8th. Finegan did not allow her to do so. On March 4, General Gardner, the new commander of the Confederate forces building a defensive line several miles west of Jacksonville, forwarded to Seymour the ambrotype with assurances that he was taking "steps" to recover the other items. "That I may not be misunderstood, it is due to myself to state that no sympathy with the fate of any officers commanding negro troops, but compassion for a widow in grief, has induced these efforts to recover for her relics which she must naturally value," he said. Seymour responded, "No kindness you can show in this connection can be construed otherwise than affecting those whom on both sides at all times we desire to shield from sorrow." When it became clear that Confederates would not give back the diary, Kate Ault Fribley returned north to the home of her father. To honor her husband's memory, she joined the National Freedmen's Relief Association and taught in one of its schools in Nashville, Tennessee.[31]

Union officers in Florida who had been on Morris Island thought that Confederates were behaving differently than they had seven months before. When the flag of truce arrived with the ambrotype from Fribley's body, Appleton observed, "That is more than they did about Shaw's things." Confederate major general James Patton Anderson eventually sent Seymour a full list of the prisoners from Olustee and, unlike Beauregard, included the names of Black soldiers. "A flag of truce from the enemy brought news that prisoners, black and white, were treated alike," Norton said. "I hope it is so, for I have sworn never to take a prisoner if my men left there were murdered." Union officers had reported many of the men on the list, including Corporal Gooding and Major Bogle, to be dead, and the information that they were alive reinforced the impression that Confederates were treating Black and white troops alike in the aftermath of Olustee. Deserters from the Confederate army who came to Jacksonville in March confirmed that white and Black Union prisoners were in Lake City and Tallahassee, where "citizens generally showed them every kindness." A private in the 1st North Carolina wrote a Northern newspaper that these reports were "perfectly reliable, and certainly most refreshing for us to hear."[32]

Although Confederates were indeed treating Blacks as prisoners of

Charles W. Fribley and Kate Ault Fribley. This photograph was taken on December 14, 1861, four days after their marriage. Although Confederate commanders dishonored Charles in burial, the intervention of the "lady" Kate prompted them to return an item found on his body. Union officials contrasted this treatment with that of Robert Gould Shaw at Fort Wagner. (David L. Richards Collection, Gettysburg, Pa.)

war, they were not transparent, of course, about the post-battle atrocities or about their purposeful neglect of the Black wounded at Olustee Station and Lake City. But Seymour was too ready to believe the reports he received from Confederate sources and was nonchalant about the possibility that his men might be mistreated. Immediately after the battle, he told a Federal surgeon that the wounded "ought to be well taken care of by the enemy" and requested the parole of his wounded only at the insistence of the surgeon. He assured the colonel of the 1st North Carolina on March 17 that "colored soldiers and their officers are treated by the Confederates precisely as are those of white Regiments." Gillmore's chief of staff, John W. Turner, an opponent of the use of Black troops in battle, categorized Seymour as one of the officers who would not "make a thing to be worshipped of the negro." Turner later testified before the Congressional Committee on the Conduct of the War that Confederates treated Blacks and whites equally and there were no outrages committed during the Florida expedition.[33]

Black soldiers and their advocates in the Department of the South, however, were more suspicious of Confederate reports and were increasingly frustrated with Seymour and Gillmore for not doing enough to ensure they received the honor and respect due to civilized combatants. Rumors circulated that Seymour's staff had asked the Confederates bearing the flag of truce with Fribley's ambrotype, "What are you going to do with our nigger soldiers?" "Hang them if President Lincoln is willing," the rebels purportedly replied. Black soldiers and the white officers in command of them thought it was important to diligently track the Confederate disposition of Black prisoners and believed that immediate retaliation for mistreatment was necessary to protect them. Some soldiers and officers spoke openly of their own intention to fight under a black flag, the signal that a combatant would not take prisoners. "How the rebels have disposed of the colored men who fell into their hands we have not heard yet, but we hope that the fear of retaliation, if not the dictates of humanity, will cause them to reconsider their threat of outlawry," surgeon Alex P. Heichhold of the 8th wrote a Philadelphia newspaper. "If not, we must act accordingly." Sgt. George E. Stephens of the 54th, a thirty-one-year-old cabinetmaker from Boston, was outraged that Confederate prisoners in Jacksonville who took an oath of allegiance to the United States were allowed to pass outside Union lines, visit their families, and potentially pass intelligence to Confederate forces. "If, while we are pampering and petting rebel prisoners, Federal prisoners are hung and enslaved, we are exchanging smiles for kicks—paying gold and honor for dross and dishonor," he said in a public letter. "As far as this regiment is concerned we will ask no quarter, and rest satisfied that we will give none," a soldier in the 55th Massachusetts wrote to the *Weekly Anglo-African*. "We are compelled to take this in our own hands."[34]

Although Federals did not yet know it, Confederate officers in Florida sent the Black prisoners from Olustee to the same place they sent their white captives. Doctors in Lake City and Tallahassee determined when prisoners were able to travel and in many cases sent them away before they were able.

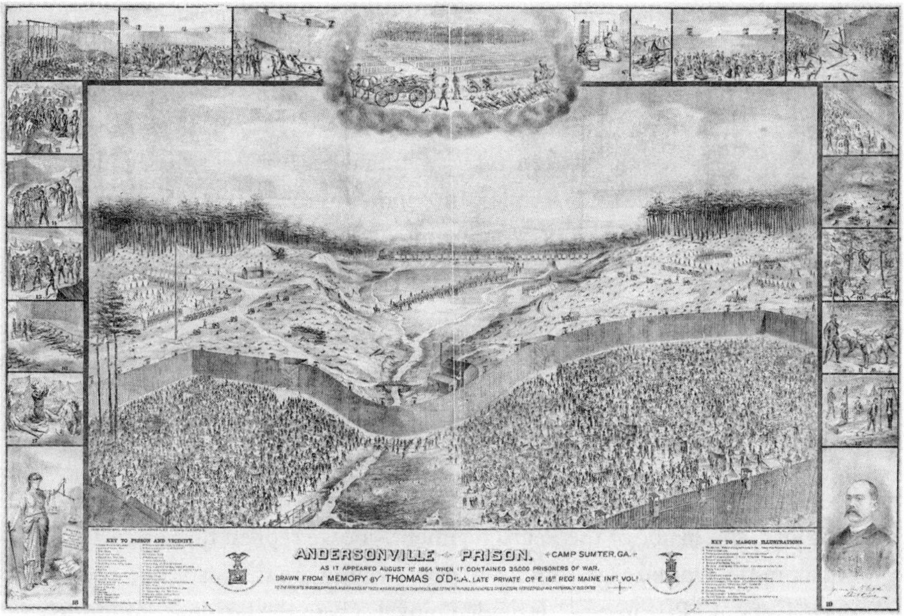


Pvt. Thomas O'Dea's drawing of Andersonville Prison as it appeared on August 1, 1864. Drawn from memory twenty years later, this famous lithograph depicts the South Gate, on the left. The Black prisoners from Olustee camped near it on the slope that descended to the ditch used as a toilet. The presence of men from the 54th Massachusetts, the 8th USCT, and the 1st North Carolina in Andersonville was a sign that retaliation had forced the Confederate government to treat them as legitimate combatants. (Library of Congress Prints and Photographs Division)

They went to Camp Sumter, the new military prison opened on February 24 in Andersonville, Georgia, and arrived there in small batches in various states of recovery from their wounds over the next five months.[35]

Confederate authorities established Camp Sumter, also known as Andersonville, to house white prisoners from the overcrowded prisons in Richmond in a remote site that they believed would be safe from the incursions of Union armies. Its isolation in the Georgia countryside also meant it was far from supplies needed to feed its inmates. It had no shelter for the men inside the open-air stockade. Typical of the complete disarray of the Confederate command structure relative to its prisons, commanders at Camp Sumter were shocked when Black men disembarked from the trains bringing prisoners on March 14. They had no warning and no instructions. Lt. Col. Alexander W. Persons, in command of the post, asked a superior what he was supposed to do. "His reply was that the question was yet in abeyance," Persons later testified, "and I think he said, 'until further orders treat them as prisoners of war.'" Seventy-one of the Black men captured at Olustee eventually ended up in Andersonville. They camped near its south gate, on a slope near the ditch prisoners used as a toilet.[36]

Confederates treated Bogle, who had two broken bones in his lower right leg, as if he were a Black private rather than a white field officer. He arrived at Andersonville on March 14 with gangrene growing in his wound. It is significant that Bogle went to Camp Sumter rather than Camp Oglethorpe, for Federal officers, located in Macon, Georgia. The customs of war required combatants to house officers in separate camps from enlisted men and to treat them with special consideration indicative of their status. His presence in Andersonville was a public shaming. Bogle was faint after his journey and went to the hospital inside the stockade. A Federal prisoner there began to bind his leg, but a Confederate surgeon said, "Send him out there with his niggers." He tried to go to the hospital again in April. The doctor asked if he was "the major of the negro regiment." Bogle replied that he "was an officer in the United States military service." "You are the man," the doctor said. "Get out." Prison officials denied him access to the hospital until June. When Bogle repeatedly requested that Confederate authorities recognize his rank, the matter went to the Confederate War Department. "No objection is known to his being placed with his privates," Assistant Secretary of War John A. Campbell decided. "He cannot complain of miscegenation."[37]

The presence of Black soldiers in Andersonville legitimized them as combatants under the laws of war, but prison officials were determined to mark them with a separate status from the white prisoners. Every single Black prisoner who arrived at Camp Sumter "was crippled in some way," as one white soldier confined there accurately observed. Confederates had two preferences for handling Black Union troops: execution or enslavement. Officers in charge of the stockade tried to create a mini–slave system for their Black prisoners. "When I was taken there I was put in the stockade and stayed there about two months, until my wound got well enough to allow me to work," Frank Mattocks, a soldier in the 1st North Carolina, said. "I was then taken out and put to work." Under the supervision of a white Federal prisoner, Otis Knight, the Black soldiers did manual labor enhancing the stockade and digging graves. At least one worked as a servant in the home of a Confederate doctor living near the prison. Confederate sergeants sometimes punished the laborers by whipping them with a leather strap attached to a staff. They gave Isaac Hawkins of the 54th, a twenty-nine-year-old sailor from Medina, New York, lashes across the entire back of his body. Black prisoners received no medical attention. "I never had my wounds dressed at all," recalled William Henry Jennings of the 8th. Thirty-three of the 106 Black soldiers eventually imprisoned at Andersonville from different battles died, which is a rate of 31 percent, close to the overall death rate of 29 percent. James Gooding, his letters to the *New Bedford Mercury* silenced by his imprisonment, was one of the three men of the 54th who died there.[38]

Florida officials, despite their brief and superficial investigation into the background of their Black prisoners and the evidence that some of the troops they had captured were former slaves, did not distinguish between the freeborn men of the 54th and 8th and the former slaves of the 1st when they sent captives to Andersonville. This was a violation of Confederate War Department policy, but they did not know it. Secretary of War James A. Seddon was always lax and inefficient in his communication with the hinterlands. Eventually authorities in Richmond noticed this mistake and tried to rectify it. One of Seddon's subordinates received a roll of the seventy-one Black Olustee prisoners in Andersonville. "Many of them admit they are slaves of persons living in eastern North Carolina," he told the secretary. "It is so inconvenient as to be almost impossible for the owners to go to Americus [ten miles from Andersonville] for the purpose of identifying and claiming them. Could they not be ordered to some more convenient place, Raleigh or Salisbury, for instance?" Seddon replied, "The demand on transportation is too great at present for this to be done, but if the request be renewed at a more favorable moment it will probably be accorded."[39]

This reply exemplifies the inconsistent mess that Confederate policy toward Black prisoners had become once the government veered away from its plans of state trials for all of them. In addition to the disagreement over the legality of the policy within the War Department bureaucracy, Seddon and Jefferson Davis were under pressure from other powerful constituencies who ignored the May 1863 congressional resolutions. Slaveholders wanted their property returned to them, and military officials wanted to employ captured Blacks on the spot as military labor working on railroads and fortifications. This had been the original policy of the Confederate Congress after Lincoln issued the preliminary emancipation proclamation in September 1862. A statute passed the next month required the secretary of war to establish depots in each state to hold slaves whom the Confederate military captured and to advertise their names in newspapers. Masters who provided proof of ownership could reclaim their slaves, and in the meantime the military could work the slaves. Some local officials in Virginia and Alabama still used the earlier plan and either ignored or were ignorant of the May 1863 resolutions that supplanted it.[40] Seddon's willingness to return the Black prisoners of the 1st North Carolina to their masters was a knowing defiance of the legislation that was supposed to guide his decision-making. The Federal retaliation, and internal discord over the appropriate policy, had effectively blocked state trials for both freeborn and formerly enslaved prisoners. Confederate officials were working their way toward a policy of putting freeborn Black soldiers in military prisons and using recaptured slaves as military laborers.

News of this inconsistency reached South Carolina governor Milledge Bonham in June. He still held as state prisoners in the Charleston Jail the soldiers from the 54th captured on Sol Legare and Morris Islands nearly a year earlier. The court he convened had declared that South Carolina did not have jurisdiction over them, but Bonham was determined to assert his authority. He read advertisements in the Richmond newspapers giving the names of slaves captured in Federal uniform in Virginia and the opportunity for owners to claim them. He wrote Seddon to ask if the Confederate government had adopted new rules that he did not know about. Rather than answer the question, Assistant Secretary of War Campbell referred the letter to the attorney general. Two months went by without a reply.[41]

While the Confederate government waffled and procrastinated over its policy toward Black captives, the Lincoln administration faced a terrible moment of decision regarding its willingness to use retaliation to protect its Black soldiers against massacres on the battlefield. Astute Union officers in Florida were suspicious that Confederates had murdered Black soldiers after Olustee. "The very small number of colored prisoners attracted immediate attention," one of them said, "as it was well known that the number left wounded on the field was large." Seymour and Gillmore, however, had not communicated such concerns to Washington, so the executive branch was unaware of the atrocities. Olustee did not force Lincoln's hand; what did was a massacre two months later at Fort Pillow, Tennessee, located on the Mississippi River forty miles north of Memphis. On April 12, Confederate troops under the command of Maj. Gen. Nathan Bedford Forrest attacked the Union garrison, comprising white soldiers from the 13th Tennessee Cavalry and portions of two Black artillery units. They murdered white and Black Union soldiers after they tried to surrender and massacred sick soldiers in the post hospital. During the battle and the executions, Confederate soldiers killed nearly two-thirds of the Black Union soldiers at Fort Pillow. They also took fifty Black prisoners, and the Confederate War Department approved local commanders' requests to put them to work on fortifications in Mobile, Alabama. Confederates took Maj. William Bradford prisoner but shot him the night after the battle and left his body fifty yards from the road on which they were marching.[42]

News of the massacre spread quickly. Unlike Olustee, where all the Union soldiers who saw the atrocities were prisoners in Confederate hands and unable to tell their story, witnesses to what happened at Fort Pillow were within the Union lines. Northern newspapers generated a furious public outcry. Lincoln addressed the "painful rumor" in an April 18 speech in Baltimore. "Having determined to use the negro as a soldier, there is no way but to give him all the protection given to any other soldier," he told the crowd. "The difficulty is not in stating the principle, but in practically applying it." He promised to investigate the facts thoroughly, and if a massacre was "conclusively proved," he promised, "the retribution shall surely come." Newspaper coverage and letters to the president indicated widespread support among the Northern public for retaliation. Republican and abolitionist papers alike blamed the slave system itself for the massacre. "In no other school could human beings have been trained to such readiness for cruelties like these," the *Liberator* noted. "Accustomed to brutality and bestiality all their lives, it was easy for them to perpetrate the atrocities." A few Northern Democratic newspapers sympathized with the Confederate troops at Fort Pillow. "Dressing a monkey in the uniform of the government," the *Portland Maine Advertiser* wrote, "cannot convert the monkey into a real soldier and attach to him the rights and immunities of a prisoner of war."[43]

Voices with powerful influence over the administration advocated retaliation. Secretary of War Edwin Stanton ordered his subordinates in the Mississippi Valley to investigate. Lt. Gen. Ulysses S. Grant, now in overall command of Union armies, instructed Maj. Gen. William Tecumseh Sherman to retaliate promptly if the investigations confirmed that men were murdered after capture. Grant decided it was now necessary to halt all prisoner exchanges with the Confederacy. Francis Lieber pressured Henry W. Halleck. "Something must be done. The negro soldier must be protected," he said. "He is a soldier; our Flag is his flag. He wears our uniform." The military's report, which included sworn affidavits from thirty-three witnesses, concluded that Confederates at Fort Pillow violated the "usages of civilized war" and "those obligations of common humanity which even barbarians and heathen tribes, in some sort observe."[44]

The Fort Pillow massacre intersected with the politics of the U.S. capital. It was a presidential election year, war-weariness was growing, the Republican Party was dividing over plans to reconstruct the Southern states, and the Democratic Party was seemingly gaining momentum in its criticism of the Lincoln administration for botching the war effort. In this context, the U.S. Congress dispatched a subcommittee to Illinois, composed of Radical Republican senator Benjamin Wade and moderate Republican congressman Daniel Gooch, to gather testimony. Wade returned to Washington on May 2 armed with both credible proof of the massacre and with sensational, gruesome accounts. The senator immediately distributed an unprecedented 60,000 copies of the committee's summary and attached to it photographs and statements from recently returned Union prisoners of war describing terrible conditions in Confederate military prisons. The gist of the report was that savage slaveholders raised in a barbaric society waged an uncivilized war. Wade's propaganda piece was designed to generate public outrage that would transform into support for a vigorous prosecution of the war and for a reconstruction policy that reconfigured Southern society. Its publication escalated the number of editorials calling for retaliation and required Lincoln's cabinet to discuss the matter.[45]

For the first time in the Civil War, high-ranking members of the Lincoln administration had to decide what they were willing to do about Confederate atrocities against Black troops perpetrated on the battlefield. They were winning a victory using a threat of retaliation and hostages to address the Confederacy's official policy of giving captured Blacks state trials. Massacres were different because individual commanders and soldiers committed them without the public sanction of the Confederate government, although killing Blacks after capture enjoyed the tacit approval and subtle encouragement of the Richmond authorities. Retaliating for the acts of individuals had the potential to escalate dramatically the war's level of violence. If the Lincoln administration decided to respond with the customary "tit for tat" equation in the case, there was a real possibility that the war would degenerate into the specter that had haunted both combatants from the start: a war of the black flag with no prisoners taken on either side. Even more frightening was the vision of a war with all prisoners executed in an endless cycle of retaliatory violence. Retaliation was supposed to restrain the overall violence of war, but if the Lincoln administration actually executed up to 295 Confederate prisoners of war in response to the Fort Pillow massacre, the opposite might happen. The president and his cabinet confronted a crisis of civilization. A war of the black flag would reveal Americans to be barbarians and not the civilized men they claimed to be. Outlaws and pirates, not honorable men, fought under a black flag.

This fear of escalating violence under a black flag pervaded the discussion in Lincoln's cabinet. On May 3, the president asked each member to give him a written opinion about the appropriate response to the Fort Pillow massacre. Secretary of the Navy Gideon Welles had mixed feelings. "The idea of retaliation—killing man for man—which is the popular noisy demand, is barbarous, and I cannot assent to it or advise it. The leading officers should be held accountable and punished, but how?" he recorded in his diary. "The policy of killing negro soldiers after they have surrendered must not be permitted, and the Rebel leaders should be called upon to avow or disavow it. . . . If they will give us no answer, or declare they will kill the negroes, or justify Forrest, shall we take innocent Rebel officers as hostages? The whole subject is beset with difficulties. I cannot yield to any inhuman scheme of retaliation."[46]

Secretary of War Stanton, in an opposite opinion, proposed selecting by lot 295 Confederate officers who were prisoners of war and, if the Confederate government refused to hand over within a given time frame those who had committed the massacre, retaliating on the hostages. Secretary of State William Henry Seward wanted to give Jefferson Davis a chance to present evidence that disproved the massacre or to disavow it. Attorney General Edward Bates wrote, "I would not have compact with the enemy for mutual slaughter—no cartel of blood and murder—no stipulation to the effect that *if you murder one of my own, I will murder one of yours*." In a meeting on May 6, Bates and Postmaster General Montgomery Blair suggested that Lincoln declare Forrest and his officers to be outlaws subject to trial and punishment when captured. Welles agreed with this plan because it "avoided communication with rebel authorities. Took the matter in our own hands." Stanton and Secretary of the Treasury Salmon P. Chase likewise decided the proposal was reasonable. "We are on the eve of an impending battle," Secretary of the Interior John P. Usher remarked. "Until the result shall have been known it seems to me to be inexpedient to take any extreme action."[47]

Lincoln considered this advice and on May 17, while waiting at the telegraph office for news of the fighting in Virginia, wrote an instruction to Stanton. The president asked the secretary of war to notify Confederate authorities that there was proof of the massacre at Fort Pillow and that Confederate officers held as prisoners of war were set aside as hostages. Lincoln said, "Blood cannot restore blood, and government should not act for revenge." He therefore wanted Stanton to ask Confederate authorities to assure him by July 1 that there would be no other massacre, and that all officers and soldiers, "whether white or colored," would be treated as honorable combatants under the laws of war in order to release the Confederate officers from their hostage status. But Lincoln apparently never sent these instructions to

Stanton but left them in the telegraph office. He was not satisfied with any option placed before him and did nothing about the Fort Pillow massacre. He told Frederick Douglass of his overarching fear regarding retaliation. "Once begun, I do not know where such a measure would stop."[48]

The inaction of the Lincoln administration contributed to the subsequent escalation of violence between white Confederate soldiers and Black Union soldiers and their officers. After Olustee, Fort Pillow, and another Confederate massacre of white and Black troops at Plymouth, North Carolina, on April 20, the race war that Confederates had feared and had created emerged. The war became more brutal because Black Union soldiers and white Confederate soldiers were no longer willing to surrender to each other. The ability to surrender to an enemy and receive protection and humane treatment was one of the essential marks of a civilized war. Instead, many Black soldiers fought under the black flag. Sherman had foreseen this outcome when he refused Grant's instruction to retaliate after Fort Pillow. "I know well the animus of the Southern soldiery, and the truth is they cannot be restrained," he said. "The effect will be of course to make the negroes desperate, and when in turn they commit horrid acts of retaliation we will be relieved of the responsibility." A comprehensive historical study found that in 1864 "soldiers increasingly chose death over surrender." The ratio of killed to captured soldiers shifted in official reports. The Battle of the Crater on July 30 at Petersburg, Virginia, exemplified the new mindset, as Black troops entered the fight yelling, "Remember Fort Pillow!" and "No Quarter!" Soldiers on both sides initially refused to accept surrenders and fought to the death in a melee that yielded relatively few prisoners.[49]

This was not civilized war. "It is against the usages of modern war to resolve, in hatred and revenge, to give no quarter," Francis Lieber stated bluntly when he wrote Article 60 of General Orders No. 100. "Modern wars are not internecine wars, in which the killing of the enemy is the object," Article 68 read. "Unnecessary or revengeful destruction of life is not lawful." Lieber's own instructions, however, contained provisions that justified the carnage between Black and white combatants in the Civil War. They allowed a combatant to put a prisoner of war to death within three days of a battle if "it be discovered that he belongs to a corps which gives no quarter." The black flag became a pervasive, though not dominant, feature of the war after the Florida expedition.[50]

The black flag now flew over the Department of the South between Black Union soldiers and white Confederate soldiers as the American crisis of civilization marked its third year. Confederates massacred on the battlefield the men they could not envision as citizens in a civilized nation. Black troops and their white officers vowed to give no quarter to the men who had declared them outlaws and refused to treat them humanely. While this unfolded, the Federal bombardment of Charleston turned portions of the city that exemplified Southern civilization into a lawless ruin. When the Confederate government decided to send white Union prisoners of war to Charleston, a new commander in the city decided to use them as human shields. This initiated a new retaliation ritual that endangered the lives of 1,600 white prisoners of war and exposed the true condition of the captives from the 54th Massachusetts.

# 5

# HUMAN SHIELDS

While Confederates in Florida gradually sent the Black prisoners captured at the Battle of Olustee to Andersonville, the Federal bombardment of Charleston continued. It was not an immediate and overwhelming display of power but a grinding and cumulative assault. Week after week, Federal heavy rifled artillery slowly pounded the jewel of Southern civilization into a ruin. Confederate signal officer Augustine Thomas Smythe watched it happen to his native city from his post in the steeple of St. Michael's cathedral and from his home at 12 Meeting Street. In November and December 1863, he and his superiors had dismissed the shelling, which did less damage to buildings than they had expected and killed only five people. "Instead of having the debris of houses staring one in the face you have to hunt up the resting places of the shells," Smythe wrote his refugee father. "This all proves how much more damage shelling actually does on paper, than in reality." Confederate officers calculated that 42 percent of the 296 shells that landed in the city in December did not explode. In January 1864, an inspector reported that 126 buildings were damaged, 41 of them only slightly. Harbor transportation was "inconvenienced" but not "practically impeded." He acknowledged that thousands of people had left the city and that this caused "considerable social distress," but the results as a whole, he concluded, were "utterly inadequate to the labors and boasts of the besieging forces." "Their Greek-fire is a great humbug," Maj. Gen. P. G. T. Beauregard wrote a subordinate. He had been doing experiments with the liquid in some of the unexploded shells. "We cannot light it most often, even with a match."[1]

Then, gradually, as the shells continued to fall month after month, adding up to 11,000 of them, ranging over different sectors of the city, essential

"Bursting of a Shell in the Streets of Charleston, South Carolina, Sketched by an English Artist." Although residents initially dismissed the impact of the Federal bombardment, the shelling eventually depopulated portions of the city and contributed to the spread of lawlessness. (*Harper's Weekly: A Journal of Civilization*, January 9, 1864, 28)

elements of civilization began to disappear: tamed nature, law and order, and the refined leisure that produced art and beauty. Portions of the city were deserted. Cows grazed the six-foot-high fennel and grass that grew up in the streets. The gaslights no longer shone at night, and Smythe found that it was no longer safe, even for a soldier, to be out alone. There were daily assaults. Thieves roamed the streets and pillaged the abandoned houses. Confederate soldiers—in league with bandit women—stripped copper and other metals from houses to sell to the Ordnance Bureau. "The city here is in a very lawless condition," Smythe wrote his mother. "It is horrible and dangerous." When a *London Times* special correspondent visited the city in March 1865, he described a wasteland (although most of the really dramatic devastation he saw was the result of an 1861 fire, not the shelling). "Fully two thirds of this once beautiful and thriving city have been reduced to ashes, the other third, fronting the sea having been so riddled by shot and shell during the last eight months as to be virtually uninhabitable."[2]

Federals believed their constant bombardment of the city sent subtextual messages about Federal resources and power. They knew that Confederates could not afford to keep pace with them. Col. Charles Ray Brayton, the chief of artillery on Morris Island, always returned from the guns "full of glee." If he fired 12 shots into the city, rebel batteries in the harbor fired at least 100 back at Morris in response. "They are wasting their precious ammunition," Maj. John Appleton of the 54th Massachusetts had written his wife from Morris in December 1863. "It must cost them something handsome, this amusement." Federals also conceived of the shells as an "avenging flame" that punished "guilty conspirators." Brayton fired 150 projectiles at Charleston on Christmas Day and shelled the firefighters attempting to put out the resulting fires.[3]

Confederates defending the city, however, read a different message. The Yankees were stymied before a defiant city and its defenses. Federals fired 8,806 shots at Fort Sumter during July 1864, and the garrison inside the collapsed earthwork still raised the Confederate flag every morning. Federals made war on women and children, the Confederates argued, because they could not defeat Confederate men. "What brutes! What cowards!" Smythe wrote his sister. "To wait until the dead of night when everybody is asleep in their beds then throw in their horrible missiles of destruction. . . . It is a shame that these scoundrels should outrage humanity to such a degree." "The Yanks have always made war upon women & children," a soldier defending James Island wrote. "It is a reproach that will always stick to them."[4]

A sense of helpless rage haunted the actions of both combatants in the Department of the South in 1864. Neither side had the resources it needed to subdue the enemy in front of it. In April, Maj. Gen. Quincy A. Gillmore and Brig. Gen. Truman Seymour departed for Virginia with the bulk of the white troops from the department to fight in the campaign to defeat Robert E. Lee's army. General Beauregard and most of the veteran Confederate soldiers in the Department of South Carolina, Georgia, and Florida quickly followed. Gillmore's replacement was Maj. Gen. John G. Foster, a competent 1846 West Point graduate who had never quite recovered from a leg wound he received in the Mexican War. He was a Catholic with a pleasant personality and a contented staff. He had been part of the U.S. Army garrison at Fort Sumter in April 1861 and had told Maj. Robert Anderson not to surrender. He still spoke of the submission with bitterness. During his command in North Carolina, Foster used his troops to raid extensively and actively, brought the war to unrepentant secessionists, and burned houses to punish rebel guerrillas.[5]

His counterpart was native Virginian and 1841 West Point graduate Maj. Gen. Samuel Jones, who had been a professor of math and artillery at his alma mater before the war. He had commanded Confederate military de-

Maj. Gen. John G. Foster, U.S. Army, and Maj. Gen. Samuel Jones, Confederate States of America. The two commanders' mishandling of the retaliation ritual brought unnecessary suffering to the prisoners of war brought to Charleston in 1864. (Library of Congress Prints and Photographs Division)

partments in Florida, east Tennessee, and southwestern Virginia. State legislators and senators in Virginia petitioned Jefferson Davis to remove Jones from command because of his "manifest errors and defects." Smythe was not confident in the appointment. "They say he was sent here as this was the easiest place, the work being all done, & they had no place else to send him."[6]

Foster and Jones chafed at their positions in command of a military sideshow stripped of troops, equipment, ammunition, and land and water transport. Foster peppered Maj. Gen. Henry W. Halleck in Washington with letters listing deficiencies — 4,000 of his Black troops were new recruits "unused to arms and ignorant of drill" — yet requesting permission for an infantry attack on Charleston or Savannah. Halleck consulted General-in-Chief Ulysses S. Grant, who granted Foster some freedom of action but emphasized that any "demonstration" in the Department of the South was a "diversion." The goal in Washington was no longer to capture Charleston but to "make raids on the enemy's lines of communication and destroy as much of them as possible." Halleck was reluctant to send anything to the Department of the South. "It is certain that the expenses of that department have been enormous without any commensurate results," he told its new commander. Jones, for his part, sent regular dispatches to Richmond with a catalog of problems. "My force is not only entirely too small for the protection of Charleston and Savannah and the railroad connecting them, but some of the troops cannot be relied on," he reported. "A part of the guard near Savannah overpowered the others yesterday and escaped to Pulaski." The whole garrison at Fort Bartow was "unsound." He did not have enough slave labor to work on the fortifications. Although his chief engineer needed 2,000 slaves, South Carolina's impressment agent had delivered only 9.[7]

Against this backdrop of frustration and futility in June 1864, Foster increased the bombardment of Charleston. His subordinates fired an average of fifty shots each day into Charleston at "irregular intervals." Jones snapped. "The enemy continue their bombardment of the city with increased vigor, damaging private property and endangering the lives of women and children," he wrote Gen. Braxton Bragg, Jefferson Davis's military advisor, on June 1. "I can take care of a party, say 50 Yankee prisoners. Can you not send me that number, including a General?" Jones asked for Truman Seymour, who had been captured in May at the Battle of the Wilderness in Virginia. He would confine the prisoners "in parts of the city still occupied by citizens, but under the enemy's fire." Bragg submitted the request to Secretary of War James A. Seddon, who looked more like a walking cadaver each day that passed. There is no record of what transpired within the Davis administration as its members considered Jones's proposal. On June 9, though, orders from Richmond instructed prison officials in Georgia to send fifty high-ranking Federal prisoners for "special use" in Charleston. On June 10, authorities at Camp Oglethorpe in Macon shipped off five brigadier generals, including Seymour, eleven colonels, twenty-five lieutenant colonels, and nine majors, the latter selected alphabetically. "These brigadiers are no loss to us as they have acted like a set of old women throughout," a Union captain at the prison commented in his diary as he watched them depart. Seymour gained no more respect in prison than he had while in command in the field.[8]

The Confederacy had decided to use human shields to force a suspension of the bombardment. This was consistent with prior practice in Charleston. A colonel defending Morris Island in July 1863 had asked permission to "hold and fortify" the island through exposing Union prisoners to fire. General Beauregard had responded that it was not consistent with the usages of war to use prisoners "as a means of defense or protection." Yet two months later, Beauregard had ordered the garrison at Fort Sumter to expose recently captured Union prisoners to the Union bombardment of the fort if there was not enough cover in the fort for both the Confederate defenders and the prisoners. A young officer stationed at Fort Sumter told his family, "We are keeping the prisoners in Sumter so when they shell they may injure their own men."[9]

The consequences of the Confederacy's decision to bring fifty Federal officers to Charleston revealed that the highest-ranking military officials on both sides were willing to mistreat enemy prisoners and ignore the rules that supposedly separated civilized combatants from barbarians. The retaliation ritual increasingly failed to restrain the violence of Civil War combatants and adjust their conduct during operations in the Department of the South. Ulterior motives and hidden agendas infected the ritual. As revenge, lawlessness, and violence escalated, many soldiers and officers in the region feared that Americans were losing their claim to a place in the civilized world. Civilization was a worldview that ordered people in relation to the natural world. "Savages" were the people on the sliding scale of progress who lived most like animals. The prisoners subjected to retaliation in Charleston Harbor—eventually numbering 1,200 of them—believed the conditions they endured as prisoners "decivilized" them. They crossed the boundary separating civilized man from natural animal.[10]

The officers and soldiers tasked with implementing retaliation against prisoners of war in the Department of the South were not unified about whether the measures taken were appropriate for a Christian civilization, especially after the U.S. War Department decided to withhold rations from 600 Confederate prisoners. A significant number of them feared that retaliation violated Christian doctrines of forgiveness and loving one's enemy. They intervened to mitigate the worst suffering of the human shields brought to Charleston. At the same time that retaliation over the treatment of prisoners of war failed, the Federal retaliation on behalf of freeborn Black soldiers succeeded in ensuring their status as legitimate combatants.

Jones notified Foster of his action on June 13. His short letter was simultaneously information and subtle accusation. He told his antagonist that five general and forty-five field officers were in the city "for safe keeping." They were "provided with commodious quarters in a part of the city occupied by non-combatants, the majority of whom are women and children," Jones wrote. "It is proper, however, that I should inform you that it is part of the city which has been for many months exposed day and night to the fire of your guns."[11]

Foster was shocked and asked Brig. Gen. Alexander Schimmelfennig for advice. The Prussian revolutionary émigré and veteran of the Battle of Gettysburg commanded the troops on Morris Island, including the 54th

Massachusetts, which had returned there from Florida. "He is in a state of chronic craving for Rebel prisoners," Appleton told his wife. "He is consumptive and a martyr to rheumatism, and quite irritable. He will send for an officer and say, 'You will bring me tree prisonair tomorrow morning, Go.'" Appleton considered him a fighter and liked him.[12]

Schimmelfennig believed that Jones had inadvertently revealed how desperate the Confederates were in defending Charleston. "In my opinion the endeavor of the enemy to force us to give up the bombardment should be the reason for its continuation. At the same time, as a means to force him to give up his barbarous practices, the simple fact of retaliation can be made effectual, as I have as many places where his shells fall as he has in Charleston where mine fall," he said. Foster agreed. On June 16, he wrote Jones to protest the "indefensible act of cruelty" that "can be designed only to prevent the continuance of our fire on Charleston." He reminded Jones that several months earlier Beauregard had told Gillmore he would remove noncombatants from the city. Charleston was a legitimate military target because it was a "depot for military supplies [with] arsenals, foundries, and factories for the manufacture of munitions of war. . . . Its wharves and the banks of the rivers on both sides of the city are lined with batteries." Foster accused Jones of violating the standards of "honorable warfare" and informed Jones that he had requested President Abraham Lincoln to send him fifty Confederate prisoners of war to put under the fire of Confederate guns. Foster then wrote to Halleck. "I think the cruel determination of the rebels to place our officers under fire is an evidence of their vindictive weakness and of the destruction the city is sustaining from our fire," he said. "This last is not so much from actual demolition as from the depopulation and desolation. Private letters speak of this and of the grass growing in the streets."[13]

Foster had initiated another ritual of retaliation, and the typical correspondence ensued. Both parties sought to convince their peer audience of civilized nations, and future historians, of the barbarity of their enemy and the righteousness of their own position. Jones provided a lengthy exposition of the ways that he claimed Union forces had violated the customs of war since the bombardment began on August 22, 1863. Gillmore had given only four hours' notice before firing the first shell into the city, which was not time to remove noncombatants; the Union fire fell randomly in the city rather than targeting the military works, so its purpose clearly was to destroy private property and kill noncombatants; Union artillerists targeted church steeples during hours of public worship. The Union bombardment was "conducted in a spirit of mere malice and cruelty" rather than with the purposeful restraint of civilized war. "The fire has been such as you very well know could not lessen by one hour the duration of this war or produce any material military result," he said. "I cannot but regard the desultory firing on this city, which you dignify by the name of bombardment, from its commencement to this hour, as unchristian, inhuman, and utterly indefensible by any law, human or divine." Jones informed Foster that he did not treat the five generals and forty-five field officers he held in the city cruelly. They had large, comfortable quarters located away from military works. He gave them the consideration due to men of their high military rank. "If you direct your guns only at the works that you distinctly specify as the object of your fire," he concluded, "the prisoners of war and their neighbors, non-combatants, women and children, among whom they live, will be in no danger whatever from the effects of your shot." Smythe was hopeful that the human shields would stop the ongoing destruction of his city. "They will hardly fire on their own men," he thought.[14]

The fifty Federal officers in Charleston were indeed living well. They were in the splendid private house of prominent Charleston attorney Michael P. O'Connor. They were free to walk the large yard, play cricket, bathe in the sea, and purchase luxury items such as coffee and sugar. "It seems a shame to treat them so well," Smythe wrote his mother. "As we have now got the credit of putting them in shell range, we ought to do so & not leave them out there where a shell does not drop once in two months." When Brig. Gen. Roswell S. Ripley found out that the prisoners employed two Black Charleston servants to cook for them, he stopped the practice. Seymour socialized with Jones's staff officers and even made sketches of Federal guns for one of them. "Strange to say I could not blow Seymour from a gun or hang him without a good deal of repugnance," the Confederate captain admitted. "Indeed I felt more inclined to ask him to dinner and show him around Charleston."[15]

In the meantime, Foster received permission from the U.S. War Department to bring fifty Confederate officers to Charleston and put them on Morris Island under the fire of Confederate guns. Implementing retaliation properly required an exact and measured response. The problem was, as communication moved up the chain, minor changes of wording in the description of what Jones had done gave Union officials in the War Department a misimpression. Part of this was Jones's fault. In his first letter to Foster, he had said that the Union prisoners were "exposed day and night to the fire of your guns," when in reality they were in a part of the city that only occasionally received shells. Therefore, Halleck received dispatches from Foster that spoke of "exposure" and "under the enemy's fire." Accordingly, on June 21, he

Michael P. O'Connor house, prison of the fifty Union officers brought to Charleston as human shields in June 1864. (Library of Congress Prints and Photographs Division)

authorized Foster to treat fifty Confederate prisoners "in precisely the same manner as the enemy treat ours—that is to be placed in positions where they will be most exposed to the fire of the rebels." Foster could put the prisoners under fire in the field, in batteries, or in vessels. Halleck ordered strict precautions to keep the Confederate prisoners from escaping, including putting them in irons. The U.S. commissary general of prisoners sent Foster two major generals, three brigadier generals, fifteen colonels, thirteen lieutenant colonels, and seventeen majors from the military prison at Fort Delaware. They arrived in Charleston Harbor on June 29 in an army steamer transport. Rear Adm. John A. Dahlgren, in charge of the Union blockade, gave permission for the steamer to anchor under the guns of the frigate USS *Wabash*.[16]

The critical addition of the word "most" to the word "exposed" in Halleck's orders to Foster threatened the equivalency that was supposed to characterize retaliation. Foster wavered between taking his responsibility of "tit for tat" seriously and simply following Halleck's orders. When the rebel prisoners arrived, he told Halleck he would double check "the degree of exposure, the kind and amount of rations, the general comforts which are given our prisoners." Three days later, however, he told Halleck he would put the prisoners in "the most exposed position." Halleck's orders to secure the prisoners also created practical problems that undermined Foster's intentions to treat the prisoners in an equivalent manner. To be under fire, the Confederate prisoners had to go on Morris Island, which housed only Union regimental camps and fortified batteries. Foster planned to put the prisoners in strong jails near Fort Gregg, but he had to build them first. Workers constructed two small wooden houses with grated windows. The buildings looked like birdcages.[17]

Union officers and soldiers on Morris had different perspectives about the danger of the position and the retaliation itself. "They will have a hot place if the rebels fire as they have been doing," Lt. Robert Newell of the 54th Massachusetts wrote. "I am not quite sure that I believe in the Government's policy of retaliation. . . . It is rather a mean business, at any rate, though perhaps necessary." A naval surgeon thought, "They are somewhat exposed but their position is such that only a chance shot would do them harm." Esther Hill Hawks was a doctor who worked with Black troops on Morris. A lieutenant at Fort Gregg told her that he hoped the rebel prisoners would never come to the island. "So barbarous," he said. "Poor sniveling fool! how quick to be compassionate when rebels are to be endangered," she thought.[18]

Foster followed the prescriptions of the retaliation ritual before he acted. He had to get official information about the exact treatment of the Union officers in Charleston. He did two things on July 1: wrote a letter to Jones about the situation with the prisoners and launched a demonstration against Charleston and its railroad line to Savannah. This multipronged attack presented a greater danger to the city than any previous Federal effort. A force of 2,000 Union infantry under Schimmelfennig, including the men of the 54th Massachusetts, advanced to the south end of James Island with the support of two monitors and several gunboats. They captured a battery and commenced entrenching. But the heat defeated them; it was 110 degrees in the shade. The skirmishers of the 54th had to lie supine in the direct sun for hours, and the soldiers guarding the fieldwork were crowded together. Within a few hours, fifty men of the 54th were unconscious from heatstroke; six officers became delirious. Major Appleton's nose dripped blood. He vomited and passed out. At the regimental hospital back on Morris Island, Appleton was "crazy as a loon." "I saw all sorts of things," he said. A little green man, fifteen inches high, sat on the floor and stared at him morning and night for several days. "The nurse is careful not to step on him," Appleton said. He was never able to return to duty. A boat attack by 1,000 men on Fort Johnson, at the opposite end of James, failed the following evening when some of the boats ran aground and incompetent regimental commanders did not support the success of the initial landing party.[19]

Another prong of Foster's attack, however, nearly achieved a breakthrough. A Union brigade of three USCT regiments and one white regiment successfully landed on John's Island, located adjacent to and to the west of James. Since the Union possessed Morris to the east and Folly to the south, the Federals were finally in position to enfilade the Confederate defensive lines on James. General Jones recognized the peril and sent panicked telegrams for help. On July 7, the Union brigade attacked strongly fortified batteries and was repulsed. Confederate reinforcements from Georgia arrived on John's Island during the action, and two days later Confederate infantry attacked the Federals' defensive field fortifications and batteries. They were repulsed. Soldiers in the 26th USCT, with permission from their colonel, fought under the black flag on John's Island. They captured a wounded private from the 2nd South Carolina and bayoneted him to death. On July 10, Foster ordered his forces to withdraw.[20]

During the ten days of combat at various locations in the city's environs, a distracted Foster and Jones corresponded about the Yankee prisoners in Charleston, writing to each other amid sending orders to meet the rapidly unfolding disasters occurring on the field. Foster sent his messages from steamer transports moving him around the rivers and islands where the action took place. It was clear he had not read Jones's earlier messages carefully, if at all. In order to implement an equivalent retaliation, Foster asked Jones to specify the "degree" of exposure of the Federal prisoners. He asked whether they were in the part of the city "most, or the least exposed, or that exposed in a medium degree." He asked for a statement from the prisoners themselves about the kind and quantity of food they received, and the kind of bedding and blankets they had. Foster promised to treat the Confederate prisoners in the "exact manner."[21]

Even before he received this message, Jones realized that he had made a mistake to use prisoners as human shields. He had provoked a public debate within South Carolina over whether bringing the Federal officers to Charleston was "right" and "expedient." Jones hoped to salvage what was turning out to be a bad situation and turn it to the Confederates' advantage. "It may happen that bringing them here may lead to a near general exchange of prisoners," he suggested. Josiah Gorgas, head of the Confederate Ordnance Bureau, thought this would be a "good solution of an awkward move." Jones received permission from the Confederate War Department to offer Foster an exchange of the officer prisoners.[22]

Jones paved the way for this new plan with the cooperation of the five Union brigadier generals who were enjoying their luxurious life in the O'Connor house. He allowed them to write two letters to Foster. The first asked Foster to provide the fifty Confederate officers in the harbor "every kindness and courtesy that you can extend them." Seymour wrote that he was "pleasantly and comfortably" situated, received "every privilege," and was not "unnecessarily exposed to fire." The second letter asked Foster to contact authorities in Washington to request an exchange for the Federal prisoners held in Georgia. The 1,500 officers at Camp Oglethorpe in Macon and the 33,000 enlisted men at Camp Sumter were suffering and dying. Jones attached a personal note to Foster expressing his willingness to exchange the officers in Charleston and to negotiate an agreement to exchange all the prisoners "languishing in confinement." Foster replied on July 4 that he reciprocated the desire to exchange the prisoners but refused to negotiate until the Union officers were withdrawn from exposure to fire. "Such a course on my part would be an implied admission that those officers are unduly exposed and treated with unnecessary rigor," Jones responded, "which they have themselves assured you . . . is not the case."[23]

The introduction of exchange into the retaliation negotiations, and the circumstances of the ten-day military operations, which temporarily took Union troops away from Morris Island, meant that the fifty Confederate prisoners remained confined in a transport steamer for four weeks. Although they were not under fire, Foster was not accurate when he assured Halleck, after receiving the message from Seymour, that the Confederates were as comfortable as the Union officers in Charleston. They were on a small boat and lived most of the time in a poorly ventilated room measuring about 25 × 45 feet. There were no chairs. The heat was intense, yet no more than twenty-five men could go on deck at a time. While on deck, the prisoners enjoyed time fishing for sharks with the Union sailors. But the meat they received with their rations was often decayed, and because the drinking water was distilled from salt water, it was, as one prisoner reported, "so warm or brackish that it would have answered better for an emetic than to allay thirst." Initially, some of their guards treated them with brutality, but when Capt. Lafayette McWilliams of the 157th New York took command, he treated them well and did his best to alleviate their condition. This would be the first but not the last time that an officer of the 157th New York would intervene on behalf of Confederate prisoners.[24]

Jones and Foster ultimately received permission from their respective governments to make a special exchange of their high-ranking prisoners.[25] The exchange extracted Jones and Foster from a situation that had gone off the rails from the start. Jones had not used the proper format of the ritual in his initial correspondence, announced that he had put prisoners under fire when he had not, and opened himself to internal criticism that he had violated the laws of war. Union authorities were already on record, in retaliation correspondence between Gillmore and Beauregard eleven months before, with their absolute conviction that the bombardment of Charleston was fully justified under the laws of war. Foster had tried to mete out an exact response, but combat distractions and the change in the conversation from retaliation to exchange caused him to neglect the prisoners he had brought to Charleston. Once his understanding of the circumstances of the Union prisoners in Charleston changed, he could not put the Confederate prisoners in the empty buildings on Morris Island, but rather than send them to Hilton Head, where he could have guarded and housed them in comfort, he left them in the uncomfortable conditions on the ship.

The exchange took place on the morning of August 3 in Charleston Harbor and revealed to Federal officials and the Northern public the current situation of the prisoners from the 54th Massachusetts captured on James Island and Fort Wagner the year before. The Federal blockading ships flew their flags and fired a salute, bands played, and the soldiers on Morris Island cheered as Foster's transport *Cosmopolitan* delivered the rebel officers and received their Yankee counterparts. While Seymour and the other brigadier generals celebrated, one of the exchanged Union field officers handed Foster a letter from forty soldiers of the 54th with a list of their names attached. Jones had confined one of the lower-ranking Yankee officers in the Charleston Jail yard, and one of the Black prisoners held there managed to smuggle him a note. "Sir: I do, in behalf of my fellow prisoners earnestly hope and pray that this may be the means, through you, Sir, of procuring our release," it read. "The privations of the white soldiers are nothing in comparison to ours, in our destitute condition, being as it were without friends, and in the enemy's hands, with an almost utter hopelessness of being released, and not having heard from our families or friends since we were captured." After delivering the original to Foster, the officer sent a copy to the *New York Tribune*. The paper published the note on August 10 and asked Massachusetts

Sojourner Truth with a photograph of grandson James Caldwell, 54th Massachusetts. Caldwell, a blacksmith from Battle Creek, Michigan, was captured on July 16, 1863, on Sol Legare Island. His name was on the list of prisoners from the 54th held in the Charleston Jail yard, published in the *New York Tribune* on August 10, 1864. The publicity forced the Confederate War Department to admit its change of policy toward freeborn Black soldiers. Caldwell was transferred to Florence Military Prison on December 8, 1864, and was exchanged in March 1865. (Library of Congress Prints and Photographs Division)

journalists to circulate widely the list of names, which included two soldiers from the 55th Massachusetts and the Black sailors from the *Isaac Smith*. A notable name was blacksmith James Caldwell, from Battle Creek, Michigan, the grandson of Sojourner Truth. "It is at any rate a relief to be assured that this number have been held as prisoners-of-war, and not summarily shot or sold into slavery," said the accompanying editorial.[26]

Technically, these soldiers of the 54th were not yet military prisoners of war, unlike their comrades captured at the Battle of Olustee, who were in the Confederate military prison at Andersonville. South Carolina governor Milledge Bonham still held these 1863 captives as state prisoners as he sought a way to put them on trial against the wishes of the Confederate War Department. He confined them in cells. They could go out into the yard during the day, but their clothing was in tatters, and prison officials fed them one small loaf of corn bread per day. They suffered from aggravated cases of scurvy. A few men received additional food for doing the dirty work around the prison. In the evening they sang mournful songs they had composed that expressed their suffering. Sgt. Robert Johnson of the 55th Massachusetts wrote a parody on the popular song "This Cruel War":[27]

When I enlisted in the army,
Then I thought 't was grand
Marching through the streets of Boston
Behind a regimental band.
When at Wagner, I was captured
Then my courage failed;
Now I'm dirty, hungry, naked,
Here in Charleston Jail.
Weeping, sad and lonely,
Oh! how bad I feel!
Down in Charleston, South Carolina,
Praying for a good, square meal.
We are longing, watching, praying,
But will not repine
Till Jeff Davis does release us,
And send us in our lines.
Then with words of kind affection
How they'll greet us there!
Wondering how we could live so long
Upon the dodger fare.

Then we will laugh, long and loudly.
Oh, how glad we'll feel
When we arrive on Morris Island
And eat a good, square meal!

Six prisoners of the 54th captured at Wagner were not in the Charleston Jail yard. Rather, they served as nurses at a hospital in Rikersville, four miles from the city, and cared for fifty sick and wounded Federal officers. Abraham Lincoln's brother-in-law Dr. George Rogers Clark Todd was the surgeon in charge. At first, he made sure the officer prisoners had clean and comfortable cots arranged in a spacious room and fed them well. Confederate prison authorities also sent enlisted men, Black and white, to this hospital. "They by this I suppose consider that they are putting into practice our ideas of negro equality," a captain from the 7th Pennsylvania Cavalry remarked. Federal soldiers reported that Todd, who had a long history of drunken rages, physically abused prisoners and whipped Black soldiers doing menial duties at the hospital.[28]

The new surge of publicity regarding the prisoners of the 54th forced the Confederate War Department to be explicit about its change in policy toward free Black Federal prisoners. Important voices from Georgia, where the 34,500 Federal prisoners in Macon and Andersonville were "eating up our subsistence," informed Secretary of War Seddon that people did not "object to the exchange of negro prisoners (not slaves)" if it meant a resumption of the cartel. Confederate commanders continually took Black prisoners who claimed to be free and wrote Seddon for instructions. "Shall any difference be made between them and white prisoners, and shall they be separated from whites in prison quarters or in hospitals?" one letter inquired. Seddon did his best to put off a definitive statement, but Bonham forced his hand. The governor wrote that he wanted a final decision about the status of the Black prisoners in Charleston. On August 31, Seddon admitted the congressional resolutions were defunct because of the "embarrassments attending this question and the serious consequences which might ensue from the rigid enforcement of the act." He instructed state governors to consider free Blacks captured in Federal uniform as prisoners of war and treat them similarly to white captives "except in some trivial particulars indicative of inferior consideration."[29]

Under intense scrutiny at two different times—the immediate aftermath of Fort Wagner and the arrival of Union officers in Charleston—and under the pressure of potential retaliation secured with hostages, the Confederate War Department never implemented the resolutions of the Confederate Congress, which required state trials for former slaves and freeborn Black men captured in Federal uniform. Neither did Seddon ever establish the proposed military courts to try white officers. He ultimately ordered his subordinates to put free Black prisoners into the Confederate prison system.[30]

The retaliation ritual swerved the Confederacy from the path leading to public mass executions and inhibited the development of a uniform practice. It inaugurated the War Department's covert preference, as Seddon informed one of his generals, "never to be inconvenienced with such prisoners." In subsequent months, Confederate soldiers executed Black soldiers and their white officers on several battlefields when they tried to surrender. Confederate military authorities re-enslaved hundreds of Black soldiers and used them for military labor but sent freeborn Black men to military prisons with white Union soldiers.[31]

Both the Union and the Confederacy now recognized the freeborn Black men of the 54th as legitimate combatants, a tacit acknowledgment that they were civilized men with a place in civilized society. Yet despite issuing retaliation orders to make this claim, the U.S. government had been slow to recognize Black men as soldiers and citizens with equal rights to their white comrades in arms. Although the men of the 54th had enlisted as soldiers in the volunteer Union army, the War Department tried to pay them as laborers. The soldiers of the 54th, owed thirteen dollars a month according to their muster contracts, refused to receive the seven dollars a month the paymasters offered them instead. They served and bled for months without pay and rejected an offer from Governor John Andrew for the state of Massachusetts to make up the difference. They wanted the U.S. government to acknowledge their honorable manhood and their standing as civilized soldiers. Before his imprisonment and death at Andersonville, Corp. James Gooding had written Abraham Lincoln. "You caution the Rebel Chieftain, that the United States knows no distinction in her Soldiers. She insists on having all her Soldiers of whatever creed or Color, to be treated according to the usages of War," he said. "Now if the United States exacts uniformity of treatment of her Soldiers from the Insurgents, would it not be well and consistent to set the example herself by paying all her *Soldiers* alike?"[32]

The protest of the 54th had been a hard road for the enlisted men, especially those with suffering families at home. "If the nation persists in such an unjust course growing from slavery and sympathy with slavery the stripes in the flag should be black as symbolical of the stains upon its once fair name," Appleton wrote. The officers sympathized with the men's plight and advocated for them but had to maintain hierarchy and discipline. In May, some men from Company A had refused to go on guard duty, and soldiers from other companies crowded around them with their muskets. Officers beat the crowd back with the butts of their pistols, while Col. Edward Hallowell aimed his weapon at each of the men detailed for guard. "Do you refuse to go on guard? One, two . . . " "No, sir," was the response from each. In a separate incident, Lieutenant Newell shot and wounded a private who refused to fall in for an expedition to capture a blockhouse. This restored obedience, but tension in the regiment simmered over the summer. Hallowell traveled to Washington with a demand that the government pay the regiment as soldiers or muster it out of the service, but Secretary of War Edwin Stanton refused to see him and rebuked Foster for allowing him to come.[33]

The same month that the Confederacy officially recognized the freemen of the 54th as soldiers, so did the United States. On August 1, the War Department issued Circular 60, which granted Black men the pay of soldiers dating from January 1, 1864. Men who swore an oath that they were free before April 19, 1861, would receive equal pay from the date of their enlistment. Appleton and other officers decried the "unjust compromise" that denigrated men who had been born slaves. Colonel Hallowell wrote a cleverly worded oath for his men: "You do solemnly swear that you owed no man unrequited labor on or before the 19th day of April, 1861. So help you God." Some slave-born men in the 54th "took the oath as freemen, by God's higher law," Capt. Luis F. Emilio wrote in the regiment's official history. "That they were compelled to take this or any oath at the last was an insult crowning the injury." Hallowell made the first muster for pay on August 31, and a month later, paymasters distributed $170,000 to the soldiers of the 54th. Some individuals received over $200. The celebration lasted for days. "The fiddle and other music long neglected enlivens the tents day and night. Songs burst out everywhere; dancing is incessant; boisterous shouts are heard, mimicry, burlesque, and carnival," an officer wrote. "Here a crowd and preacher; there a crowd and two boxers; yonder, feasting and jubilee."[34]

Being recognized as a legitimate combatant in August 1864 had a dark side; it meant a military prison if captured. Officers and soldiers who suffered that fate experienced a personal crisis of civilization. Union and Confederate prisoners, especially those chosen as the subjects of retaliation, believed that captivity decivilized them. Prison reduced men to a savage state and turned some of them into animals. Most Americans in the mid-nineteenth century believed in a strict line that divided superior humans from lower animals. Humans uniquely possessed eternal souls, reason, language, and religion. It was the task of a refined gentleman living in civilization to separate himself from the brutish beasts who lived in the untamed natural world. He subdued instinctual passions and practiced physical modesty. He was clean, because as John Stuart Mill had written, dirtiness, "more than anything else, renders man bestial." There was even a difference between "civilized tasting" and "animalistic feeding." American elites used food to mark social class. In the United States, slaves ate unbolted (unsifted) cornmeal, while elites ate bread baked with refined white flour.[35]

Prison life destroyed the boundary between the human and the animal. "This is the roughest pen that ever civilized man was put in," a prisoner at Andersonville wrote. "Here all is bestial, just like a hog pen, & hogs we must be, for like hogs we live, like hogs we act." This understanding of captivity shaped the experience of the next round of Union and Confederate officers put under fire. During negotiations for the exchange of the original fifty, Confederate prison officials decided to send an additional 600 Union officers to Charleston from Camp Oglethorpe, where most of the 1,500 prisoners lived outside without shelter and ate unbolted cornmeal with their fingers like slaves. Lice, a variety of vermin associated with poverty and inferiority, swarmed over the bodies of the captives. Because every prisoner had them, the Federal officers were past the shame they initially felt. It was now a mark of gentlemanly cleanness to strip naked each day and go hunting for "greybacks." The men who had become beasts, though, did not even bother to fight the lice anymore. It was harder every day for the prisoners to subdue their animal instincts. "The want of all authority and discipline is daily becoming apparent," an elite Federal from Maine recorded in his diary. "Angry disputes and even fisticuffs are getting quite common. It is indeed degrading for two officers to settle their troubles by pounding each other, yet it cannot be denied by the gravest philosophers that it is a more natural than refined method of proceeding. Then, too, there is a sort of demoralizing influence in this manner of life that makes a man feel more like fighting than doing anything more useful or dignified." Officers with money and self-discipline did everything they could to preserve the boundary: they purchased food from outside the prison, obtained books, and studied foreign languages.[36]

Conditions for Federal officers deteriorated when they arrived in Charleston. General Jones was horrified when the Confederate War Department notified him that an additional 600 Union officers were on the way to the city. He protested that he did not have guards for more prisoners and that their arrival would complicate his negotiations with General Foster. Prison officials had no viable alternatives, though, so the prisoners arrived on July

29. Jones put them in the Charleston Jail yard, which was about an acre of ground enclosed by a twenty-foot-high wall. The sound of cannon booming and shells screaming overhead from the Union bombardment of the city was a constant. Shells regularly hit the ground near the yard—one officer counted thirty in a single day. Although some of the Federals had no shelter to protect them from the sun during the day and thunderstorms at night, officials issued tents to a number of them. The rations included fresh meat—the first in three months for some of the prisoners—and those with money purchased watermelon, tomatoes, and potatoes. "We are falling in love with the Charleston officials," one officer wrote his wife on August 2. "They use us very kindly thus far—much more so than anywhere else." Then the fifty exchanged Confederate officers who had been on the U.S. Army steamer for four weeks arrived in the city and told what had happened to them. On August 6, prison officials notified the Union officers in the jail yard that they were now the objects of retaliation for Foster's mistreatment of the Confederate prisoners. Rations changed from fresh meat to lard and wormy rice.[37]

Federal officers in the Charleston Jail yard lived outside of civilization for the next few weeks. Inside their "pen," the prisoners from the 54th searched for scraps of food. "They 'root' around and eat just such articles as a hog in a farmer's yard," a sympathetic officer observed. "They are certainly the most patriotic sufferers I have yet seen in the war." At dusk, the murderers, thieves, and prostitutes confined in the jail itself went wild. "The criminals shouted like hungry beasts in a zoo, pounded with sticks on the floor or on the bars of the windows, and rattled the bolts and bars of the doors—violently," a Federal prisoner wrote. One "screech[ed] like an animal" for half an hour each evening. The yard was filthy with refuse and vermin. "It was the most revolting place that civilized humanity ever occupied and lived," was the consensus. Outside the "pen" was the Burnt District, a deserted section of the city destroyed during an 1861 fire. Occasionally some Black people camped there. The only glimpse of human elevation above the animal was the singing of the prisoners of the 54th. "No race so delicately sensitive to the emotional can be essentially coarse and barbarous," a Federal from New York thought.[38]

There is no record that Jones notified Foster of this retaliation. Foster, in the meantime, conducted a correspondence with his superiors that revealed motives and subtext to his correspondence with Jones that had nothing to do with retaliation for putting prisoners under fire. He informed Halleck that an additional 600 Union officers were in Charleston and accurately identified the reasons: Charleston was the only secure place in the region to hold prisoners of war, and Confederate officials thought their presence would induce Foster to make further exchanges. Foster recognized that Confederate authorities did not bring the 600 to Charleston with the intention of putting them under fire.[39] Foster also thought he recognized an opportunity. He did not agree with the Lincoln administration's policy of halting general prisoner exchanges until the Confederacy agreed to recognize all Black soldiers as prisoners of war. As the commander of the Department of the South, he was the first to receive news about the condition of Union prisoners in Andersonville. Foster had an underlying agenda: he wanted to work out an exchange of all the Union prisoners whom the Confederacy moved into South Carolina. Failing that, he wanted his government to take substantive action to alleviate the suffering of the Union soldiers in Andersonville.

Foster asked permission to arrange the exchange of the Andersonville prisoners. He told Halleck that he would notify Jones that no more exchanges would be made in Charleston Harbor, with a hint that his government might make exchanges at the Savannah River. "The effect of this is to induce them to remove our officers from Charleston to Savannah, so that our fire may be continued on the city without the risk of hurting our friends," he said. "I have, however, taken pains to ascertain where our prisoners are confined so as to direct the fire to the other parts." Halleck replied four days later that Secretary of War Stanton was sending Foster 600 rebel officers to be exposed to fire and "treated in the same manner" as the 600 Union officers were treated in Charleston. "No exchanges will be made without special instructions from the War Department," he cautioned.[40]

Halleck's instruction to treat the 600 Confederate prisoners "in the same manner" indicated a subtle shift in the goals of the War Department for the retaliation in Charleston. This would not just be about putting prisoners under fire; it would be about the suffering and sickness of Union prisoners throughout the Confederacy. The Lincoln administration was under immense pressure from members of Congress, from newspapers, and from the public to renew the prisoner exchange. Calls to implement retaliation against Confederate prisoners held in Northern prisons also came from every direction. In May, Secretary of War Stanton had issued orders to reduce the rations of all Confederate prisoners by 20 percent, which fell short of his goal of feeding them precisely the same rations that Union prisoners in the Confederacy received.[41]

The exchange of the fifty Union officers increased the pressure on the administration to retaliate because two of the five generals wrote to the War Department with accounts of the terrible suffering of Union prisoners in Georgia. Truman Seymour believed that Southern soldiers could live on cornmeal, but Northern men, "except in an almshouse," were never "reduced to the common rule of the diet of the Southern race." His letter liberally employed the animal metaphor. "At Andersonville the scene would disgust a race of cannibal barbarians," he said. "Scores die daily from sheer neglect, and with as little care; less than a rotten sheep would meet at the hands of a brutal owner." Seymour urged retaliation against all Confederate prisoners in Union hands. "Why should not the rebel prisoners be treated exactly like our own?" he asked. "My firm conviction is that the Southern authorities believe we do not dare to give like treatment to their captured. It would perhaps disgrace us . . . [but] the South can be compelled to treat [prisoners] well. Give Confederate prisoners the same measure of humanity that they mete out to us and there will soon be no dread or apprehension respecting the prisoners' life." Seymour suggested that Federal officers recently returned from Southern prisons should form a commission to draw up the rules for retaliation based upon their recent experience. Maj. Gen. Daniel Sickles wrote Lincoln with an alternative proposition. He believed retaliation would not work because the Confederate government could not adequately supply food, clothes, or medicine to its own troops. Foster should receive authorization to negotiate with Jones an arrangement for each side to provide supplies for its prisoners held by the other. Commissioner for Exchange Ethan Allen Hitchcock endorsed on this letter that he had evidence Confederate guards in Richmond stole the supplies sent for Union prisoners a few months before. "The only sure remedy for the abominations practiced in the South by the enemy is to defeat his armies," he concluded in the phrase that had become his mantra.[42]

Foster wanted to exchange prisoners; Stanton wanted to retaliate. Both used the arrival of the 600 Union prisoners in Charleston to pursue contradictory goals related to the broader question of prisoner exchange and treatment. On August 15, Foster initiated a second retaliation ritual regarding prisoners under the fire of guns, but his real purpose was to work with Jones to arrange an exchange. He threatened to put 600 Confederate prisoners under fire unless Jones removed the Union officers, and he requested information from Jones as to the number and rank of the prisoners. On August 20, Jones replied that the 600 prisoners were in Charleston merely because it was a convenient location. The United States was the combatant that treated prisoners cruelly, he asserted, because it denied its soldiers a fair and honorable exchange. Jones then offered to exchange every prisoner of war in his department—which included Andersonville—for an equal number of Confederate prisoners. This was exactly what Foster expected and desired.[43]

But Foster had completely misread the commitment of the decision makers in the Lincoln administration to the policy of holding Confederate prisoners of war. On August 18, Union general-in-chief Ulysses S. Grant had nixed all ideas of a general exchange on military grounds. He echoed the position that Hitchcock had been circulating in the War Department for over a year and had communicated to him back in April. "If we commence a system of exchange which liberates all prisoners taken, we will have to fight until the whole South is exterminated," Grant explained. "If we hold those caught they amount to no more than dead men." Grant believed that resuming exchanges could lead to Union major general William T. Sherman's defeat in operations around Atlanta and compromise his own campaign in Virginia. "Please inform Foster that in no circumstances will he be authorized to make exchange of prisoners of war," Grant wrote Stanton. "Exchanges simply reinforce the enemy at once."[44]

Foster was now stuck, because of his public letter to Jones, implementing a retaliation he knew was false. On August 25, the U.S. steamer *Crescent* arrived in Port Royal bearing 600 Confederate officers who had been prisoners at Fort Delaware. Foster had to put them on Morris Island under fire, but he faced a serious security issue because of the dearth of troops in his department. Fifty men were easy to guard, but 600 men posed a threat to forts and batteries that were not secure against assault. In addition, Jones might send troops to rescue such a large number. Foster ordered his subordinates to build a secure stockade, and in the meantime, as happened before, the 600 Confederate officers remained on the cramped confines of a small ship. Jones, for his part, once he received word from Foster that there would be no exchange, repeatedly begged his government to remove the 600 Union officers from Charleston. Instead, he received notice on September 5 that 600 more officers and thousands of privates were on their way from the prisons in Georgia. Sherman had captured Atlanta, and it was no longer safe to keep Union prisoners in the state.[45]

The 600 Confederate officers landed on Morris Island on September 7 and left civilization behind. In their view, their captors were barbarians, and they lived like animals. The most traumatic part of their experience, they believed, was being under the guard of the Black soldiers of the 54th Massachusetts and 21st USCT. These troops marched them down the beach, over the buried body of Robert Gould Shaw, and into the stockade between Fort Strong (formerly Fort Wagner) and Fort Gregg. It reminded one prisoner of the "rude cor[r]al such as we used to brand our cattle." Sixteen Black sentinels stood on platforms ten feet above the ground and watched the Confederates inside the enclosure. The prisoners lived in A-tents arranged into streets. A Black sergeant was in charge of each street; he called the roll three times a day, distributed the rations, and enforced the rules. Prisoners could not have lights burning at night, go out in the streets after dark (except to visit the barrels set up as toilets), or congregate in groups of more than ten. The sergeants had authority to shoot Confederate prisoners who disobeyed their orders, and on at least two occasions they did so. A calcium light on the parapet of Wagner shone into the camp at night so the sentinels could observe the prisoners. "They appear to be very peaceful and quiet," 1st Sgt. Burrill Smith, a Boston laborer, wrote of his charges. "Being they are officers they are of the first-class traitors."[46]

Honor required the Confederate officers to act with self-controlled coolness rather than reveal the internal humiliation they felt. "At the stockade the captives gave no trouble, and readily conformed to the rules," Captain Emilio wrote. "They have had the good sense not to insult their guards," Charles E. Briggs, the surgeon of the 54th said. "Our men sustain their character." A Confederate major who fought at Wagner on July 18, 1863, even shared reminiscences with officers of the 54th and confirmed particulars about Robert Gould Shaw's burial. Underneath the polite demeanor, however, the Confederates seethed with rage. Some Federals perceived this. "It cuts them very much to be ordered around by those they have been used to consider the same as Cattle," a naval officer who visited the stockade observed. Confederate prisoners drew from the vocabulary of civilization to describe their captors. "The privates were *niggers* of the deepest dye, and betrayed all the ignorance, villainy, and cruelty peculiar to barbarians," one later wrote. "Black, uncouth, and barbarous as they were, we soon found they were far preferable to the white officers who commanded them," another said. "If physiognomy be an index of character, then certainly those officers were villainous."[47]

Confederate prisoners used the symbolism of the human/animal divide to describe what feeding—they could not call it eating—was like inside the stockade. Foster had obtained accurate information about the official ration and other details of the living condition of the Union officers in the Charleston Jail yard, many of whom did not have tents or blankets. He ordered an equivalent ration and thus informed Jones: the prisoners would get half a pound of salt meat, one-fifth of a pint of rice, half a pound of hard bread, one-fifth of a pint of beans, and some salt or vinegar. This was half of the ration issued to U.S. soldiers stationed on Morris Island, but the food itself was the same furnished to the soldiers of the 54th. The quality was often poor—

moldy meat and wormy bread. Prisoners with money could purchase molasses and cake from the sutler who came inside the stockade once a week. The Confederate officers felt intense hunger pangs that disrupted their sleep, and they sickened because of the scanty diet. They were treated, and acted, like animals. The sergeants gave them rations "as if throwing them to the dogs." "Many officers here forget their dignity and position and when edibles are brought it frequently looks as if hogs were running pell mell over each other for corn," prisoner James B. McCreary told his diary. Some prisoners "rooted deep in the sand in search of grass nuts." When the Union medical director for Morris Island, Surgeon John Milton Hawks, visited the stockade and saw the condition of the prisoners, he successfully petitioned Foster to add tea and soft bread to the diet of the sickest men. "The officers [of the 54th] do not find it agreeable to guard scantily fed men, the health of many of whom is giving way under their diets," Surgeon Briggs said. "I hope we shall not long be obliged to resort to this retaliation."[48]

Once again, as was the case in July with the fifty officers from each side, there was no equivalency between the position of the Union officers in Charleston and that of the Confederate officers on Morris, as proper retaliation required. This time, some of the disparities were to the Confederates' advantage; some were to the Union. There were fewer Confederate officers under fire than Union officers, who now numbered 1,500 and were in the Charleston Jail yard and the workhouse/insane asylum. On the other hand, 300 of these Union officers gave their parole not to escape and moved to comfortable quarters in the Roper Hospital (a smaller but unknown number were paroled to the Marine Hospital). Here the prisoners entered civilization again and lived like gentlemen. They slept on beds in separate rooms, lounged on verandas, walked the gardens without Confederate guards to annoy them, purchased food and luxury items from the peddlers who congregated outside the gate, read literature at night under the light of gas lamps, and enjoyed the ministrations of the Sisters of Mercy, who visited with books, grapes, and peaches.[49]

What was supposed to matter most was the degree of danger to the prisoners from the shells that fell around their prisons. The officers on both sides faced equal danger—which was very little. Weapons technology and the skill of artillerists ensured precision in firing shells. Both sides aimed their fire so as not to hit their own men. The sound and fury was dramatic. Shells passed overheard and landed nearby frequently. Fragments occasionally fell into the areas where prisoners were and caused narrow escapes but killed no one. Union lieutenant Morris C. Foot was the only injury. He suffered a slight

"Quarters of the Union Officers Exposed to Federal Fire in Charleston, Sketched by One of the Officers." This sketch reflects the common depiction of Charleston as a wasteland: depopulated and bleak, with grass growing in the street. (*Harper's Weekly: A Journal of Civilization*, August 27, 1864, 549)

wound when a stray shell crashed through the roof of the east wing of Roper Hospital while he was eating dinner and grazed his elbow. The prisoners quickly learned they had nothing to fear and enjoyed watching the fireworks display in the sky at night and listening to the scream of the projectiles. "It was a gratifying sound," one Union officer recalled. "It seemed like hearing from a Christian, civilized land to listen to the songs of those honest, patriotic shells. . . . Each one screamed in the ears of every rebel '*There's no rest for the wicked.*'" A Confederate officer wrote, "One of our greatest pleasures was to watch the shells at night, darting through the air like shooting stars, and in predicting how near to us they would explode."[50]

By the beginning of October, Jones and Foster were in a standoff that neither wanted and that could accomplish no adjustment of the behavior of either side. Events that month in Virginia, however, indicated to the U.S. War Department for the first time that Confederate authorities had adjusted their policy regarding freeborn Black soldiers and the white officers of Black troops. On October 9, Confederates paroled and released to the Union exchange agent three lieutenants captured in command of Black troops. "These are the first deliveries of this class of prisoners," the agent wrote General Hitchcock. Several days later, during an exchange of naval prisoners,

Confederates delivered Orin H. Brown, William H. Johnson, William Wilson (the New Yorkers from the captured *Isaac Smith*) and two other Black sailors from the Charleston Jail yard.[51]

Lee twice put in writing to Grant the new Confederate policy. On October 3, he proposed to exchange prisoners from the armies operating in Virginia. "I intend to include all captured soldiers of the United States of whatever nation and color under my control," he said. "Deserters from our service and negroes belonging to our citizens are not considered subjects of exchange and were not included in my proposition." Grant rejected the offer. "The Government is bound to secure to all persons received into her armies the rights due to soldiers," he said. Two weeks later, during a retaliation correspondence resulting from Confederates using Black prisoners to labor on fortifications around Richmond, Lee admitted that if "colored soldiers not slaves" were included in the work party, it was a "mistake" made without the sanction of the Confederate War Department and would be "corrected."[52]

Meanwhile, it became untenable for Confederate authorities to keep thousands of prisoners in Charleston. In addition to the 1,500 Federal officers, there were 5,000 Federal privates from Andersonville in the Charleston race course at the fairgrounds. Jones did not have space or troops to guard the prisoners sent him from Georgia. Federals fired into Charleston every fifteen minutes, and the shells reached the upper parts of the city. To make matters worse, a yellow fever epidemic erupted in the city. The Confederate officer in charge of Roper Hospital and his adjutant died from the disease. "Great fright every sick man thinks he has it," one of the prisoners confined in Roper noted in his diary. Confederate prison authorities sent the Federal officers to Columbia on October 5. The prisoners marched down King Street to the train station. "The streets are grown up to grass and weeds," one of them noted with satisfaction. "Charleston is reaping her reward for secession."[53]

The Federal enlisted men went to Florence. Thirty-nine prisoners from the 54th joined their white counterparts there after Governor Bonham finally turned them over to Confederate military authorities on December 8. The transfer from the Charleston Jail yard to Florence acknowledged their status as legitimate combatants, but conditions in the military prison were not an improvement. It was a twenty-three-acre stockade with no shelter for its 12,362 inmates. Six of the acres were uninhabitable swamp. Union prisoners who had taken an oath of allegiance to the Confederacy, nicknamed "Galvanized Yankees" by other prisoners in the Department of the South, guarded the men of the 54th on the trains from Charleston to Florence and stole their blankets. The commandant at Florence disarmed the Galvanized Yankees and put them in the stockade. "Then the fun began, as the Galvanized Yanks had Confederate uniforms on, they were easily spotted," prisoner Charlie Mosher recorded in his diary. "The darks had to fight to recover their stuff. I saw one 'dark' strike one of them such a blow that the fellow changed ends in a twinkling. It is needless to say that the 'darks' gained the day as well as their goods." Twelve of the 54th prisoners died in the Florence stockade, including midwesterners Henry Worthington and William Henry Harrison, two of the defendants in Bonham's September 1863 state trial. The mortality rate in three months at Florence was four times greater than the mortality rate the prisoners of the 54th had sustained in their seventeen months in the Charleston Jail yard.[54]

Foster received official notice that the Federal prisoners were no longer in Charleston from the new Confederate commander for the Department of South Carolina, Georgia, and Florida, Lt. Gen. William J. Hardee (Jones was demoted to command of a subdistrict). The Georgia-born 1838 West Point graduate had written the U.S. Army's 1855 infantry tactics manual for commissioned officers and had served as a division and corps commander in Confederate armies in Arkansas, Tennessee, and Georgia. He was a warm friend of Jefferson Davis and did not place the strategic importance on Charleston that its residents did. "The people of Charleston, though in many respects to be admired, are so entirely wrapped up in their own State and City as to be unmindful of the wants of other portions of the country," he wrote the Confederate president. "To them Charleston is the Confederacy, and to save Charleston they are willing that Lee should give up Richmond, or any other section of the Confederacy so that their selfish ambition might be gratified." After Foster heard from Hardee, he removed the 600 Confederate officers from the stockade on Morris Island. A battalion of the 54th escorted them to the pier and turned them over to their new guardians, the 157th New York. Transports took them to their new prison, Fort Pulaski, Georgia, situated on the mouth of the Savannah River, on October 22. Foster moved 200 from there to the prison barracks on Hilton Head a month later.[55]

The War Department subjected these 600 Confederate officers to a ration retaliation that has completely escaped the notice of academic Civil War historians, who believe that the United States never implemented a tit-for-tat retaliation on the issue of feeding prisoners. When Foster did not get the exchange of prisoners that he hoped for, he turned to his second plan, a retaliation designed to address the physical suffering of Union prisoners in South Carolina from the poor rations they received. He had been appalled to hear of the animal condition of the Federal prisoners passing through the streets of Charleston. "All tenderness for each other seemed to be blunted by the brutalizing effect of starvation and misery," he told Halleck. "The strong would crowd out the weak in the struggle for food."[56] This time, Foster's views aligned with that of his superiors. Halleck and Stanton wanted to move beyond the ration reduction that was already in place. Although they had not been successful in convincing either Hitchcock or Lincoln's cabinet to agree, affairs in the Department of the South offered an opportunity to apply this retaliation on a small scale in the region where Union prisoners received the worst rations.

The decision to deliberately malnourish prisoners of war reflected Halleck and Foster's belief that the Civil War was a crisis for American civilization. Halleck thought that Confederate treatment of its prisoners was the most savage aspect of the war. As the army's published expert on the customs of war, however, he also thought that legal retaliation imposed an uncrossable line: a civilized combatant could not commit a savage act under any circumstances. If the United States gave its prisoners rations that could not sustain life, it was a barbaric act. Could the United States use retaliation to protect its soldiers in Confederate prisons and preserve its reputation among civilized nations? Halleck thought it was possible. He considered the honor of the United States—"the verdict of history"—when he recommended on October 16 that the rations issued to rebel prisoners "be made nearly as possible the same" as that issued to Union prisoners. Confederate prisoners could perform labor if they wanted to receive additional food. "Rebel authorities say they are unable to furnish their soldiers or our prisoners with the same ration we do, but have a bill of fare which they pretend to supply prisoners, poor and scanty it is true, but sufficient to support life and to prevent any serious sufferings from hunger," he said. "Let us give this same fare to their officers and men in our hands. No one can complain of this. The rebels do not follow their pretended bill of fare and often reduce it to cause starvation and death, but we as a civilized and Christian people cannot do this." The United States had a duty "to humanity, to history, and to the world," he claimed, to enforce the laws of war that required the Confederacy to supply its prisoners with adequate food.[57]

Foster went beyond the retaliation that Halleck recommended and crossed the line his superior drew. He decided to give the 600 Confederate officers in his hands the same rations that Union prisoners in South Carolina actually received. "Any measure you may in future exercise toward the Union prisoners in your power, whether of severity or leniency," Foster wrote Hardee on October 17, "will be reciprocated by me and a corresponding change of treatment extended to the Confederate prisoners in my power." He bypassed the prescriptions of the retaliation ritual in this communication. It was general and vague. Foster did not accuse Hardee of violating a particular custom of war, did not give a statement of the ration that he believed Confederates issued, and did not give Hardee an opportunity to explain.[58]

The Federal prisoners in Columbia knew that Foster intended to protect them. On November 12, thirty-nine Union officers sent Hardee a petition about the terrible conditions they endured in an open field without shelter and with no meat in their rations. "Our government has already found it necessary to retaliate, in behalf of union prisoners of war, by reducing the rations allowed to your fellow citizens in northern prisons," it read. "We deprecate the necessity of inflicting additional retaliation by turning . . . Southern officers out of their prison shelters, & subjecting them to treatment as nearly as possible identical with that which we receive." The petitioners listed the "torments" of their situation in Columbia. The Confederate colonel commanding the camp endorsed the petition. "The complaints within are but too well founded," he wrote. Unless Hardee acted to remedy the problems, it was "in vain to expect our gallant officers who are prisoners, will be fed & warmed & clothed." Confederate officers in charge of inspecting prisons in South Carolina likewise worried about retaliation. "The shocking condition of these poor wretches," one wrote, "is calculated to bring reproach upon our government. . . . Policy and a regard for our own poor fellows in the hands of the Yankees would suggest such prisoner treatment to those already in our power as we would have them show to ours." Hardee took action to improve the ration, but in the meantime, dozens of Union officers escaped from Columbia and reported conditions there to Foster.[59]

Once he had testimony of the situation in Columbia, Foster on November 21 ordered a ration retaliation for the 400 Confederate officers in Pulaski and the 200 in the barracks at Hilton Head. Two days later, Grant ordered Foster to suspend the bombardment of Charleston. "This is not intended to prohibit the throwing of an occasional shell into Charleston, if circumstances should require," Halleck explained. "The object is to economize ordnance stores." Foster's initial orders about the retaliation miscarried, however, and thus from October 22 to December 15, the Confederate officers experienced kind treatment from Col. Philip P. Brown Jr., who commanded Pulaski, and his regiment of the 157th New York who made up the prison guards. Brown instilled the values of professionalism and Christian gentility into his command and intended to treat his Confederate prisoners according to those values. His orders prohibited profanity, required soldiers to deport themselves with full military etiquette, and mandated attendance at divine service on the Sabbath. He provided the prisoners with rations equal to that of his men, tried to secure blankets and supplies for them, made sure their holding cells were clean, required them to bathe weekly, allowed forty prisoners at a time to walk outside the casemate on a parole of honor, and ensured the guards treated the prisoners with courtesy and respect.[60]

Brown represented a prominent perspective in the Department of the South that married Christianity to civilization. The two did not have to go together, as the ancient Greeks exemplified. Many military officers who were devout Christians believed that the biblical worldview trumped the secular customs of war when the two came into conflict. Jesus taught forgiveness and love of enemy, and the Federals who read the Bible and prayed daily often concluded that retaliation of any kind was incompatible with Jesus's teachings, as Sophia Hawthorne had written to Ethan Allen Hitchcock when he asked for her opinion about withholding rations from Confederate prisoners. During the debate about the appropriate response to the Fort Pillow massacre, an anonymous writer for the newspaper published on Morris Island, *The Swamp Angel*, made the same case that she did. The "eye for eye, tooth for tooth" doctrine belonged to "the old Mosaic dispensation" and smacked "somewhat of barbarism." He asked, "Why should we perpetuate horrors, because the brutal followers of a reckless leader have done so?" A *Christian* civilization would "withhold the vengeful bayonet from the prostrate foe and retaliate deeds of blood with offices of mercy."[61]

Foster first learned that retaliation was not in place at Pulaski when the *Charleston Courier* published a letter to Brown complimenting him on his care of the prisoners. "Praise from the enemy is the last thing that an officer should seek, or permit to be bestowed on him," Foster wrote him. "These officers were sent to this department for the purposes of retaliation." If Brown treated them "in precisely the same manner" that Confederates treated Union prisoners, "very few compliments would have been extended to you." Brown responded that he never received any instructions about how to treat his prisoners, an excuse that Foster's chief of staff found incredible. "It is perfectly well understood by every officer in this department that these prisoners were sent here for the purpose of retaliation to be treated precisely the same as our officers and for no other reason," he lectured. He claimed his office sent repeated instructions about the precise ration to issue. He directed Brown to implement the ration that escaped Union officers reported were the rations in Columbia: one pint of unbolted cornmeal every five days, half a pint of molasses per day, half a pint of rice occasionally for five days, three tablespoons of salt every five days, and "no meat or grease whatsoever." Brown could substitute half a pound of bread for the rice.[62]

Brown balked at the orders and did his best, consistent with his professional ethic of obeying orders, to mitigate the treatment the Confederate officers received. He asked detailed questions of Foster's chief of staff in order to delay implementation: Should he issue bread rather than rice one day in five or more often? What was the definite quantity of salt, since tablespoons were not the same size? He had already issued enough of the previous ration to last several days—should he take that away? It would take a while for his quartermaster to find unbolted cornmeal. After a few days, however, Brown obeyed his orders. It was particularly frustrating for Brown because Foster had taken steps to sicken 600 prisoners at the same time that national authorities exchanged 12,000 of the sickest prisoners held on each side. Union and Confederate officials made the deliveries in Charleston and Savannah Harbors.[63]

The prisoners at Pulaski suffered intense hunger pangs under the new regimen, and forty-two of them quickly developed scurvy. Their teeth loosened, their gums turned black, they developed spots on their limbs, and their muscles contracted. They fainted frequently. Many of the prisoners killed and ate the cats who roamed the fort. The guards of the 157th openly expressed their sympathy with the prisoners, and although they would not overtly disobey orders, they took small steps to help. Some of the New Yorkers put bread or a piece of meat on the end of their bayonets and dared the rebels to take it off, "always holding their guns in such a position that the meat or bread could be taken off by the prisoners," a grateful Confederate officer recalled. The post quartermaster clandestinely distributed a barrel of fish to the sickest men. Capt. Wash Nelson, a Virginia artillery officer, recalled that he killed and ate three cats at Pulaski. "My last was a kitten, tender and nice," he said. "A compassionate Yankee soldier gave it to me. I was cooking at the stove by the grating which separated us from the guard. This soldier hailed me, 'I say—are you one of them fellers that eats cats!' I replied yes. 'Well, here is one I'll shove through if you want it.' 'Shove it through,' I answered and in a very few minutes that kitten was in frying order." Because the prisoners respected Brown, they agreed not to kill his beloved pet cat. Half of the prisoners got sick. A medical inspector in the Department of the South reported to Foster after an inspection of the prison barracks at

Hilton Head that the ration was "insufficient to support life in health for any lengthened period."[64]

Prisoners were at the heart of the crisis of civilization during the American Civil War. Unionists believed that military prisons in Georgia and South Carolina reduced 35,000 men to an animal condition and exposed the barbarity of their Confederate captors. Charleston's slow descent into a lawless wasteland caused General Jones to use prisoners as a human shield against the Federal bombardment. The horror that General Foster felt when he contemplated the savage acts of his enemy caused him to also commit a savage act: providing his prisoners with a ration that he knew would cause them sickness and potential death. The fact that a Federal commander risked the lives and health of prisoners of war as official policy marked the escalation of retaliation in the Department of the South beyond the bounds of civilized war. Maj. Gen. William Tecumseh Sherman's army arrived on the scene at the same time and raised new problems for the officers and soldiers struggling to retain their place in civilization. Federal pillagers threatened the sanctity of civilized womanhood, and Confederate soldiers murdered prisoners and planted hidden land mines in public roads. When Sherman executed forty-three Confederate prisoners as an act of retaliation, the crisis of civilization reached its apex.

# 6

# PILLAGERS AND ASSASSINS

Henry Hitchcock, the thirty-five-year-old nephew of Ethan Allen Hitchcock, joined the Union army in October 1864. He was late, because his uncle had advised him that he was more valuable to the Union cause in the political rather than the military realm, but after three years of regret, he decided to do his duty. He insisted on getting a commission and going to the front. "Here is a young fellow spoiling for a fight," his uncle told Secretary of War Edwin Stanton. Ethan secured a place for his nephew as the military secretary on the staff of his friend and admirer Maj. Gen. William Tecumseh Sherman. Henry joined the Army of the Tennessee and the Army of Georgia, with a combined force of 60,000 infantry and 5,500 cavalry, as they prepared to march east from Atlanta toward the territory in Georgia encompassed in the Department of the South. He immediately commenced an investigation to determine whether Sherman's army fought a civilized war. He was a lawyer, and he used his profession's methods, interviewing the principals, collecting evidence, and debating both sides of the question.[1]

Henry had long conversations with Sherman and was enamored with the general's intellect and powerful personality. The sharp-nosed, bright-blue-eyed Sherman talked "continually and with immense rapidity." He was restless and fidgety. He used "hyperbole for emphasis" and enjoyed phrasing his opinions to deliver the maximum shock value. He did not listen to others' opinions. He smoked at least six cigars a day, was an avid reader, and conducted an immense personal correspondence. "I never passed a more amusing or instructive day," an officer in the Department of the South wrote of time spent with Sherman, "but at his departure I felt it a relief and experienced almost an exhaustion after the excitement of his vigorous presence."[2]

The intense general was experienced in retaliation rituals; he had participated in them during all of his previous campaigns. Because he had fought in the West, most involved his practice of treating guerrillas in Tennessee and Mississippi as "wild beasts unknown to the usages of war." When Confederate officers had threatened to retaliate by executing Union prisoners after Sherman's troops had summarily executed guerrillas or burned houses located near a guerrilla attack, Sherman had never given an inch. He told his superiors he would "make no concessions to the authorities of that government which has turned loose bands of men without uniforms — without any marks of a soldier's calling — to do their will." He had chosen Confederate prisoners by lot and held them as hostages for the lives of Union prisoners, and it had always worked.[3]

Sherman explained to Hitchcock that he fought against the population of the Confederacy, men and women, who spawned and protected guerrillas, sustained its armies, and destroyed the law and order of their legitimate government, the United States of America. "This war is on our part a war *against anarchy*," he told Henry. Sherman's goals for the march to Savannah were to change the base of his army so that it could join Lt. Gen. Ulysses S. Grant in Virginia, destroy Georgia's war resources, prove the weakness of the Confederate government, demoralize soldiers from Georgia fighting in Virginia, and break the will of slaveholding Confederate women whose activities supported the war. "Sherman is perfectly right — the only possible way to end this unhappy and dreadful conflict . . . is to make it *terrible beyond endurance*," Henry told his family. "Our enemies have shown themselves *devils* in the spirit which ever began this most unprovoked and inexcusable rebellion. There is nothing for it but 'to fight the devil with fire.'" Henry emphasized that he did not mean "wanton barbarity nor useless destruction." "It is neither barbarous nor useless, but just and indispensable, to utterly destroy everything, no matter whose, or what, or whom that does or can uphold, sustain or encourage this gigantic crime," he explained. "There is no peace else for this generation or the next."[4]

Hitchcock was comfortable with immense destruction of property; the honor of the army he had joined depended on who did the destroying and why. He understood one essential element of civilized war: the regulation of men that restrained violence. The hierarchical organization of an army was supposed to control soldiers through orders and strict discipline that would ensure that the destruction an army committed was deliberate, targeted, and necessary, rather than expansive, indiscriminate, and wasteful. The orders of officers, rather than the whims of individual soldiers, should govern an army's behavior. Civilized armies foraged; barbarians pillaged.

The lawyer was pleased that Sherman's initial orders for foragers, dictated to him and issued November 9, 1864, from Kingston, Georgia, conformed to the civilized requirement of regulation, discipline, and deliberation. Sherman's instruction "expressly defines and limits the discretion of the corps commanders to whom *alone* is committed the question of destruction," Hitchcock summarized. "All private soldiers are expressly forbidden *to enter any* house even to forage." Brigade commanders organized the foraging parties, who worked under the command of "discreet" officers and stayed near the route of the army's march. Soldiers could not enter dwellings or "commit any trespass," although they could gather vegetables and drive in stock that were in sight of their camp during a halt in the march. The orders permitted cavalry and artillery soldiers to take horses, mules, and wagons freely but asked them to discriminate between the "hostile" rich and the "neutral or friendly" poor people of Georgia. Sherman ordered his foragers to "refrain from abusive or threatening language" and "endeavor to leave with each family a reasonable portion for their maintenance." He cautioned in special orders that if soldiers who were not foragers straggled, they were vulnerable to capture by hostile citizens. Corps and brigade commanders supplemented these instructions with additional controls to prevent straggling and plundering. The 17th Corps had orders that "no raw or drafted men will be detailed as foragers."[5]

Once the army started on the march, however, Hitchcock agonized over the evidence he collected that the army was violating its orders. Sherman divided his force into two wings (each with two corps). Maj. Gen. Oliver O. Howard, an 1854 West Point graduate and evangelical Christian, commanded the right wing, which included Maj. Gen. Frank P. Blair Jr.'s 17th Corps. Blair, like Hitchcock, was a Republican lawyer from St. Louis who had played a prominent political role in keeping Missouri in the Union in 1861. Sherman and Hitchcock rode with the left wing, under command of Maj. Gen. Henry W. Slocum, an 1852 West Pointer who had also studied law before the war. Sherman and Slocum moved southeast from Atlanta in a feint toward Augusta but eventually turned south to Milledgeville, the state capital. Howard's wing marched toward Macon. There was no organized Confederate army in Howard's or Slocum's way, merely a small cavalry force under Maj. Gen. Joseph Wheeler and the old men and young boys of the Georgia militia.[6]

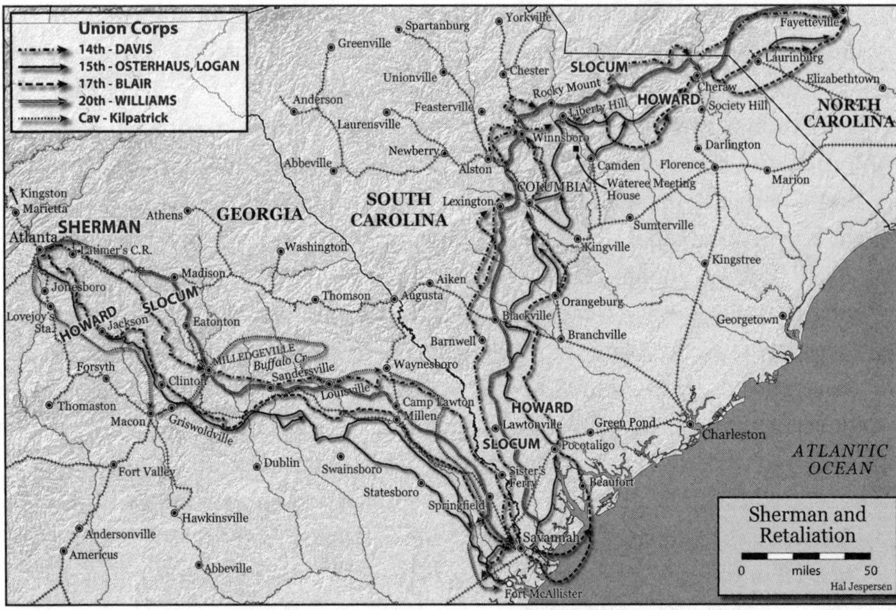


Hitchcock experienced the march as a crisis of civilization. It challenged his complacent view that his army and his nation were civilized; it revealed to him that officers had different interpretations of the rules that civilized men supposedly shared. He feared the march had revealed the savage nature of Union soldiers, the inconsistency of Sherman, and his own inability to determine what was right. An excessive number of soldiers, he thought, undisciplined by their line officers, operated outside the regulations and straggled, pillaged, and burned. There were savage individuals in every army, Confederate and Union officers acknowledged, and no commander could prevent, although he must punish, isolated acts of savagery. Hitchcock worried that the sheer number of "irregularities" reflected on the honor of Union officers. He obsessed over the discipline of the army, asked for the perspective of every officer he encountered on the march, and advocated for civilized restraint in nightly debates over the conduct of the campaign. The variety of opinion he recorded in his journal from different men revealed that the officers of Sherman's army were not equally committed to the restraints of civilized war and did not agree about the power it was possible for them to exercise over volunteer citizen soldiers in a republican army.

Hitchcock noticed that Sherman and a group of brigade commanders claimed that stragglers committed all the depredations of the army. On November 13, when Hitchcock expressed outrage that the Marietta courthouse was on fire (burning public buildings was clearly a violation of the laws of war), Sherman pointed to some stragglers and said, "There are the men who do this. Set as many guards as you please, and they will slip in and set fire. . . . I never ordered burning of any dwelling—didn't order this, but can't be helped. I say *Jeff. Davis* [the Confederate president] *burnt them.*" Hitchcock watched closely for stragglers during the next several days. On November 16, as Slocum's wing passed through Latimer's Crossroads, he debated Sherman's aide-de-camp, Capt. Lewis M. Dayton, who contended, "We should do whatever and as bad as the rebs, even to *scalping.*" "His view not important, save as *typical,*" Hitchcock wrote. That night in camp, with a house burning in the distance, Lt. Col. Charles Ewing explained to Hitchcock that it was impossible to control straggling and depredations unless generals in the field were able to execute guilty soldiers, but Lincoln himself reviewed all death sentences and gave clemency to almost all cases. "It is a great mistake," Hitchcock thought. "Such 'mercy' damages *us.*" When Georgia citizens shot some stragglers on November 18, Hitchcock thought it "served 'em right." He decided that it was impossible to entirely prevent soldiers from entering houses, since that would require a guard at every house, and "we *cannot* stop for that."[7]

Hitchcock also noticed that some division and brigade commanders enforced discipline better than others, however, and it made him wonder if Sherman could have reined in his army better than he did. On November 20, Hitchcock questioned the staff of Jefferson C. Davis's 14th Corps, who assured him that soldiers of that corps had not burned any dwelling on that day's march. Davis that day arrested two soldiers who stole dresses from a house. His provost marshal tied the men to a wagon, each wearing one of the dresses with the word "stolen" marked on it, and made them walk behind the wagon to the jeers of their comrades. Davis told Hitchcock that Sherman was the problem—ordinary soldiers in the army believed that "Uncle Billy" wanted them to straggle, plunder, and burn, and said so to their officers. "I am bound to say I think Sherman lacking in enforcing discipline," Hitchcock decided. The 3rd Wisconsin called roll at every halt in the march and court-martialed in the field all its stragglers. Every regiment could and should do this, he thought. "I do not see why this army cannot be kept in better trim as to stragglers," Hitchcock noted. "I am much dissatisfied with this." He believed the laws of war allowed the Union army to do enough "damage" to "teach a terrible lesson" to the enemy. "But I would find a way to stop anything beyond."[8]

Through almost four years of combat, Union and Confederate offi-

Maj. Gen. William Tecumseh Sherman and his staff in May 1865, men who had different interpretations of the rules of civilized war. Sherman is seated in the center of the photograph. Maj. Gen. Quincy A. Gillmore is seated, third from the left. Maj. Gen. Oliver O. Howard is the full-bearded man standing behind Sherman. Maj. Gen. Henry W. Slocum is the second man to the right of Howard. (Library of Congress Prints and Photographs Division)

cials professed to fight a civilized war. The emphasis on these declarations in the scholarly literature has obscured the simultaneous expressions of deep-seated fears that civilization was failing. Hitchcock concluded to his sorrow that savage acts abounded during the Federal invasion of Georgia and South Carolina in the winter of 1864–1865. Union soldiers pillaged and burned houses and slaughtered thousands of dogs. Confederate officials planted mines underneath the roads. Confederate soldiers killed prisoners of war, and South Carolina citizens killed foragers of the Union army. The reality of events on the ground, he thought, threatened the honorable reputation of both sides.

Hitchcock meticulously recorded the unfolding crisis of civilization that he observed. It culminated in February 1865, when Sherman executed forty-three prisoners of war in South Carolina as an act of retaliation for the murder of his foragers. Retaliation often functioned to end breaches of the laws of war and de-escalate violence.[9] In the cases of Sherman's executions and Maj. Gen. John G. Foster's decision to deprive 600 Confederate prisoners of a ration necessary for health, retaliation contributed to, rather than restrained, an escalating cycle of violence in the Department of the South. In effect, Sherman ultimately gave his Confederate enemy permission to kill Union soldiers caught pillaging. Juxtaposed against these failures, the ongoing retaliation over the recognition of freeborn Black citizens as Federal soldiers reached its successful conclusion when the Confederate Congress officially changed its laws and the prisoners of the 54th Massachusetts finally returned home.

Hitchcock decried the soldiers who had transformed into pillagers, and he condemned his rebel opponents for becoming murders and assassins. "The rebs *killed after surrender* the prisoners they took," he reported on November 23. "If this proves true, Sherman will retaliate, *and we must not be taken prisoners*. I confess I don't expect any mercy if captured; and the worse of it is that the 'foraging' or pillaging of our men is bound to bring this about." Union soldiers who straggled in Georgia were temporarily isolated from the main columns. On occasion, Wheeler's cavalry or local citizens captured stragglers and killed them after they had surrendered. Sometimes, dead Union soldiers were mutilated or had their throats cut from ear to ear. Shannon's Scouts, a detail of forty-five men from Terry's Texas Rangers, executed "marauders" caught in the act of robbing and burning homes. One of the scouts claimed his unit executed 100 Union prisoners in a two-week period. Wheeler's cavalrymen also killed Union prisoners captured in skirmishes or who were members of officially detailed foraging parties. On December 1, Sherman instructed his cavalry commander, Brig. Gen. Judson Kilpatrick, to carefully investigate and corroborate information about murdered prisoners, to notify Wheeler by flag of truce, and to retaliate with hanging or mutilation, man for man, without regard to rank. There is no evidence that Kilpatrick did so in Georgia.[10]

Confederate officials were increasingly frustrated and desperate. When Maj. Gen. Howell Cobb reported to Jefferson Davis on November 17 that his militia forces were falling back rapidly and were "too weak to resist" Sherman, Davis ordered Cobb to obstruct the roads, burn bridges, and plant "sub-terra shells," or land mines. The Confederate president, who often operated in the realm of fantasy at this stage of the war, wrote that land mines "will be effective to check an advance." Gen. Robert E. Lee, who could not spare any men from Virginia, told Davis the Georgia "population must turn out." The state's senators and congressmen published proclamations to the people asking them to remove all provisions from Sherman's path or burn them, destroy roads and bridges, and turn out under arms to harass Sherman's veterans. "You have now the best opportunity ever yet presented to destroy the enemy," one read. "Every citizen with his gun, and every negro with his spade and axe, can do the work of a soldier. You can destroy the enemy by retarding his march. Georgians, be firm!"[11]

Confederate men and women placed enormous significance on the fact that they could not stop Yankee soldiers from entering and looting their homes. In the mindset of civilization through which they understood the world, men were "shamed" and women "outraged" when soldiers "violated" domestic spaces. When Southerners accused Federals of conducting a savage war in Georgia, they used language loaded with sexual imagery, even when no rape occurred. Slaveholding Southerners prided themselves on a chivalric civilization where patriarchs protected white women within the domestic spaces of which their male kin were the masters. When Union pillagers ransacked women's bedrooms, they intentionally sent a powerful message of their own mastery over Southern men and their disregard for the claims of Southern women to be "ladies" worthy of respect. When Yankee soldiers appeared on a woman's doorstep in Georgia, civilization as she knew it had collapsed.[12]

A comparative perspective, however, highlights the boundaries Union soldiers would not cross. Sherman's soldiers did not kill Georgia women because they knew that honorable and civilized men, in contrast to barbarians, recognized the value of refined white women. During this time, however, soldiers in the U.S. Army and the state militias fought a series of Indian wars in the West and committed several indiscriminate massacres, notably at Bear River in Idaho (January 29, 1863) and Sand Creek in Colorado (November 29, 1864). Killing women, and even children, something unthinkable in the war between the Union and the Confederacy, was possible in the Indian wars because Indian women and children lived outside of, and posed a threat to, civilization. For Union soldiers, the discourse of civilization trumped that of gender.[13]

The Confederate decision to defend Georgia with "sub-terra shells" provoked the greatest outrage from Union officers. Sherman retaliated, without using the formal ritual, when his army encountered burned bridges or land mines. Consistent with his previous practice in Missouri, Tennessee, and Mississippi, Sherman held citizens accountable when locals obstructed his army or ambushed his soldiers. On November 23, he ordered commanding officers to "deal harshly with inhabitants nearby" when bridges were destroyed "to show them that it is to their interest not to impede our movements." If Confederates burned forage and corn, commanders should burn houses and barns. Sherman's subordinates debated the proper application of this policy. On November 25, Slocum's wing found a burned bridge over Buffalo Creek (six miles west of Sandersville). Locals proffered various stories about who did it. Ewing advocated burning a nearby house. Hitchcock opposed this action unless there was evidence that the owner was involved in the destruction. "In war everything is right which prevents anything," Sherman broke in. "If bridges are burned, I have a right to burn all houses near it." "Beg pardon, General," Hitchcock replied. "Indiscriminate punishment is not just." "Well, let him look to his own people," Sherman countered. "If they find that their burning bridges only destroys their own citizens' houses they'll stop it." Hitchcock let the matter drop and later decided that Sherman was right "to a certain extent." "Some things can be reached only in that way—hence it is right to retaliate for murder of prisoners by killing in return."[14]

Hitchcock unequivocally agreed that placing land mines on a public road, as opposed to use in defending a fortification, was an act of assassination that violated the laws of war and did not object when Sherman used Confederate prisoners of war to clear them. On December 9, as the 17th Corps marched on the road to Savannah, two sub-terra shells (the Federals called them torpedoes) exploded, killing a horse and wounding several men of the 1st Alabama Cavalry (Union). The blast tore off the foot of a lieutenant. Sherman and Hitchcock rode up shortly afterward. Part of an unexploded shell was visible. Blair arrived on the scene with a squad of Confederate prisoners whom he intended to use to dig up the remaining shells. Two of them begged Sherman to intervene. He refused. "He told them their people had put these things there to assassinate our men instead of fighting them fair," Hitchcock noted in his journal. "He did exactly right. . . . They run away, refuse to defend the road, but leave hidden in an open public road, without warning or chance of defense, these murderous instruments of assassination—contrary to every rule of civilized warfare." The prisoners, without injury, uncovered seven more shells, buried in a line directly across the road and rigged to explode with the pressure of a footfall.[15]

If sub-terra shells triggered the outrage of Union generals, reports from Union prisoners of war who escaped from locations in Macon and Millen, Georgia, and Columbia, South Carolina, activated rage and vengeance in Sherman's foot soldiers. Unique to Civil War campaigns, Union soldiers in Georgia traveled by abandoned Confederate prison camps and saw what conditions there were like. Several hundred Union prisoners escaped when Confederates moved them from Georgia to South Carolina, and many soldiers in Sherman's army spoke with returned prisoners who told harrowing tales of living like an animal while dogs guarded and pursued them. Throughout their march, Sherman's men killed dogs in vast numbers and left them lying on the roadside or in yards. They knew that dogs were a linchpin of slaveholders' police power over enslaved people. While his men shot ten dogs on a plantation, Capt. John Henry Otto of the 21st Wisconsin lectured their weeping mistress. "The boys are only executing your police, your nigger catchers," he said. "They have the foolish notion that it is barbarous and brutal to hunt a human being with voracious wild beasts."[16]

Events in Georgia intensified the passions on both sides that the rules of civilized war were designed to subdue. Sherman's army was burning with hatred and revenge when its advance units reached the outskirts of Savannah on December 11. Two days later, a division of the 15th Corps captured Fort McAllister, located below the city, in an attack that took fifteen minutes. Sherman made contact with the Federal blockading fleet and met with Foster, whose Black troops, including the 54th Massachusetts, had been raiding near the Charleston and Savannah Railroad in order to occupy Confederate troops in the Charleston vicinity. Sherman allowed Savannah's Confederate defenders, a 9,000-man army under Lt. Gen. William J. Hardee, to escape and rendezvous in South Carolina. "I could go on and smash South Carolina all to pieces," he wrote Grant from Savannah. "Charleston is now a mere desolated wreck, and is hardly worth the time it would take to starve it out." Confederates expected him to attack Augusta or Charleston next. He proposed instead to march to Columbia, and then to Raleigh, North Carolina. "The game is then up with Lee," Sherman said.[17]

Sherman was frank with his superiors about his intention to make war on the people of South Carolina. "I attach more importance to these deep incisions into the enemy's country, because this war differs from European wars in this particular," he told Maj. Gen. Henry Halleck on December 24. "We are not only fighting hostile armies, but a hostile people, and must make old and young, and rich and poor, feel the hard hand of war." Halleck wanted Sherman to capture Charleston but granted him the power to decide his own future. "I hope that by some accident the place may be destroyed," he told his triumphant subordinate, "and if a little salt should be thrown upon the site it might prevent the growth of future crops of nullification and secession." Sherman assured Halleck, "The truth is the whole army is burning with an insatiable desire to wreak vengeance upon South Carolina. I almost tremble at her fate, but feel that she deserves all that seems in store for her."[18]

While Grant, Halleck, and Sherman considered questions of punishment and vengeance on the campaign level in December 1864, the U.S. Senate and the Northern public considered them on the national level. Unaware that Foster was malnourishing Confederate prisoners in Fort Pulaski and Hilton Head, Republican senator Morton S. Wilkinson of Minnesota introduced a resolution on December 20 to provide *all* Confederate prisoners with rations, clothing, medical attention, and personal exposure to the elements exactly equivalent to those that Union prisoners received. The Senate's military affairs committee recommended that former Union prisoners of war should conduct the retaliation. The U.S. War Department had already taken the first step in that direction by appointing Brig. Gen. Henry Wessels to be the new commissary general of prisoners over the territory east of the Mississippi River. He was one of the fifty Union officers who had been placed under fire in Charleston, and he had urged the Lincoln administration to retaliate ever since his return to Union lines.[19]

During the subsequent debate, supporters of the resolution among the Northern public used the same language of de-civilization that Union prisoners used. Ordinary Northern women expressed to Abraham Lincoln their horror that Confederate prison pens turned men into animals. Mrs. A. Moor wrote to the president from Greenwich, New York, where a young man released from Andersonville during the exchange of sick prisoners died with the U.S. flag wound around his body. He had brought home his last day's ration, "a small quantity of corn meal ground in the ear, poorer than our men give their horses and hogs." Young Northern men in the South were "stretched upon the ground or upon a board without shelter for weeks suffering from sickness and pain covered with vermin." They died "as an animal dies." Moor supported the proposed retaliation as "the most effective and speediest means" of relieving the suffering of Union soldiers. "It is repulsive and sickening to the human heart to think that we are caring for those bloodthirsty rebels and traitors," she said.[20]

For the next two weeks, senators debated the question at the heart of the matter: could the United States do such a thing and maintain its honor? "I say we cannot do what is proposed and stand as a civilized people among the nations of the earth," Indiana Democrat Thomas A. Hendricks said. "The earthquake has its power, the lightening has its power, the tornado has its power, but there is a power greater than all, and that is the judgment of the civilized world. I do defer to the judgment of the civilized world." Massachusetts Republican Charles Sumner, renowned for his speeches against the barbarity of slavery, agreed. "It would be injurious at home, for it would barbarize the whole community," his alternative resolutions read. "It could have no other result than to degrade the national character and the national name." The people of the United States "renounce all vengeance and every evil example, and plant themselves firmly on the sacred landmarks of Christian civilization." Ethan Allen Hitchcock and Francis Lieber publicly agreed with Sumner, who also received fifty letters of support from ordinary Christians across the country. The retaliation proposal failed in the Senate; there was no interest in the House of Representatives, and no widespread support from the press or the public. Civilian officials of the United States backed away from tit-for-tat retaliation, just as they had done in the aftermath of the Fort Pillow massacre.[21]

The Senate discussion brought Foster into the spotlight and raised the question of whether military officers had the authority to retaliate on prisoners of war without permission of Congress. Senator James Rood Doolittle, from Wisconsin, used precedent from the War of 1812 to claim that Congress had authority over retaliation. The Constitution gave Congress the power to "define and punish" offenses "against the law of nations," he argued, and therefore "legislation is necessary in order to treat prisoners differently than the rules and regulations require." Doolittle had recently spoken with a captain from his state who had escaped from the Confederate military prison in Columbia after being under fire in Charleston. Doolittle told his colleagues that Foster had notified Confederate authorities that he would treat Confederate prisoners in an equivalent manner to their treatment of Union prisoners. This revelation provoked a question from Senator John B. Henderson of Missouri. "If Congress has entire power over the question and Congress has not directed retaliation to be exercised, how could an officer in the field undertake to say that he would retaliate in that way?" he asked. Doolittle replied, "He took the responsibility of doing it; that is all I can say on the subject. I confess I had supposed that the discretion was in the commanders of our armies; but now I have doubts on the subject." Henderson commented, "I can tell the Senate that the military commanders in the West have exercised the power since the beginning of the war. It has never been doubted there." Legal expert and former attorney general of the United States Reverdy Johnson, the senator from Maryland, closed the discussion with his opinion that military officers in the field had the authority and the duty to exercise retaliation on prisoners of war when necessary.[22]

Once the national debate turned against a retaliation in kind for the treatment of Union prisoners and Foster felt the scrutiny of Congress, medical inspectors in the Department of the South intervened to stop the sufferings of the 600 Confederate officers held in the casemate of Fort Pulaski and in barrack cells at Hilton Head. The prisoners were subsisting on a ration that a Federal doctor believed was "insufficient to support life in health for

Provost buildings, Hilton Head, that confined 200 of the Confederate officers subjected to Maj. Gen. John G. Foster's ration retaliation. (Library of Congress Prints and Photographs Division)

any lengthened period." They received a quarter of a pound of bread, ten ounces of cornmeal (much of it husks and weevils), and half a pint of pickles every five days. Prisoners with money could purchase other food from a sutler, but many of the prisoners did not have money. They ate rats and cats. A new Confederate prisoner in Hilton Head was George P. Harrison, who had been a brigade commander at the Battle of Olustee and the commander of the Confederate military prison at Florence, South Carolina. Sherman's army scooped him up while he was visiting his plantation in Georgia in early December. "To avoid freezing to death when the weather is cold much of the night is spent running up and down the building to keep up the circulation," he wrote the Georgia representative to the Confederate Congress. "This is done by almost the entire prison." The Union provost marshal allowed Harrison to send the letter. "Whilst he enforces with fidelity the orders of his Government, he is deeply anxious that Federal prisoners in Confederate prisons might be better treated, so as to bring about an amelioration of the Confederate prisoners here."[23]

Foster conceded the futility of the retaliation and wanted to get the Confederate officers out of his department. On January 26, Secretary of War Stanton, who was in Savannah to confer with Sherman, ordered the provost marshal at Hilton Head to add four ounces of meat and four ounces of potatoes to each ration. "At last there is a little decrease in the severity of our treatment," prisoner Samuel Horace Hawes told his diary. No one immediately communicated this change to Col. Philip P. Brown Jr., the genteel officer of the 157th New York still in command at Pulaski. One reason may have been Foster's declining health. "I would favor the removal of Foster on the ground of physical disability," Sherman told Stanton. "We want a man who is not confined to his quarters."[24]

Maj. Gen. Quincy A. Gillmore, accompanied by his usual entourage of newspaper reporters and civilian admirers, returned to command the Department of the South, although Sherman and Grant thought he "frittered" away any troops sent him and cost the government unnecessary expense. Brown took initiative when he learned of the appointment. On February 10, he asked the commander of the District of Savannah, Bvt. Maj. Gen. Cuvier Grover, to use his influence with Gillmore to revoke the retaliation orders. "Considerations of humanity require that something should be done without delay," he wrote. Grover sent a medical inspector to Pulaski and reported the results to department headquarters on February 10. "They are in a condition of great suffering and exhaustion for want of sufficient food and clothing," he said.[25]

There was now a clamor of voices at Gillmore's headquarters demanding to end the retaliation completely and give the Confederate officers a full ration. Lt. Col. Stewart L. Woodford of the 127th New York, a district inspector for the provost marshal general's office, expressed succinctly the essential problem. "Their number is so small that retaliation inflicted upon them can have no real effect in ameliorating the condition of the large number of our officers held in so horrid a condition at Columbia," he said, "and simply causes suffering to a small number here without at present any good resulting." Gillmore agreed. On February 12, the Confederate prisoners at Pulaski received a full ration, and on the 20th, so did the officers at Hilton Head. "Today the spirits of the men were raised by an appearance of 'big rations,'" prisoner Richard H. Adams said. "I have already had one square meal and tomorrow will have a big pot of bean soup."[26]

Foster's ration retaliation was not an act of civilized war; it was an act of vengeance. As Lieber had explained in the national debate, two criteria marked the difference between legitimate retaliation and revenge: the likelihood that the act would compel a change in the enemy's behavior and the requirement that a combatant could not commit a savage act. Foster's orders to feed prisoners rations that would sicken them violated Article 56 of General Orders No. 100: "A prisoner of war is subject to no punishment for being a public enemy, nor is any revenge wreaked upon him by the intentional infliction of any suffering, or disgrace, by cruel imprisonment, want of food, by mutilation, death, or any other barbarity." Because he never engaged in a formal retaliation ritual with his Confederate counterpart over the ration issue, and because his action was unpublicized, there was no chance that it would change Confederate behavior. Foster's ration deprivation, which lasted two months, most certainly caused suffering. It is impossible, however, to determine its role in the deaths of the thirteen Confederate prisoners buried at Fort Pulaski and the five buried at Hilton Head.[27]

When Sherman's army invaded South Carolina, it was likely its officers and soldiers would unleash hatred and vengeance on its citizens. Lieber, who reminded his friend Halleck about the customs of war during every military campaign, worried that it would be so. "I implore everyone who has anything to say or to do in the matter, to stay the hand of mere ruthless revenge," he wrote on February 11. "My name is not namby-pamby. I even insist upon sternness . . . but let it be manly, unflinching yet un-impassioned sternness. Let Sherman, if such a thing be possible, levy the heaviest contributions, let him blow the negroes into all directions like a storm, let him lay the yoke of retribution heavy on the offenders of that offending State, but let there not be ruthless burning, killing, violating women by soldiers." Halleck seemingly agreed. "South Carolina has been the viper's nest of this rebellion. Her people have advised and assisted in the starvation and murder of our prisoners of war," he wrote. "She should be punished and that strongly and severely; but there should be no revengeful cruelty or ruthless ravaging." He cautioned, however, "Individual acts of excess and cruelty . . . cannot be entirely prevented." This would become the official excuse for what happened later.[28]

During Sherman's invasion of South Carolina the level of pillaging and burning escalated, as increasing numbers of Union soldiers abandoned restraint. This increased the subsequent Confederate murders of foragers. Sherman ordered Slocum's left wing to cross the Savannah River at Sister's Ferry. The worst winter rains in two decades had turned the river into a lake, and it took Slocum until the end of January 1865 to make the movement. When his advance units entered the state, sub-terra shells, planted all along the roads, exploded, killing one man and wounding several more. "Our soldiers regarded the act of placing them in a highway where no contest was anticipated as something akin to poisoning a stream of water," Slocum said. "If that section of South Carolina suffered more severely than any other, it was due in part to the blundering of people who were more zealous than wise." Howard's wing took water transport from Savannah to Beaufort, South Carolina, located on Port Royal Island, and then moved overland to Pocotaligo. Blair's 17th Corps captured the Confederate fortifications there, took control of the Charleston and Savannah Railroad, and made contact with a portion of the 54th Massachusetts, proud to be the first troops in the Department of the South "to meet the stalwart Westerners" in the field. The two wings of Sherman's army then headed toward Columbia from their respective locations.[29]

Official orders for Sherman's army in South Carolina maintained the distinction between authorized foraging and illegal pillaging and required line officers to control their men. Howard and Blair issued stringent orders against stealing and did their best to enforce them. Many Union soldiers upheld their commitment to the restraints of civilized war and were appalled at the behavior of their comrades who ransacked houses, insulted women, and set fire to dwellings and fences. Many line officers and soldiers, however, believed that South Carolina deserved special punishment and reveled in the opportunity to plunder and burn the state that had started the war.

The rank and file of Sherman's army, as they observed the scale of pillaging, were as divided over the treatment of South Carolina as Sherman's officers had been over the treatment of Georgia. William W. Prichard, a noncommissioned officer in the 9th Pennsylvania Cavalry, argued with himself, a position that was common among Union soldiers. He thought burning houses "partakes of the barbarous," yet he thought Confederates initiated the barbarities. "They starve our prisoners with the land full of everything, and all classes of citizens and soldiers co-incide with the agreement to kill them off by the lingering process of starvation. Is our treatment of their noncombatants worse than their treatment of ours?" he asked himself. "However, I do not burn—do not steal or plunder; being conscientiously opposed to it, I need not do it and I will not do it." On one day, a tiny part of him was glad that "the day of humiliation" had come to "rank rebels." On another, the cruelty of house burning rankled him to the core. "If we are defeated on this campaign . . . I shall assign as the reason the wanton destruction of private property and the savageness with which this campaign is conducted," he wrote on February 9. If he were in charge, he would destroy all public property, supplies for the Confederate army, unoccupied residences, and cotton. Nothing more. "I did not enlist to fight women and children and I shall never raise my hand to assist in any such nefarious business." After considering the justification that Confederates were the first to commit the "wrongs" that he saw all around him, he rejected the thought. "If we were to retaliate in kind for every wrong that the rebels commit, this war would soon assume the no quarter system."[30]

Despite the efforts of restrained officers and soldiers, as Sherman's army moved north from the burned city of Columbia on February 20, the destruction of the countryside was immense. Although the Federals had not started the initial fires that erupted in the capital city, and many Federal soldiers had tried to fight them, the pillagers in Sherman's army had burned houses, ransacked and vandalized personal property, and insulted and abused residents. Events in Columbia escalated the saturnalia of vengeance as the army marched on. Women and children, with household goods of all descriptions, were scattered in the fields as far as Prichard's eye could see. "The rebels burn all the corn and forage; we burn the cotton and outhouses," he said. "The infantry coming in the rear burn the houses, and there is nothing left." The divisions of Sherman's army, marching along parallel roads, extended in width 100 miles across the countryside. "*Everything*—I say *everything*" was destroyed. Soldiers set farm fences on fire, and the blaze raced along for miles without going out. "The roads catch fire; the grass in the fields catches fire, and everything burns up. I have sometimes thought that the very Devil was in the elements." The sun turned red from the smoke. On February 20, General Howard, who had openly wept at the destruction he witnessed, wrote Blair and Maj. Gen. John A. Logan, who commanded the 15th Army Corps. "These outrages must be stopped at all hazards, and the thieves and robbers who commit them be dealt with severely and summarily," he said. "I call upon you and all the officers and soldiers under you, who have one spark of honor or respect for the profession which they follow, to help me put down these infamous proceedings and to arrest the perpetrators."[31]

A portion of Sherman's army was out of control, and his officers and soldiers who cared the most about the restraints of civilized war recognized it. Confederates in South Carolina were out of control, too. They had been unable to muster any effective military defense against the invasion. No one was in charge. Gen. P. G. T. Beauregard was back in the state, but Jefferson Davis had not given him formal authority over Hardee and the troops Hardee commanded in the Department of South Carolina, Georgia, and Florida. Beauregard had scattered 20,000 "demoralized" troops to defend Augusta, Branchville, and Charleston and provided Sherman with a relatively clear path to Columbia. Sherman was a logistical genius who knew how to move an army through weather and over obstacles of terrain. His army's movements and speed shocked and confused his Confederate opponents. As the Yankees marched north from Columbia through Winnsboro and headed east toward Cheraw, Confederate cavalry attacked foraging parties and other detachments from the main columns. They regularly murdered prisoners after capture.[32]

In the midst of the increasingly unrestrained violence, General Kilpatrick initiated a retaliation ritual. Sherman's short and scrawny cavalry commander had spent three months in prison for bribery early in the war and openly kept Black and white mistresses in his headquarters during the march through South Carolina. His creative cursing was legendary. On February 22, after the army had pillaged Winnsboro and burned private homes, he sent a flag of truce to his counterpart, Joseph Wheeler, and delivered a letter about the murder of eighteen Union soldiers. First, Kilpatrick stated the facts, as he understood them. A Texas regiment under a lieutenant colonel and armed with Spencer carbines killed an infantry lieutenant and eight Union soldiers after they had surrendered and were disarmed. Further, unknown parties murdered nine Federal cavalrymen—five in a barnyard, three in an open field, and one in a road—and slit the throats of two from ear to ear. Kilpatrick then gave Wheeler until sundown the next day to make a satisfactory explanation. If that were not forthcoming, he would shoot eighteen Confederate prisoners. Additionally, if Wheeler's troops did not treat his men as prisoners of war "in every way," his retaliation would extend to burning every house that his scouting parties could reach. "Nor will I be responsible for the conduct of my soldiers, who will not only be allowed, but encouraged to take a fearful revenge," he concluded. "I know of no other way to intimidate cowards." Although Kilpatrick followed some elements of the retaliation ritual in his message, such as providing his opponent an opportunity to explain, he mistakenly conflated retaliation with revenge.[33]

Wheeler's response exemplified how the retaliation ritual was supposed to function as a tool to de-escalate violence. "I am much shocked at the statements," he wrote Kilpatrick the same day. "I am satisfied that you are mistaken in the matter." He claimed that none of his Texas regiments fit the description. "I will have the matter promptly investigated and see that full justice is done," he promised. "Should the report, however, by any means prove correct, I prefer that the retaliation be inflicted upon the parties guilty of the misdeed, and not upon innocent persons." It was not right for Kilpatrick to shoot eighteen innocent prisoners because he found eighteen of his own men dead, Wheeler claimed, and notified his antagonist that he would regard such an action as murder and respond accordingly. "Your threat to burn every house as far as your scouts can extend is of too brutal a character for me, and I think for my Government, to reply to."[34]

Wheeler's response should have ended matters. Kilpatrick was satisfied. He assured Wheeler that he trusted him to investigate and discover the guilty parties. He provided additional details about the Texas regiment from

Brig. Gen. Judson Kilpatrick. He initiated a retaliation ritual to protect prisoners from his cavalry command after Confederates murdered nine Union horsemen after surrender and slit the throats of two of them. (Library of Congress Prints and Photographs Division)

the statement of his eyewitness, one of his scouts, who claimed, "The general conversation of your men was that they would take no more prisoners." Kilpatrick stood by his threat to burn houses and promised to retaliate man for man if Union soldiers continued to be murdered but would take no action for the present because of Wheeler's assurances. Kilpatrick then made an extraordinary promise that addressed the unspoken subtext to their previous conversation. "If stragglers from my command are found in the houses of citizens committing any outrages whatever, my own people are directed to shoot them on the spot," he wrote, "and of course I expect officers and soldiers of your command to do the same."[35] Kilpatrick thus put on the record that he understood the civilized usages of war and that he and his opponent alike would enforce them on Union soldiers.

The matter did not rest there, however. Kilpatrick reported the deaths to Sherman, of course, and included an important detail about the murder of the infantrymen he had omitted when he wrote Wheeler. "We found their bodies all together and mutilated, with paper on their breasts, saying 'Death to Foragers.'" Sherman thought this was worth drawing a line in the sand. He was confident that the usages of war permitted his army to forage the countryside and drew upon historical precedent. "Now it is clearly our war right to subsist our army on the enemy," he told Howard. "Napoleon always did it, but could avail himself of the civil powers he found in existence to collect forage and provisions by regular impressments. We cannot do that here, and I contend if the enemy fails to defend his country we may rightfully appropriate what we want. If our foragers act under mine, yours, or other proper orders, they must be protected." Like Kilpatrick, however, Sherman recognized that foragers should not be protected if they "enter dwellings" or "commit wanton waste." "If the people resist our foragers I will not deem it wrong," he proclaimed, "but the Confederate army must not be supposed to be the champion of any people." He instructed Howard to take life for life if any of his foragers were murdered and to leave a record of each case.[36]

On February 23, Sherman ordered Kilpatrick to shoot eighteen Confederate prisoners at once in retaliation for the murder of the foragers. "It is petty nonsense for Wheeler and Beauregard and such vain heroes to talk of our warring against women and children," he wrote. "If they claim to be men they should defend their women and children and prevent us reaching their homes." Sherman wanted to send two messages with the retaliatory execution: his army would "use the produce of the country as we please" and would protect its foragers. "I want the foragers to be regulated and systematized so as not to degenerate into common robbers," he reiterated. He instructed Kilpatrick to leave the executed Confederates on the roadside with a label on their bodies announcing the intention to kill man for man. "If our foragers commit excess, punish them yourself, but never let an enemy judge between our men and the law," Sherman said. "For my part I want the people of the South to realize the fact that they shall not dictate laws of war or peace to us. If there is to be any dictation we want our full share."[37]

Another group of executions quickly followed. On February 24, a Federal scout found the bodies of twenty-one infantrymen in a ravine three miles from Feasterville. They were naked and their throats cut. Another scout found a soldier of the 92nd Illinois Mounted Infantry hung to the limb of a tree. Murders of Union soldiers in the area were the work of Confederate cavalrymen, portions of the 1st Regiment of South Carolina Infantry, and citizens who lived there. They vented their rage and frustration at being unable to defend their homes and stop Sherman's army on isolated parties of foragers and stragglers. "After leaving Columbia, we hung about the front & flanks of the Enemy during his march upon Cheraw . . . cutting to pieces numerous parties, who called themselves 'foraging parties,' but whose object was in fact plunder," a member of the 1st Regiment wrote his family. "The intense pleasure of chasing, & killing these fiends, taken often in the act of committing crimes upon women too dreadful to mention, is beyond description."[38]

Sherman initiated a retaliation ritual on February 24 with Lt. Gen. Wade Hampton III, who commanded all the Confederate cavalry forces in South Carolina. Hampton exemplified the planter culture of his native state. He possessed immense wealth invested in land and slaves and ordered his life around the values of paternalism, honor, and chivalry. A few months before, while serving as the cavalry commander of the Army of Northern Virginia during the defense of Petersburg, Hampton led a raid that marched 100 miles and stole 2,468 cattle from behind Union lines. He had held his dying son in his arms on a Virginia battlefield. He was a die-hard rebel. "No suffering which can be inflicted by the passage over our country of the Yankee armies can equal what would befall us if we return to the Union," he told Jefferson Davis. "We shall live under a base and vulgar tyranny. *No* sacrifice would be too great to escape this train of horrors and I think it far better for us to fight to the extreme limits of our country, rather than to reconstruct the Union upon *any terms*." The Yankees had burned his residences in Columbia and stolen mementos from them a few days before. "I hate to see my men take these devils who have done all these evil deeds, prisoners," he told his sister. His code of chivalry "demanded blood vengeance, not magnanimity."

Lt. Gen. Wade Hampton III. Hampton was a die-hard rebel who believed that his soldiers were justified in killing Federal pillagers and did not stop them when they killed Federal foragers as well. Sherman executed forty-three Confederate prisoners of war in retaliation. (Courtesy of the South Caroliniana Library, University of South Carolina, Columbia)

In Virginia, when Confederate soldiers had slit the throats of some Yankee looters, Hampton wrote Lee that he "was glad to learn of the vandals' fate." Hampton allowed his men to ignore the laws of war, eschewing investigation and courts-martial to determine the guilt or innocence of Federal prisoners, and sanctioned murder.[39]

Sherman wrote Hampton that he had official reports that his foraging parties were murdered after capture and provided details of the locations. Sherman then violated a fundamental protocol of the ritual. Rather than give Hampton an opportunity to explain whether these were unsanctioned or official acts, he informed his enemy that he had ordered the execution of an equivalent number of prisoners. "I hold about 1000 prisoners captured in various ways, and can stand it as long as you," he wrote. Then Sherman made a crucial acknowledgment that in similar situations deterred other Union officers from executing any Confederate prisoners. "I hardly think these murders were committed with your knowledge, and would suggest that you give notice to the people at large that every life taken by them simply results in the death of one of your Confederates." Most officers in the Civil War declined to retaliate against innocent prisoners of war if the original atrocity was not an official act of the enemy leadership. Retaliation in such a case could not effect a change in policy because the barbarities were not official policy. Sherman, however, as he had stated to Hitchcock in Georgia, thought that the people of the Confederacy would police themselves if they truly believed a terrible punishment on their soldiers or community would inevitably follow.[40]

In this communication, when Sherman assumed that citizens committed the murders without Hampton's knowledge, he actually gave the Confederate general too much credit. Although there is no existing evidence that Hampton ordered the execution of Federal foragers, cavalry under his command acted in accordance with his stated beliefs. The fact that regularly enlisted Confederate soldiers killed Federal prisoners after capture clearly violated the laws of war. Under the customs practiced throughout the American Civil War, Sherman was justified in holding Hampton responsible for the behavior of his men through a retaliatory act, including the execution of prisoners.

Sherman's message to Hampton followed the ritual's protocol in one way, albeit with Sherman's unique style. In 1863, when Beauregard wrote to Gillmore about the sack of Darien and other Union raids along the South Carolina–Georgia coast, he had quoted Emer de Vattel, provided several historical references, and used the words "civilization" and "savagery" multiple times. Sherman in 1865 was blunt and direct. "Of course you cannot question my right to forage of the country," he said. "It is a war right as old as history." He quoted no authority, although he knew the books better than many Civil War commanders did, and argued without example that "the manner of exercising it varies with circumstances." Immediately after asserting the legality of foraging, Sherman broke retaliation's etiquette again. "I have no doubt this is the occasion of much misbehavior on the part of our men, but I cannot permit an enemy to judge or punish with wholesale murder," he wrote. Sherman admitted that his men did wrong.[41]

The retaliation ritual prompted Sherman to proclaim again the distinction between official foraging and unauthorized pillaging that his army blurred during its march north from Columbia. His correspondence reflected the internal debates within his army as much as it did external diplomacy with his enemy. The struggle to balance competing desires to fight a civilized war and to punish South Carolina was apparent in Sherman's complex response when Confederate citizens and soldiers murdered foragers. He intended to protect his foragers who followed the rules, but he would not protect stragglers and pillagers. He let his army know it. On February 25, a circular instructed corps and division commanders to retaliate life for life if foragers were killed after capture and to keep a record. "I want the foragers, however, to be kept within reasonable bounds for the sake of discipline," Sherman ordered. "I will not protect them when they enter dwellings and commit wanton waste, such as woman's apparel, jewelry, and such things as are not needed by our army." He publicly announced what he had communicated privately to Kilpatrick: if citizens of South Carolina resisted pillagers, "I will not deem it wrong." His division commanders recognized another reason to reassert discipline over the foragers: the force of Confederate cavalry on the army's flanks had increased in recent days and was picking up large numbers of foragers and stragglers. Orders to "keep men well in hand" and "in condition to meet an attack" flowed to the lower ranks.[42]

Hampton, in the meantime, had not yet received Sherman's message but learned through his own channels about the retaliatory executions. Col. George Gibbs Dibrell, a division commander under Wheeler, heard from slaves that the Yankees had hung eighteen Confederates between Wateree Meeting House and Rocky Mount in retaliation for the killing of their soldiers. "I have sent a scout down this side of the creek to learn certainly," he reported to Hampton on February 26. The next day, Sherman's letter arrived at Hampton's headquarters.[43]

Hampton's response reflected his code of chivalric vengeance in defense of property and female dependents. He accused Sherman of murder. If Sherman's foraging parties were "murdered" after capture, and Sherman responded in a like manner, then Sherman was guilty of murder. "I beg to assure you that for every soldier of mine 'murdered' by you," he wrote, "I shall have executed at once two of yours, giving in all cases preference to any officers who may be in my hands." Hampton claimed that he knew nothing about the deaths of Sherman's foragers and gave no orders to kill any prisoners after capture. "I do not believe that my men killed any of yours," he said, "except under circumstances in which it was perfectly legitimate and proper that they should kill them." Hampton made this assertion without any investigation of the circumstances of the killings. Hampton played an important part in the escalating violence in South Carolina because he made no attempt to stop the war crimes his subordinates committed.[44]

Hampton characterized Union foragers as thieves who robbed citizens and fired their houses. "To check this system, which is justly execrated by every civilized nation, I have directed my men to shoot down all of your men who are caught burning houses." Sherman was a "disgrace [to] the profession of arms" because he allowed his men "to destroy private dwellings." Hampton agreed that an army had the right to forage. "But there is a right, older, even, than this, and one more inalienable—the right that every man has to defend his home." He drew from the major rhetorical devices Confederates used to accuse Yankees of savagery. He hoped old men and young boys would shoot the "wild beasts" who insulted their women. "The Indian scalped his victim regardless of age or sex, but with all his barbarity he always respected the persons of his female captives," he said. "Your soldiers, more savage than the Indian, insult those whose natural protectors are absent." He set aside fifty-six Union prisoners of war as hostages. On March 1, Beauregard approved Hampton's order "to that vandal Sherman. The system of retaliation must be carried out at any cost."[45]

Sherman never responded to Hampton's message. His only reaction was a note to Howard on March 1: "I had an original communication from Wade Hampton yesterday." Forty-two Confederate prisoners of war were already dead, and another execution would follow the next day.[46] Sherman's retaliation orders were in place to protect his foragers, and he intended to use them. He did not care if Confederates killed his pillagers, who were indeed behaving barbarously, and he was on record as saying so. Sherman, as always, thought and acted outside the box. He violated the protocols of retaliation in South Carolina in 1865 and ignored the elements of the ritual that often served to de-escalate violence. On the other hand, since the record indicates that Hampton did not care if his men killed Yankee prisoners and refused to investigate the Federal allegations or hold his command responsible for their actions, Sherman's executions could be justified within the customs of war. Because of the extent of Confederate war crimes in South Carolina and his unflinching response to them, Sherman executed more prisoners of war during an active campaign than any other field commander of the American Civil War.[47]

Sherman fully understood the customs of war that the world expected of him. He expended copious amounts of ink during his campaigns justifying his actions, putting on record the restraints he demanded of his soldiers, and continually adjusting his orders to ensure the official records, if not the actual behavior of his soldiers, would hold up under scrutiny. As the retaliation ritual of February 1865 unfolded, Sherman amended the conduct of his army, conceded the Confederate perspective on his stragglers, and, like Kilpatrick had done, gave the Confederate army permission to kill any of his soldiers caught pillaging houses.

Only one of Sherman's subordinates retaliated for the death of a forager after Sherman received Hampton's message. On March 1, Confederates beat to death Pvt. Robert M. Woodruff, Company H, 30th Illinois Infantry, "a regularly detailed forager," near a bridge on the road to Cheraw. Blair ordered the 17th Corps's provost marshal to select one Confederate prisoner and shoot him. On March 2, Confederate prisoners captured by the 30th Illinois and held in a corral in that regiment's camp drew lots from a hat. A Methodist preacher, conscripted into the Confederate army, drew the black mark. The officer of the 30th Illinois charged with the execution, Maj. William C. Rhoads, initially refused to obey the order but complied when superiors threatened him with a court-martial. He detailed twelve men from Company H to form the firing squad, filled six rifles with blanks and six with balls, and gave the prisoner a chance to pray with a Baptist chaplain. Rhoads asked the prisoner if he had anything to say. "I was forced into the army, never was in battle, never wished the Yankees any harm," the man said. "I have a large family, all girls. I have been a local Methodist preacher." The soldiers of the 30th Illinois attending the execution wept openly in sympathy. "The man of Co. H that was killed, was not well thought of," the regimental historian wrote years later, "and many regrets were heard that a good man was killed for him." Rhoads gave the command, the squad opened fire, and five bullets struck the prisoner's body. He was buried with a marker enumerating the details of his death. In 1912, the Baptist chaplain who prayed with the prisoner still thought March 2, 1865, was the saddest day of his life and vividly remembered crying in his tent and begging not to participate in the execution.[48]

The regimental historian of the 30th Illinois remembered that the execution stopped the killing of foragers from his regiment. That was coincidentally true. Historians echo such memories and claim that the retaliation stopped the murder of foragers, although the lack of documentation on the Confederate side makes it difficult to determine the consequences of the executions. The killing of foragers clustered around the dates of February 22–March 2, numbering about sixty during that time. There is no record of Sherman's subordinates retaliating after March 2. Timing is an important element to the story.[49]

A change in orders and in the behavior of Union soldiers when Sherman's army crossed into North Carolina four days later may be the best way to account for the reduction in forager murders. After the advance units of the 17th Corps took Cheraw, South Carolina, on March 3, Sherman suggested that new rules would apply in North Carolina. On March 6, he instructed Slocum to tell citizens on the approach to Fayetteville that he would "deal harshly" with the town if any bridges were burned, but if there were no resistance, he would deal "generously" with the people. "We will dispose of all public stores and property but spare private houses . . . and keep the foragers from insulting families by word or rudeness," Sherman ordered. "It might be well to instruct your brigade commanders that we are now out of South Carolina and that a little moderation may be of political consequence to us in North Carolina." The next day, as the first units of his wing crossed the state border, Slocum complied. "All officers and soldiers of this command are reminded that the State of North Carolina was one of the last States that passed the ordinance of secession, and that from the commencement of the war there has been in this State a strong Union party," General Orders No. 8 read. "It should not be assumed that the inhabitants are enemies to our Government, and it is to be hoped that every effort will be made to prevent any wanton destruction of property, or any unkind treatment of citizens."[50]

Commanders of the right wing of Sherman's army, always the most outspoken against pillaging and house burning, used Sherman's attitude regarding North Carolina and an orgy of pillaging by the soldiers of the 17th Corps as they approached the state line to crack down. Blair reported to Howard on March 7 that soldiers pillaged every house on his line of march, breaking open trunks and stealing jewelry. "There is no cure except the entire cessation of foraging," he wrote. "The system is vicious and its results utterly deplorable." Sherman had told Blair that he would forbid foraging and would pay citizens for what his army took in North Carolina.[51]

On March 8, in light of this change in policy, Howard issued new orders. He allowed only one foraging party, of sixty men, for each division. The foragers could not advance beyond the lead infantry guard or spread more than five miles from a column's flank. They had to turn surplus animals over to their corps' quartermaster. This requirement struck a blow at pillagers, who had acquired excess horses and mules and used them to independently range across the South Carolina countryside. Howard charged divisions with organizing a provost guard and placing guards "at every house on the line of march." Blair added additional controls for the 17th Corps. "The state of North Carolina is to a great extent loyal," Special Orders No. 63 declared, "and as such, a marked difference should be made in the manner in which we treat the people, and the manner in which those of South Carolina were treated. Nothing should be taken from them except what is absolutely necessary for the use of the army." Foragers could not separate from the group or enter houses. He ordered division commanders to confiscate animals from soldiers "not authorized to be mounted" and created division patrols to "arrest and dismount all mounted men found away from the line of march, unless they are regularly detailed foragers with their officers." During the next few days, line officers of the 15th and 17th Corps arrested men absent their commands without orders. The 1st Division of the 15th Corps made such soldiers dig deep wells and refill them, over and over.[52]

Confederates murdered foragers in disproportionately high numbers, and Federals executed forty-three prisoners of war, an aberration for the American Civil War, because conditions in South Carolina in February 1865 made for a perfect storm. Sherman and Hampton were unique personalities, Union soldiers possessed a particular hatred for the state, fringe elements on both sides had been committing atrocities for months, and Confederate men seethed with hatred and frustration at their inability to defend their families and homes. In this moment, retaliation against prisoners of war exemplified, rather than defused, the local dynamic of violence.

Juxtaposed against this failure of a local retaliation ritual was the crowning success of the long-unfolding national retaliation ritual over the Confederacy's 1863 threat to prosecute freeborn Black Union soldiers for inciting slave insurrection. On February 8, 1865, the Confederate government officially changed its policy and amended its original resolutions. The Confederate Congress passed a resolution that substituted the phrase "employ our negro slaves" for the original phrase "employ negroes in war against the Confederate states" in its statement of how the United States violated the precepts of civilized war. Legislators repealed the sections that required military courts to execute or punish white officers and that required Confederate officers to deliver Black prisoners to state authorities. Two weeks later, Confederate exchange agents delivered fourteen Black U.S. soldiers to the Union exchange agent in Virginia, an act that proclaimed the Black men's status as prisoners of war. Historians who assert that the United States resumed exchange without concessions from the Confederate government overlook these two important events. The Union retaliation on behalf of Black men who were citizens of Northern states, involving hostages from South Carolina and a refusal to exchange prisoners, had worked. It had taken eighteen months, but the Confederate government adjusted its policy and put it on record for the world to see.[53]

The U.S. War Department, aware of the pending legislation in the Confederate Congress, agreed to renew the general exchange of prisoners. Grant authorized his subordinates on February 5 to exchange all prisoners of war held in the Department of the South. Twenty-seven prisoners from the 54th Massachusetts were still alive in the Confederate military prison at Florence, despite deteriorating conditions there throughout the winter. Its commandant, Lt. Col. John F. Iverson, reported that 3,000 of his 7,000 Federal prisoners were sick. They had no clothes, and he did not have enough rations to distribute. Maj. Archibald Bogle, the wounded officer captured at the Battle of Olustee in command of the former slaves of the 1st North Carolina, was also still alive. When Confederate prison authorities evacuated Andersonville during Sherman's march through Georgia, they sent Bogle under special escort to Camp Lawton, a forty-two-acre camp for enlisted men near Millen, Georgia, intended to be the largest in the world. A Confederate officer there instructed the clerk not to register Bogle's name in order to inhibit any chance of his exchange. Bogle eventually joined his Black enlisted comrades from the Battle of Olustee in the prison pens of South Carolina.[54]

The designated exchange point for the Federal prisoners held in Florence was Wilmington, North Carolina. On February 15, Confederate officials removed all of the prisoners who were able to travel, including the men from the 54th. A train took them to Cheraw, where the line terminated. The prisoners marched eighty-three miles from there to a station on the North Carolina Railroad, where cars took them to Goldsboro, North Carolina. They were turned out into an open field. Bogle received a parole. About 360 of the sick prisoners were put in a makeshift hospital on the fairgrounds outside of town. Confederate prison officials, no strangers to the suffering of Federal prisoners, reported that the "neglect, filth, and squalor" of this place was unequaled in their experience. It was a "state of affairs that I felt disgraced our character for humanity," admitted one of them. On February 22, a Federal army captured Wilmington. Between February 26 and March 4, Confederate officials delivered 8,684 prisoners of war, 120 of them Black Union soldiers, at a railroad crossing on the Northeast Cape Fear River. On March 4, all of the Confederate officers brought to the Department of the South for retaliation sailed north from Fort Pulaski and Hilton Head to the Fort Delaware military prison to await their exchange.[55]

The prisoners from the 54th arrived in boxcars that stopped right at the point where guard outposts marked the extent of the Federal lines outside Wilmington. "I did not believe we would be paroled until within an hour of the time we were," one white prisoner recalled. "What made me believe at last was seeing a colored soldier on picket by the side of the railroad, with Uncle Sam's uniform on." As the prisoners exited the trains, a Confederate and Union agent counted them, placing a hand on each man's shoulder and yelling out the number. They walked to the camps of Federal regiments stationed at the river, whose men had made banners wreathed in evergreens that read "We Welcome You Home Our Brothers" and had prepared rations and coffee for them. When the liberated prisoners saw the U.S. flag, the Federal guards presenting arms, and the welcome banner, tumult erupted. Men leaped in the air "like ballet dancers," shouted, fell down on the side of the road and "wept like children," waved hats and caps, and "hugged and cried." Of the thirteen soldiers of the 54th captured on Sol Legare Island on July 16, 1863, the first prisoners from the regiment, nine survived to participate in this happy moment.[56]

The Union prisoners who were former slaves, with a few exceptions, such as Frank Mattocks, an enlisted man from the 1st North Carolina who survived Andersonville and Florence, were excluded from the exchanges that occurred near the end of the war. The Confederate government did not hold trials for them and publicly execute them in mass numbers, as its original resolutions threatened, but it never conceded they were legitimate soldiers. The Confederate military always viewed and treated them as servile insurrectionists and recovered property. Confederate soldiers often murdered them on the battlefield. When captured, Confederate military officials used them as slave laborers, returned them to their former owners, or sold them at auction. There were at least 2,323 Black captives from forty-eight different USCT regiments; the Confederate military enslaved 1,900 of them. The United States recovered 201 Black prisoners through exchange and 384 through liberation by Union forces. The number of Black soldiers who died while in Confederate military captivity is a confirmed 273, but the probable total is 686, a mortality rate double that of white captives.[57]

A few of the 54th's prisoners exchanged at Wilmington returned to their regiment before it mustered out. One of these was Daniel States, the Pennsylvania farmer whose life was saved at Fort Wagner by the Confederate officer who wrote down the names of his guards. Two others were Edward Johnson, a laborer from Evansville, Indiana, and George Morris, a seaman from Philadelphia, both captured at the Battle of Olustee and survivors of Andersonville (three of the ten soldiers from the 54th confined in Camp Sumter died there). They found the 54th on occupation duty in Charleston, camped along the lines of the abandoned Confederate defensive works that ran through the graves of Magnolia Cemetery.[58]

Black soldiers of the Union army entered Charleston on February 18 after Confederate troops had evacuated the city during the previous night. The lieutenant colonel of the 21st USCT accepted the mayor's surrender. The city was on fire; Confederate troops had torched cotton bales piled in the public squares, a railroad depot exploded, and the blazes spread to private houses. The lower part of the city was deserted. "The effect of our firing on

"Marching On: the 55th Massachusetts Colored Regiment Singing 'John Brown's March' in the Streets of Charleston." (*Harper's Weekly: A Journal of Civilization*, March 18, 1865, 165)

the houses was much more disastrous than I had supposed, far more so than at Vicksburg," one of Gillmore's staff officers wrote. "In some streets there is scarcely a house whose walls and roofs are not torn in great holes." Black and Irish citizens of Charleston greeted the occupying Union soldiers. "The scene at the wharf was perfectly indescribable," he said. "The band played Dixie and the negroes went perfectly wild, shouting, dancing, beside themselves with excitement."[59]

Two ceremonies marked the death of the Confederacy in Charleston. On March 21, the freed people in the city held a parade to celebrate the "Burying of Slavery." The band of the 21st USCT and the enlisted men of that regiment marched first. One float portrayed a slave block with two Black people chained to it, and behind that came a hearse bearing a sign, "Slavery is dead. Rebellion killed it." Women and children who attended the new public schools established in the city marched next, singing "John Brown's Body" and carrying banners reading, "We Know no Masters but Ourselves." On April 14, U.S. government officials and Northern dignitaries, including abolitionist William Lloyd Garrison and celebrity pastor Henry Ward Beecher, gathered at Fort Sumter to watch Bvt. Maj. Gen. Robert Anderson raise the U.S. flag that he had lowered on the same date in 1861. The ceremonies concluded the next day with a jubilee at Zion Church, where an elderly freedman gave a welcome speech to Garrison that dissolved the visitors to tears.[60]

As white Southerners looked upon these scenes of celebration, they did not just see the end of a political movement for independence, or the end of a labor system, or the end of white supremacy. They saw the collapse of civilization itself.

CONCLUSION

# THE CRISIS OF CIVILIZATION

Retaliation, the method provided by the customs of war to negotiate the conduct of civilized war, was in the spotlight from 1861 to 1865. Officers and soldiers in the Union and Confederate armies feared that a civil war would destroy their civilization and unleash the darkest passions of men. Properly conducting the retaliation ritual preserved honor before a watching civilized world, demonstrated a commitment to a set of rules that guaranteed one's place in civilization, and revealed the atrocious acts of the enemy. Confederates used retaliation to express their outrage when the Union armed "savage" Blacks for servile insurrection, bombarded residential areas of cities, and unleashed pillagers who entered the homes of civilized women. Officers of the United States used retaliation to protect the freeborn Black men who wore the Federal uniform and the Union prisoners turned into animals under the treatment given them by their captors.

During Reconstruction, the rhetoric of civilization and savagery continued to shape political and social debates over the conduct of the war and the postwar task of rebuilding Southern civilization. Both sides insisted they had fought a civilized war and that the other side had not. This reflected the continued importance of vindicating honor and winning the narrative before domestic political audiences, the civilized nations of the world, and future scholars who would pronounce the verdict of history. Robert Gould Shaw's parents had to defend the honor of their son in a *Harper's Weekly* notice on September 3, 1870. The rector of St. Andrew's church in Darien, Georgia, had recently published a national appeal asking for aid for his parish. It claimed that "without an engagement, the town of Darien, Georgia, was taken and burned by the United States colored troops, Colonel SHAW, Fifty-Fourth

Massachusetts Regiment, commanding." The Shaws published their son's correspondence that revealed his own outrage over the burning and his request never again to participate in "barbarous" destruction. The rector's response, in the October 1 issue, acknowledged the colonel's "blamelessness" and his parents' tacit admission that it was a "disgrace to burn a defenseless town."[1]

The Republican Party used the Confederate treatment of prisoners of war as the overarching symbol to represent the barbarity of the rebellion. Congress conducted an investigation in 1869 that concluded that rebel atrocities were "characteristics of savage life." Confederates "professedly aspire to civilization" but instead had "failed" to "master old passions, traditions, and prejudices." The House report provided a historical survey of war practices among "Savage and Half-Civilized Tribes and Nations." "The savage is the worst and lowest state of society," it read. "Their practices in war are governed by the passions or prejudices of each individual or tribe, since they have no well-organized society, no code of morals, no restraining influences of religion and no recognized international law." Savages murdered prisoners of war as soon as captured, sold them like stock, enslaved them, treated them with cruel severity, and subjected them to the "will of the captor or the master." Republicans dedicated the rest of the report to show that savage Confederates did all of those things to their prisoners. During congressional debates and local election campaigns through the 1870s, Republicans used Confederate massacres of Black troops and savage treatment of white prisoners to justify policies designed to remake the barbaric South into an image of the civilized North.[2]

Black veterans of the U.S. Army, especially those prominent in the Republican Party, proclaimed the message that their wartime restraint, in contrast with the barbarity of Confederates, proved their civilized status and their claim to equal political rights. The Grand Army of the Republic, the powerful postwar veterans' organization, commissioned Joseph T. Wilson, a veteran of the 2nd Louisiana Native Guards and the 54th Massachusetts, to write an official history of Black troops in the Civil War. Wilson had been severely wounded at the Battle of Olustee. *The Black Phalanx*, published in 1888 to wide acclaim, centered on the contrast between "barbaric" Confederates who "waged a war of extermination against the negro soldier" and the moral discipline of the USCT. Wilson dedicated the book to the "Brave Men Who Commanded the Black Phalanx." "You were outlawed by the decrees of Jefferson Davis," he wrote. "The record of the Black Phalanx, invites the scrutiny of all who have been disposed to taunt you for associating

"The Last of the First Negro Soldiers: The First South Carolina Volunteers." During Reconstruction, Black veterans insisted that their restraint during the Civil War proved their civilized status, their manhood, and their claim to equal political rights. (From the Penn School Collection, Wilson Library, University of North Carolina at Chapel Hill. Permission granted by Penn Center, Inc., St. Helena Island, S.C.)

with 'armed barbarians.' No massacre of vanquished foe stains the banners of those who followed you, giving quarter but receiving none. It was your teaching that served as a complete restraint against retaliation, though statesmen hinted it would be just. Your training developed patriotism and courage, but not revenge."[3]

Southerners insisted that only Confederate soldiers maintained honor and civilization throughout the conflict. The Immortal 600, the postwar club of the Confederate officers brought to Morris Island and subjected to the ration retaliation at Fort Pulaski and Hilton Head, folded the "savage" treatment they received into the Lost Cause narrative. They published narratives that highlighted the brutality of the "bestial" Black guards from the 54th Massachusetts, "savages" unfit for political rights, and the vindictive behavior of Yankee officers, barbarians unworthy of imposing terms on a defeated South.[4]

William Tecumseh Sherman and Wade Hampton continued their rhetorical dueling over Sherman's conduct in South Carolina through the 1880s. It began when Hampton showed up to the surrender negotiations at Bennett Place, North Carolina, carrying a freshly cut switch rather than a sword, a "weapon" appropriate for "children, slaves, and impudent Yankees, not honorable warriors." Henry Hitchcock recognized the "carefully calculated insult" and was appalled. "His whole demeanor was marked with the easy 'well-bred' essentially vulgar insolence which is characteristic of *that* type of 'gentleman,'" he said. "A man of polished manners, scarcely veiling the utter arrogance and selfishness which marks his class, and which I hate with a perfect hatred." Hampton dedicated the rest of his life to vindicating his personal honor and that of the Confederate cause. Yankees would always be, in his mind, house-burning pillagers. The free Black man, he said, might "elevate himself in the scale of civilization," but only if he deferred to the paternalistic leadership of propertied white elites. The Black troops who occupied South Carolina during Reconstruction were a "horde of barbarians, brutal negro troops, under their no less brutal and more degraded Yankee officers." Sherman, for his part, publicly blamed Hampton for the burning of Columbia in a published report of June 1865 and cited an order from P. G. T. Beauregard to burn cotton in the city before Confederate troops evacuated. Hampton had transmitted it with his signature, but he thought the order unwise and convinced Beauregard to countermand it, although the second order was issued too late to stop Confederate troops from firing piles of cotton in the street. Sherman's accusation "enraged Hampton more than any other event in his life," his biographer concludes. "The highest duty of the chivalric knight was home defense. It was the ultimate slander." Hampton sent a long letter to the *New York Day Book* that "explicitly called Sherman a liar and a violator of ladies." The controversy prompted discussion in the U.S. Senate and popular Northern newspapers and journals and resulted in an 1873 joint United States–British investigation of the Columbia fire.[5]

Despite the ubiquitous presence of the rhetoric of civilization and savagery in the postwar period in public speeches, newspaper editorials, works of literature, private correspondence, and personal diaries, historians who write about Reconstruction in the South generally minimize the language in favor of gender, race, or economic interpretations. Important as these are, we need to do a better job of placing the overarching model of civilization into our analysis. It was foundational to nineteenth-century Americans and was the lens through which most of them viewed the world around them; they folded gender and race into the civilization construct, not vice versa. It was a holistic worldview that applied across all aspects of their lives, from eating to fighting war. It ordered their place in the natural world, incorporated their relationship with animals, and encompassed how they viewed the entire trajectory of human history. Reconstruction was not just a process of reunification, or a reassertion of white supremacy, or a restructuring of labor, or a political blip in the story of capitalism's triumph. It was an attempt to rebuild a new civilization on the ashes of an old one.[6]

The U.S. Army, for its part, never again used the ritual of retaliation to shape its campaigns. In the latter half of the nineteenth century, it was engaged in projects of empire, spreading civilization across the North American Plains and across the seas to the people in Puerto Rico and the Philippines. Army commanders saw only savage or barbaric enemies who were not worthy of the honorable rituals conducted between civilized equals. In the Great Plains, the War Department used military commissions to execute Indians for violating the laws of war and held Indians as prisoners indefinitely, while its soldiers massacred women and children. In the Philippine War (1899–1902), there was no formal correspondence with the enemy guerrillas, who were not considered legal combatants. Army commanders there were concerned with the honor of the United States and insisted that American troops follow the laws of war. They issued General Orders No. 100 immediately after landing on the islands, enforced its provisions, and court-martialed officers for violations. Local commanders executed guerrillas on the spot if they were captured with arms in their hands or conducted retaliatory burnings of houses and buildings located near an attack, but these actions were sanctioned under General Orders No. 100 and did not require discussion with the enemy.[7]

When the United States fought against foes its army commanders considered civilized—Spain in Cuba in 1898 and Germany in the Great War in 1918—retaliation rituals had already faded away. The judgments of the civilized world had been codified and formalized. European nations used General Orders No. 100 as the basis for a conference in Brussels in 1874 that produced the International Declaration Concerning the Laws and Customs of War. The peace conferences at The Hague in 1899 and 1907 created treaties that bound signatories to conduct war and treat prisoners according to a detailed set of rules. International tribunals and war crime commissions took the place of formal retaliation rituals. They judged disputes between nations, ensured the proper treatment of prisoners of war, and punished offenders who violated the laws of war.[8]

Retaliation rituals also ended because they had a mixed record in the American Civil War. Both sides could provide evidence that it worked: the United States had backed away from John Pope's orders, and the Confederacy had granted combatant status to Black citizens of the North. It also failed. Confederates remained convinced that former slaves had no place in civilized war (or civilized society), and nothing had stopped them from re-enslaving Black Union soldiers and massacring them on the battlefield. The Union bombardment turned parts of Charleston into a wasteland. Sherman's army brought the war inside the domestic spaces of white women. Conditions in the prisons of both sides turned men into animals. Ethan Allen Hitchcock was ultimately right. Retaliation could not and did not solve the fundamental issues at stake between the combatants. The fighting did that.

By using retaliation, both combatants in the American Civil War self-consciously made their case to subsequent generations and requested the verdict of history. Union and Confederate officers believed that historians who read their correspondence dispassionately would determine who was civilized and who was savage. They never dreamed those categories would fade away from American culture and from historical analysis. This book has returned the focus to the mental constructs of Civil War combatants and to the war as they experienced it. It was the crisis of their civilization.

# NOTES

## ABBREVIATIONS

| | |
|---|---|
| AHEC | U.S. Army Heritage and Education Center, Carlisle, Pa. |
| APWV | John W. M. Appleton Papers, West Virginia and Regional History Center, Morgantown |
| CWD | Civil War Documents Collection, U.S. Army Heritage and Education Center, Carlisle, Pa. |
| EAHLC | Ethan Allen Hitchcock Papers, Library of Congress Manuscript Division, Washington, D.C. |
| FLP | Francis Lieber Papers, Huntington Library, San Marino, Calif. |
| GO | General Orders |
| JBM | Journal of James B. McCreary, Midwest Manuscript Collection, Newberry Library, Chicago |
| LOC | Library of Congress Manuscript Division, Washington, D.C. |
| MHS | Massachusetts Historical Society, Boston |
| NARA | National Archives and Records Administration, Washington, D.C. |
| OLS | Battle of Olustee.org |
| *OR* | U.S. War Department, *The War of the Rebellion: A Compilation of the Official Records of the Union and Confederate Armies*, 127 vols., Washington, D.C.: Government Printing Office, 1880–1901 |
| RG | Record Group |
| SCL | South Caroliniana Library, University of South Carolina, Columbia |
| SPLC | Edwin McMasters Stanton Papers, Library of Congress Manuscript Division, Washington, D.C. |
| VHS | Virginia Historical Society, Richmond |
| VMI | Virginia Military Institute Archives Digital Collections |

## INTRODUCTION

1. Emilio, *Brave Black Regiment*, 222–23; Higginson, *Army Life in a Black Regiment*, 111; Saxton, *Regiment Remembered*, 109.

2. Dahlgren, *Memoir of John A. Dahlgren*, 533; Schwartz, *Woman Doctor's Civil War*, 90; Prince, *Letters and Diary of Henry W. Prince*, 86; McMichael, *Autograph and Diary*, entry of September 8, 1864; entry of September 7, 1864, JBM; Richard H. Adams Jr. Civil War Prisoner of War Diary, entry of September 7, 1864, VMI; Williams and Kutzler, *Prison Pens*, 128; Fontaine, *Prison Life*, 24.

3. Foster to Saxton, September 2, 1864, *OR*, ser. 2, vol. 7: 712; diary entries of September 7–9, 1864, Samuel Horace Hawes Papers, VHS; McGrath, *History of the 127th New York*, 104; Fulkerson, "Prison Experience of a Confederate Soldier," 137–38.

4. GO No. 100, April 24, 1863, *OR*, ser. 3, vol. 3: 151.

5. Although Civil War scholars have recently produced several first-rate studies that consider the international laws of war and include some discussion of retaliation, this is the first book-length study of the subject published by an academic press. Its characterization of retaliation as a ritual and its assertion that retaliation shaped practice on the ground in every military campaign is original. The most important works that helped shape my thinking are Sheehan-Dean, *Calculus of Violence*, and Dilbeck, *A More Civil War*. For an excellent case study of retaliatory violence in the irregular Civil War, see Myers, *Executing Daniel Bright*. For a discussion of retaliation in the context of an argument that President Lincoln "did not authorize or condone any violations of the laws of war against enemy civilians" (119), see Carnahan, *Lincoln on Trial*. For a good overview of retaliation as part of prisoner policy but without discussing those involved in military campaigns, see Sanders, *While in the Hands of the Enemy*. Springer, *America's Captives*, discusses the precedent of retaliation in the American Revolution and the Mexican War. A study of retaliation published by a nonacademic press presents several cases to claim that both sides committed atrocities, but none of the cases is placed in cultural or military context. See Speer, *War of Vengeance*.

6. The behavior of partisans and guerrillas produced many retaliation incidents in Virginia, Kentucky, Tennessee, Missouri, Arkansas, Mississippi, and Louisiana. Federal military officials often summarily executed captured guerrillas and responded to guerrilla attacks with punitive policies against citizens. They arrested men and women, burned houses within a given radius of a guerrilla attack, confiscated foodstuffs, and ordered retaliatory executions against prisoners of war. Jefferson Davis and his West Point–trained general officers tried to rein in irregular warfare, but they also thought that citizens had the right to take up arms in self-defense when their neighborhoods were invaded. Because Davis and his cabinet believed that Federal armies had oppressed and maltreated citizens since the opening of hostilities, they used retaliation when the U.S. Army targeted citizens during anti-guerrilla operations. Because the Confederate government disapproved of the actions of guerrillas in many cases, retaliation incidents over guerrillas had a different dynamic than other issues. Confederate senator Henry Foote (Mississippi) introduced a bill in August 1862 to retaliate for the protection of partisan rangers, but it was referred to a committee and never passed. For a discussion of retaliation and guerrillas, see Foote, "Sternest Feature of War"; Sheehan-Dean, *Calculus of Violence*, 73–79, 380; Myers, *Executing Daniel Bright*; and Mountcastle, *Punitive War*.

7. For an exploration of the varying patterns of violence across space and time, see Sheehan-Dean, *Calculus of Violence*. Lee's discussion of the fruitfulness of identifying factors that restrain and factors that escalate violence in a given conflict has also influenced this book; see *Barbarians and Brothers*. For a study that emphasizes restraint, see Neely, *Civil War and the Limits of Destruction*. For studies that emphasize violence, see Nelson, *Ruin Nation*; Cashin, *War Stuff*; Berry, *Weirding the War*; and Royster, *Destructive War*.

8. Anyone interested in the laws of war should consult Neff, *Justice in Blue and Gray*; Sheehan-Dean, *Calculus of Violence*; and Witt, *Lincoln's Code*.

9. This worldview differentiated humans from animals with criteria such as literacy, religion, highly complex social organization, agriculture (especially commercial as

opposed to subsistence), art and music, mastery over nature, cleanliness, refined manners, and the like. The list of criteria was long. The category of "barbarian" indicated people who had mastered some but not all of the necessary achievements. Some civilizations were "higher" than others in terms of advancing toward the full human potential. Scholars working at the end of the twentieth century and the beginning of the twenty-first have shown that race, gender, and labor are important categories of analysis for understanding American society during this period. Labor structure, gender arrangements, and race were part of a much broader picture of civilization that nineteenth-century Americans considered in evaluating their world. My thinking about the worldview of civilization has been shaped particularly by the following works: K. Thomas, *Man and the Natural World*; Bushman, *Refinement of America*; Bederman, *Manliness and Civilization*; Berry, *All That Makes a Man*; and DeMello, *Animals and Society*.

10. For a thorough consideration of Confederate rhetoric that demonized Yankees and continually accused them of savagery and atrocities, see Rable, *Damn Yankees!* Rable considers public rhetoric regarding retaliation on pp. 106–8.

11. Mitchell, in *Vacant Chair*, identified the importance of self-control contrasted with its opposite as a key feature of Northern thinking from the start of the war.

12. For centuries, philosophers and theologians have sought to place constraints on the violence of war. Augustine in the fourth century, Thomas Aquinas in the Middle Ages, and Francisco Suárez, Alberico Gentili, and Francisco de Vitoria in the sixteenth century wrote about "just" war—wars that were morally justified. In the early medieval period, however, monarchs and churchmen believed that if war was fought for pious ends, there was no limit to how it could be waged. In the ninth and tenth centuries, ecclesiastics tried to limit intra-Christian violence and to direct warfare toward pagan Vikings, Hungarians, and Muslims. The first step toward the modern laws of war was the Peace and Truce of God movements in France that attempted to define and protect noncombatants. The next step occurred during the Age of Chivalry, when knightly custom and legal theory derived from Roman law created a formal system of military law in the twelfth through fourteenth centuries. While theologians mostly wrote about whether a war should be fought at all, secular philosophers concentrated on laws for conducting war, and armies developed legal codes to govern conduct of troops. In the European early modern period, when the Continent emerged from the wars of religion, international relations specialists such as Hugo Grotius abandoned the question of whether a war was justified. Writers accepted war as part of international politics but wrote increasingly of restraints that should govern the conduct of armies. Social and economic factors also influenced the rise of "limited war" as a concept. In the seventeenth and eighteenth centuries, monarchs fought for political power rather than ideology and used paid professional armies. Napoleonic warfare, despite its citizen armies and ideological fervor, was more limited in many ways than wars in earlier centuries, although examples of commanders and armies abandoning restraint were common in both periods. By the nineteenth century, there was a broad consensus in the middle-class culture of the Atlantic World that war should be as moral and humane as possible. Europeans applied *guerre mortelle* (no rules and indiscriminate slaughter of the enemy) to rebels, infidels, and savages. For helpful overviews of the Western traditions that informed nineteenth-century American thinking about civilized war, see Howard, Andreopoulos, and Shulman, *Laws of War*; Corey and Charles, *Just War Tradition*; Cowdrey, "Peace and Truce of God"; and Lynn, *Battle*.

13. Sheehan-Dean notes that historical examples and analogies helped ordinary

Americans make sense of the Civil War. He demonstrates that the Napoleonic wars were the benchmark, the contemporary Crimean War a common reference, and the Indian Rebellion of 1857 a frequently used parallel when Americans discussed precedents for civilized and savage behaviors. See *Calculus of Violence*, 18–19, 36, 67. For a good introduction to the concept of honor in the Civil War era, see Foote, *Gentlemen and the Roughs*; Elder, *Sacred Mirror*; C. Smith, *American Honor*; K. Greenberg, *Honor and Slavery*; and Wyatt-Brown, *Honor and Violence*.

14. Halleck, "Retaliation in War," 110; Lincoln to Rosecrans, November 19, 1864, in Basler, *Collected Works*, 8:116; Seddon to Ould, June 24, 1863, *OR*, ser. 2, vol. 6: 41–47; Younger, *Inside the Confederate Government*, 53; Sheehan-Dean, *Calculus of Violence*, 40–42. Dilbeck, *A More Civil War*, delineates how the moral demands of Christianity influenced limitations on retaliation as he considers the question of whether the Union waged a just war (92–98). Carnahan, *Lincoln on Trial*, offers evidence that Lincoln "was continually concerned that military actions be undertaken only for valid military reasons, and never for motives of revenge or cruelty" (33).

15. Randolph to Harris, June 29, 1862, *OR*, ser. 2, vol. 4: 793–94; Younger, *Inside the Confederate Government*, 170; Jones to Randolph, April 22, 1862, Randolph to Jones, April 24, 1862, and Randolph to Anderson, May 18, 1862, *OR*, ser. 2, vol. 3: 565, 855–58; Croffut, *Fifty Years in Camp and Field*, 457; Halleck to Ludlow, July 2, 1863, *OR*, ser. 2, vol. 6: 73.

16. GO No. 49, February 27, 1862, *OR*, ser. 2, vol. 3, pt. 1: 334; Halleck, "Retaliation in War," 107–13.

17. Lieber to Halleck, June 2, 1863, box 27, and April 19 and December 21, 1864, box 28, FLP.

18. Butler to Patrick, October 12, 1864, GO No. 126, October 13, 1864, Grant to Butler, October 20, 1864, and GO No. 134, October 20, 1864, *OR*, ser. 1, vol. 42, pt. 3: 185, 216–17, 285–86; Sparks, *Inside Lincoln's Army*, 429; J. Jones, *Rebel War Clerk's Diary*, 313. When Lieber read about this retaliation in the *New York Times*, he wrote Halleck that Benjamin Butler, the Union general responsible for initiating it, was wrong to think that putting POWs to labor on fortifications violated the laws of war. Halleck acknowledged Lieber's point but responded that recent practice in European wars was not to require labor of prisoners. Lieber to Halleck, October 15, 1864, box 28, and Halleck to Lieber, October 16, 1864, box 10, FLP.

19. Lieber to Halleck, April 19, 1864, box 28, FLP; Lee to Seddon, July 18, 1864, *OR*, ser. 2, vol. 7: 473; Sheehan-Dean, "*Lex Talionis*," 174–75. Sheehan-Dean demonstrates that officers and civilians throughout the North and South were aware of retaliation's place in international law and its parameters. Global military theory strongly influenced their thought and behavior.

20. GO No. 13, December 4, 1861, and GO No. 48, February 26, 1862, *OR*, ser. 2, vol. 1: 233–36, 267–68; Halleck, "Retaliation in War," 110–12. The U.S. Army's official 1914 guide to the laws of war still maintained this position: "Persons guilty of no offence whatever may be punished as retaliation for the guilty acts of others." See Carnahan, *Lincoln on Trial*, 53.

21. Davis to Lee, July 31, 1862, and GO No. 54, August 1, 1862, *OR*, ser. 2, vol. 4: 830–31, 836–37; Stanton to Lincoln, May 5, 1864, box 42, reel 14, Letterbooks 1863–1865, SPLC; Halleck, "Retaliation in War," 115–18. Evidence from the retaliation ritual presented in this book challenges Carnahan's point that the concept of "command responsibility" did not arise until after World War II. See *Lincoln on Trial*, 7, 98. Although no writer in the Civil War used this term or defined the concept in a twentieth-century manner, Jefferson

Davis and others believed that commanders were responsible for the atrocities their men committed and could be punished for them through the retaliation ritual.

22. Thomas to Hood, January 13, 1865, *OR*, ser. 2, vol. 8: 64–65; Grant to Lee, March 14, 1865, and Lee to Grant, March 23, 1865, *OR*, ser. 2, vol. 8: 393, 425.

23. Crist, Dix, and Williams, *Papers of Jefferson Davis*, 8:339 and 11:369.

24. Ethan A. Hitchcock, Biographical Sketch of Class of 1817, Ethan Allen Hitchcock Papers, West Point Military Academy, Special Collections; undated autobiographical manuscript, box 8, EAHLC.

25. Hitchcock to Stanton, November 9, 1863, and Halleck to Stanton, November 15, 1863, *OR*, ser. 2, vol. 6: 486, 523–24; Stanton to Hitchcock, November 9, 1863, box 41, reel 14, Letterbooks 1863–1865, SPLC.

26. Hitchcock to Mann, November 15, and Mann to Hitchcock, November 18, box 3, EAHLC; Hoar to Hitchcock, November 19, 1863, Hitchcock Papers, West Point Military Academy; Hawthorne to Hitchcock, November 16 and 22, box 11, W. A. Croffut Papers, LOC.

27. Hitchcock to Mann, November 23, 1863, box 3, EAHLC; Dilbeck, *A More Civil War*, 112–13; Gillispie, *Andersonvilles of the North*, 232. For a perspective that Stanton and Radical Republicans vindictively manipulated public reporting of the condition of returned Union prisoners in the spring of 1864 in order to rouse public opinion in favor of retaliation, see Pickenpaugh, *Captives in Gray*, 189; and Marvel, *Lincoln's Autocrat*, 309.

28. Sheehan-Dean argues that the Civil War "witnessed few of the cycles of retributive killing that have marked other conflicts" because of its decentralized nature. Rogue commanders enacted unsanctioned violence, but the cooling-off period and diplomacy inherent in retaliation negotiations caused attention to wane, and authorities could usually plausibly deny culpability. *Calculus of Violence*, 333, 353. For Hitchcock's perspective, see Paragraphs of Endorsements, Ethan Allen Hitchcock, June 1–11, 1863, box 3, EAHLC; and Ethan Allen Hitchcock Memoir, box 9, W. A. Croffut Papers, LOC.

## CHAPTER 1

1. Miller, *Lincoln's Abolitionist General*, viii, 79, 264; Hunter to Stanton, June 23, 1862, *OR*, ser. 3, vol. 2: 196–98; Hunter to Stanton, April 30, 1863, box 11, reel 4, SPLC.

2. Foote, *Seeking the One Great Remedy*, 53–87; Foote, "Rich Man's War"; Duncan, *Blue-Eyed Child of Fortune*, 1–18, 176–86.

3. Sawtelle to Dear Parents, November 13, 1861, box 102, folder 13, Orlando P. Sawtelle Papers, CWD; Kingsley to Dear Mother, December 13, 1861, box 66, folder 2, Caroll E. Kingsley Papers, CWD; Symonds, *Lincoln and His Admirals*, 37, 69; McPherson, *War on the Waters*, 41–48, 134; R. Browning, *Success Is All That Was Expected*, 41.

4. National Freedmen's Relief Association, *National Freedmen's Relief Association*, 3–10; W. Rose, *Rehearsal for Reconstruction*, 3–29; Foote, *Seeking the One Great Remedy*, 91–92; Manning, *Troubled Refuge*, 78–80.

5. GO No. 9, Headquarters Expeditionary Corps, February 6, 1862, *OR*, ser. 1, vol. 6: 222–23.

6. GO No. 17, March 6, 1863, *OR*, ser. 1, vol. 14: 1020–21.

7. Higginson, *Army Life in a Black Regiment*, 211–14; Looby, *Thomas Wentworth Higginson*, 280–81; Benham to De La Croix, May 6, 1862, Hunter to Stevens, May 8, 1862, and Pierce to Chase, May 12, 1862, *OR*, ser. 3, vol. 2: 29–30, 52–54.

8. GO No. 11, Department of the South, May 9, 1862, *OR*, ser. 1, vol. 14: 341; Ely to Stevens, Wright, etc., May 11, 1862, and Pierce to Hunter, May 11, 1862, *OR*, ser. 3, vol. 2: 29–31, 54–56; Holland, *Letters and Diary of Laura M. Towne*, 41.

9. Pierce to Hunter, May 11 and 13, 1862, *OR*, ser. 3, vol. 2: 56.

10. Wells to Pierce, n.d., and Phillips to Pierce, May 13, 1862, *OR*, ser. 3, vol. 2: 58–60.

11. Pierce to Chase, May 12, 1862, *OR*, ser. 3, vol. 2: 52–53.

12. "By the President of the United States: A Proclamation," May 19, 1862, *OR*, ser. 3, vol. 2: 42–43.

13. Andrew to Stanton, May 19, 1862, *OR*, ser. 3, vol. 2: 45.

14. Hunter to Stanton, May 31, 1862, and Stanton to Hunter, June 9, 1862, *OR*, ser. 1, vol. 14: 348–50.

15. Hess, *Field Armies and Fortifications*, 245–47; McPherson, *War on the Waters*, 138–41; Symonds, *Lincoln and His Admirals*, 201–2; R. Browning, *Success Is All That Was Expected*, 101–2.

16. Hess, *Field Armies and Fortifications*, 246–47.

17. Stanton to Grow, June 14, 1862, *OR*, ser. 3, vol. 2: 147–48; Cozzens and Girardi, *Memoirs of General John Pope*, 12.

18. Hunter to Stanton, June 23, 1862, *OR*, ser. 3, vol. 2: 197–98.

19. Hunter to Stanton, June 23, 1862.

20. Miller, *Lincoln's Abolitionist General*, 106.

21. Stanton to Saxton, June 16, 1862, box 7, reel 3, SPLC; Stanton to Hunter, June 16, 1862, *OR*, ser. 3, vol. 2: 152–53.

22. Sears, *Papers of George B. McClellan*, 344, 352, 354, 381, 388; Rafuse, *McClellan's War*, 5, 123, 130–31, 172–77.

23. Gienapp and Gienapp, *Diary of Gideon Welles*, 43; Croffut, *Fifty Years in Camp and Field*, 455. The portrait of Stanton in Marvel's biography, *Lincoln's Autocrat*, is entirely negative.

24. Rafuse, *McClellan's War*, 212; Matsui, *First Republican Army*, 3–20; Cozzens, *General John Pope*, 36–37, 72–75; Hennessy, *Return to Bull Run*, 6.

25. Eby, *Virginia Yankee*, 67; Donald, *Inside Lincoln's Cabinet*, 96; Cozzens and Girardi, *General John Pope*, 114–20.

26. For literature on Abraham Lincoln and Congress's path toward emancipation, see Guelzo, *Lincoln's Emancipation Proclamation*; Foner, *Fiery Trial*; and Oakes, *Freedom National*. For the role of McClellan's Peninsula Campaign, see Brasher, *Peninsula Campaign*.

27. Duncan, *Blue-Eyed Child of Fortune*, 209.

28. Duncan, 218, 221.

29. GO No. 5, July 18, 1862, in *OR*, ser. 1, vol. 12, pt. 2: 50; GO No. 13, July 25, 1862, in *OR*, ser. 1, vol. 12, pt. 3: 509.

30. GO No. 7, July (?), 1862, and GO No. 11, July 23, 1862, in *OR*, ser. 1, vol. 12, pt. 2: 51–52.

31. GO No. 14, 1st Army Corps, Army of Northern Virginia, July 27, 1862, *OR*, ser. 1, vol. 4: 293; King to Patrick, July 27, 1862, and Schriver to Devin, July 28, 1862, *OR*, ser. 1, vol. 12, pt. 3: 511, 515; Sutherland, "Abraham Lincoln," 577–78.

32. Crist, Dix, and Williams, *Papers of Jefferson Davis*, 8:305; J. Jones, *Rebel War Clerk's Diary*, 1:5, 144, 147, 152; Lee to Jackson, July 27, 1862, and Lee to Stuart, July 30, 1862, in *OR*, ser. 1, vol. 12, pt. 3: 919–20.

33. Dix to Stanton, July 23, 1862, *OR*, ser. 2, vol. 4: 266–68.

34. Davis to Lee, July 31, 1862, *OR*, ser. 2, vol. 4: 830–31; Cooper, *Jefferson Davis*, 29, 32–35, 40, 119, 140, 155, 249–50, 255, 354.

35. Lee to General Commanding U.S. Army, Washington, August 2, 1862, *OR*, ser. 2, vol. 4: 328–29.

36. Lee to General Commanding U.S. Army.

37. Davis to Lee, July 31, 1862, GO No. 54, August 1, 1862, and Message of Jefferson Davis to Congress, August 18, 1862, *OR*, ser. 2, vol. 4: 830–31, 836–37, 854–55.

38. Sears, *Papers of George B. McClellan*, 388–89; Rafuse, *McClellan's War*, 247–48.

39. Military Notebook, H. W. Halleck Papers, LOC; Marszalek, *Commander of All Lincoln's Armies*, 2, 36–37, 60, 98, 104–8, 128–36, 141–42, 152–53; Rafuse, *McClellan's War*, 242–43.

40. Halleck to Lieber, February 3 and 11, 1862, box 9, and Lieber to Halleck, multiple letters in box 27, FLP; Mack and Lesesne, *Lieber and the Culture of the Mind*, 1–6.

41. Halleck to Lee, August 7, 1862, *OR*, ser. 2, vol. 4: 350.

42. Hunter to Stanton, August 10, 1862, *OR*, ser. 3, vol. 2: 346; Saxton to Stanton, August 16, 1862, box 8, reel 3, SPLC; Higginson, *Army Life in a Black Regiment*, 211–14; S. Taylor, *Black Woman's Civil War Memoirs*, 29–40; Schafer, "War-Time Letters from Seth Rogers," October 20, 1863.

43. Saxton to Stanton, August 16, 1862, box 8, reel 3, SPLC.

44. Stanton to Saxton, August 25, 1862, and Halleck to Brannan, August 28, 1862, box 8, reel 3, SPLC.

45. GO No. 60, Confederate War Department, August 21, 1862, *OR*, ser. 1, vol. 14: 599; Neff, *Justice in Blue and Gray*, 67.

46. Report of Witcher, 21st Virginia, August 13, 1862, Report of Dobyns, 42nd Virginia, and Report of Garnett, August 15, 1862, *OR*, ser. 1, vol. 12, pt. 2: 201–3; Turner, "Major Charles A. Davidson," 30; Krick, *Stonewall Jackson*, 160–61, 183, 246–49, 264, 275.

47. Report of Gordon, *OR*, ser. 1, vol. 12, pt. 2: 808; Gordon, *Brook Farm to Cedar Mountain*, 331–32; Report of Andrews, 2nd Massachusetts, *OR*, ser. 1, vol. 12, pt. 2: 154; Duncan, *Blue-Eyed Child of Fortune*, 229–30; Krick, *Stonewall Jackson*, 274.

48. Russell to My Dear Parents, September 30, 1862, Henry Sturgis Russell Civil War Letters, MHS; Return of Casualties in the Union Forces, Cedar Mountain, Report of Williams, August 16, 1862, Report of Crawford, August 14, 1862, and Report of Andrews, August 11, 1862, *OR*, ser. 1, vol. 12, pt. 2: 137, 145–46, 152, 154; Krick, *Stonewall Jackson*, 287.

49. Order No. 2, August 27, 1862, Letters and Orders Issued, C. S. Military Prison, Richmond, Va., January 1862–December 1863, chap. 9, vol. 99½, RG 109, NARA; Entry 130, Daybook of Prisoners Received in Richmond, and Entry 132, Register of Captured Federal Officers Confined in Libby Prison, RG 249, NARA; Russell to Alex, August 11, 1862, and to My Dear Parents, September 30, 1862, Henry Sturgis Russell Civil War Letters, MHS; entries of August 12, 15, and 17, 1862, William D. Wilkins Diary, Clarke Historical Library, Central Michigan University, Mount Pleasant; Sheehan-Dean, *Calculus of Violence*, 67.

50. Duncan, *Blue-Eyed Child of Fortune*, 230, 232, 235.

51. Donald, *Inside Lincoln's Cabinet*, 113, entry of August 15, 1862; Sutherland, *Seasons of War*, 172–73; Cozzens, *General John Pope*, 98–99.

52. GO No. 19, August 14, 1862, *OR*, ser. 1, vol. 12, pt. 3: 573. For a discussion of self-control and manhood, see Foote, *Gentlemen and the Roughs*, 56–57. Legal historian Stephen Neff believes that the legality of Pope's orders to subsist on the countryside was

"doubtful." International law allowed for requisitions—the taking of private property from enemy civilians—in cases "of *actual* need" and obligated armies to be moderate and take only what was absolutely necessary. Pope's orders were doubtful because his commissary could have supplied his army and his orders to issue vouchers only to loyal people indicated the policy was about collective punishment of rebels more than actually supplying his army. See Neff, *Justice in Blue and Gray*, 94–95.

53. Ruggles to Sigel, August 16, 1862, *OR*, ser. 1, vol. 12, pt. 3: 577; Sparks, *Inside Lincoln's Army*, 122–23. Joan E. Cashin, in *War Stuff*, argues that "official policy had little impact on restraining armies" during the American Civil War. Soldiers were in competition with civilians for resources and took what they needed throughout the war. She argues that Pope's orders, intended to give soldiers latitude but also to protect citizens and the environment, did not work in practice. Her book is about "the inability of policy to constrain human misconduct" (3–4). This chapter and subsequent ones show that the retaliation ritual at times caused commanders on the ground to enforce policy. In her discussion of Pope's orders and soldier behavior—for example, on pp. 70 and 118–19—Cashin does not address retaliation or the corps- and brigade-level actions that cracked down on soldiers.

54. GO No. 107, August 15, 1862, in O'Brien and Diefendorf, *General Orders*, 366; Halleck to McClellan, August 13, 1862, *OR*, ser. 2, vol. 4: 381.

55. Letcher to Randolph, August 15, 1862, *OR*, ser. 2, vol. 4: 849–50.

56. Order No. 2, August 27, 1862, C. S. Military Prison, Richmond, Va., January 1862–December 1863, chap. 9, vol. 99½, RG 109, NARA.

57. Russell to My Dear Parents, September 30, 1862, Russell Civil War Letters; entries of August 20, August 24, September 11, 1862, Wilkins Diary, Clarke Historical Library; Petition to Winder, September 8, 1862, *OR*, ser. 2, vol. 4: 873.

58. Duncan, *Blue-Eyed Child of Fortune*, 245.

59. Ould to Thomas, September 24, 1862, and Mulford to Van Buren, September 25, 1862, *OR*, ser. 2, vol. 4: 552, 562.

60. Ould to Thomas, September 24, 1862, and Mulford to Van Buren, September 25, 1862. Section IV of GO No. 84 of the Confederate War Department, November 2, 1862, officially rescinded the parts of GO No. 54 that applied to Pope and his officers (*OR*, ser. 2, vol. 4: 939). Russell to My Dear Parents, September 30, 1862, Russell Civil War Letters; Duncan, *Blue-Eyed Child of Fortune*, 248.

61. Sanders, in his discussion of the breakdown of prisoner exchange, makes this point about the Pope retaliation episode; see *While in the Hands of the Enemy*, 146–47. The first Black U.S. soldiers taken prisoner by Confederates were men of the 1st Kansas Colored Infantry captured at Island Mound, Missouri, on October 29, 1862. See Newhall, "'Under the Rebel Lash,'" 29.

62. Saxton to Stanton, October 29, 1862, *OR*, ser. 3, vol. 2: 695; Looby, *Thomas Wentworth Higginson*, 147–48, 169, 178; Holland, *Letters and Diary of Laura M. Towne*, 93–94; Higginson, *Army Life in a Black Regiment*, 214; S. Taylor, *Black Woman's Civil War Memoirs*, 41.

63. Saxton to Mitchel, October 26, 1862, *OR*, ser. 1, vol. 14: 189; 33rd USCI Regimental Descriptive Book, vol. 1, 33rd USCI Regimental Books, RG 94, NARA.

64. Beard to Saxton, November 10 and 22, 1862, and Saxton to Stanton, November 12 and 25, 1862, in *OR*, ser. 1, vol. 14: 189–94.

65. Beard to Saxton, November 10 and 22, 1862, and Saxton to Stanton, November 12

and 25, 1862. For a discussion of courage, coolness, and fears that Blacks did not possess civilized manhood, see Foote, *Gentlemen and the Roughs*.

66. Mercer to Jordan, November 14, 1862, *OR*, ser. 2, vol. 4: 945–46; J. Jones, *Rebel War Clerk's Diary*, 191, 312; Younger, *Inside the Confederate Government*, 33; Cooper, *Jefferson Davis*, 415.

67. Seddon to Beauregard, November 30, 1862, in *OR*, ser. 2, vol. 4: 954.

68. GO No. 111, December 24, 1862, *OR*, ser. 2, vol. 5: 795–97. Caroline Wood Newhall argues that the overarching Confederate policy toward Black prisoners was to view them and treat them as recaptured property. She demonstrates that ultimately the Confederacy enslaved most of its Black war captives and used the principle of postliminy under the laws of war to justify its perspective. See "'Under the Rebel Lash,'" 6–7, 57–59.

69. Report of Stanton, December 1, 1862, *OR*, ser. 3, vol. 2: 911–12. Robert Ould, the Confederate agent for exchange, had told his counterpart, William H. Ludlow, that Confederate authorities would "retain all the commissioned officers of the United States" they captured if the United States did not respond to their demands regarding Black troops and the execution of a citizen of New Orleans. The Davis administration had demanded the punishment of Maj. Gen. Benjamin Butler, in charge of the occupation of that city, as a condition of the parole and exchange of U.S. officers. Ludlow wrote Stanton that the United States should therefore retain all of the Confederate officers it held. Ould to Ludlow, November 29, 1862, box 9, reel 4, Ludlow to Stanton, December 28, 1862, and Stanton to Ludlow, December 28, 1862, box 10, reel 4, SPLC. Halleck ordered the commander of every Union military department not to release Confederate officers on parole; see December 30, 1862, *OR*, ser. 2, vol. 5: 130. For a discussion of the precedents and legality of emancipating and arming slaves, see Sheehan-Dean, *Calculus of Violence*, 282.

## CHAPTER 2

1. Higginson, "Barbarism and Civilization"; Looby, *Thomas Wentworth Higginson*, 13–15, 87, 175; Higginson, *Army Life in a Black Regiment*, 191.

2. GO No. 1, November 25, 1862, 33rd USCI Regimental Order Book, vol. 5, 33rd USCI Regimental Books, RG 94, NARA.

3. Historian Keith P. Wilson first noted the fruitfulness of comparing Higginson, Shaw, and Montgomery and called for further research. I am grateful for his essay. As he pointed out, "The question that troubled the minds of those at the vanguard of the abolition movement was not simply would Blacks fight but how would they fight? Would they be influenced by the frontier abolitionism of Montgomery or the civilized combat of Higginson and Shaw?" See "In the Shadow of John Brown," 307. Historian Andrew F. Lang also has an interesting discussion of these three commanders. He uses Shaw as an example of the citizen-soldiers who worried that occupation and anti-guerrilla warfare undermined the republican military tradition and made barbarous plunderers out of citizen-soldiers. Lang discusses the difference between Shaw and Montgomery as one concerning their approach to the "insurgent presence" in occupied areas. As we will see in this chapter, however, Montgomery's and Shaw's regiments were not used to combat guerrillas but to attack the property of slaveholders. Guerrillas were not a factor in the Union expeditions on the Georgia–South Carolina coast. See *In the Wake of War*, 125–27.

4. Looby, *Thomas Wentworth Higginson*, 106; GO No. 11, January 1, 1863, 33rd USCI Regimental Order Book, vol. 5, 33rd USCI Regimental Books, RG 94, NARA.

5. Higginson, *Army Life in a Black Regiment*, 40–41, 197; Schafer, "War-Time Letters from Seth Rogers," entries of December 27, 1862, and January 16, 1863.

6. Pearson, *Letters from Port Royal*, 154; Galloway, *One Battle Too Many*, 163; Schafer, "War-Time Letters from Seth Rogers," entries of January 3 and 17, 1863.

7. Higginson to Saxton, February 1, 1863, *OR*, ser. 1, vol. 14: 195–98; entry of Jacob Jones and Thomas Fields, 33rd USCI Regimental Descriptive Book, vol. 1, 33rd USCI Regimental Books, RG 94, NARA; Schafer, "War-Time Letters from Seth Rogers," entries of January 26 and 27 and February 5, 1863.

8. Looby, *Thomas Wentworth Higginson*, 93; Schafer, "War-Time Letters from Seth Rogers," entries of January 27 and 28, 1863.

9. Higginson to Saxton, February 1, 1863, *OR*, ser. 1, vol. 14: 195–98; Looby, *Thomas Wentworth Higginson*, 93–95; Schafer, "War-Time Letters from Seth Rogers," entry of January 30, 1863.

10. Higginson to Saxton, February 1, 1863, and Saxton to Stanton, February 2, 1863, *OR*, ser. 1, vol. 14: 194–98; Schafer, "War-Time Letters from Seth Rogers," entry of February 1, 1863.

11. The full text of this letter is in the appendix of Dew, *Apostles of Disunion*, which also provides an excellent discussion of the mentality of secession leaders. The assumption that the end of slavery would bring about a race war was foundational to the European settlement of the Atlantic World. Historian Kay Wright Lewis explores how the English massacred men, women, and children in their wars against "savage" and "barbaric" peoples—the Irish in Ireland and enslaved Africans and Indians in the Western Hemisphere—who were perceived as a dangerous threat. "Historically, the term 'extermination' was used to describe the envisioned slaughter of large populations of white and Black people in the Atlantic World," Lewis explains. White Southerners believed that whites would have to resort to exterminatory violence to defend themselves against slave revolt and maintain racial control. The language of extermination and the pervasive violence of slavery was always "present and traumatic" for enslaved people, who shaped their resistance strategies in consideration of the threat of extermination hanging over their heads. See *Curse upon the Nation*, 3–4.

12. Extract from President's Message, January 12, 1863, *OR*, ser. 2, vol. 5: 807.

13. Extract from President's Message; Jordan to Cate, January 21, 1863, Entry 107, Misc. Letters, box 7, RG 249, NARA.

14. Semmes, *Report of the Judiciary Committee*; *Journal of the Congress of the Confederate States of America*, 3:51, 99, 112, 155, 203, 210. Robert Garlick Hill Kean, head of the Confederate Bureau of War, thought Davis's proclamation was "futile": "The state courts cannot try and punish POWs and no court could permit an indictment to be found on the facts which could be produced." See Younger, *Inside the Confederate Government*, 39–40. Neff's discussion of the international laws of war informed my interpretation that Semmes was correct in his reading of the law; see *Justice in Blue and Gray*, 71.

15. *Journal of the Congress of the Confederate States of America*, 3:211.

16. No. 74, Joint Resolution on the Subject of Retaliation, *OR*, ser. 1, vol. 28, pt. 2: 235–36; *Journal of the Congress of the Confederate States of America*, 3:319, 333, 361, 386–87. In addition to the Department of the South, there were situations regarding Black troops in Missouri and Alabama in May 1863. In Missouri, Confederate guerrillas killed and mutilated some unarmed Black soldiers of the 1st Kansas captured while foraging. The Union commander burned the farm where this occurred and the surrounding area in

retaliation and eventually shot a rebel prisoner when the guerrillas killed a Black soldier. Because these were guerrillas, not members of the Confederate army whose activities were officially sanctioned, this remained a local incident. See Stith, *Extreme Civil War*, 101–3. Confederates in Alabama captured some white officers of Black troops and some Alabama residents who had enlisted in the Union army and thus were "levying war against the state and inciting slaves to rebellion." The governor of Alabama wanted to try the white enlisted men, and Confederate secretary of war James Seddon wanted to try the white officers, but the prisoners were accidently exchanged by subordinates. See Seddon to Shorter, May 23, 1863, *OR*, ser. 2, vol. 5: 955.

17. Montgomery to Hatch, May 2, 1864, 34th USCI Regimental Letter, Order, and Endorsement Book, vol. 3, and James Montgomery entry, 34th USCI Regimental Descriptive Book, vol. 1, 34th USCI Regimental Books, RG 94, NARA; K. Wilson, "In the Shadow of John Brown," 308–10; Duncan, *Blue-Eyed Child of Fortune*, 356; Schafer, "War-Time Letters from Seth Rogers," entries of February 24 and 25, 1863.

18. Montgomery to Thomas, May 26, 1863, 34th USCI Regimental Letter, Order, and Endorsement Book, vol. 3, 34th USCI Regimental Books, RG 94, NARA; K. Wilson, "In the Shadow of John Brown," 309, 318; Alfred Marple letter, April 19, 1863, Alfred Marple Diary and Letters, SCL; Looby, *Thomas Wentworth Higginson*, 158; Duncan, *Blue-Eyed Child of Fortune*, 339, 362, 366, 369.

19. Saxton to Stanton, March 6 and March 14, 1863, *OR*, ser. 1, vol. 14: 423, 226; Schafer, *Thunder on the River*, 144–45.

20. GO No. 1, March 10, GO No. 2, March 11, GO No. 4, March 14, GO No. 9, March 21, and Special Orders No. 1, March 12, 1863, 33rd Regimental Order Book, vol. 5, 33rd USCI Regimental Books, RG 94, NARA; Finegan to Jordan, March 20, 1863, *OR*, ser. 1, vol. 14: 837; Schafer, "War-Time Letters from Seth Rogers," entry of March 12, 1863. Higginson allowed women and children to pass in and out of his lines freely. On March 17, Finegan notified Higginson that he had twenty-four hours to remove the women and children from the town, with a clear implication that he made the request so that he could attack Jacksonville. Higginson escorted 150 women to Finegan's lines, and about 200 remained in Jacksonville. Higginson did not force women and children out of town, because he had not received a formal notice that the enemy intended to attack. See McCormick to Higginson, March 17, Higginson to McCormick, March 18, and Finegan to Jordan, March 20, 1863, *OR*, ser. 1, vol. 14: 838–39; and Schafer, "War-Time Letters from Seth Rogers," entries of March 14, 16, 15, 17, and 19, 1863.

21. Special Orders No. 1 on March 12, 1863, 33rd USCI Regimental Order Book, vol. 5, 33rd USCI Regimental Books, RG 94, NARA; Schafer, *Thunder on the River*, 146. The performance of the companies of the 2nd under fire was impressive considering that they had had weapons only for two days and had not had time for any drilling. See Schafer, "William Lee Apthorp."

22. Schafer, *Thunder on the River*, 147–48.

23. The following works have particularly shaped my thinking about gender and civilization: Berry, *All That Makes a Man*; Bederman, *Manliness and Civilization*; Bushman, *Refinement of America*; A. Greenberg, *Manifest Manhood*; Nelson, *Ruin Nation*; Clinton and Silber, *Battle Scars*; and Hoganson, *Fighting for American Manhood*.

24. GO No. 1, 2, 4, in 33rd USCI Regimental Order Book, vol. 5, 33rd USCI Regimental Books, RG 94, NARA; Schafer, "War-Time Letters from Seth Rogers," entries of March 14 and 17, 1863; Schafer, *Thunder on the River*, 147–49.

25. Looby, *Thomas Wentworth Higginson,* 110; Schafer, "War-Time Letters from Seth Rogers," entries of March 14, 15, and 16, 1863.

26. Schafer, "William Lee Apthorp"; Schafer, "War-Time Letters from Seth Rogers," entries of March 14, 15, and 27, 1863.

27. Russell to Finegan, April 2, 1863, *OR,* ser. 1, vol. 14: 860–61; Schafer, "William Lee Apthorp"; Schafer, "War-Time Letters from Seth Rogers," entry of March 28, 1863; Looby, *Thomas Wentworth Higginson,* 121.

28. GO No. 32, March 27, 1863, 33rd USCI Regimental Order Book, vol. 5, 33rd USCI Regimental Books, RG 94, NARA; Saxton to Stanton, April 4, 1863, *OR,* ser. 3, vol. 3: 117; Hunter to Halleck, February 11, 1863, Halleck to Hunter, February 15 and 16, 1863, Foster to Halleck, February 16, 1863, Halleck to Foster, February 17, 1863, Special Orders No. 97, February 19, 1863, Hunter to Halleck, February 24, 1863, *OR,* ser. 1, vol. 14: 396, 401–11; Symonds, *Lincoln and His Admirals,* 205; R. Browning, *Success Is All That Was Expected,* 154–63; Dahlgren, *Memoir of John A. Dahlgren,* 388.

29. Schafer, "War-Time Letters from Seth Rogers," entry of March 29, 1863; Schafer, "William Lee Apthorp"; Schafer, *Thunder on the River,* 159–61.

30. Russell to Finegan, April 2, 1863, and Beauregard to Seddon, March 30, 1863, *OR,* ser. 1, vol. 14: 860, 850.

31. Special Orders No. 18, April 2, 1863, *OR,* ser. 1, vol. 14: 863.

32. Ash, *Firebrand of Liberty,* 201; Lincoln to Hunter, April 1, 1863, *OR,* ser. 1, vol. 14: 435; Looby, *Thomas Wentworth Higginson,* 145. According to Lang, who has an excellent analysis of Black troops, garrisoning, and occupation, 64 percent of USCT units "exclusively performed garrison duty." *In the Wake of War,* 130–31. Some of the language in this paragraph was published previously in Lorien Foote, "Review of *Firebrand of Liberty,*" *Journal of Southern History* 76 (February 2010): 164–65.

33. Hunter to Davis, April 23, 1863, in Crist, Dix, and Williams, *Papers of Jefferson Davis,* 9:152; Hunter to Stanton, April 25, 1863, *OR,* ser. 1, vol. 14: 448; Hunter to Lincoln, May 27, 1863, *OR,* ser. 2, vol. 5: 711–12; Miller, *Lincoln's Abolitionist General,* 124, 131.

34. Looby, *Thomas Wentworth Higginson,* 151; Stephens to Davis, June 12, 1863, in Crist, Dix, and Williams, *Papers of Jefferson Davis,* 9:153, 215.

35. Ould to Ludlow, May 22, 1863, and Ludlow to Ould, May 25, 1863, *OR,* ser. 2, vol. 5: 691, 702–3.

36. Entries of June 1, 3, 1863, Ethan Allen Hitchcock Memoir, box 9, W. A. Croffut Papers, LOC; note on envelope, June 1, 1863, box 3, EAHLC; Hitchcock to Stanton, June 7, 1863, *OR,* ser. 2, vol. 5: 754; Holt to Lieber, July 15, 1863, box 11, FLP.

37. Halleck to Ludlow, July 15, 1863, *OR,* ser. 2, vol. 6: 118; J. Jones, *Rebel War Clerk's Diary,* 389; Hoffman to Hitchcock, June 27, 1863, box 3, EAHLC. Although the retaliation ritual over Burnside's execution began in May, Confederate officials did not select the prisoners by lot until July 7. The lots fell to Capt. Henry Sawyer, 1st New Jersey Cavalry, and Capt. John Flinn, 51st Indiana. Once that occurred, the Lincoln administration officially notified the Davis administration on July 15 that it had reserved William Henry Fitzhugh Lee for execution. The standoff lasted until March 14, 1864. Another problem for the Davis administration was that it had selected the Federal prisoners by lot. As Sawyer and Flinn pointed out, if Davis wanted to retaliate for Burnside's actions, he should have selected prisoners from Burnside's command or the two Federal officers whom the Confederacy held in a prison in Atlanta for recruiting in Tennessee. The head of the Confederate Ordnance Bureau, Josiah Gorgas, agreed that the "solution of the

difficulty" was the execution of the Atlanta prisoners rather than Sawyer and Flinn. See Special Orders No. 160, July 4, 1863, and Turner to Winder, July 7, 1863, C. S. Military Prison, Richmond, Va., January 1862–December 1863, chap. 9, vol. 99½, RG 109, NARA; Sawyer and Flinn to Winder, July 11, 1863, Entry 107, Misc. Letters, box 11, RG 249, NARA; Wiggins, *Journals of Josiah Gorgas*, 76; and Dilbeck, *A More Civil War*, 114–16.

38. Andrew to Stanton, April 1, Hunter to Andrew, May 4, and Andrew to Stanton, May 16, 1863, *OR*, ser. 3, vol. 3: 110, 190–91, 209; Duncan, *Blue-Eyed Child of Fortune*, 286; Foote, *Seeking the One Great Remedy*, 106–12.

39. Hunter to Lincoln, April 25, May 22, 1863, *OR*, ser. 1, vol. 14: 447, 456–57. Hunter wanted to arm liberated slaves — not the men who would form regiments, of course — with pikes. Militant abolitionists like John Brown had also wanted to distribute pikes to slaves to help them foment insurrection. For a discussion of contrasting cultural views of the pike, see Phillips, *Looming Civil War*. Abolitionists believed the pike was a civilized, European weapon that could be used on the defensive with minimal training to fight for freedom. Confederates saw pikes as "African spears, barbaric, offensive weapons" (117).

40. Hunter to Stanton, June 3, 1863, *OR*, ser. 1, vol. 14: 463; Montgomery to Hunter, June 3, 1863, 34th USCI Regimental Letter, Order, and Endorsement Book, vol. 3, 34th USCI Regimental Books, RG 94, NARA; Walker to Jordan, June 17, 1863, and Lay to Jordan, June 24, 1863, *OR*, ser. 1, vol. 14: 290–91, 306; Alfred Marple diary entry, June 3, 1863, Marple Diary and Letters, SCL; Clinton, *Harriet Tubman*, 163–73. Montgomery recruited two companies for the 2nd from the slaves liberated during this raid. Montgomery to Hatch, May 2, 1864, 34th USCI Regimental Letter, Order, and Endorsement Book, vol. 3, 34th USCT Regimental Books, RG 94, NARA.

41. Hunter to Stanton, April 30, 1863, box 11, reel 4, SPLC; W. S. Walker to Jordan, June 17, 1863, and Lay to Jordan, June 24, 1863, *OR*, ser. 1, vol. 14: 290–91, 306; Alfred Marple diary entry, June 3, 1863, Marple Diary and Letters, SCL; Schafer, "William Lee Apthorp"; Looby, *Thomas Wentworth Higginson*, 282.

42. Walker to Jordan, June 17, 1863, and Lay to Jordan, June 24, 1863, *OR*, ser. 1, vol. 14: 290–91, 306; Circular, May 29, 1863, HQ 3rd Military District, *OR*, ser. 1, vol. 14: 307; K. Wilson, "In the Shadow of John Brown," 309.

43. Lieber to Halleck, November 13, 1862, February 20 and May 20, 1863, box 27, Halleck to Lieber, February 23, 1863, box 9, and Hitchcock to Lieber, March 6, 1863, box 11, FLP; Special Orders No. 399, December 17, 1862, box 3, EAHLC; Sheehan-Dean, *Calculus of Violence*, 182; Neff, *Justice in Blue and Gray*, 58; Dilbeck, *A More Civil War*, 5, 86, 95; Springer and Robins, *Transforming Civil War Prisons*, 16. For Halleck's role in drafting the code, see McCurry, *Women's War*, 43–53.

44. Article 14, Article 15, Article 16, Article 29, GO No. 100, Avalon Project.

45. Article 42, Article 43, Article 57, and Article 58, GO No. 100, Avalon Project. Several scholars have excellent discussions of the code, its governing principles, its relationship to previous treatises, and its concept of military necessity. Witt, *Lincoln's Code*, 170–82, 234–40; Dilbeck, *A More Civil War*, 69, 74, 88–92; Neff, *Justice in Blue and Gray*, 60–62; Sheehan-Dean, *Calculus of Violence*, 17, 180–81.

46. Neff, *Justice in Blue and Gray*, 57, 130–31; Sheehan-Dean, *Calculus of Violence*, 182; Dilbeck, *A More Civil War*, 91.

47. Seddon to Ould, June 24, 1863, *OR*, ser. 2, vol. 6: 45; Younger, *Inside the Confederate Government*, 68.

48. Hunter to Montgomery, June 9, 1863, *OR*, ser. 1, vol. 14: 466–67.

49. Hunter to Montgomery, June 9, 1863.

50. Hunter to Montgomery, June 10, 1863, Hunter to Lincoln, May 27, 1863, and Hunter to Welles, May 27, 1863, *OR*, ser. 2, vol. 5: 711–13, 770; Hunter to Halleck, June 10, 1863, *OR*, ser. 1, vol. 14: 467. Articles 54 and 55 of GO No. 100 pronounced, "Hostages are rare in the present age" and defined a hostage as a "person accepted as a pledge for the fulfillment of an agreement concluded between belligerents." Historian Aaron Sheehan-Dean notes that local Union commanders held civilians hostage "to negotiate conclusions to specific incidents." His discussion of "civilian pawns" does not deal with the many officers and soldiers held hostage by both sides during retaliation rituals. See *Calculus of Violence*, 199–201.

51. Ludlow to Ould, June 14, 1863, *OR*, ser. 2, vol. 6: 17.

52. Hunter to Andrew, June 3, 1863, *OR*, ser. 1, vol. 14: 462; Duncan, *Blue-Eyed Child of Fortune*, 35, 289–90, 300, 313, 359–60; C. Davis, *Black Soldiers*, 32–33; Adams, *On the Altar of Freedom*, 51.

53. Thomas to Mercer, June 13, 1863, and Report of Lane, June 19, 1863, *OR*, ser. 1, vol. 14: 317–19; Duncan, *Blue-Eyed Child of Fortune*, 342–43; Adams, *On the Altar of Freedom*, 29; John Appleton to Mary Appleton, June 14, 1863, box 2, APWV. There may have been an element of revenge, which also violated GO No. 100, in the actions of the 2nd at Darien. Rumor spread among Union troops that one of the captains in the 2nd had lived in Darien and was run out of town for his Union sentiments. Alfred Marple diary entry, June 15, 1863, and letter, June 18, 1863, Marple Diary and Letters, SCL.

54. Duncan, *Blue-Eyed Child of Fortune*, 343–44; Higginson to Father, June 16, 1863, Francis Lee Higginson Letters, Digital Library of Georgia; Looby, *Thomas Wentworth Higginson*, 292.

55. John Appleton to Mary Appleton, June 7, 11, 14, 19, 1863, box 2, and Military Memoir, p. 224, box 3A, APWV; Emilio to Parents, June 12, 1863, and Mother to Emilio, July 13, 1863, box 1, folder 12, Luis F. Emilio Papers, MHS.

56. Lowell to Shaw, June 20, 1863, and Lowell to Whiting, June 26, 1863, in Emerson, *Letters of Charles Russell Lowell*, 262, 265–66.

57. Looby, *Thomas Wentworth Higginson*, 153.

58. Emilio to Parents, June 12, 1863, box 1, folder 12, Emilio Papers, MHS; Adams, *On the Altar of Freedom*, xxii–xxxi, 29, 31; Egerton, *Thunder at the Gates*, 21–23; Barr, "Corporal James H. Gooding."

59. Hester, *Yankee Scholar*, 89, 160–69; Looby, *Thomas Wentworth Higginson*, 209–10; Schafer, "War-Time Letters from Seth Rogers," entries of February 13, May 27, and October 25, 1863.

60. Schafer, "William Lee Apthorp." Lang, *In the Wake of War*, writes that Black men viewed the war of occupation as an opportunity "to cleanse the South of its slaveholding character, to eliminate the symbols of white supremacy, and to erase the artifacts of plantation life" (172).

61. Duncan, *Blue-Eyed Child of Fortune*, 348–49, 354–78; K. Wilson, "In the Shadow of John Brown," 321–24. In the aftermath of Darien, Shaw became fascinated with Montgomery and developed an admiration for him. As Higginson and Rogers had before him, he loved to listen to stories of exploits in Kansas. Eventually, Montgomery convinced Shaw that he acted under Hunter's orders when he destroyed Darien. Shaw claimed to have seen letters to that effect. If so, then Hunter issued private orders to Montgomery that contradicted his official correspondence. This would confirm, rather than contradict,

Hunter's concern with honor and reputation, which is a projection of image rather than a reflection of internal virtue. It could also be that Shaw saw letters where Hunter outlined his raiding strategy of destroying resources and assumed that such orders sanctioned Montgomery's actions. The War Department issued orders to relieve Hunter from command on June 3, but it seems that Hunter was not immediately notified, and the command did not change until June 12. Miller, *Lincoln's Abolitionist General*, 145–46.

62. Williams, *Beauregard*, 1–15, 51–54, 67.

63. Beauregard to Gillmore, July 4, 1864 [1863], *OR*, ser. 1, vol. 28, pt. 2: 11–13. Vattel's discussion of waste, destruction, ravaging, and burning calls for hard war conducted with moderation. He allowed "waste of a country," destroying provisions, and foraging so the enemy "may not find a subsistence there." This promotes the main object of the war. But, "those who tear up the vines and cut down the fruit-trees are looked upon as savage barbarians, unless they do it with a view to punish the enemy for some gross violation of the law of nations. They desolate a country for many years to come, and beyond what their own safety requires. Such conduct is not dictated by prudence, but by hatred and fury." Vattel does say that a civilized combatant may sack a town under two conditions: chastising an unjust and barbarous nation and creating an uninhabitable barrier if a combatant is unable to check the incursions of the enemy any other way. The general rule in his text is this: "All damage done to an enemy unnecessarily, every act of hostility which does not tend to procure victory and bring the war to a conclusion, is a licentiousness condemned by the law of nature." Vattel, *Law of Nations*, 570, 573.

## CHAPTER 3

1. Duncan, *Blue-Eyed Child of Fortune*, 383; Adams, *On the Altar of Freedom*, 38. Shaw misdated his letter July 15.

2. For Gillmore's plans, see Wise, *Gate of Hell*, 34, 63; Symonds, *Lincoln and His Admirals*, 243; R. Browning, *Success Is All That Was Expected*, 220; and Dahlgren, *Memoir of John A. Dahlgren*, 396. For the raid of the 1st South Carolina, see Looby, *Thomas Wentworth Higginson*, 294; GO No. 59, July 12, 1863, 33rd USCI Regimental Letter, Order, and Endorsement Book, vol. 3, 33rd USCI Regimental Books, RG 94, NARA; and Higginson to Saxton, July 11, 1863, Report of Aiken, July 12, 1863, and Report of White, July 11, 1863, *OR*, ser. 1, vol. 28, pt. 1: 194–98.

3. Terry to Smith, July 16, 1863, Report of Davis, July 31, 1863, and Report of Colquitt, July 17, 1863, *OR*, ser. 1, vol. 28, pt. 1: 583–87, 755; Duncan, *Blue-Eyed Child of Fortune*, 385; Adams, *On the Altar of Freedom*, 36; Emilio to Father, July 15 and 16, 1863, box 1, folder 12, Emilio Papers, MHS; Alfred Marple Diary, entry of July 16, 1863, Marple Diary and Letters, SCL.

4. John Appleton to Mary Appleton, July 1, 16, and 17, 1863, box 2, APWV; Report of Colquitt, July 17, 1863, and Jeffords to Molony, July 18, 1863, *OR*, ser. 1, vol. 28, pt. 1: 588, 591; Emilio, *Brave Black Regiment*, 57–62; Adams, *On the Altar of Freedom*, 37; Duncan, *Blue-Eyed Child of Fortune*, 385; Marszalek, *Diary of Miss Emma Holmes*, 281. Emilio's narrative names Sgt. James D. Wilson, although the published roster in Emilio's appendix names the sergeant of Company H who was killed on July 16, 1863, as Joseph D. Wilson.

5. Theodore A. Honour, a bookkeeper at the Bank of Charleston and a private in the 25th South Carolina (Eutaw) Volunteers, wrote that when his company chased the Federal soldiers into the marsh, "it was now that we found that we had been fighting nothing but

negroes." Honour to Beckie Honour, July 16, 1863, Theodore A. Honour Papers, SCL; Hagood to Nance, July 18, 1863, *OR*, ser. 1, vol. 28, pt. 1: 586; Hagood to Nance, July 16, 1863, *OR*, ser. 2, vol. 6: 123–24; Emilio, *Brave Black Regiment*, 396; Peronneau to Nance, July 19, 1863, *OR*, ser. 2, vol. 6: 132. The captured men were Lemuel Blake (age 21, farmer from West Chester, Pa.), James Caldwell (19, blacksmith from Battle Creek, Mich.), George Counsel (26, laborer from West Chester, Pa.), John W. Dickinson (30, laborer from Galesburg, Ill.), William Henry Harrison (22, teamster from Battle Creek, Mich.), Sgt. Walter A. Jeffries (38, laborer from Cincinnati, Ohio), John Leatherman (24, seaman from Ypsilanti, Mich.), Joseph Proctor (24, cook from Chambersburg, Pa.), Enos Smith (30, laborer from Easton, Pa.), Frederick Wallace (20, barber from Cincinnati, Ohio), Corp. Armistead Williams (36, laborer from Detroit, Mich.), James O. Williams (35, laborer from Carlisle, Pa.), and Henry W. Worthington (18, laborer from Defiance, Ohio).

6. Beauregard to Cooper, July 17, 1863, *OR*, ser. 2, vol. 6: 125; Marszalek, *Diary of Miss Emma Holmes*, 281; Williams, *Beauregard*, 52–53, 171; Wise, *Gate of Hell*, 89–90.

7. Gillmore Memorial, from Proceedings of the American Society of Civil Engineers, Quincy A. Gillmore Papers, AHEC; Wise, *Gate of Hell*, 33, 39, 120; Gray and Ropes, *War Letters*, 275–78; Dahlgren, *Memoir of John A. Dahlgren*, 7–9, 123, 137, 152, 183, 287; Symonds, *Lincoln and His Admirals*, 191; R. Browning, *Success Is All That Was Expected*, 216.

8. Serrell to Gillmore, September 10, 1863, *OR*, ser. 1, vol. 28, pt. 1: 230; Dahlgren, *Memoir of John A. Dahlgren*, 398–99; Orlando P. Sawtelle to Parents, July 11, 1863, Orlando P. Sawtelle Papers, box 102, folder 13, CWD; Wise, *Gate of Hell*, 64–79; Symonds, *Lincoln and His Admirals*, 243; McPherson, *War on the Waters*, 173; Hess, *Field Armies and Fortifications in the Civil War*, 252–53.

9. Turner to his Father, July 13, 1863, box 1, John W. Turner Papers, AHEC; Duncan, *Blue-Eyed Child of Fortune*, 362, 386; Emilio to Father, July 18, 1863, box 1, folder 12, Emilio Papers, MHS; Report of Davis, July 31, 1863, *OR*, ser. 1, vol. 28, pt. 1: 584–85. Strong had told Shaw on June 28 that he was "very desirous to have the negro troops take their part in whatever is done" (Duncan, *Blue-Eyed Child of Fortune*, 362).

10. Entry of July 18, 1863, William A. Gyles Papers, SCL; Duncan, *Blue-Eyed Child of Fortune*, 362; Seymour to Turner, November 10, 1863, *OR*, ser. 1, vol. 28, pt. 1: 347; Wise, *Gate of Hell*, 93–100; Dahlgren, *Memoir of John A. Dahlgren*, 402–3.

11. Emilio, *Brave Black Regiment*, 73–79; Adams, *On the Altar of Freedom*, 39, 51; Appleton Military Memoir, pp. 56–57, box 3A, APWV; Wise, *Gate of Hell*, 101–5, 118; Emilio to Parents, July 22, 1863, box 1, folder 12, Emilio Papers, MHS; Hess, *Field Armies and Fortifications*, 258. Charles Cowley, the judge advocate of the South Atlantic Blockading Squadron, noted in his history that the 54th started forward on the step "left oblique," a very difficult maneuver. He wrote that "naturally enough these new troops crowded badly on the center, so that Shaw had to halt twice to dress ranks before they took the double quick." See Cowley, *Leaves from a Lawyer's Life*, 99–100. Supporting regiments such as the 7th New Hampshire likewise did not fire their guns during their advance on Wagner. See Abbott to Gillmore, August 16, 1863, *OR*, ser. 1, vol. 28, pt. 1: 365.

12. For Union reports, see Emilio, *Brave Black Regiment*, 80–85; Appleton Military Memoir, pp. 58–60, box 3A, APWV; Hallowell to Seymour, November 7, 1863, and Seymour to Turner, November 10, 1863, *OR*, ser. 1, vol. 28, pt. 1: 362, 347; C. Davis, *Black Soldiers*, 36–37; and Adams, *On the Altar of Freedom*, 38. For Confederate reports, see entry of July 18, 1863, Gyles Papers, SCL; Report of De Pass, July 19, 1863, McKethan to Taliaferro, July 20, 1863, Blake to Gaillard, July 20, 1863, Taliaferro to Nance, July 21, 1863,

and Crawley to Taliaferro, July 22, 1863, *OR*, ser. 1, vol. 28, pt. 1: 417–19, 525, 545, 549, 570. For excellent scholarly accounts of the battle at Wagner on July 18, see Wise, *Gate of Hell*, 101–5; and Hess, *Field Armies and Fortifications*, 256–58.

13. Appleton Military Memoir, pp. 61–62, box 3A, APWV; Knight to Taliaferro, July 20, 1863, Ripley to Jordan, July 22, 1863, Abbott to Gillmore, August 16, 1863, Hallowell to Seymour, November 7, 1863, and Seymour to Turner, November 10, 1863, *OR*, ser. 1, vol. 28, pt. 1: 347–48, 362, 364–65, 373, 524.

14. Abbott to Gillmore, August 16, 1863, Hallowell to Seymour, November 7, 1863, and Seymour to Turner, November 10, 1863, *OR*, ser. 1, vol. 28, pt. 1: 347, 364–65, 373, 524; Hess, *Field Armies and Fortifications*, 256–58; Wise, *Gate of Hell*, 106–14.

15. Taliaferro to Nance, July 21, 1863, *OR*, ser. 1, vol. 28, pt. 1: 419; Jordan to Ripley, July 19, 1863, Beauregard to Cooper, July 21, 1863, Gillmore to Beauregard, August 5, 1863, Hagood to Jordan, August 11, 1863, and Beauregard to Gillmore, August 18, 1863, *OR*, ser. 1, vol. 28, pt. 2: 37–38, 46–47, 210, 214; Wise, *Gate of Hell*, 111–13.

16. Ripley to Jordan, July 22, 1863, *OR*, ser. 1, vol. 28, pt. 1: 373; Hagood to Jordan, August 11, 1863, *OR*, ser. 1, vol. 28, pt. 2: 47; C. Davis, *Black Soldiers*, 39; Wise, *Gate of Hell*, 115–16.

17. Jordan to Crowell, July 23, 1863, and Roman to Jordan, August 7, 1863, *OR*, ser. 2, vol. 6: 146, 187; Emilio, *Brave Black Regiment*, 400–402; Marszalek, *Diary of Miss Emma Holmes*, 287; *Petition in Favor of the Sisters of Our Lady of Mercy*, 11–12, 19–20. Caroline Wood Newhall's research shows that 198 Black prisoners received medical care from their Confederate captors. She argues, "This reveals a de facto policy of preserving the lives of black prisoners as property to be used toward the war effort." See "'Under the Rebel Lash,'" 64–65.

18. Emilio, *Brave Black Regiment*, 401–3; Wise, *Gate of Hell*, 116.

19. Gillmore to Beauregard, July 20, 1863, and Beauregard to Gillmore, July 22, 1863, *OR*, ser. 1, vol. 28, pt. 2: 21, 25.

20. Hagood to Nance, July 22, 1863, Gillmore to Beauregard, July 22, 1863, and Anderson to Nance, July 24, 1863, *OR*, ser. 1, vol. 28, pt. 2: 26, 47, 226–27; Ripley to Jordan, August 1, 1863, and Report of Beauregard of Operations on Morris Island, September 18, 1864, *OR*, ser. 1, vol. 28, pt. 1: 78, 376; Wise, *Gate of Hell*, 122–23; Emilio, *Brave Black Regiment*, 403.

21. Adams, *On the Altar of Freedom*, 41–42; Emilio, *Brave Black Regiment*, 393. Laura M. Towne, a Northern teacher who helped nurse wounded soldiers of the 54th in a hospital in Beaufort, wrote that when it was yet unknown what happened to Shaw, the men were "all greatly excited about him, hoping, fearing, disregarding their own wounds in anxiety for him." See Holland, *Letters and Diary of Laura M. Towne*, 114.

22. Gillmore to Beauregard, August 5, 1863, *OR*, ser. 1, vol. 28, pt. 2: 37–38.

23. Beauregard to Gillmore, August 18, 1863, *OR*, ser. 1, vol. 28, pt. 2: 45–46.

24. Confederate treatment of Black Union soldiers captured at the Battle of Milliken's Bend in Louisiana in June 1863 did not come before President Lincoln for decision. Confederate troops captured about fifty Black soldiers and two white officers. The Confederate commander of the Trans-Mississippi, Lt. Gen. Edmund Kirby Smith, instructed his subordinates not to take Black prisoners in the future. He said there was "propriety" in "giving no quarter to armed negroes and their officers. In this way we may be relieved of a disagreeable dilemma." If soldiers or officers did capture Black troops, Smith instructed his subordinates to turn them over to state authorities for trial. "Should negroes thus taken be executed by the military authorities capturing them it would certainly provoke retaliation. By turning them over to civil authorities to be tried

by the laws of the State no exception can be taken." The Confederate War Department disapproved of Smith's policy of no quarter. Secretary of War Seddon suggested a policy that violated the congressional retaliation resolutions. He told Smith to take prisoners and return them to their owners. "A few examples might perhaps be made, but to refuse them quarter would only make them, against their tendencies, fight desperately." When Union commander Maj. Gen. Ulysses S. Grant wrote Maj. Gen. Richard Taylor to inquire if Confederates had hanged a white captain and several Black soldiers after capture at Milliken's Bend, Taylor denied it. He wrote Grant that he would investigate and punish the parties if it turned out to be true and said that he was required to turn all Blacks captured in arms to the civil authorities for trial. Grant accepted the denial and the matter went no further. See Smith to Taylor, June 13, 1863, Anderson to Taylor, June 13, 1863, Smith to Cooper, June 16, 1863, and Halleck to Ludlow, July 2, 1863, *OR*, ser. 2, vol. 6: 21–22, 73; Grant to Taylor, June 22, 1863, Taylor to Grant, June 27, 1863, and Grant to Taylor, July 4, 1863, *OR*, ser. 1, vol. 24, pt. 3: 425, 443 469; Pickenpaugh, *Captives in Blue*, 186–87; and Burkhardt, *Confederate Rage*, 60–62.

25. Holt to Lieber, July 15, 1863, box 11, FLP; Emerson, *Letters of Charles Russell Lowell*, 289; Johnson to Lincoln, July 31, 1863, Freedmen and Southern Society Project, http://www.freedmen.umd.edu/hjohnson.html; Egerton, *Thunder at the Gates*, 166–67, 381. Johnson, the daughter of an escaped slave from Louisiana, lived in Buffalo, New York. Her son was not identified in the letter, although she stated he was not captured at Wagner. Egerton has not been able to identify her son from the roster of the 54th. No soldier named Johnson listed Buffalo as his residence. He was probably one of the three Johnsons in the regiment who were from New York State.

26. Lieber to Halleck, August 3, 1863, box 27, FLP; Emerson, *Letters of Charles Russell Lowell*, 289; GO No. 100, Avalon Project. Massachusetts senator Charles Sumner also pressured Stanton. Stanton to Sumner, August 4, 1863, box 40, reel 14, Letterbooks 1863–65, SPLC.

27. Halleck to Lieber, August 4, 1863, box 9, FLP; Burlingame and Ettlinger, *Inside Lincoln's White House*, 69; GO No. 252, July 31, 1863, *OR*, ser. 2, vol. 6: 163. Lieber did not like Halleck's alteration. "Hard labor inflicted for the selling of a U.S. soldier will not be allowed to continue beyond the time when peace is concluded. But an enslaved solider will remain a slave—he and his posterity forever," he wrote Halleck. "How is this retaliation? Where is the principle Tit for Tat which characterizes retaliation?" Halleck responded, "It by no means follows that those of the rebels put at hard labor are to be released at the end of the war. . . . It is useless now to anticipate the condition of things after the war is over. . . . Perhaps, in this case, it is as well to begin as mildly as possible."

28. Stanton to Andrew, August 8, 1863, box 40, reel 14, Letterbooks 1863–1865, SPLC.

29. List of Prisoners Captured from the U.S. Army and Navy near Charleston 11 July to 6 Aug 1863, dated August 16, 1863, Entry 107, Misc. Letters, box 7, RG 249, NARA. In this document, Confederates give the number of dead buried in front of Wagner on July 19 as 600 officers and men.

30. Brown, Johnson, Wilson to U.S. Consul, Nassau, June 30, 1863, *OR*, ser. 2, vol. 6: 171. Confederates reported they captured eleven officers, 105 men, and "three negroes." Brown and Johnson were "very slightly" wounded. The three men were serving as wardroom stewards on the *Isaac Smith*. See Report of Conover, May 7, 1863, List of killed and wounded on board steamer *Isaac Smith*, Report of Yates, February 1, 1863, List of Prisoners from Steamer *Isaac Smith*, U.S. Naval War Records Office, *Official Records*, ser. 1, vol. 13:

563–71. Orin H. Brown was a barber born in Brewster Station, New York, who enlisted as a landsman at age twenty-two on September 26, 1862. William H. Johnson was born in Brooklyn, New York, and was unemployed when he enlisted as a landsman on October 29, 1858. William Wilson was born in New York, New York, and was a seventeen-year-old waiter when he enlisted as a 1st Class Boy. The date for Wilson's enlistment in the National Park Service Soldier and Sailor's Database is September 7, 1863, but the year must be 1862, as indicated in his letter to the U.S. Consul.

31. Stanton to Hitchcock, August 8, 1863, box 3, EAHLC; Welles to Stanton and Hitchcock endorsement of Brown letter, August 3, 1863, *OR*, ser. 2, vol. 6: 171; Stanton to Welles, August 8, 1863, box 40, reel 14, Letterbooks 1863–1865, SPLC. One of the hostages, C. J. McDowell, 2nd South Carolina Cavalry, wrote from Carroll Prison in Washington, D.C., on February 1, 1864, asking for permission to write Richmond to secure the exchange of the Black sailors in Charleston. McDowell to Hoffman, February 1, 1864, *OR*, ser. 2, vol. 6: 904–5.

32. J. Jones, *Rebel War Clerk's Diary*, 2:13. Jones, however, thought the "free negroes" were taken on Morris Island.

33. Beauregard to Cooper, July 21, 1863, Seddon to Beauregard, July 22, 1863, Bonham to Beauregard, July 22, 1863, Beauregard to Seddon, July 23, 1863, Bonham to Seddon, July 23, 1863, Beauregard to Cooper, July 24, 1863, Beauregard to Bonham, July 29, 1863, and Seddon to Bonham, August 1, 1863, *OR*, ser. 2, vol. 6: 134, 139, 145–47, 159, 169.

34. Younger, *Inside the Confederate Government*, 91; Campbell endorsement on Bonham to Beauregard, July 22, 1863, *OR*, ser. 2, vol. 6: 140. Kean, like all other officials in the Confederate War Department, thought, "It is quite clear that the enlistment of our slaves is a barbarity which no people, who regarded anything save the gratification of a devilish lust of revenge and hatred, could tolerate on the principle, the use of savages, which Chatham denounced and the Declaration of Independence recorded as infamous. It is also contrary to public law, since the Pandects." Kean also thought that slaves captured in arms against their lawful owners could either suffer the "penalties of municipal law for their revolt" or "simply be returned to their masters." Further, Kean believed that white officers who commanded former slaves should not be treated as prisoners of war. He noted that "all exchanges have stopped and each side is hording up prisoners as the subjects of retaliation" (92).

35. Foote, *Seeking the One Great Remedy*, 120–27.

36. Bonham to Seddon and endorsement, August 8 and 10, 1863, Seddon to Bonham, August 14, 1863, and Seddon to Bonham, September 1, 1863, *OR*, ser. 2, vol. 6: 190–94, 202, 245; Westwood, "Captive Black Union Soldiers," 38–40.

37. Bonham to Seddon and endorsement, August 8 and 10, 1863, Seddon to Bonham, August 14, 1863, and Seddon to Bonham, September 1, 1863, *OR*, ser. 2, vol. 6: 190–94, 202, 245.

38. Westwood, "Captive Black Union Soldiers," 38–51; Emilio, *Brave Black Regiment*, 345, 373–78; Egerton, *Thunder at the Gates*, 168. Egerton notes that Worthington's father was from Virginia and so he may have been born there, but "if he had been a slave, he was freed at an early age."

39. Edward McCrady Legal Journal, 1863, Conner Family Papers, South Carolina Historical Society, Charleston; Bonham to Seddon, August 23, 1864, *OR*, ser. 2, vol. 7: 673; Westwood, "Captive Black Union Soldiers," 38–51; Emilio, *Brave Black Regiment*, 345, 373–78.

40. Jordan provided this information years after the war when Luis Emilio investigated the fate of the prisoners of the 54th for his regimental history. See Emilio, *Brave Black Regiment*, 404–5. The military court in Mobile claimed that Dow could not be tried for acts committed prior to the adoption of the congressional resolutions on May 1, 1863. For more on the Dow case, see Military Court, Maury's Corps, Mobile, Alabama, August 22, 1863, *OR*, ser. 2, vol. 6: 269–70, and related correspondence in the volume.

41. J. Jones, *Rebel War Clerk's Diary*, 2:26; Younger, *Inside the Confederate Government*, 102; Meredith to Hitchcock, August 25, 1863, *OR*, ser. 2, vol. 6: 225. Meredith did not initially recognize what Ould was trying to communicate to him. He did not connect the statement to the 54th and dismissed it because "their laws put slave and free upon the same footing."

42. Report on Artillery Operations before Forts Wagner and Sumter from the 26th day of July to the 7th day of September, 1863, Col. John W. Turner, Chief of Artillery, Morris Island, box 2, Turner Papers, AHEC; Dahlgren, *Memoir of John A. Dahlgren*, 405–6; Orlando P. Sawtelle to Parents, July 23, 1863, box 102, folder 13, Sawtelle Papers, CWD; Wise, *Gate of Hell*, 119–20, 156, 217–18; Hess, *Field Armies and Fortifications*, 259–61; McPherson, *War on the Waters*, 173.

43. Montogmery to Hatch, May 2, 1864, 34th USCI Regimental Letter, Order, and Endorsement Book, vol. 3, RG 94, NARA; Emilio, *Brave Black Regiment*, 125; Brooks to Gillmore, December 10, 1863, Turner Papers, AHEC; Briggs to Mother, August 1, 1863, box 1, folder 8, Charles E. Briggs Letters, MHS; Special Orders No. 493, August 24, 1863, *OR*, ser. 1, vol. 28, pt. 2: 62; Adams, *On the Altar of Freedom*, 46; Brooks to Gillmore, September 27, 1863, *OR*, ser. 1, vol. 28, pt. 1: 298; Redkey, *Grand Army of Black Men*, 35–37; Alfred Marple to Wife, September 5, 1863, Marple Diary and Letters, SCL; Galloway, *One Battle Too Many*, 229–31; Wise, *Gate of Hell*, 132–45.

44. Circular, Engineer's Office, September 10, 1863, and Brooks, Siege Journal, Morris Island, Note No. 19, *OR*, ser. 1, vol. 28, pt. 1: 328–29. The responses of the six engineers are a study in nineteenth-century racial attitudes and the belief that race determined certain traits. "I should liken the white man to the horse (often untractable and balky); the black man to the ox," Capt. Joseph Walker, of the 1st New York Engineers, wrote in his response. "It seems to me there is a hard, nervous organization at the bottom of the character of the white, and a soft, susceptible one at the bottom of the character of the black." Walker thought the "character of the white" ran to extremes from "bull-dog courage" to "pitiful cur," while the "black character" is "uniformity and mediocrity." See *OR*, ser. 1, vol. 28, pt. 1: 330. The responses of the engineers enraged Col. Norwood P. Hallowell of the 55th Massachusetts, another Black regiment that fought in the Department of the South. "In the matter of 'enthusiasm' the engineers are altogether at fault. In five minutes you can excite a regiment of blacks into a pitch of enthusiasm that will carry everything before it, provided you yourself are sincere; provided you respect and trust them and they respect and trust you," he wrote, "provided always you know how to spell and pronounce the word 'negro'—that sure test and gauge of refinement in an American." See C. Davis, *Black Soldiers*, 47.

45. Brooks to Gillmore, December 10, 1863, Turner Papers, AHEC.

46. Serrell to Gillmore, September 10, 1863, *OR*, ser. 1, vol. 28, pt. 1: 230–35; Stryker, "Swamp Angel," 72–74; Wise, *Gate of Hell*, 148–50; Hess, *Field Armies and Fortifications*, 270.

47. Gillmore to Beauregard, August 21, 1863, *OR*, ser. 1, vol. 28, pt. 2: 57–58.

48. Report on Artillery Operations before Forts Wagner and Sumter, and Turner to

Father, October 24, 1863, box 2, Turner Papers, AHEC; Stryker, "Swamp Angel," 73; Ripley, *Siege Train*, 16; Wise, *Gate of Hell*, 148, 169–70. Article 19 of GO No. 100 did not require notification. It read: "Commanders, whenever admissible, inform the enemy of their intention to bombard a place, so that the noncombatants, and especially the women and children, may be removed before the bombardment commences. But it is no infraction of the common law of war to omit thus to inform the enemy. Surprise may be a necessity." For a broader discussion of the Union practice of bombarding cities in context of the laws of war, see Sheehan-Dean, *Calculus of Violence*, 192–96; and Carnahan, *Lincoln on Trial*, 106–7.

49. Basler, *Collected Works*, 4:344; 5:181, 240; 6:107, 145, 255, 270, 421.

50. Turner to Father, October 24, 1863, box 1, Turner Papers, AHEC; Report of Gillmore, February 28, 1864, *OR*, ser. 1, vol. 28, pt. 1: 30; Gray and Ropes, *War Letters*, 189–91; Wise, *Gate of Hell*, 169; Phelps, *Bombardment of Charleston*, 10.

51. Beauregard to Pickens, October 3, 1862, *OR*, ser. 1, vol. 14: 617; Emerson and Stokes, *Days of Destruction*, 51; Marszalek, *Diary of Miss Emma Holmes*, 279, 294, 297; Bonham to Beauregard, August 12, 1863, and Beauregard to Bonham, August 15, 1863, *OR*, ser. 1, vol. 28, pt. 2: 276, 283–84; Wise, *Gate of Hell*, 81; Phelps, *Bombardment of Charleston*, 58–59. For a wonderful example of an argument between a husband and wife over her desire to stay in Charleston and have him visit her there at the risk of their lives, and her request that he apply for furloughs to visit her in Charleston in mid-August, see the correspondence in the Honour Papers, SCL.

52. Beauregard to Gillmore, August 22, 1863, *OR*, ser. 1, vol. 28, pt. 2: 58–59.

53. Beauregard to Cooper, August 22, 1863, J. G., Consul of S. M. Catolica, to Gillmore, August 22, 1863, and Walker to Gillmore, August 22, 1863, *OR*, ser. 1, vol. 28, pt. 2: 61, 300. Beauregard told Cooper that the consuls "have protested against this barbarous course."

54. Gillmore to Beauregard, August 22, 1863, Gillmore to Spanish Consul, August 22, 1863, and Gillmore to Walker, August 22, 1863, *OR*, ser. 1, vol. 28, pt. 2: 60–62. Gillmore's three letters arrived at Battery Wagner under flag of truce at noon on August 23. A boat was not available to take them across the harbor until 3:00 P.M. After the Union messengers had left, General Hagood received instructions from Beauregard to open any letter from Gillmore in the presence of the men delivering it and return it to Gillmore "if couched in discourteous or offensive language. The enemy's communications must be hereafter, confined to a simple and explicit statement of what he demands or wants." See Hagood to Jordan, August 23, 1863, *OR*, ser. 1, vol. 28, pt. 2: 303.

55. Report on Artillery Operations, box 2, Turner Papers, AHEC; Ripley, *Siege Train*, 18–19; Report of Gillmore, February 24, 1864, and Extract from Daily Reports of Yates, *OR*, ser. 1, vol. 28, pt. 1: 33–34, 528–29; Marszalek, *Diary of Miss Emma Holmes*, 300; Middleton to Wife, August 23, 24, 25, 1863, Williams Middleton Papers, SCL; Theodore Honour to Wife, August 22, 24, 1863, Honour Papers, SCL; Smith, Smith, and Childs, *Mason Smith Family Letters*, 62–63.

56. *Charleston Mercury*, August 28, 1863; *London Times*, September 14, 1863, 7.

57. Adams, *On the Altar of Freedom*, 63–64.

58. Gillmore to Dahlgren, August 30, 1863, Gillmore Papers, AHEC; Report on Artillery Operations, box 2, Turner Papers, AHEC; Gillmore to Halleck, October 11, 1863, *OR*, ser. 1, vol. 28, pt. 2: 105; Dahlgren, *Memoir of John A. Dahlgren*, 408–13; Ripley, *Siege Train*, 12; R. Browning, *Success Is All That Was Expected*, 242–43, 249–50, 287–88; Symonds, *Lincoln and His Admirals*, 245–47; McPherson, *War on the Waters*, 178; Hess, *Field Armies and Fortifications*, 263, 285.

59. Beauregard to Cooper, September 6, 1863, *OR*, ser. 1, vol. 28, pt. 2: 343; Report on Artillery Operations, box 2, Turner Papers, AHEC; Hess, *Field Armies and Fortifications*, 273–82; Wise, *Gate of Hell*, 194–204.

60. Hess, *Field Armies and Fortifications*, 282–85; Wise, *Gate of Hell*, 212; Alfred Marple to Wife, September 24, 1863, Marple Diary and Letters, SCL.

61. Stanton to Tilghman, November 17, 1863, box 42, reel 14, Stanton to Sumner, November 24, 1863, box 41, reel 14, and Tilghman to Stanton, December 25, 1863, box 20, reel 7, Letterbooks 1863–1865, SPLC; GO No. 77, September 17, 1863, and GO No. 105, November 25, 1863, *OR*, ser. 1, vol. 28, pt. 2: 95, 123; Alfred Marple to Wife, November 19, 1863, Marple Diary and Letters, SCL; Looby, *Thomas Wentworth Higginson*, 339. Higginson wrote, "Nothing can be more certain than that Gillmore allowed the colored troops to be most unreasonably used, as to fatigue duty, not from any hostility but from inattention. . . . The fact of a second order being issued by him on the subject instead of vindicating condemns him, for in military usage the remedy for a neglected order is not a second order but a court-martial." Historian Andrew F. Lang identifies the elements of the "race-based garrisoning philosophy" that Lincoln established in the Emancipation Proclamation: those of the USCT "would concentrate in humid, unhealthy regions thought to be ideal for men of African descent; black military service would encompass labor and fatigue assignments; the occupation duties of black soldiers would release white soldiers to fight at the front; and military discipline would be regulated according to the army's new racial hierarchy." See *In the Wake of War*, 144.

62. Prisoners of 54th Massachusetts to Beauregard, November 16, 1863, *OR*, ser. 2, vol. 6: 527.

63. Hitchcock to Gillmore, December 2, 1863, *OR*, ser. 2, vol. 6: 630–31; Smith to Higginson, December 12, 1863, 33rd USCI Regimental Letter and Order Book, vol. 3, 33rd USCI Regimental Books, RG 94, NARA. Hitchcock sent a similar inquiry to the "Commanding Officer Port Hudson, LA" on December 2 (see *OR* citation above). Hitchcock had evidence that "two colored lads" taken prisoner with troops of the 42nd Massachusetts in Galveston, Texas, had been sold into slavery and that two Union officers of Black troops were sentenced for "negro stealing" by a Virginia state court. Hitchcock endorsement on letter from Lt. John Roberts, a POW at Camp Groce, Tex., November 2, 1863, and Hitchcock to Stanton, November 24, 1863, *OR*, ser. 2, vol. 6: 54, 557. The "two colored lads" were cousins Charles Fairfax Revaleon, the grandson of a Revolutionary War soldier, and Charles Gerrish Amos. Hitchcock did not forget them and sought to find them in June 1865. Both Revaleon and Amos returned safely to Massachusetts in July. See Hitchcock to Andrew, May 31, 1865, Hitchcock to Canby, June 5, 1865, and Ware to Hitchcock, July 11, 1865, *OR*, ser. 2, vol. 8: 587, 640, 703.

64. John Appleton to Mary Appleton, June 19, 1863, box 2, and Appleton Military Memoir, p. 195, box 3A, APWV; Egerton, *Thunder at the Gates*, 29–31.

65. John Appleton to Mary Appleton, December 7, 1863, box 2, APWV.

66. Hallowell to Smith, December 13, 1863, and Gillmore to Hitchcock, December 29, 1863, *OR*, ser. 2, vol. 6: 775–76; Emilio, *Brave Black Regiment*, 328; Adams, *On the Altar of Freedom*, 64.

67. Gillmore to Halleck and Stanton, December 14 and 15, 1863, and By Order of the Secretary of War, December 22, 1863, *OR*, ser. 1, vol. 28, pt. 2: 127–29, 135; John Appleton to Mary Appleton, December 7 and 8, 1863, box 2, APWV.

## CHAPTER 4

1. Norton, *Army Letters*, 202; *Sunbury American*, March 5, 1864, 2; Coles, "Far from the Fields of Glory," 91–92; "Kate Ault Fribley," Lycoming County Women's History Project (online); Richards, *Civil War Tales*, 50.

2. Photographs of records from the NARA about Lt. Col. William N. Reed are available on the Battle of Olustee website under the entries "William N. Reed" (http://battleofolustee.org/pics/william_n_reed_35th_usct.htm) and "Thirty-fifth United States Colored Troops" (http://battleofolustee.org/35th_usct.html). "Death of Major Archibald Bogle," *Boston Journal*, March 2, 1864, 2, column 1, OLS; Coles, "Far from the Fields of Glory," 97.

3. John Appleton to Mary Appleton, February 7, 1864, box 2, APWV; Emilio, *Brave Black Regiment*, 148–55.

4. Gillmore to Seymour, February 11, 1864, and Finegan to Jordan, February 26, 1864, *OR*, ser. 1, vol. 35, pt. 1: 282, 330–31; Schafer, *Thunder on the River*, 179.

5. Gillmore to Halleck, January 31, 1864, GO No. 24, February 15, 1864, and Special Orders No. 13, February 17, 1864, *OR*, ser. 1, vol. 35, pt. 1: 279, 481–82; Turner to Father, February 7, 1864, box 1, Turner Papers, AHEC. Gillmore was a political ally of Secretary of the Treasury Salmon P. Chase, who was trying to gain the Republican 1864 presidential nomination and who was working with corrupt Florida tax commissioner Lyman Stickney to gain electoral votes through the readmission of Florida. President Lincoln also hoped to boost his reelection bid through the expedition and sent his private secretary John Hay along on the expedition to register voters. See Coles, "Far from the Fields of Glory," 21–33, 67; and Schafer, *Thunder on the River*, 176–77.

6. John Appleton to Mary Appleton, February 8, 13, 14, 1864, box 2, APWV; "History and Diary Extracts of Pvt. William P. Woodlin," 8th USCT, OLS; Schafer, *Thunder on the River*, 182.

7. John Appleton to Mary Appleton, February 18, 1864, box 2, APWV; *Boston Herald*, March 2, 1864, 4, OLS; Egerton, *Thunder at the Gates*, 216–19. Egerton provides a detailed account of the incident. Four soldiers committed the rape: Pvts. John M. Smith, Spencer Lloyd, John Wesley Cork, and an unnamed soldier who was never identified or caught. The men were known troublemakers in the regiment. The victim was Sarah Hammond, who testified that the men came to her house and told her that the Federal army was disbursing rations. When she left her house with her baby, the men accosted her and took turns raping her. She testified against them in front of the four-person tribunal who tried the soldiers. Cork and Lloyd questioned their accuser during the proceedings. Capt. William Anthorp of the 34th USCT defended the accused. Esther Hill Hawks, who wrote of the execution in her diary and was an advocate of racial equality, noted that other soldiers "sobbed aloud" when the men were hung and thought Seymour displayed "utter heartlessness" because he did not apply the same penalty to "white officers and men who have been guilty of the same offense towards black women." See Schwartz, *Woman Doctor's Civil War*, 61.

8. Although there is nothing in the written record to indicate whether Confederate troops heard about the incident, it is reasonable to assume they did based on the way intelligence normally spread to Confederate armies. Records on the Confederate side are particularly sparse for the Florida campaign.

9. Seymour to Gillmore, February 11 and 17, 1864, Gillmore to Seymour, February 18,

1864, Seymour to Turner, February 22, 1864, and Gillmore to Halleck, March 7, 1864, *OR*, ser. 1, vol. 35, pt. 1: 276–77, 282–87; Schafer, *Thunder on the River*, 178–84; Coles, "Far from the Fields of Glory," 65–66, 85; Nulty, *Confederate Florida*, 114–23, 213–16.

10. Finegan to Turner, February 13, 1864, Beauregard to Finegan, February 19, 1864, Finegan to Jordan, February 26, 1864, and Beauregard to Cooper, March 25, 1864, *OR*, ser. 1, vol. 35, pt. 1: 325–26, 331, 322, 620; Schafer, *Thunder on the River*, 185; Coles, "Far from the Fields of Glory," 98–100.

11. John Appleton to Mary Appleton, February 24, 1864, box 2, APWV; Seymour to Turner, February 22, 1864, and Report of Grant, April 27, 1864, *OR*, ser. 1, vol. 35, pt. 1: 286–87, 338–39; Emilio, *Brave Black Regiment*, 158; Schafer, *Thunder on the River*, 186; Coles, "Far from the Fields of Glory," 114, 124; Nulty, *Confederate Florida*, 124.

12. Finegan to Jordan, February 26, 1864, Report of Colquitt, February 26, 1864, and Report of Harrison, February 22, 1864, *OR*, ser. 1, vol. 35, pt. 1: 331, 343, 348–49; Coles, "Far from the Fields of Glory," 123–25; Nulty, *Confederate Florida*, 128–34.

13. Report of Hawley, n.d., Report of Abbott, February 27, 1864, and Report of Seymour, March 25, 1864, *OR*, ser. 1, vol. 35, pt. 1: 304, 311, 288; *Boston Herald*, March 2, 1864, 4, OLS; Gray and Ropes, *War Letters*, 308; Coles, "Far from the Fields of Glory," 127–28; Nulty, *Confederate Florida*, 107–8, 136–40, 205–9. Before going to Florida, one wing of the 7th New Hampshire had Spencer repeating rifles, and the unit was trained to use them. Before the battle, the regiment was ordered to give these weapons to a mounted infantry unit and received many unserviceable single-shot rifles in exchange. The new recruits never had time to train in loading and firing the old type of weapon. The 7th was demoralized when it went into battle. There was ongoing controversy between Hawley and the men of the 7th for decades after the Battle of Olustee about whether he gave a wrong order or whether his order was misheard. Broadwater argues that Union artillery was too far forward because there was no other option. The forest of trees that made up the battlefield obstructed the guns' fire. At a distance, shells would have struck the trees instead of the infantry. See *Battle of Olustee*, 114.

14. Norton, *Army Letters*, 197–98, 200; Report of Bailey, February 24, 1864, *OR*, ser. 1, vol. 35, pt. 1: 311–12; Letter from Surgeon A. P. Heichhold, February 23, 1864, published in the *Christian Recorder*, March 12, 1864, Letter from Sgt. Maj. Rufus S. Johns, March 24, 1864, published in the *Christian Recorder*, April 16, 1864, and History and Diary Extracts of Pvt. William P. Woodlin, OLS. Norton provides an excellent summary of how Seymour and Hawley mishandled their new troops.

> No braver men ever faced an enemy. To make these men fight well, I would have halted them out of range of the firing, formed my line, unslung knapsacks, got my cartridge boxes ready, and loaded. Then I would have moved up to the support of a regiment already engaged. I would have had them lie down and let the balls and shells whistle over them till they got a little used to it. Then I would have moved them to the front, told them to get as close to the ground as they could and go in. Just the other thing was done. . . . If there is a second lieutenant in our regiment who couldn't plan and execute a better battle, I would vote to dismiss him for incompetency. (202–3)

15. Norton, *Army Letters*, 198–99, 204; John Appleton to Mary Appleton, February 24, 1864, box 2, APWV; Report of Bailey, February 24, 1864, Bailey to Hall, March 10, 1864, Report of Lewis, March 10, 1864, and Report of Ely, March 10, 1864, *OR*, ser. 1, vol. 35, pt. 1: 311–14; Letter from Surgeon A. P. Heichhold, February 23, 1864, OLS.

16. John Appleton to Mary Appleton, February 24, 1864, box 2, APWV; Report of Bailey, February 24, 1864, Bailey to Hall, March 10, 1864, Report of Lewis, March 10, 1864, and Report of Ely, March 10, 1864, *OR*, ser. 1, vol. 35, pt. 1: 311–14; Letter from Surgeon A. P. Heichhold, February 23, 1864, OLS. The reports of the artillery officers near the 8th USCT that confirm some details but minimize their own poor performance are in the same volume of the *OR* cited above: Report of Langdon, March 25, 1864 (316–18), and Report of Myrick, February 24, 1864 (319).

17. Letter of 2nd Lt. Hugh W. Barclay, February 25, 1864, published in the *Athens Southern Banner*, March 9, 1864, and in the *Boston Herald*, March 2, 1864, 4, OLS; Return of Casualties in the Engagement near Olustee, Report of Colquitt, February 26, 1864, Finegan to Jordan, February 26, 1864, Report of Harrison, February 22, 1864, and Report of Grant, April 27, 1864, *OR*, ser. 1, vol. 35, pt. 1: 298, 331, 340, 344, 349; Coles, "Far from the Fields of Glory," 135–38; Nulty, *Confederate Florida*, 145–65, 203.

18. Letter from Surgeon A. P. Heichhold, February 23, 1864, OLS; Emilio, *Brave Black Regiment*, 162. When Heichhold evacuated the battlefield, he prioritized Black wounded men. When some remonstrated that white wounded should also be removed, he replied, "I know what will become of the white troops who fall into the enemy's possession, but I am not certain of the fate of the colored troops." See letter of Rufus S. Jones, sergeant major of 8th USCT, March 20, 1864, published in the *Christian Recorder*, April 16, 1864, in Redkey, *Grand Army of Black Men*, 42.

19. Report of Hallowell, March 1, 1864, and Report of Hawley, *OR*, ser. 1, vol. 35, pt. 1: 315, 298, 304; Emilio, *Brave Black Regiment*, 162–67; Coles, "Far from the Fields of Glory," 141–42; Nulty, *Confederate Florida*, 156–58, 168.

20. Report of Hallowell, March 1, 1864, Report of Casualties at Olustee, and Report of Hawley, *OR*, ser. 1, vol. 35, pt. 1: 315, 298, 304; Emilio, *Brave Black Regiment*, 162–67; John Appleton to Mary Appleton, February 23, 1864, box 2, APWV; Coles, "Far from the Fields of Glory," 141–42; Nulty, *Confederate Florida*, 156–58, 168.

21. Emilio, *Brave Black Regiment*, 161–69, 424–25; Report of Hallowell, March 1, 1864, and Report of Harrison, February 22, 1864, *OR*, ser. 1, vol. 35, pt. 1: 315, 350; John Appleton to Mary Appleton, February 24, 1864, box 2, APWV; Letter from E. D. W., 54th Mass., March 13, 1864, published in the *Christian Recorder*, April 2, 1864, and Letter from Corp. Henry Shackleford, February 20, 1864, published in the *Atlanta Intelligencer*, March 2, 1864, OLS.

22. The scholarship that has particularly shaped my thinking on the distinction in U.S. warfare between war against "savage" Indians and war against "civilized" combatants is Grenier, *First Way of War*; Neely, *Civil War and the Limits of Destruction*; and Kinsella, *Image before the Weapon*. In his comprehensive history of the U.S. Army Officer Corps from 1810 to 1846, Samuel J. Watson points out that the national standing army in that period did not have a history of massacres against Indians; rather, it was citizen-soldiers, volunteers, and militia who perpetrated them. Officers believed atrocities threatened social order and hierarchy and were often enacted against frontiersmen whose violence was out of control. For the regular army, he concludes, "neither Sand Creek nor Wounded Knee was characteristic of the decades between 1783 and 1846." See *Peacekeepers and Conquerors*, 8. For scholarship on the Civil War and Native peoples, see Nelson, *Three-Cornered War*; Kelman, *Misplaced Massacre*; Wooster, *American Military Frontiers*; Confer, *Cherokee Nation in the Civil War*; Hauptman, *Between Two Fires*; Josephy, *Civil War in the American West*; and Utley, *Frontiersmen in Blue*.

23. Lee, *Barbarians and Brothers*, 3–4, 240–41; Urwin, *Black Flag over Dixie*; Burkhardt, *Confederate Rage*.

24. James Jordan to Louisa, February 21, 1864, original in Vol. 2, Letters from Confederate Soldiers, United Daughters of the Confederacy Collection, Georgia State Archives, and Capt. Winston Stephens to His Wife, February 21, 1864, OLS; *Voice from Rebel Prisons*, 4; Palmer, *History of the Forty-Eighth Regiment*, 136.

25. Report of Casualties at Olustee, *OR*, ser. 1, vol. 35, pt. 1: 298; Coles, "Shooting Niggers Sir," 77. For Confederate discussion of who was to blame for the desultory pursuit of Union forces, see reports and communication in *OR*, ser. 1, vol. 35, pt. 1: 331, 353–54. An excellent discussion of the treatment of wounded Black Union soldiers at Olustee, with a full discussion of the relevant primary sources and an estimate of numbers, is in Coles's dissertation, "Far from the Fields of Glory," 155–67, and in his chapter in Urwin, *Black Flag over Dixie*, 77. Coles estimates that twenty-five to fifty wounded men were murdered on the battlefield. Burkhardt, in *Confederate Rage*, p. 90, estimates seventy-five. I am inclined to agree with the lower approximation. Neither Coles nor Burkhardt seemed to have found the letter from William B. Rodman to James A. Seddon cited below in note 36, which indicates that seventy-one Black Olustee prisoners made it to Andersonville.

26. Finegan to Turner, February 23, 1864, *OR*, ser. 1, vol. 35, pt. 1: 327; *Voice from Rebel Prisons*, 4–7; Coles, "Far from the Fields of Glory," 164–69; Nulty, *Confederate Florida*, 183.

27. Finegan to Jordan, February 26, 1864, *OR*, ser. 1, vol. 35, pt. 1: 331; *Memphis Daily Appeal*, April 1, 1864, p. 1, and Archibald Bogle entry, OLS; *Voice from Rebel Prisons*, 4; U.S. House of Representatives, *Trial of Henry Wirz*, 326–27.

28. Colquitt to Beauregard, March 5, 1864, Gardner to Beauregard, March 5, 1864, Taliaferro to Beauregard, March 5, 1864, and Beauregard to Cooper, March 7, 1864, *OR*, ser. 1, vol. 35, pt. 2: 335–39.

29. Report of Casualties at Olustee, *OR*, ser. 1, vol. 35, pt. 1: 298; John Appleton to Mary Appleton, February 24, 1864, box 2, APWV; Emilio, *Brave Black Regiment*, 170–74; Seymour to Turner, February 21, 1864, *OR*, ser. 1, vol. 35, pt. 1: 488; Beauregard to Cooper, March 6, 1864, *OR*, ser. 1, vol. 35, pt. 2: 333–34; Nulty, *Confederate Florida*, 184; Schafer, *Thunder on the River*, 186–89.

30. Seymour to the general commanding Confederate Forces, Florida, February 23, 1864, and Finegan to Seymour, February 24, 1864, *OR*, ser. 1, vol. 35, pt. 1: 329–30; Nulty, *Confederate Florida*, 184.

31. Seymour to Finegan, February 25, 1864, and Finegan to Seymour, February 26, 1864, *OR*, ser. 1, vol. 35, pt. 1: 493, 496; Gardner to Seymour, March 4, 1864, and Seymour to Gardner, March 4, 1864, *OR*, ser. 1, vol. 35, pt. 2: 7–8; *Sunbury American*, April 2, 1864, 2; "Kate Ault Fribley," Lycoming County Women's History Project. The line officers of the 8th wanted to instigate an affair of honor with the provost marshal of the Department of the South because of his unchivalrous treatment of Kate Ault Fribley. According to Lieutenant Norton, the provost marshal told her that Fribley had rashly exposed himself, and the officers of the 8th were as badly scared as the men. "It is all an infamous lie, and there is more than one officer in the regiment ready to tell him so at the first opportunity," Norton wrote on March 9. "The man who could coolly tell a poor widow alone in this country that her husband was killed by his own fault is a brute to say the least." Norton, *Army Letters*, 204.

32. John Appleton to Mary Appleton, March 5, 1864, box 2, APWV; Emilio, *Brave Black Regiment*, 183; Norton, *Army Letters*, 201, 210–11; Seymour to Turner, March 2, 1864, *OR*,

ser. 1, vol. 35, pt. 2: 3; Letter to Editor, *Worcester Aegis and Transcript*, from R., pvt. in the 1st North Carolina, written March 14, 1864, and published April 2, 1864, 4, and Letter from Capt. James W. Grace to the *New Bedford Mercury*, February 25, 1864, published March 9, 1864, OLS.

33. Report of Majer, February 24, 1864, *OR*, ser. 1, vol. 35, pt. 1: 301; Archibald Bogle, OLS; John W. Turner to Father, February 7, 1864, box 1, Turner Papers, AHEC; Coles, "Far from the Fields of Glory," 176–77.

34. John Appleton to Mary Appleton, March 8, 1864, box 2, APWV; Letter from Surgeon A. P. Heichhold, February 23, 1864, OLS; Redkey, *Grand Army of Black Men*, 45, 49–50, 54.

35. Marvel, *Andersonville*, 41–42, 111–12; Futch, *History of Andersonville Prison*; Coles, "Far from the Fields of Glory," 170.

36. Testimony of Alexander W. Persons, August 30 and September 28, 1865, in U.S. House of Representatives, *Trial of Henry Wirz*, 460; R. Davis, "Escape from Andersonville"; Marvel, *Andersonville*, 41–42, 111–12. The number seventy-one comes from Rodman to Seddon, May 27, 1864, *OR*, ser. 2, vol. 7: 174.

37. Archibald Bogle, OLS; *Voice from Rebel Prisons*, 4; U.S. House of Representatives, *Trial of Henry Wirz*, 326–27; Gibbs to Campbell, June 5, 1864, *OR*, ser. 2, vol. 7: 198.

38. Mahood, *Charlie Mosher's Civil War*, 219, 225; Testimony of Frank Maddox, 35th USCT, September 5, 1865, Testimony of William Henry Jennings, 8th USCT, September 6, 1865, Testimony of John Fisher, 8th USCT, September 11, 1865, and Testimony of Lewis Dyer, 12th USCT, September 23, 1865, in U.S. House of Representatives, *Trial of Henry Wirz*, 176–80, 187–88, 279–80, 408–9; Emilio, *Brave Black Regiment*, 183, 355; Rodman to Seddon, May 27, 1864, *OR*, ser. 2, vol. 7: 174; Marvel, *Andersonville*, 105, 155; Egerton, *Thunder at the Gates*, 230–32; Barr, "Loathsome Diseases and Principles," 117–18; "African Americans at Andersonville," Andersonville National Historic Site (online). According to Caroline Wood Newhall's research in pension and compiled service records, Pvt. Frank Mattocks had been enslaved in White Oak, North Carolina. His captor at Olustee told him to pretend to be free so he would not be killed. He gave his name as Ben Harbine and claimed to be part of the 54th Massachusetts. See "'Under the Rebel Lash,'" 168.

39. Rodman to Seddon, May 27, 1864, *OR*, ser. 2, vol. 7: 174.

40. Seddon to Davis, February 3, 1864, *OR*, ser. 2, vol. 6: 913. Newhall has an extended analysis of the Confederate policy of re-enslaving Black captives. The October 18, 1862, congressional resolution was intended to protect slaveholders' property rights and established depots to house recaptured slaves so that their enslavers could reclaim them. The camps were not originally intended to house Black prisoners captured in arms. President Davis issued GO No. 25 on March 6, 1863, to implement the resolution. GO No. 25 was notably used in Virginia and Alabama. Newhall argues that this policy "provided a set of guidelines that military leaders ultimately replicated when handling black POWs." See "'Under the Rebel Lash,'" 40–42, 57–60, 99–100.

41. Bonham to Seddon, June 24, 1864, *OR*, ser. 2, vol. 7: 409; Westwood, "Captive Black Union Soldiers," 46.

42. Hatch to Hitchcock, September 25, 1864, *OR*, ser. 2, vol. 7: 876; Crist, Dix, and Williams, *Papers of Jefferson Davis*, 10:358; Maury to Cooper, May 20, 1864, *OR*, ser. 2, vol. 7: 155; Cimprich, *Fort Pillow*, 78–87; Silkenat, *Raising the White Flag*, 156–59.

43. Basler, *Collected Works*, 7:302; Tap, *Fort Pillow Massacre*, 67–70; Cimprich, *Fort Pillow*, 89–90; Frisby, "'Remember Fort Pillow!,'" 118–22.

44. Lieber to Halleck, April 19, 1864, box 28, FLP; Simpson, *Let Us Have Peace*, 58; Cimprich, *Fort Pillow*, 96.

45. Frisby, "'Remember Fort Pillow!,'" 104–25; Cimprich, *Fort Pillow*, 97.

46. Gienapp and Gienapp, *Diary of Gideon Welles*, 402.

47. Gienapp and Gienapp, 402; Stanton to Lincoln, May 5, 1864, box 42, reel 14, Letterbooks 1863–1865, SPLC; Cimprich, *Fort Pillow*, 99; Tap, *Fort Pillow Massacre*, 71–74; Ward, *River Run Red*, 321–23; Wills, *River Was Dyed with Blood*, 159–60; Burkhardt, *Confederate Rage*, 119; Sheehan-Dean, *Calculus of Violence*, 286.

48. Lincoln to Stanton, May 17, 1864, in Basler, *Collected Works*, 7:302; Silkenat, *Raising the White Flag*, 160; Frisby, "'Remember Fort Pillow!,'" 121; Cimprich, *Fort Pillow*, 101; Ward, *River Run Red*, 323; Tap, *Fort Pillow Massacre*, 79. Aaron Sheehan-Dean notes that Lincoln's reluctance to act also stemmed from his "continuing belief that the Confederate rank and file were held in the army against their will, and retaliation would only alienate them from the Union. The political consideration at the heart of the war constrained how Lincoln responded." See *Calculus of Violence*, 286.

49. Burkhardt, *Confederate Rage*, 120–21; Sheen-Dean, *Calculus of Violence*, 287; Silkenat, *Raising the White Flag*, 168, 179–80, 297. Newhall argues that there were "higher rates of capture and survival among black POWs than is currently understood" ("'Under the Rebel Lash,'" 23). Because Confederates viewed Black soldiers as property, they desired to re-enslave them, an objective that placed limits around the massacre of Black soldiers. She documents the capture of 2,273 Black prisoners and the enslavement of 1,900 of them by the Confederate military.

50. Articles 60, 66, and 68, GO No. 100, Avalon Project. Local Union commanders who remained in Florida continued to press the War Department to retaliate for Olustee. On July 27, Brig. Gen. William Birney captured nineteen Confederate prisoners in a raid and requested that they be held as hostages and for the exchange of "colored soldiers only." On September 25, Brig. Gen. John P. Hatch wrote to Ethan Allen Hitchcock, "It is now known that most of the wounded colored men were murdered on the field [at Olustee]." He had information that Georgia regulars and Georgia volunteers in Colquitt's brigade committed the "outrages." "As many of these troops are now in our hands as prisoners, an investigation of the circumstances might easily be made," he said. There is no record that Hitchcock replied. See Hatch to Hitchcock, *OR*, ser. 2, vol. 7: 876; and Report of Birney, *OR*, ser. 1, vol. 35, pt. 1: 420–21.

## CHAPTER 5

1. Emerson and Stokes, *Days of Destruction*, 16–17, 79; "Extract from Journal of Operations," December 18 and 25, 1863, and Bryan to Roman, January 6, 1864, *OR*, ser. 1, vol. 28, pt. 1: 181–85, 682–84; Beauregard to Anderson, November 12, 1863, Beauregard to Norris, November 18, 1863, and Beauregard to Cooper, November 22 and December 1, 1863, *OR*, ser. 1, vol. 28, pt. 2: 501, 511–15, 531.

2. Smythe's letters to his parents chart the breakdown of law and order from its beginnings in February 1864 to its complete collapse by the end of the year. Emerson and Stokes, *Days of Destruction*, 25–26, 91, 100–105, 111, 117–18, 124, 134–38; Ripley, *Siege Train*, 127, 234; Rhett to Jordan, March 4, 1864, *OR*, ser. 1, vol. 28, pt. 1: 686; Smith, Smith, and Childs, *Mason Smith Family Letters*, 72. The estimate of 11,000 shells is in Phelps,

*Bombardment of Charleston*, 150. Quote from the *London Times* is in C. Bennett, *Resolute Rebel*, 269.

3. John Appleton to Mary Appleton, December 19 and 31, 1863, box 2, and Appleton Military Memoir, pp. 123, 138–39, box 3A, APWV; December 19, 1863, "Extract from Journal of Operations," Report of Rhett, January 1, 1864, *OR*, ser. 1, vol. 28, pt. 1: 182, 684; Adams, *On the Altar of Freedom*, 95.

4. Emerson and Stokes, *Days of Destruction*, 86; Theodore A. Honour to Beckie Honour, October 4, December 2 and 26, 1863, Honour Papers, SCL; Ripley, *Siege Train*, 99; Ames to Dean, July 27 and August 16, 1864, *OR*, ser. 1, vol. 35, pt. 2: 191, 241; Huguenin to Jones, August 1, 1864, *OR*, ser. 1, vol. 35, pt. 1: 232.

5. Gray and Ropes, *War Letters*, 320, 439–53; Emilio, *Brave Black Regiment*, 193; McGrath, *History of the 127th New York Volunteers*, 102–3. I am grateful to Shane Makowicki, doctoral candidate at Texas A&M University, for sharing insights about Foster from his own dissertation research that I used for my portrait here.

6. S. Jones, *Siege of Charleston*, 5–6; Crist, Dix, and Williams, *Papers of Jefferson Davis*, 10:5; Emerson and Stokes, *Days of Destruction*, 115.

7. Foster to Halleck, June 7, 15, 21, 22, 23, 1864, Halleck to Foster, June 11 and 29, 1864, Jones to Johnston, June 15, 1864, Jones to Bonham, June 29, 1864, and Jones to Cooper, July 29, 1864, *OR*, ser. 1, vol. 35, pt. 2: 114, 124, 130–31, 142, 145–46, 155–56, 532, 543, 596; Jones to Bragg, June 14, 15, 1864, *OR*, ser. 1, vol. 35, pt. 1: 120–21.

8. Foster to Halleck, June 15 and 22, 1864, *OR*, ser. 1, vol. 35, pt. 1: 12–13; Jones to Bragg, June 1, 1864, and Cooper to Cobb, June 9, 1864, *OR*, ser. 2, vol. 7: 185, 217; Racine, *"Unspoiled Heart,"* 155.

9. Jordan to Branch, July 18, 1863, and Beauregard to Elliott, September 9, 1863, *OR*, ser. 2, vol. 6: 129, 275; Smith, Smith, and Childs, *Mason Smith Family Letters*, 66.

10. The insight that soldiers experienced captivity during the Civil War as a "decivilizing" process belongs to Kutzler, *Living by Inches*.

11. Jones to Foster, June 13, 1864, *OR*, ser. 1, vol. 35, pt. 2: 132.

12. Appleton Military Memoir, pp. 223, 228, 244, box 3A, APWV.

13. Schimmelfennig to Burger, June 15, 1864, and Foster to Jones, June 16, 1864, *OR*, ser. 1, vol. 35, pt. 2: 131–34; Foster to Halleck, June 16, 1864, *OR*, ser. 2, vol. 7: 371.

14. Jones to Foster, June 22, 1864, *OR*, ser. 1, vol. 53: 104; Emerson and Stokes, *Days of Destruction*, 109. The number of noncombatants killed in the Federal shelling was not documented by Confederate officials or civilian sources, and it is impossible to estimate casualties from the given records. A Confederate report of January 4, 1864, put the count as five people killed and eight wounded due to shell fire up to that point, but that was the last official count. See *OR*, ser. 1, vol. 28: 683.

15. Emerson and Stokes, *Days of Destruction*, 23, 109–13; Swift, *My Experiences as a Prisoner of War*, 14–20; Ripley to Jones, June 25, 1864, *OR*, ser. 2, vol. 7: 415–16; Stokes, *Immortal 600*, 43.

16. Foster to Halleck, June 16, 1864, Strong to Halleck, June 19, 1864, Halleck to Foster, June 21, 1864, and Hoffman to Strong, June 23, 1864, *OR*, ser. 1, vol. 35, pt. 2: 135, 141, 143, 147; Dahlgren, *Memoir of John A. Dahlgren*, 459. GO No. 255, September 12, 1864, *OR*, ser. 2, vol. 7: 805 has the list of the fifty officers.

17. Foster to Halleck, June 27 and 30, 1864, and Burger to Schimmelfennig, June 27, 1864, *OR*, ser. 1, vol. 35, pt. 2: 150–51, 157; Foster to Halleck, July 8, 1864, *OR*, ser. 2, vol. 7: 447.

18. Newell to Father, July 22, 1864, Robert R. Newell Letters, Boston Public Library; Webber to Wife, July 19, 1864, Samuel Gilbert Webber Papers, SCL; Schwartz, *Woman Doctor's Civil War*, 87.

19. Foster to Halleck, July 7, 1864, and Jones to Cooper, July 4, 1864, *OR*, ser. 1, vol. 35, pt. 1: 14–15, 121; Emilio, *Brave Black Regiment*, 204–5; Appleton Military Memoir, pp. 250–53, box 3A, APWV. The role of the heat in defeating the various parts of Foster's demonstration is a ubiquitous comment in Union soldiers' accounts of the event. It was clearly an unusually oppressive heat. Soldiers note the number of men "prostrated with heatstroke" and the "terrible suffering" from the heat and use phrases such as "hot as blazes." A soldier in the 144th New York recorded, "The Col. was sunstroke during the engagement. The field across which they charged was about 3/4 of a mile and they were out of breath before they could get near enough to fire at them." See, for example, Saxton, *Regiment Remembered*, 106, 113; Prince, *Letters and Diary of Henry W. Prince*, 159; M. L. S. Jackson Diary, box 61, folder 11, CWD; and Alfred Marple to Wife, July 8, 1864, Marple Diary and Letters, SCL.

20. Another prong of the attack was designed to destroy the railroad between Charleston and Savannah. A force of 1,200 infantry sailed up the Edisto River, landed at White Point, and marched toward the railroad. The heat, a small Confederate force, and the incompetence of the brigade commander halted the effort after only five miles. Foster to Halleck, July 7 and 12, 1864, Jones to Cooper, July 4, 5, 7, 8, 10, 11, 12, and August 22, 1864, Jones to Jefferson Davis, July 7, 1864, and Robertson to Stringfellow, July 14, 1864, *OR*, ser. 1, vol. 35, pt. 1: 14–17, 121–25, 143; Jones to Johnston, July 2 and 8, 1864, Jones to McLaws, July 2, 1864, Jones to Beauregard, July 8, 1864, and Jones to Bragg, August 19, 1864, *OR*, ser. 1, vol. 35, pt. 2: 546, 552, 570, 612.

21. Foster to Jones, July 1, 1864, *OR*, ser. 1, vol. 35, pt. 2: 163.

22. Jones to Cooper, June 24, 1864, *OR*, ser. 2, vol. 7: 410; Wiggins, *Journals of Josiah Gorgas*, 126–27.

23. Foster to Jones, July 1, 1864, Wessells, Seymour, Scammon, Heckman, and Shaler to Foster, July 1, 1864, Jones to Foster, July 1, 1864, Foster to Seymour, July 4, 1864, Foster to Jones, July 4, 1864, and Jones to Foster, July 13, 1864, *OR*, ser. 1, vol. 35, pt. 2: 161–64, 174–75.

24. Foster to Halleck, July 7, 1864, *OR*, ser. 1, vol. 35, pt. 2: 170; Smith to Seddon, August 18, 1864, *OR*, ser. 2, vol. 7: 612–13; Duke, *Reminiscences*, 375–76; Matthews, *Basil Wilson Duke*, 170–71.

25. Davis to Jones, July 14, 1864, and Halleck to Foster, July 19, 1864, *OR*, ser. 2, vol. 7: 378, 467.

26. "Colored Soldiers in South Carolina," *New York Daily Tribune*, August 10, 1864, 5; Emilio, *Brave Black Regiment*, 218; Appleton Military Memoir, p. 263, box 3A, APWV; Webber to wife, August 4, 1864, Webber Papers, SCL; Dahlgren, *Memoir of John A. Dahlgren*, 471; Foster to Halleck, August 4, 1864, *OR*, ser. 1, vol. 35, pt. 2: 212–13; Barr, "Loathsome Diseases and Principles," 106–7.

27. Johnson gave the lyrics to Federal officers who were confined in the Charleston Jail yard in August and September. Both Federal officers and Confederate inspection reports attest to the condition of the Black prisoners. For the lyrics, see Glazier, *Capture*, 148. For conditions, see Racine, *"Unspoiled Heart,"* 204; Trautman, *Twenty Months in Captivity*, 101; John Ogden Reminiscences, Wisconsin Veterans Museum, Madison; Cooper, *In and Out of Rebel Prisons*, 116; and Bryan to Jordan, January 15, 1864, and Soule to Roman, March 21, 1864, *OR*, ser. 2, vol. 6: 843, 1079.

28. Entries of August 29 and September 10–19, 1864, Heber S. Thompson Diary, SCL; Berry, *House of Abraham*, 42, 166–69. Conditions in this hospital deteriorated when Confederate prison authorities sent sick prisoners from Andersonville there in September after Sherman captured Atlanta. It was overcrowded with men dying from dysentery and scurvy.

29. Cobb to Seddon, June 6, 1864, Carrington to Seddon, August 11, 1864, Campbell to Seddon, August 21, 1864, Bonham to Seddon, August 23, 1864, and Seddon to Bonham, August 31, 1864, *OR*, ser. 2, vol. 7: 203, 583, 673, 703–4.

30. This was because of the case of Union major general Neil Dow, a prominent temperance advocate who commanded Black troops in Florida and then Louisiana. After he was captured, a Confederate military court in Mobile, Alabama, tried him on August 22, 1863, under the Confederate congressional resolutions. Because of his influence and a public outcry in the Northern states, Union authorities had taken a hostage for his safety. The court decided it could not try an officer for acts done prior to the adoption of the resolutions. The court's decision, and the flurry of Confederate correspondence over the case, reflected the fear of what would happen should the Confederacy actually execute a white officer of Black troops. See *OR*, ser. 2, vol. 6: 269–70, for the trial record. James G. Hollandsworth Jr. found that by the summer of 1864, Confederate authorities treated white officers from Black units as they did officers of white regiments. His research found thirty officers from Black units who were held in Confederate military prisons and exchanged and eleven officers who were probably executed on the spot after capture (nine of these in Tennessee or Louisiana). See "Execution of White Officers."

31. Endorsement of Seddon, June 13, 1864, *OR*, ser. 2, vol. 7: 204. My conclusion that the Union's retaliation prevented the Confederacy from enacting its favored policies agrees with Sheehan-Dean, *Calculus of Violence*. For the view that the Union failed to protect its Black soldiers because the United States did not retaliate when Confederates massacred or brutalized Blacks on the battlefield, see Burkhardt, *Confederate Rage*; and Steplyk, *Fighting Means Killing*.

32. Adams, *On the Altar of Freedom*, 118–19; Appleton Military Memoir, pp. 126, 236, box 3A, SPWV; Emilio, *Brave Black Regiment*, 190.

33. John Appleton to Mary Appleton, March 20 and 22, 1864, box 2, and Appleton Military Memoir, pp. 210, 223, 226–27, 235, box 3A, APWV; Emilio, *Brave Black Regiment*, 190–91, 217; Newell to Mother, May 2, 1864, Newell to "My Dear Will," May 14, 1864, Newell to Mother, June 8, 1864, and Newell to Father, July 22, 1864, Newell Letters, Boston Public Library; Anderson to Hartwell, June 17, 1864, and Foster to Halleck, July 7, 1864, *OR*, ser. 1, vol. 35, pt. 2: 139, 168.

34. GO No. 120, August 18, 1864, Records, U.S. Army, Department of the South, SCL; Emilio, *Brave Black Regiment*, 220–21, 227–28; Briggs to Mother, October 4, 1864, box 1, folder 15, Briggs Letters, MHS; John Hawks to Esther Hill Hawks, September 28, 1864, and Smith to Esther Hill Hawks, November 3, 1864, Esther Hill Hawks Papers, LOC.

35. Kutzler, *Living by Inches*, 61, 107, 110; K. Thomas, *Man and the Natural World*, 32–41; DeMello, *Animals and Society*, 37–41; M. Smith, *Smell of Battle*.

36. Kutzler, *Living by Inches*, 62–4, 111; Racine, *"Unspoiled Heart,"* 148, 157–58, 167; Trautman, *Twenty Months in Captivity*, 90; Nathaniel Rollins to Timothy O'Howe, January 26, 1865, Nathaniel Rollins Papers, Wisconsin Historical Society, Madison.

37. Jones to Cooper, July 26, 1864, *OR*, ser. 2, vol. 7: 502; Rollins to O'Howe, January 26, 1865, and 1864 Journal of Nathaniel Rollins, Rollins Papers, Wisconsin Historical Society;

Racine, *"Unspoiled Heart,"* 172–75; Allen and Allen, *"Guest" of the Confederacy*, 120–28; entries of July 26–August 7, 1864, Civil War Diaries of Francis Trowbridge Sherman, University of Virginia Library, Special Collections.

38. Racine, *"Unspoiled Heart,"* 204; Kutzler, *Living by Inches*, 97; Cooper, *In and Out of Rebel Prisons*, 258–59; Glazier, *Capture*, 140–41, 152; Trautman, *Twenty Months in Captivity*, 98–100.

39. Foster to Halleck, August 18, 1864, *OR*, ser. 1, vol. 35, pt. 2: 247.

40. Foster to Halleck, August 4, 1864, *OR*, ser. 1, vol. 35, pt. 2: 213; Halleck to Foster, August 8, 1864, *OR*, ser. 2, vol. 7: 567.

41. Pickenpaugh, *Captives in Gray*, 190; Marvel, *Lincoln's Autocrat*, 309; Gillispie, *Andersonvilles of the North*, 232.

42. Seymour to Hoffman, August 10, 1864, Wessells to Thomas, August 9, 1864, and Sickles to Lincoln, August 10, 1864, *OR*, ser. 2, vol. 7: 570–75.

43. Foster to Jones, August 15, 1864, *OR*, ser. 1, vol. 35, pt. 2: 235; Foster to Jones, August 15, 1864, Foster to Halleck, August 15, 17 [19], 1864, and Jones to Foster, August 20, 1864, *OR*, ser. 2, vol. 7: 598, 615–16, 625. Foster's ulterior motive was present in concurrent messages to Halleck. He informed his superior that he would transmit any Confederate proposal for the exchange of prisoners to the War Department. At the same time, he forwarded petitions from Union officers held in Charleston describing the conditions in Andersonville and requesting that the government exchange the suffering private soldiers in that camp.

44. Grant to Butler, August 18, 1864, *OR*, ser. 2, vol. 7: 607; Grant to Stanton, August 21, 1864, *OR*, ser. 1, vol. 35, pt. 2: 254. Union and Confederate War Departments had trouble with Foster and Jones, who negotiated "special" exchanges of individuals in their departments, continually broached the subject of exchange with their superiors, appointed local "agents of exchange," and delivered a substantial number of packages sent from private sources to prisoners in their care. They tried to dictate policy at the local level and interfered with national arrangements. Grant and Halleck ordered Foster to stop these practices; Seddon did the same to Jones. The correspondence about this is substantial. See, for example, Grant to Stanton, August 21, 1864, Halleck to Foster, September 30 and November 3, 1864, Seddon to Jones, September 30, 1864, Foster to Hoffman, November 5, 1864, and Foster to Halleck, November 11, 1864, *OR*, ser. 2, vol. 7: 662, 895, 899, 1087, 1095, 1119.

45. Schimmelfennig to Foster, August 18, 1864, and Burger to Schimmelfennig, August 23, 1864, *OR*, ser. 1, vol. 35, pt. 2: 250, 256; Foster to Jones, September 4, 1864, Cooper to Jones, September 5, 1864, and Jones to Seddon, September 5, 1864, *OR*, ser. 2, vol. 7: 763, 773.

46. Saxton to Foster, September 8, 1864, and Foster to Scammon, October 3, 1864, *OR*, ser. 1, vol. 35, pt. 2: 275, 308–10; Huguenin to Nance, September 8, 1864, *OR*, ser. 1, vol. 35, pt. 1: 241; Foster to Halleck, September 13, 1864, *OR*, ser. 2, vol. 7: 819; Emilio, *Brave Black Regiment*, 222–24; McGrath, *History of the 127th New York*, 104; Smith to Hawks, September 18, 1864, Hawks Papers, LOC; Fontaine, *Prison Life*, 24; Emerson and Stokes, *Days of Destruction*, 118, 120; Williams and Kutzler, *Prison Pens*, 129; McMichael, *Autograph and Diary*, entry of September 7, 1864; entry of September 7, 1864, JBM; entries of September 7 and 9, 1864, Adams Prisoner of War Diary, VMI.

47. Emilio, *Brave Black Regiment*, 223, 226–27; Briggs to Emma Briggs, September 11, 1864, box 1, folder 15, Briggs Letters, MHS; Greer to Mother, October 2, 1864, folder 31,

George S. Greer Family Papers, Mariners' Museum Library, Newport News, Va.; Williams and Kutzler, *Prison Pens*, 128; Fuzzlebug (the pseudonym for John Dunkle), *Prison Life*, 29. Historian Kelly D. Mezurek argues that placing Black guards over Confederate prisoners was an intentional indignity that served the retaliation agenda. Confederates believed this violated the prohibition in U.S. GO No. 100, Article 75, against not subjecting prisoners of war to "intentional suffering or indignity." See "'De Bottom Rails on Top Now,'" 139–40. For a discussion of how these 600 Confederate officers narrated their experience after the war, see Riotto, "As Happy a Man."

48. Foster to Saxton, September 12, 1864, Taylor to Gurney, September 9, 1864, and Taylor to Hallowell, October 6, 1864, *OR*, ser. 1, vol. 35, pt. 2: 278, 285, 312; Foster to Jones, September 15, 1864, and Burger to Saxton, September 24, 1864, *OR*, ser. 2, vol. 7: 826, 869; Foster to Halleck, September 19 and October 4, 1864, and Saxton to Burger, September 27, 1864, *OR*, ser. 1, vol. 35, pt. 1: 24, 81; McGrath, *History of the 127th New York*, 104; Emilio, *Brave Black Regiment*, 224; Williams and Kutlzer, *Prison Pens*, 129–30; McMichael, *Autograph and Diary*, entries of September and October 1864; entries of September 15, October 17, 21, 1864, JBM; Fuzzlebug, *Prison Life*, 34; diary entry of September 20, 1864, Hawes Papers, VHS; John Milton Hawks to Esther Hill Hawks, September 18 and 28, 1864, Hawks Papers, LOC; Briggs to Mother, September 21, 1864, box 1, folder 15, Briggs Letters, MHS.

49. Rollins to O'Howe, January 26, 1865, and 1864 Journal of Nathaniel Rollins, Rollins Papers, Wisconsin Historical Society; Racine, *"Unspoiled Heart,"* 176–215; Allen and Allen, *"Guest" of the Confederacy*, 129–30; entries of September 22–30, 1864, James E. Wenrick Diary, Historical Society of Pennsylvania, Online Collection; entries of August 10–September 19, 1864, Civil War Diaries of Francis Trowbridge Sherman, University of Virginia Library; Trautman, *Twenty Months in Captivity*, 101–4; Glazier, *Capture*, 156–59; *Petition in Favor of the Sisters of Our Lady of Mercy*, 12–13.

50. Rollins to O'Howe, January 26, 1865, Rollins Papers, Wisconsin Historical Society; Williams and Kutzler, *Prison Pens*, 129. For Union accounts, see Ogden Reminiscences, Wisconsin Veterans Museum; Racine, *"Unspoiled Heart,"* 184, 187, 196, 208–9; Allen and Allen, *"Guest" of the Confederacy*, 130–39; entries of September and October 1864, Wenrick Diary, Historical Society of Pennsylvania, Online Collection; entries of September and October 1864, Civil War Diaries of Francis Trowbridge Sherman, University of Virginia Library; Trautman, *Twenty Months in Captivity*, 101; and Glazier, *Capture*, 141–60. For Confederate accounts, see entries of September and October 1864, JBM; A. Edgar, *Reminiscences*, 144; entries of September and October 1864, Adams Prisoner of War Diary, VMI; Fulkerson, "Prison Experience," 139; and McMichael, *Autograph and Diary*, entries of September and October 1864. There was another equivalency in the treatment of the prisoners under fire. Both sides sent and received letters and received boxes sent from friends and families. Foster and Jones were diligent to ensure that officers received packages; indeed, a member of Foster's staff recorded the transmission of items across the lines and made sure that the Confederate officers signed for their items. On October 3, for example, seventeen Confederate officers received boxes that contained tobacco, clay pipes, cooked food, sundry articles (items such as soap), a mattress, a pillow, a coat, and twenty-seven sacks of bread. On the same date, a member of Jones's staff signed for eighty-two boxes that the U.S. Sanitary Commission sent to Union prisoners in Charleston (officers and privates), which included towels, handkerchiefs, quilts, bed sacks, and food for the officers. Prisoners on both sides who came from wealthy families or who had local

contacts received greenbacks, gold, and banknotes to purchase supplies. Voluminous records of the exchange of packages and letters can be found in Entry 4277, Letters Received by the Provost Marshal, Entry 4311, Agent of Exchange Register of Letters Received, Entry 4312, Agent of Exchange Press Copies of Letters Sent, Entry 4315, Agent of Exchange Letters Received, and Entry 4316, Lists of Union POWs to Whom Money Was Forwarded, RG 393, NARA. Diaries of prisoners also confirm receipt of packages and boxes—entries regarding this are ubiquitous.

51. Mulford to Hitchcock, October 9, 1864, and Butler to Hoffman, October 18, 1864, *OR*, ser. 2, vol. 7: 956, 1007. The correspondence does not name the five Black sailors, but since the five were "all the negroes captured of our naval service," it is logical to assume that these were the five sailors held in the Charleston Jail. Other correspondence suggests that the seamen from the *Isaac Smith* were still prisoners in January 1865. Admiral Dahlgren wanted to include them in a local exchange of prisoners he was arranging, but it could be that the records of the Naval Department were not up to date on the situation. See Welles to Stanton, January 30, 1865, and Dana to Welles, February 18, 1865, *OR*, ser. 2, vol. 8: 146, 257. Federal census records, as accessed on Ancestry.com through the Texas A&M University Libraries, indicate that all three men returned to New York. Orin H. Brown resumed his prewar profession as a barber and was living in Westfield, New York, in 1870. In 1900, both William H. Johnson and William Wilson lived in Manhattan. Johnson had married in 1865. Wilson was a single laborer living in lodgings.

52. Lee to Grant, October 3, 1864, Grant to Lee, October 3, 1864, Seddon to Lee, October 15, 1864, and Lee to Grant, October 19, 1864, *OR*, ser. 2, vol. 7: 914, 991, 1011. Seddon and Lee used historical precedent from the American Revolution and the War of 1812 to claim that "slaves in arms" revert to their former owners if captured. Grant argued that he had to protect "all persons" received into the army of the United States. "When acknowledged soldiers of the Government are captured, they must be treated as prisoners of war, or such treatment as they receive inflicted upon an equal number of prisoners held by us," he said. Grant approved a retaliation to put Confederate prisoners to work on a Federal canal that was under fire of Confederate guns. Lee therefore removed the Black prisoners at work on the Confederate fortifications. There had indeed been eleven freeborn Black soldiers at work (see Turner to Hatch, October 14, 1864, *OR*, ser. 2, vol. 7: 987–88). Grant then removed the Confederate prisoners at the canal. Lee told Seddon, "The issue is therefore made in regard to recaptured slaves, though the necessity of pressing it for the present is avoided." (See Lee to Seddon, October 23, 1864, *OR*, ser. 2, vol. 7: 1029–30.)

53. Foster to Halleck, October 4, 1864, *OR*, ser. 1, vol. 35, pt. 1: 25; Foster to Scammon, October 3, 1864, *OR*, ser. 1, vol. 35, pt. 2: 310; Allen and Allen, *"Guest" of the Confederacy*, 138–39; Glazier, *Capture*, 160; Rollins to O'Howe, January 26, 1865, Rollins Papers, Wisconsin Historical Society; Racine, *"Unspoiled Heart,"* 220; Jones to Cooper, September 23, 1864, *OR*, ser. 2, vol. 7: 866.

54. Emilio, *Brave Black Regiment*, 419–24; Pickenpaugh, *Captives in Blue*, 196–97, 202–5; Basile, *Diary of Amos E. Stearns*, 85–88; Westwood, "Captive Black Union Soldiers," 48; Mahood, *Charlie Mosher's Civil War*, 277; Pickett to Hardee, October 12, 1864, and Rutherford to Andrews, November 5, 1864, *OR*, ser. 2, vol. 7: 972–73, 1097–98. Civil War officials and modern historians refer to Confederate prisoners who took an oath of allegiance to the United States as "Galvanized Yankees" and to Union prisoners who were released to fight in Confederate regiments as "Galvanized Confederates." Prisoners in

the Department of the South, however, referred to the former Union soldiers who wore Confederate gray as "Galvanized Yankees."

55. Hardee to Davis, January 29, 1865, in Crist, Dix, and Williams, *Papers of Jefferson Davis*, 11:359; Foster to Halleck, October 13, 1864, *OR*, ser. 1, vol. 35, pt. 1: 26; Hardee to Foster, October 13, 1864, Foster to Hardee, October 15, 1864, Foster to Halleck, October 20, 1864, and Foster to Hardee, October 31, 1864, *OR*, ser. 2, vol. 7: 981–82, 990, 1016, 1073; Emilio, *Brave Black Regiment*, 230. Foster did not immediately remove the 600 Confederate officers from their position on Morris because the Black prisoners of the 54th were still under fire, but he did not explain this to his Confederate counterpart.

56. Foster to Halleck, September 25, 1864, *OR*, ser. 2, vol. 7: 875.

57. Halleck to Lieber, October 16, 1864, box 10, FLP; Halleck, "Retaliation in War," 113–14.

58. Foster to Hardee, October 17, 1864, *OR*, ser. 2, vol. 7: 1007.

59. Petition to Lt. Gen. Hardee from C. S. Military Prison, Columbia, S.C., November 12, 1864, and Fragment of Endorsements, folder 27, Hutson Lee Papers, South Carolina Historical Society, Charleston; Chilton to Saunders, November 26, 1864, *OR*, ser. 2, vol. 7: 1162; "Statements Forwarded by Capt. Appleton, Provost Marshal[,] Morris Island[,] of U.S. Soldiers who came into our lines on the 5th Nov 1864 at Long Island SC, Having escaped from the Southern Confederacy," Entries 4294 and 4295, Record Book of the Office of the Provost Marshal General, Hilton Head, South Carolina, RG 393, NARA.

60. Foster to Halleck, November 21, 1864, and Halleck to Foster, November 23, 1864, *OR*, ser. 1, vol. 44: 517, 535; GO No. 96, October 31, 1864, Regimental Order Book, vol. 5, and GO No. 19, November 6, 1864, Regimental Order Book, vol. 6, 157th New York Regimental Books, RG 94, NARA; October 28, 1864, Col. Brown Entry, Entry 4311, Agent of Exchange Register of Letters Received, RG 393, NARA; Saxton, *Regiment Remembered*, 110, 151; Adams Prisoner of War Diary, VMI; Williams and Kutzler, *Prison Pens*, 132; diary entries of October and November 1864, Hawes Papers, VHS; McMichael, *Autograph and Diary*, entries of November 1864, JBM.

61. May 26, 1864, issue of *The Swamp Angel*, box 3A, APWV.

62. Burger to Brown and Brown to Burger, December 12, 1864, and Burger to Brown, December 15, 1864, *OR*, ser. 1, vol. 44: 700, 725; Brown to Burger, December 15, 1864, Regimental Letter Book, vol. 3, 157th New York Regimental Books, RG 94, NARA. Foster knew that rations for Confederate soldiers in South Carolina were not consistently better than the fare prisoners received. Deserters from the Confederate army, who regularly came into Union lines from September to December 1864, told interrogators about the rations Confederate soldiers received. For example, John Reynolds told the Union provost marshal on October 17, "Our rations are poor consisting of 1 pound of corn meal and ⅓ pound of bacon and a gill of molasses." See interviews in Entry 4277, Letters Received by Provost Marshal, 1862–65, RG 393, NARA.

63. Brown to Burger, December 16 and 19, 1864, Regimental Letter Book, vol. 3, 157th New York Regimental Books, RG 94, NARA. Under intense pressure from the Northern public, Union authorities proposed the exchange of "sick and invalid officers and men who in the judgement of the party holding them, shall be unfit for duty and likely to remain so for 60 days." Butler to Ould, September 9, 1864, and Mulford to Butler, November 29, 1864, *OR*, ser. 2, vol. 7: 793, 1169; entries of November 13, 28, December 2, 11, 12, 13, 1864, Thompson Diary, SCL; Pickenpaugh, *Captives in Blue*, 228; Sanders, *While in the Hands of the Enemy*, 260–63.

64. Williams and Kutzler, *Prison Pens*, 132–34; McMichael, *Autograph and Diary*, entries of January and February 1865; Fulkerson, "Prison Experience," 140–42; Woodford to Burger, February 11, 1865, Entry 4312, Agent of Exchange Press Copies of Letters Sent, 208DS, RG 393, NARA; Stokes, *Immortal 600*, 96–97.

## CHAPTER 6

1. Hitchcock, *Marching with Sherman*, v–vi, 6–7; Bailey, "Home Front Becomes Battle Front."

2. This portrait of Sherman is based upon Gray and Ropes, *War Letters*, 427–28; Cozzens and Girardi, *Memoirs of General John Pope*, 91–92; Kennett, *Sherman*, 23–30, 98–110; Marszalek, *Sherman*, 334; and McDonough, *William Tecumseh Sherman*, 239. Robert L. O'Connell provides an important reminder to anyone seeking to interpret Sherman: he was "to an extraordinary degree, theatrical." See *Fierce Patriot*, xiii.

3. Sherman to Pemberton, November 18, 1862, and Sherman to Rawlins, November 19, 1862, *OR*, ser. 2, vol. 4: 723–24, 729; Foote, "Sternest Feature of War," 88–89.

4. Hitchcock, *Marching with Sherman*, 35, 73; Bailey, "Home Front Becomes Battle Front"; Frank, *Civilian War*, 3–11; Sherman, "Grand Strategy," 255; Sherman, *Memoirs*, 697; McDonough, *William Tecumseh Sherman*, 555, 562, 585; O'Connell, *Fierce Patriot*, 152.

5. Hitchcock, *Marching with Sherman*, 58; Special Field Orders No. 120, November 9, 1864, *OR*, ser. 1, vol. 39, pt. 3: 713; GO No. 64, Headquarters 17th Army Corps, November 14, 1864, *OR*, ser. 1, vol. 44: 459; Report of Langley, Commanding Third Brigade, Second Division, 14th Army Corps, January 3, 1865, *OR*, ser. 1, vol. 44: 199; O. Howard, *Autobiography*, 2:77–78. Historian Lee Kennett found in the *OR* at least fifty orders issued during the first month of Sherman's march to supplement SFO 120. See *Sherman*, 270. Sherman's orders were compatible with the international customs of war; see Sheehan-Dean, *Calculus of Violence*, 247–48; Vattel, *Law of Nations*, 566–75; and Articles 15, 17, 21, 44, GO No. 100, Avalon Project.

6. Bailey, "Home Front Becomes Battle Front."

7. Hitchcock, *Marching with Sherman*, 53–73.

8. Hitchcock, 76–87, 134. Published reports by officers who agreed with Hitchcock abound. Representative was Lt. Col. James W. Langley, 125th Illinois, who commanded the 3rd Brigade, 2nd Division, 14th Corps. He wanted to dismiss all the company commanders who "by their passiveness encourage their men to throw aside the restrictions of discipline, and become outlaws and brigands." See *OR*, ser. 1, vol. 44: 201. Other accounts agree with Hitchcock that Howard enforced stricter discipline on his wing than Slocum did on his wing. He issued general orders against pillaging with a penalty of death, had them read to soldiers regularly, organized courts-martial of soldiers who pillaged, and gave officers authority to shoot pillagers on the spot if caught in the act. See, for example, Jackson, *Colonel's Diary*, 166–70; and Kellogg, *Army Life of an Illinois Solider*, 326.

9. Sheehan-Dean, *Calculus of Violence*, 333.

10. Kilpatrick to Sherman, November 30, 1864, and Dayton to Kilpatrick, December 1, 1864, *OR*, ser. 1, vol. 44: 585, 601; Hitchcock, *Marching with Sherman*, 56, 87, 98, 109; Burkhardt, *Confederate Rage*, 221–24; entries of November and December 1864, Ephraim Franklin Bower Diary, box 16, folder 3, CWD. Wheeler claimed that Union soldiers believed false rumors that his cavalry took no prisoners and thus refused to surrender, which accounted for the large proportion killed. His men had "no alternative" but to shoot

or saber men to prevent their escape. This is a reasonable explanation that undoubtedly applied to some cases, but there is ample evidence in both Union and Confederate official and private accounts that Confederates killed Union soldiers after surrender. See Report of Wheeler, December 24, 1864, *OR*, ser. 1, vol. 44: 411.

11. Cobb to Davis and Cobb to Cooper, November 17, 1864, Davis to Cobb, November 18, 1864, "To the People of Georgia," November 18, 1864, Davis to Browne, November 22, 1864, and Fielden to Jones, December 9, 1864, *OR*, ser. 1, vol. 44: 861–67, 880, 943; Lee to Davis, November 19, 1864, in Crist, Dix, and Williams, *Papers of Jefferson Davis*, 11:171.

12. Nelson, *Ruin Nation*, 62–99; Frank, *Civilian War*, 71.

13. Kinsella, *Image before the Weapon*, 19–20, 83–93. Historians who study Union soldiers during the march through Georgia characterize their behavior in different ways. Reid Mitchell argues that soldiers labeled their enemy as savage from the start of the war, which only escalated their sense of the foe's barbarity. Northern soldiers perceived Southerners and their landscape as inferior, which shaped their willingness to wage war on the population. See *Civil War Soldiers*. Joseph Glatthaar's study of Union veterans in Sherman's army found that these men bitterly resented the Southern people, whom they blamed for the war. Intense hatred for the enemy and vengeance for the sufferings of Union soldiers inspired them to feel justified in destroying property on a wide scale. See *March to the Sea and Beyond*. Mark Grimsley argues that the basic moral value of Union soldiers inspired some restraints on their behavior. They implemented a "directed severity" that targeted those they felt most deserved it and protected some private property. See *Hard Hand of War*. O'Connell insists that historians assess Sherman's generalship by his actions rather than by his "vast opinion." In a comparative perspective, O'Connell thinks Sherman "got the big things right." Foraging-based campaigns in world history are often accompanied by generalized rape and slaughter, but not in the case of Sherman's march. See *Fierce Patriot*, xix, 151–52, 160. For an emphasis on the devastation and destruction of soldiers, see Royster, *Destructive War*.

14. Special Field Orders No. 127, November 23, 1864, *OR*, ser. 1, vol. 44: 527; Hitchcock, *Marching with Sherman*, 91–93.

15. Hitchcock, *Marching with Sherman*, 160–62; Sherman, *Memoirs*, 670; Sherman to Webster, December 23, 1864, *OR*, ser. 1, vol. 44: 791; Jackson, *Colonel's Diary*, 171; Harwell and Racine, *This Fiery Trail*, 66–67. Francis Lieber argued that it was not unlawful for a combatant to place shells in fortifications before they abandoned them in order to kill the first enemy troops that entered. "The soldier within me revolts at the thing. It seems so cowardly. The jurist within me cannot find arguments to declare it unlawful. National battles are no Quixotic tournaments," he told Halleck. "Nothing more common in sieges than undermining and blowing up the enemy, or pitfalls." Lieber to Halleck, August 24, 1863, box 27, FLP.

16. Gould and Kennedy, *Memoirs of a Dutch Mudsill*, 329–30; Hitchcock, *Marching with Sherman*, 143, 177; entry of February 23, 1865, William W. Prichard Journal, box 94, folder 8, CWD; Report of Grumbach, 149th Ohio, *OR*, ser. 1, vol. 44: 320; Rubin, *Through the Heart of Dixie*, 51. Howard, because bloodhounds had bitten soldiers in his command, gave permission to kill them. Report of Howard, November 23, 1864, *OR*, ser. 1, vol. 44: 67. For the use of dogs as symbolism, see John Campbell, "Seminoles."

17. Sherman to Stanton, December 13, 1864, Foster to Grant, December 14, 1864, and Sherman to Grant, December 16, 22, 24, 1864, *OR*, ser. 1, vol. 44: 6–7, 700–701, 713, 727, 797; Marszaleck, *Sherman*, 307.

18. Halleck to Sherman, December 16 and 18, 1864, and Sherman to Halleck, December 24, 1864, *OR*, ser. 1, vol. 44: 729, 741, 799.

19. Neely, *Civil War and the Limits of Destruction*, 171–90; Pickenpaugh, *Captives in Gray*, 220–21; GO No. 280, November 11, 1864, *OR*, ser. 2, vol. 7: 1117. Neely argues that the Senate debate was a political ploy; the more radical Republicans used the issue of treatment of prisoners to undermine rumored peace negotiations. He does not seem aware of Foster's ration retaliation in the Department of the South.

20. Moor to Lincoln, January 13, 1865, Abraham Lincoln Papers, reel 90, LOC.

21. Hendricks, *Retaliation of Rebel Prisoners*, 9; *Treatment of Prisoners of War*, 3–4; Croffut, *Fifty Years in Camp and Field*, 471–72; Halleck to Lieber, February 5, 1865, box 10, FLP; Neely, *Civil War and the Limits of Destruction*, 182, 190; Sheehan-Dean, *Calculus of Violence*, 334–36; Dilbeck, *A More Civil War*, 126–27. Neely, Sheehan-Dean, and Dilbeck emphasize that the Senate debate reflects the general determination of Union authorities to follow the laws of war, to impose restraints on violence, and to avoid mere vengeance. Dilbeck highlights the Christian ideals that permeated how Northerners thought about what was just in war. I agree with this conclusion in general, but none of these scholars seems to be aware of Foster's simultaneous ration retaliation and its implications.

22. *Congressional Globe*, January 27, 1865, 459–60; Joslyn, *Immortal Captives*, 218.

23. Burger to Lord, December 19, 1864, *OR*, ser. 2, vol. 7: 1246; Harrison to Hartridge, January 9, 1865, *OR*, ser. 2, vol. 8: 50–51; entries of November 1864–February 1865, Adams Prisoner of War Diary, VMI; diary entries of November–December 1864, Hawes Papers, VHS.

24. Foster to Halleck, January 8, 1865, *OR*, ser. 1, vol. 42, pt. 2: 27; Woodford to Thompson, January 26, 1865, Woodford to Cuvier, February 7, 1865, and Woodford to Burger, February 11, 1865, Entry 4312, Agent of Exchange Press Copies of Letters Sent, 208DS, RG 393, NARA; Sherman to Stanton, February 2, 1865, in Simon, *Papers of Ulysses S. Grant*, 13:353.

25. Brown to Kike, February 10, 1865, and Grover to Brown, February 10, 1865, Regimental Letter Book, vol. 3, 157th New York Regimental Books, RG 94, NARA; Grover to Asst. Adj. Gen. Department of the South, February 1, 1865, *OR*, ser. 2, vol. 8: 163. I believe the date given in the *OR* for the Grover letter to the Department of the South is incorrect, as the content makes sense only in relation to Brown and Grover's February 10 correspondence. For Grant's and Sherman's opinions of Foster and Gillmore, see Grant to Sherman, February 1, 1865, and Grant to Halleck, February 6, 1865, in Simon, *Papers of Ulysses S. Grant*, 13:349, 380.

26. Woodford to Burger, February 11, 1865, Entry 4312, Agent of Exchange Press Copies of Letters Sent, 208DS, RG 393, NARA; Gillmore to Halleck, February 13, 1865, *OR*, ser. 1, vol. 42, pt. 2: 412–13; entry of February 20, 1865, Adams Prisoner of War Diary, VMI; diary entry of February 20, 1865, Hawes Papers, VHS.

27. The website for Fort Pulaski National Monument comments that the 13 Confederate officers who died there were buried on site at Cockspur Island. Most of them died of dehydration due to dysentery. According to Confederate captain Henry C. Dickerson, who kept a diary in Pulaski and obtained a list of sick, 156 of the 311 prisoners there were classified as sick on February 6. A partial list of illnesses were recorded as follows: scurvy (42), chronic dysentery (37), coughs and throat disease (43), in hospital (8). Dickerson claimed that in actuality only about 20 men in the entire prison were well enough to endure the rigors of military duty. In addition to the 18 deaths at Pulaski and Hilton Head,

25 men died immediately after the prisoners left the Department of the South. See Stokes, *Immortal 600*, 89–91, 98; and Joslyn, *Immortal Captives*, 265, 290.

28. Lieber to Halleck, February 11, 1865, box 28, and Halleck to Lieber, February 18, 1865, box 10, FLP.

29. Slocum, "Sherman's March," 684; entry of February 1, 1865, Prichard Journal, box 94, folder 8, CWD; entry of February 1, 1865, Isaac C. Nelson Diary, box 20, Civil War Times Illustrated Collection, AHEC; Emilio, *Brave Black Regiment*, 266; Harwell and Racine, *This Fiery Trail*, 82, 87; Sherman, "Grand Strategy," 258; Marszalek, *Sherman*, 318.

30. Entries of February 8 and 9, 1865, Prichard Journal, box 94, folder 8, CWD. Two of the most useful sources for assessing different perspectives are Kellogg, *Army Life of an Illinois Soldier*; and Harwell and Racine, *This Fiery Trail*.

31. Entry of February 20, 1865, Prichard Journal, box 94, folder 8, CWD; Howard to Blair and Logan, February 20, 1865, *OR*, ser. 1, vol. 47, pt. 2: 506; Harwell and Racine, *This Fiery Trail*, xxx; O. Howard, *Autobiography*, 2:128; Kellogg, *Army Life of an Illinois Soldier*, 342. The best assessment of events in Columbia remains Lucas, *Sherman and the Burning of Columbia*. Jacqueline Glass Campbell argues that the Union army did not break the will of Southern women during the march through South Carolina but rather reinvigorated their commitment to the Confederacy. See *When Sherman Marched North from the Sea*.

32. Beauregard to Cooper, April 15, 1865, entry 116, box 2, Papers of P. G. T. Beauregard, RG 109, NARA; Barrett, *Sherman's March through the Carolinas*, 49, 96–98; Grimsley and Simpson, *Collapse of the Confederacy*, 41–47, 71–72; Williams, *Beauregard*, 248–51.

33. Kilpatrick to Wheeler, February 22, 1865, *OR*, ser. 1, vol. 47, pt. 1: 860; Quimby, *Perfect Scout*, 13; Andrew, *Wade Hampton*, 272.

34. Wheeler to Kilpatrick, February 22, 1865, *OR*, ser. 1, vol. 47, pt. 1: 860. Historian George S. Burkhardt points out that the men of Shannon's Scouts—a detachment of the 8th Texas (Terry's Texas Rangers) that used Spencer's repeaters—were under Wheeler's command, and he believes they "undoubtedly" murdered the Federal infantrymen. Some of Wheeler's cavalrymen, freed in a field prisoner exchange, complained to him about the behavior of Shannon's Scouts. See *Confederate Rage*, 227.

35. Kilpatrick to Wheeler, February 23, 1865, *OR*, ser. 1, vol. 47, pt. 1: 861.

36. Kilpatrick to Dayton, February 22, 1865, and Sherman to Howard, February 23, 1865, *OR*, ser. 1, vol. 47, pt. 2: 533, 537.

37. Sherman to Kilpatrick, February 23, 1865, *OR*, ser. 1, vol. 47, pt. 2: 544.

38. Kilpatrick to Sherman, February 24, 1865, *OR*, ser. 1, vol. 47, pt. 2: 554–55; Smith, Smith, and Childs, *Mason Smith Family Letters*, 201. Jonathan M. Steplyk argues that "the phenomenon of 'death to foragers' atrocities stands out as grossly disproportionate acts of violence," because the sign belied the supposed "crime" of the Federals killed. Since foraging was legitimate under the customs of war, Confederates should have labeled their victims "with a more damning epithet," such as "thieves" or "vandals." See *Fighting Means Killing*, 157.

39. Hampton to Davis, April 19, 1865, box 26, reel 9, SPLC; Andrew, *Wade Hampton*, xii, 227, 234–38, 254, 267, 269–71; Quimby, *Perfect Scout*, 119.

40. Sherman to Hampton, February 24, 1865, *OR*, ser. 1, vol. 47, pt. 2: 546.

41. Sherman to Hampton, February 24, 1865.

42. Circular, Headquarters Department and Army of the Tennessee, February 25, 1865, and Woodhall to Woods, Hazen, Smith, and Corse, February 25, 1865, *OR*, ser. 1, vol. 47, pt. 2: 566–68, 570; entry of February 25, 1865, in Kellogg, *Army Life of an Illinois Soldier*, 352;

entry of February 27, 1865, Charles G. Ward Diary, SCL. Charles W. Wills also reported that on this date John E. Smith, commanding the 3rd Division of the 15th Army Corps, shot four prisoners in retaliation for the murder of four foragers of the division. I have not found confirmation of this in official records.

43. G. G. Dibrell to Hudson, February 26, 1865, *OR*, ser. 1, vol. 47, pt. 2: 1283.

44. Hampton to Sherman, February 27, 1865, *OR*, ser. 1, vol. 47, pt. 2: 596–97.

45. Hampton to Sherman, February 27, 1865, and Beauregard to Hampton, March 1, 1865, *OR*, ser. 1, vol. 47, pt. 2: 596–97, 1300.

46. Sherman to Howard, March 1, 1865, *OR*, ser. 1, vol. 47, pt. 2: 628. Union and Confederate sources verify that Kilpatrick executed eighteen Confederate prisoners of war. Kilpatrick wrote Sherman that he would retaliate for the execution of the cavalryman of the 92nd Illinois. Sherman told Hampton that he had ordered the execution of prisoners for the twenty-one infantrymen near Feasterville, and although I have not found other records of the execution, there is no reason to doubt that they took place. Division commander John E. Smith executed two Confederate prisoners for the murder of two Federals after they had surrendered (skirmishers witnessed the initial murders). As discussed below, on March 2, the 30th Illinois in the 17th Corps executed one Confederate prisoner. Multiple sources confirm this execution.

47. Brig. Gen. Stephen G. Burbridge executed a cumulative fifty-seven prisoners in Kentucky as acts of retaliation between July and December 1864. He had issued GO No. 59 on July 16, 1864, which proclaimed that Federal authorities would publicly shoot four guerrillas for every unarmed Union citizen murdered. Although Burbridge executed some men the Confederacy claimed as soldiers, he also executed guerrillas with no official connection to the Confederate army, which meant they were not considered legitimate combatants and were not officially classed as prisoners of war. For names and details of these executions, see De Falaise, "Burbridge's Command in Kentucky." Retaliatory executions of one or two prisoners of war by field commanders was periodic during the Civil War, and the number of such incidents is impossible to count. U.S. departmental authorities in Missouri selected by lot and executed six Confederate prisoners of war in October 1864 because a field officer in Confederate major general Sterling Price's command had handed six Union prisoners over to a guerrilla chieftain who executed them. In October 1864, George Armstrong Custer executed six prisoners from John Singleton Mosby's partisan command in Virginia in retaliation for the unlawful death of a Union officer. Mosby executed six prisoners from Custer's command in retaliation, and the executions stopped. See Foote, "Sternest Feature of War," 89–90; and Sheehan-Dean, *Calculus of Violence*, 332–33.

48. Special Orders No. 56, March 2, 1865, *OR*, ser. 1, vol. 47, pt. 2: 649; McDonald, *History of the 30th Illinois*, 99–101. The text of the special order mistakenly identifies the dead forager as belonging to the 13th Illinois.

49. My count of 60 comes from adding up the numbers given in this narrative based on the official retaliation correspondence. Anne Sarah Rubin states that Wheeler's Cavalry executed 110 foragers in South Carolina, but it is unclear from her footnotes where those numbers come from. See *Through the Heart of Dixie*, 36. Burkhardt believes Confederates killed 50 Federals after they had surrendered (his count includes soldiers and not just foragers). See *Confederate Rage*, 230.

50. Sherman to Slocum, March 6, 1865, GO No. 8, Headquarters Left Wing, March 7, 1865, *OR*, ser. 1, vol. 47, pt. 2: 704, 719.

51. Blair to Howard, March 7, *OR*, ser. 1, vol. 47, pt. 2: 717–18.

52. Van Dyke to Logan and Blair, March 7, 1865, Special Field Orders No. 56, Headquarters Department and Army of the Tennessee, March 8, 1865, Special Orders No. 63, Headquarters 17th Army Corps, March 10, 1865, and Blair to Van Dyke, March 11, 1865, *OR*, ser. 1, vol. 47, pt. 2: 714–18, 728, 760, 783; Kellogg, *Army Life of an Illinois Soldier*, 359; entry of March 12, 1865, Ward Diary, SCL.

53. Joint Resolution to Amend a Joint Resolution Entitled "Joint Resolution on the Subject of Retaliation," February 8, 1865, *OR*, ser. 2, vol. 8: 197; Mulford to Hitchcock, February 23, 1865, box 4, EAHLC. U.S. naval commanders in the West Gulf Blockading Squadron used Lee's October 1864 letter to Grant agreeing that free Blacks would be treated as prisoners of war to gain combatant status for Black sailors and soldiers in the Confederacy's Trans-Mississippi Department. See Crocker to Palmer, February 27, 1865, *OR*, ser. 2, vol. 8: 316. The Confederate change in policy occurred a month before the Confederate government decided to arm slaves for its own army, although the legislation occurred too late in the war to be implemented. For a treatment of the Confederate debate over arming slaves, see Levine, *Confederate Emancipation*.

54. Grant to Stanton, January 21, 1865, in Simon, *Papers of Ulysses S. Grant*, 13:290; Grant to Foster, February 5, 1865, Entry 4204, Letters Sent by the Assistant Inspector General, RG 393, NARA; Iverson to Booth, February 13, 1865, *OR*, ser. 2, vol. 8: 218; Emilio, *Brave Black Regiment*, 97; Testimony of Archibald Bogle, in U.S. House of Representatives, *Trial of Henry Wirz*, 327; Marvel, *Andersonville*, 221–22.

55. Abbott to Campbell, March 5, 1865, *OR*, ser. 2, vol. 8: 358; Foote, *Yankee Plague*, 121–26. Confederates exchanged the free Black prisoners held in Salisbury Prison, North Carolina, the last of the prisoners held there. There were nineteen Black Union soldiers at the prison on March 3, when they were sent for exchange to Richmond. See "List of Prisoners sent from this Post on Exchange, Salisbury," *OR*, ser. 2, vol. 8: 455. For the departure of the Confederate prisoners, who were not actually released until June 1865, see Grant to Mulford, March 21, 1865, in Simon, *Papers of Ulysses S. Grant*, 14:220; entry of March 4, 1865, Adams Prisoner of War Diary, VMI; and Williams and Kutlzer, *Prison Pens*, 135.

56. Foote, *Yankee Plague*, 126. Emilio, *Brave Black Regiment*, 398–99, has the exchange point for the men of the 54th as Goldsboro. They were certainly paroled there, but all other Union and Confederate records indicate that the deliveries and exchange of Black prisoners held in South Carolina took place at Wilmington. Of the sixty-two known POWs from the 54th, there are thirty-five known survivors. See Newhall, "'Under the Rebel Lash,'" 232.

57. Newhall, "'Under the Rebel Lash,'" 10, 90–92, 110, 125, 146, 169, 230; Emilio, *Brave Black Regiment*, 430–31; Hitchcock to Stanton, November 22, 1865, *OR*, ser. 2, vol. 8: 804; U.S. House of Representatives, *Report on the Treatment of Prisoners of War*, 742–55. Newhall has done extensive research in pensions and compiled service records to provide the first solid numbers for Black prisoners from the Union army. Of the 2,273 Black prisoners she has positively identified, at least 1,587 survived captivity. Her records indicate that 357 Black POWs attempted escape. She confirms 14 Black POWs sold at auction and 19 reclaimed by former enslavers, although she estimates the latter number may be as high as 270. She confirms 271 deaths as military captives (not all of these would have occurred in a military prison).

58. Emilio, *Brave Black Regiment*, 284, 98–99, 424–25. Before these men reported to

the regiment, the 54th had occupied Charleston; participated in Potter's Raid from Georgetown, South Carolina, in April 1865, which destroyed railroad rolling stock and brought 3,000 freed people to Georgetown; and then returned to Charleston. Emilio, p. 430, says that there might have been eleven prisoners from the 54th in Andersonville, although his list of names on pp. 424–25 provides ten names. I have gone with Emilio's verified numbers throughout. For the story of the 54th's occupation of Charleston, its operations in South Carolina in 1865, and the postwar lives of its veterans, see Egerton, *Thunder at the Gates*.

59. Burton, *Siege of Charleston*, 318–21; Gray and Ropes, *War Letters*, 459–60; McGrath, *History of the 127th New York*, 150–52.

60. Stanton to Anderson, March 28, 1865, box 43, reel 14, Letterbooks 1863–1865, SPLC; McGrath, *History of the 127th New York*, 152–57; Holland, *Letters and Diary of Laura M. Towne*, 159; Schwartz, *Woman Doctor's Civil War*, 127–31; Prince, *Letters and Diary of Henry W. Prince*, 168–69.

## CONCLUSION

1. "Burning of Darien, Georgia," *Harper's Weekly*, September 3, 1870, 563; "The Burning of Darien, Georgia," *Harper's Weekly*, October 1, 1870, 627.

2. U.S. House of Representatives, *Report on the Treatment of Prisoners of War*, 8–9, 11–17; Cloyd, *Haunted by Atrocity*, 24–45.

3. J. Wilson, *Black Phalanx*, dedication. Wilson had much in common with his comrade James Gooding, who had died at Andersonville. Wilson was born in the South, lived in New Bedford, Massachusetts, traveled the world on a whaler, and wrote for newspapers and journals. As Gooding had done in his articles for the *New Bedford Mercury*, Wilson in *The Black Phalanx* referenced the British lashing Sepoys to cannons in his discussion of historical precedents for barbaric behavior (320). It is easy to picture the two men discussing history, civilization, and retaliation over the campfires. For a brief biography of Wilson, see Varon and the *Dictionary of Virginia Biography*, "Joseph T. Wilson."

4. Fulkerson, "Prison Experience"; Fuzzlebug, *Prison Life*; Murray, *Immortal Six Hundred*; Fontaine, *Prison Life*; A. Edgar, *Reminiscences*; Riotto, "As Happy a Man."

5. Hitchcock, *Marching with Sherman*, 310; Andrew, *Wade Hampton*, 294, 306, 312, 317–20, 332. Wade Hampton's actions during the war became part of the Republican Party's 1868 efforts to discredit the Democratic Party. The Democratic Party "harbored" war criminals like Wade Hampton, "the murderer of Union prisoners," proclaimed one Republican politician. See Ferrell, "'Nation Cannot Now Be Entrusted.'"

6. Online forums on the state of the field regarding Reconstruction in the *Journal of the Civil War Era*, for example, discuss labor, capitalism, law, gender, religion, race, politics, periodization, geography, and Indigenous peoples as significant topics. The word "civilization," despite its central importance to nineteenth-century Americans, is notably absent among the themes that historians of Reconstruction consider. See Harlow, "Forum." In his forum, Fitzhugh Brundage points out that opponents believed Reconstruction was a "dangerous threat to the foundations of civilization itself" but drops the term in favor of considering other aspects of analysis. Brundage argues for a longer and more flexible periodization of Reconstruction, extending it backward and forward from its traditional period of 1865–77. I think that considering how Americans incorporated Reconstruction into what they saw as the unfolding forward progression

of civilization across time could be an important part of that project. See Brundage, "Reconstruction in the South." Reconstruction historians, like Civil War historians, take the term "civilization" for granted. The word appears frequently in their books when they quote nineteenth-century Americans, but they rarely subject the language or the concept to sustained analysis within their narratives.

7. Witt, *Lincoln's Code*, 327–37, 353–65; Kinsella, *Image before the Weapon*, 18; Linn, *Philippine War*.

8. Karsten, *Law, Soldiers, and Combat*; Howard, Andreopoulos, and Shulman, *Laws of War*.

# BIBLIOGRAPHY


## PRIMARY SOURCES

### *Manuscript Collections*

*Boston Public Library*
Robert R. Newell Letters
*Clarke Historical Library, Central Michigan University, Mount Pleasant*
William D. Wilkins Diary
*Digital Library of Georgia*
Francis Lee Higginson Letters, 1863
*Historical Society of Pennsylvania, Online Collection*
James E. Wenrick Diary
*Huntington Library, San Marino, Calif.*
Francis Lieber Papers
John S. Pope, *Correspondence between Generals Pope and Halleck in Relation to Prisoners Captured at Corinth*, s.l., s.n., 1870–1879?, call # 56155, Rare Books
*Library of Congress Manuscript Division, Washington, D.C.*
W. A. Croffut Papers
H. W. Halleck Papers
Esther Hill Hawks Papers
Ethan Allen Hitchcock Papers
Abraham Lincoln Papers
Edwin McMasters Stanton Papers
*Mariners' Museum Library, Newport News, Va.*
George S. Greer Family Papers
*Massachusetts Historical Society, Boston*
Charles E. Briggs Letters
Luis F. Emilio Papers
Henry Sturgis Russell Civil War Letters
*National Archives and Record Administration, Washington, D.C.*
Record Group 94, Records of the Adjutant General's Office
33rd USCI Regimental Books
34th USCI Regimental Books
157th New York Regimental Books
Entry 363, Letters Received by Adj. Gen. Thomas Relating to Colored Troops

Record Group 109, War Department Collection of Confederate Records
Letters and Orders Issued, Confederate Military Prison, Richmond, Va., January 1862–December 1863
Papers of General P. G. T. Beauregard, 1864–1865
Papers of Major General Sam Jones, 1864–1865
Record Group 153, Records of the Judge Advocate General
Court-Martial of Capt. Daniel D. Latham
Record Group 249, Records of the Commissary General of Prisoners
Entry 47, Daily Reports of Federal POWs in Richmond, 1861–1865
Entry 107, Misc. Letters
Entry 126, Daybooks of POWs in Richmond
Entry 130, Daybook of Prisoners Received in Richmond
Entry 132, Register of Captured Federal Officers Confined in Libby Prison
Entry 135, Correspondence, Circulars, and Orders of the Confederate Military Prison at Richmond
Record Group 393, Part I, Records of Army Continental Commands
Department of the South
Entry 4204, Letters Sent by the Assistant Inspector General
Entry 4214, Register of Letters Received by the Assistant Inspector Gen.
Entry 4270, Letters Sent by Provost Marshal General, May 1864–October 1865
Entry 4275, Endorsements Sent by Provost Marshal General July 1863–July 1865
Entry 4276, Register of Letters Sent by Provost Marshal General
Entry 4277, Letters Received by Provost Marshal, 1862–1865
Entry 4292, Lists of Confederate POWs
Entries 4294 and 4295, Record Book of the Office of the Provost Marshal General in Hilton Head, South Carolina
Entry 4311, Agent of Exchange Register of Letters Received
Entry 4312, Agent of Exchange Press Copies of Letters Sent
Entry 4313, Endorsements Sent by the Agent of Exchange, October 1864–March 1865
Entry 4315, Agent of Exchange Letters Received
Entry 4316, Lists of Union POWs to Whom Money Was Forwarded

*Newberry Library, Chicago*
Midwest Manuscript Collection
Journal of James B. McCreary

*New England Historic Genealogical Society Digital Collections*
Leander Gage King Papers

*South Carolina Historical Society, Charleston*
Erastus W. Everson Papers
Hutson Lee Papers
Edward McCrady Legal Journal, 1863, Conner Family Papers
Edward B. Middleton Diary, Cheves-Middleton Papers

*South Caroliniana Library, University of South Carolina, Columbia*
P. G. T. Beauregard Papers
Milledge Luke Bonham Papers
Frederick L. Childs Papers
George Gordon DeGroot Papers

Felix H. Dover Papers
William A. Gyles Papers
James Mobley Hill Diary
Theodore A. Honour Papers
Alfred Marple Diary and Letters
William L. McArthur Letter
Williams Middleton Papers
Records, U.S. Army, Department of the South
James M. Shattuck Papers
Hiram Teed Papers
Heber S. Thompson Diary
Orville Upton Papers
Charles G. Ward Diary
Philip A. Warner Papers
Samuel Gilbert Webber Papers
*University of Virginia Library, Special Collections, Charlottesville*
Civil War Diaries of Francis Trowbridge Sherman
*U.S. Army Heritage and Education Center, Carlisle, Pa.*
Curtis R. Burke Papers
James and Francis Carman Papers
Civil War Document Collection
J. Henry Beatty Papers, Commissary Dept., Folly Island (box 7, folder 3)
Ephraim Franklin Bower Diary, 23rd Mo. (box 16, folders 3–5)
Reminiscences of Jonathan W. W. Boynton, 157th N.Y. (box 13, folder 11)
John Calvin Burce Papers, 9th Maine (box 18, folder 2)
William A. Clark, 1st S.C. Heavy Artillery (box 23, folder 10)
James Clegg, 3rd R.I. Heavy Artillery (box 23, folder 15)
Henry T. Coleman Correspondence, 52nd Pa. (box 24, folder 14)
Robert Dysart Diary, 144th N.Y. (box 34, folder 16)
John Guest Papers, 97th Pa. (box 50, folder 7)
M. L. S. Jackson Diary, 144th N.Y. (box 61, folder 11)
Caroll E. Kingsley Papers, 7th Conn. (box 66, folder 2)
John C. Murry Papers, 157th N.Y. (box 83, folder 18)
James B. Post Papers, 95th N.Y. (box 93, folders 3–5)
William W. Prichard Journal, 9th Pa. Cavalry (box 94, folder 8)
Fredrick Ranger Papers, 22nd N.Y. (box 95, folders 15–16)
Report on Brig. Gen. Roswell S. Ripley (box 98, folder 13)
Allan S. Rose Letter, 56th N.Y. (box 100, folder 8)
John W. Sanborn Papers, 4th N.H. (box 102, folder 5)
Orlando P. Sawtelle Papers (box 102, folder 11–13)
James O. Sheppard Papers, 6th S.C. Cavalry (box 104, folder 10)
Edward Shuey Papers, 97th Pa. (box 105, folder 12)
Theodore W. Skinner Papers, 112th N.Y. (box 106, folders 20–22)
Civil War Times Illustrated Collection
Isaac C. Nelson Diary, 89th Ohio, Box 20
E. Watt Webber and Thomas B. Webber Correspondence, 2nd Ky., Box 28
Quincy A. Gillmore Papers

William Gladstone Papers
Diary of Edward Sewell, 6th Conn.
Harrisburg Civil War Round Table Collection
Haas-Jones-Curry Family Papers
William F. Howard Papers
Henry A. C. Anderson Diary, 127th N.Y.
Lewis Leigh Collection, Union Folders
George C. Remey Papers
John W. Turner Papers
*Virginia Historical Society, Richmond*
E. L. Cox Diary
Samuel Horace Hawes Papers
*Virginia Military Institute Archives Digital Collections*
Richard H. Adams Jr. Civil War Prisoner of War Diary, 1863–1865
*U.S. Military Academy Library, Special Collections*
P. G. T. Beauregard Papers
Braxton Bragg Papers
George Washington Cullum Papers
Henry Wager Halleck Papers
Ethan Allen Hitchcock Papers
John Pope Papers
*West Virginia and Regional History Center, Morgantown*
John W. M. Appleton Papers
*Wisconsin Historical Society, Madison*
Nathaniel Rollins Papers
*Wisconsin Veterans Museum, Madison*
John Ogden Reminiscences

## *Newspapers and Journals*

*Boston Evening Transcript*
*Charleston Mercury*
*Congressional Globe*
*Daily National Intelligencer*
*Harper's Weekly: A Journal of Civilization*
*The Liberator (Boston, Ma.)*
*London Times*
*Maine Farmer (Augusta, Me.)*
*Newark Daily Advertiser*
*New York Daily Tribune*
*New York Semi-Weekly Tribune*
*Salem Register*
*San Francisco Daily Evening Bulletin*
*Semi-Weekly Raleigh Register*
*Sunbury (Pa.) American*

## *Published Works*

Adams, Virginia Matzke, ed. *On the Altar of Freedom: A Black Soldier's Civil War Letters from the Front*. Amherst: University of Massachusetts Press, 1991.

Allen, Robert D., and Cheryl J. Allen, eds. *A "Guest" of the Confederacy: The Civil War Letters and Diaries of Alonzo M. Keeler, Captain, Company B, Twenty-Second Michigan Infantry*. Nashville, Tenn.: Cold Tree Press, 2008.

Basile, Leon, ed. *The Civil War Diary of Amos E. Stearns, a Prisoner at Andersonville.* East Brunswick, N.J.: Associated University Presses, 1981.

Basler, Roy P., ed. *Collected Works of Abraham Lincoln.* 8 vols. New Brunswick, N.J.: Rutgers University Press, 1953.

Beauregard, P. G. T. "Torpedo Service in Harbor and Water Defenses of Charleston." *Southern Historical Society Papers* 5 (April 1878): 146–61.

Bosson, Charles P. *History of the Forty-Second Regiment Infantry, Massachusetts Volunteers, 1862, 1863, 1864.* Boston: Mills, Knight, and Co., 1886.

Burlingame, Michael, and John R. Turner Ettlinger, eds. *Inside Lincoln's White House: The Complete Civil War Diary of John Hay.* Carbondale: Southern Illinois University Press, 1997.

Cooper, Alonzo. *In and Out of Rebel Prisons.* Oswego, N.Y.: R. J. Oliphant, 1888.

Cowley, Charles. *Leaves from a Lawyer's Life Afloat and Ashore.* Lowell, Mass.: Penhallow Printing, 1879.

Cozzens, Peter, and Robert I. Girardi, eds. *The Military Memoirs of General John Pope.* Chapel Hill: University of North Carolina Press, 1998.

Crist, Lynda Lasswell, Mary Seaton Dix, and Kenneth H. Williams, eds. *The Papers of Jefferson Davis.* Vols. 8–11. Baton Rouge: Louisiana State University Press, 1996–99.

Croffut, W. A., ed. *Fifty Years in Camp and Field: Diary of Major-General Ethan Allen Hitchcock, U.S.A.* New York: Knickerbocker Press, 1909.

Dahlgren, Madeleine Vinton. *Memoir of John A. Dahlgren, Rear-Admiral United States Navy.* Boston: J. R. Osgood and Company, 1882.

Davis, Cynthia Quentin, ed. *Black Soldiers in the War of the Slaveowners' Rebellion: Selected Letters and Papers of Norwood P. Hallowell.* Hyde Park, Mass.: MassPrinting, 1963.

Donald, David, ed. *Inside Lincoln's Cabinet: The Civil War Diaries of Salmon P. Chase.* New York: Longmans, Green, 1954.

Denison, Frederic. *Sabres and Spurs: The First Regiment Rhode Island Cavalry in the Civil War.* N.p., published by the First Rhode Island Cavalry Association, 1876.

Dowdy, Clifford, and Louis H. Manarin, eds. *The Wartime Papers of R. E. Lee.* New York: Bramhall House, 1961.

Duke, Basil. *Reminiscences of General Basil W. Duke, C.S.A.* New York: Doubleday, Page, 1911.

Duncan, Russell, ed. *Blue-Eyed Child of Fortune: The Civil War Letters of Colonel Robert Gould Shaw.* Athens: University of Georgia Press, 1992.

Dwight, Elizabeth A., ed. *Life and Letters of Wilder Dwight.* Boston: Ticknor and Fields, 1868.

Eby, Cecil D., Jr., ed. *A Virginia Yankee in the Civil War: The Diaries of David Hunter Strother.* Chapel Hill: University of North Carolina Press, 1961.

Edgar, Alfred Mallory. *My Reminiscences of the Civil War with the Stonewall Brigade and the Immortal 600.* Edited by Steve Cunningham. Charleston, W.Va.: 35th Star Publishing, 2011.

Emerson, Edward D. *Life and Letters of Charles Russell Lowell.* Cambridge, Mass.: Riverside Press, 1907.

Emerson, W. Eric, and Karen Stokes, eds. *Days of Destruction: Augustine Thomas Smythe and the Civil War Siege of Charleston.* Columbia: University of South Carolina Press, 2017.

———. *Faith, Valor, and Devotion: The Civil War Letters of William Porcher DuBose*. Columbia: University of South Carolina Press, 2010.

Emilio, Luis F. *A Brave Black Regiment: History of the Fifty-Fourth Regiment of Massachusetts Volunteer Infantry, 1863–1865*. 2nd ed. Boston: Boston Book Company, 1894.

Fontaine, Lamar. *The Prison Life of Major Lamar Fontaine, One of the Immortal Six Hundred*. Clarkesdale, Miss.: Daily Register Print, 1910.

Fulkerson, Abram. "The Prison Experience of a Confederate Soldier." *Southern Historical Society Papers* 22 (January–December 1894): 128–47.

Fuzzlebug, Fritz. *Prison Life during the Rebellion: Being a Brief Narrative of the Miseries and Sufferings of Six Hundred Confederate Prisoners Sent from Fort Delaware to Morris Island to Be Punished*. Singer's Glen, Va.: Joseph Funk's Sons, 1869.

Galloway, Richard P., ed. *One Battle Too Many: The Writings of Simon Bolivar Hulbert, Private, Company E 100th Regiment, New York State Volunteers, 1861–1864*. Gaithersburg, Md.: Olde Soldier Books, 1987.

Gienapp, William E., and Erica L. Gienapp, eds. *The Civil War Diary of Gideon Welles: Lincoln's Secretary of the Navy. The Original Manuscript Edition*. Urbana: Knox College Lincoln Studies Center and the University of Illinois Press, 2014.

Glazier, Willard W. *The Capture, the Prison Pen, and the Escape*. Albany: J. Munsell, 1866.

Gordon, George H. *Brook Farm to Cedar Mountain in the War of the Great Rebellion, 1861–1862*. Boston: James R. Osgood and Company, 1883.

Gould, David, and James B. Kennedy, eds. *Memoirs of a Dutch Mudsill: The "War Memories" of John Henry Otto, Captain, Company D, 21st Regiment Wisconsin Volunteer Infantry*. Kent, Ohio: Kent State University Press, 2004.

Gray, John Chipman, and John Codman Ropes. *War Letters, 1862–1865, of John Chipman Gray and John Codman Ropes*. Cambridge, Mass.: Riverside Press, 1927.

Halleck, Henry Wager. "Retaliation in War." *American Journal of International Law* 6, no. 1 (January 1912): 107–18.

Harwell, Richard, and Philip N. Racine, eds. *This Fiery Trail: A Union Officer's Account of Sherman's Last Campaign*. Knoxville: University of Tennessee Press, 1986.

Hendricks, Thomas A. *Retaliation of Rebel Prisoners: Speech of Hon. Thomas A. Hendricks in the United States Senate January 24, 1865, upon the Consideration of the Joint Resolution Advising Retaliation*. Washington, D.C., 1865.

Hester, James Robert, ed. *A Yankee Scholar in Coastal South Carolina: William Francis Allen's Civil War Journals*. Columbia: University of South Carolina Press, 2015.

Holland, Rupert Sargent, ed. *Letters and Diary of Laura M. Towne*. New York: Negro Universities Press, 1969.

Howard, Oliver Otis. *Autobiography of Oliver Otis Howard*. 2 vols. New York: Baker and Taylor, 1907.

Higginson, Thomas Wentworth. *Army Life in a Black Regiment and Other Writings*. New York: Penguin Books, 1997.

———. "Barbarism and Civilization." *Atlantic Monthly*, January 1861, 51–61.

———. "The First Black Regiment." *The Outlook*, July 2, 1898, 521–31.

Hitchcock, Henry. *Marching with Sherman: Passages from the Letters and Campaign Diaries of Henry Hitchcock*. Edited by M. A. DeWolfe Howe. Lincoln: University of Nebraska Press, 1995.

Hotchkiss, Jedediah. *Make Me a Map of the Valley: The Civil War Journal of Stonewall*

*Jackson's Topographer*. Edited by Archie P. McDonald. Dallas: Southern Methodist University Press, 1973.

Jackson, Oscar L. *The Colonel's Diary: Journals Kept before and during the Civil War by the Late Colonel Oscar L. Jackson*. N.p., privately printed, 1922.

Jones, J. B. *A Rebel War Clerk's Diary at the Confederate States Capital*. 2 vols. Edited by Howard Swiggett. New York: Old Hickory Bookshop, 1935.

Jones, Samuel. *The Siege of Charleston and the Operations on the South Atlantic Coast in the War amongst the States*. New York: Neale Publishing Co., 1911.

Jordan, William B., Jr., ed. *The Civil War Journals of John Mead Gould, 1861–1866*. Baltimore, Md.: Butternut and Blue, 1997.

*Journal of the Congress of the Confederate States of America, 1861–1865*. 7 vols. Washington, D.C.: Government Printing Office, 1904.

Kellogg, Mary E. *Army Life of an Illinois Soldier, Including a Day by Day Record of Sherman's March to the Sea: Letters and Diary of the Late Charles W. Wills*. Washington, D.C.: Globe Printing Company, 1906.

Lieber, Francis, and G. Norman Lieber. *To Save the Country: A Lost Treatise on Martial Law*. Edited by Will Smiley and John Fabian Witt. New Haven, Conn.: Yale University Press, 2019.

Looby, Christopher, ed. *The Complete Civil War Journal and Selected Letters of Thomas Wentworth Higginson*. Chicago: University of Chicago Press, 2000.

Mahood, Wayne, ed. *Charlie Mosher's Civil War: From Fair Oaks to Andersonville with the Plymouth Pilgrims (85th N.Y. Infantry)*. Hightstown, N.J.: Longstreet House, 1994.

Marszalek, John F., ed. *The Diary of Miss Emma Holmes, 1861–1866*. Baton Rouge: Louisiana State University Press, 1979.

McDonald, Granville B. *A History of the 30th Illinois Veteran Volunteer Regiment of Infantry*. Sparta, Ill.: Sparta News, 1916.

McGrath, Franklin. *The History of the 127th New York Volunteers "Monitors" in the War for the Preservation of the Union—September 8, 1862–June 30, 1865*. N.p., n.d.

McMichael, James Robert. *Autograph and Diary, J. R. McMichael's Book: Bought July 15th, 1864, at Fort Delaware, Del*. N.p., privately published. Available from The American Civil War: Letters and Diaries database accessed through Texas A&M University Libraries.

Murray, J. Ogden. *The Immortal Six Hundred*. Winchester, Va.: Eddy Press, 1905.

National Freedmen's Relief Association. *National Freedmen's Relief Association, Organized in the City of New York, on the 22nd February, 1862*. New York: Wm. C. Bryant, 1862.

Norton, Oliver Willcox. *Army Letters, 1861–1865*. Chicago: O. L. Deming, 1903.

Oakey, Daniel. "Marching Through Georgia and the Carolinas." In *Battles and Leaders of the Civil War*, vol. 4, edited by Robert Underwood Johnson and Clarence Clough Buel, 671–78. New York: Century Co., 1888.

O'Brien, Thomas M., and Oliver Diefendorf. *General Orders of the War Department, Embracing the Years 1861, 1862, and 1863*. Vol. 1. New York: Derby and Miller, 1864.

Palmer, Abraham J. *The History of the Forty-Eighth Regiment New York Volunteers in the War for the Union, 1861–1865*. Brooklyn, N.Y.: Veterans Association of the Regiment, 1885.

Pearson, Elizabeth Ware. *Letters from Port Royal, 1862–1868*. New York: Arno Press, 1969.

*Petition of the Members of the Legislature of South Carolina to the Congress of the U.S. States in Favor of the Sisters of Our Lady of Mercy, Charleston, S.C., for the Rebuilding of Their Orphan Asylum, Partially Destroyed during the Bombardment of the City*. Charleston: Edward Perry, 1870.

Pike, James. *The Scout and the Ranger: Being the Personal Adventures of Corporal Pike of the 4th Ohio Cavalry*. Cincinnati, Ohio: J. R. Hawley, 1865.

Prince, Helen Wright, ed. *Civil War Letters and Diary of Henry W. Prince, 1862–1865*. N.p.: William W. Prince and Barry F. Prince, 1979.

Quaife, Milo M., ed. *From the Cannon's Mouth: The Civil War Letters of General Alpheus S. Williams*. Detroit, Mich.: Wayne State University Press, 1959.

Quimby, George W. *The Perfect Scout: A Soldier's Memoir of the Great March to the Sea and the Campaign of the Carolinas*. Edited by Anne Sarah Rubin and Stephen Murphy. Tuscaloosa: University of Alabama Press, 2018.

Racine, Philip N., ed. *"Unspoiled Heart": The Journal of Charles Mattocks of the 17th Maine*. Knoxville: University of Tennessee Press, 1994.

Redkey, Edwin S., ed. *A Grand Army of Black Men: Letters from African-American Soldiers in the Union Army, 1861–1865*. Cambridge: Cambridge University Press, 1992.

Ripley, Warren, ed. *Siege Train: The Journal of a Confederate Artilleryman in the Defense of Charleston*. Columbia: University of South Carolina Press, 1986.

Saxton, William. *A Regiment Remembered: The 157th New York Volunteers, from the Diary of Capt. William Saxton*. Cortland, N.Y.: Cortland County Historical Society, 1996.

Schafer, Dan. "War-Time Letters from Seth Rogers, M.D.[,] Surgeon of the First South Carolina[,] afterwards the Thirty-Third U.S.C.T., 1862–1863." Florida History Online. https://www.unf.edu/floridahistoryonline/Projects/Rogers/index.html.

———. "William Lee Apthorp, Montgomery's Raids in Florida, Georgia, and South Carolina." Florida History Online. https://www.unf.edu/floridahistoryonline/montgomery/index.html.

Schwartz, Gerald, ed. *A Woman Doctor's Civil War: Esther Hill Hawks' Diary*. Columbia: University of South Carolina Press, 1984.

Sears, Stephen W., ed. *The Civil War Papers of George B. McClellan: Selected Correspondence 1860–1865*. New York: Da Capo Press, 1992.

Semmes, Thomas J. *Report of the Judiciary Committee on the Resolution in Regard to Retaliation on Captured Officers through State Tribunals*. Senate Report No. 2. Richmond, Va.: Confederate States of America, 1863.

Sherman, William T. "The Grand Strategy of the Last Year of the War." In *Battles and Leaders of the Civil War*, vol. 4, edited by Robert Underwood Johnson and Clarence Clough Buel, 247–59. New York: Century Co., 1888.

———. *Memoirs*. Edited by Charles Royster. New York: Library of America, 1990.

Simon, John Y., ed. *The Papers of Ulysses S. Grant*. Vols. 11–14. Carbondale: Southern Illinois University Press, 1984–85.

Slocum, Henry W. "Sherman's March from Savannah to Bentonville." In *Battles and Leaders of the Civil War*, vol. 4, edited by Robert Underwood Johnson and Clarence Clough Buel, 681–95. New York: Century Co., 1888.

Smith, Daniel E. Huger, Alice R. Huger Smith, and Arney R. Childs, eds. *Mason Smith Family Letters, 1860–1868*. Columbia: University of South Carolina Press, 1950.

Sparks, David S., ed. *Inside Lincoln's Army: The Diary of Marsena Rudolph Patrick, Provost Marshal General, Army of the Potomac*. New York: Thomas Yoseloff, 1964.

Stevenson, Brenda, ed. *The Journals of Charlotte Forten Grimké*. New York: Oxford University Press, 1988.

Stryker, William S. "The Swamp Angel." In *Battles and Leaders of the Civil War*, vol. 4, edited by Robert Underwood Johnson and Clarence Clough Buel, 72–74. New York: Century Co., 1888.

Swift, F. W. *My Experiences as a Prisoner of War. A Paper Prepared and Read before Michigan Commandery of the Military Order of the Loyal Legion of the United States, December 1st, 1866*. Detroit, Mich.: Wm. S. Ostler, 1888.

Taylor, Susie King. *A Black Woman's Civil War Memoirs: Reminiscences of My Life in Camp with the 33rd U.S. Colored Troops, Late 1st South Carolina Volunteers*. Edited by Patricia W. Romero. Princeton, N.J.: Markus Wiener, 1988.

Thornton, Mary Lindsay, ed. "The Prison Diary of Adjutant Francis Atherton Boyle, C.S.A." *North Carolina Historical Review* 39, no. 1 (Winter 1962): 58–84.

Trautman, Frederic, ed. and trans. *Twenty Months in Captivity: Memoirs of a Union Officer in Confed. Prisons, by Bernhard Domschcke*. Rutherford, N.J.: Fairleigh Dickinson University Press, 1987.

*Treatment of Prisoners of War. Speech of Hon. Charles Sumner, in the Senate of the United States, January 29th, 1865, on the Resolution of the Committee on Military Affairs, Advising Retaliation in Kind for Rebel Cruelties to Prisoners*. New York: New York Young Men's Republican Union, 1865.

Turner, Charles W., ed. "Major Charles A. Davidson: Letters of a Virginia Soldier." *Civil War History* 22, no. 1 (March 1976): 16–40.

U.S. House of Representatives. 40th Congress, 2nd Session. *Trial of Henry Wirz*. Executive Document No. 23, December 7, 1867.

———. 40th Congress, 3rd Session. *Report on the Treatment of Prisoners of War, by the Rebel Authorities during the War of the Rebellion*. Report No. 45. Washington, D.C.: Government Printing Office, 1869.

U.S. Naval War Records Office. *Official Records of the Union and Confederate Navies in the War of the Rebellion*. 30 vols. Washington, D.C.: Government Printing Office, 1894–1922.

U.S. War Department. *The War of the Rebellion: A Compilation of the Official Records of the Union and Confederate Armies*. 127 vols. Washington, D.C.: Government Printing Office, 1880–1901.

Vattel, Emer de. *The Law of Nations*. Edited by Béla Kapossy and Richard Whatmore. Carmel, Ind.: Liberty Fund, 2008.

*Voice from Rebel Prisons; Giving an Account of Some of the Horrors of the Stockades at Andersonville, Milan and Other Prisons. By a Returned Prisoner of War*. Boston: Press of G. Rand and Avery, 1865.

Weiner, Marli F., ed. *A Heritage of Woe: The Civil War Diary of Grace Brown Elmore, 1861–1868*. Athens: University of Georgia Press, 1997.

Welles, Gideon. *Diary of Gideon Welles*. 3 vols. Cambridge, Mass.: Riverside Press, 1911.

Wiggins, Sarah Woolfolk, ed. *The Journals of Josiah Gorgas, 1857–1878*. Tuscaloosa: University of Alabama Press, 1995.

Williams, Timothy J., and Evan A. Kutzler, eds. *Prison Pens: Gender, Memory, and Imprisonment in the Writings of Mollie Scollay and Wash Nelson, 1863–1866*. Athens: University of Georgia Press, 2018.

Wilson, Joseph T. *The Black Phalanx: A History of the Negro Soldiers of the United States in the Wars of 1775–1812, 1861–'65*. Hartford, Conn.: American Publishing Company, 1888.

Younger, Edward, ed. *Inside the Confederate Government: The Diary of Robert Garlick Hill Kean*. Baton Rouge: Louisiana State University Press, 1985.

## SECONDARY SOURCES

### *Published Works*

Andrew, Rod, Jr. *Wade Hampton: Confederate Warrior and Southern Redeemer.* Chapel Hill: University of North Carolina Press, 2008.

Armstrong, Warren B. *For Courageous Fighting and Confident Dying: Union Chaplains in the Civil War.* Lawrence: University Press of Kansas, 1998.

Ash, Stephen V. *Firebrand of Liberty: The Story of Two Black Regiments That Changed the Course of the Civil War.* New York: W. W. Norton, 2008.

———. *When the Yankees Came: Conflict and Chaos in the Occupied South, 1861–1865.* Chapel Hill: University of North Carolina Press, 1995.

Augst, Thomas. *A Clerk's Tale: Young Men and Moral Life in Nineteenth-Century America.* Chicago: University of Chicago Press, 2003.

Ayers, Edward L. *Vengeance and Justice: Crime and Punishment in the 19th-Century American South.* New York: Oxford University Press, 1984.

Bailey, Anne J. "Home Front Becomes Battle Front: Sherman's March to the Sea." In *The Oxford Handbook of the Civil War,* edited by Lorien Foote and Earl J. Hess. New York: Oxford University Press, 2021.

———. *War and Ruin: William T. Sherman and the Savannah Campaign.* Wilmington, Del.: Scholarly Resources, 2003.

Barr, Christopher. "Corporal James H. Gooding." Andersonville National Historic Site. Accessed March 12, 2020. https://www.nps.gov/ande/learn/historyculture/j-h-gooding.htm.

———. "Loathsome Diseases and Principles: Conceptualizing Race and Slavery in Civil War Prisons." In *Crossing the Deadlines: Civil War Prisons Reconsidered,* edited by Michael P. Gray, 101–24. Kent, Ohio: Kent State University Press, 2018.

Barrett, John G. *The Civil War in North Carolina.* Chapel Hill: University of North Carolina Press, 1963.

———. *Sherman's March through the Carolinas.* Chapel Hill: University of North Carolina Press, 1956.

Barton, Michael. *Goodmen: The Character of Civil War Soldiers.* University Park: Pennsylvania State University Press, 1981.

Bederman, Gail. *Manliness and Civilization: A Cultural History of Gender and Race in the United States, 1880–1917.* Chicago: University of Chicago Press, 1995.

Beilein, Joseph M., Jr. *Bushwhackers: Guerrilla Warfare, Manhood, and the Household in Civil War Missouri.* Kent, Ohio: Kent State University Press, 2016.

Beilein, Joseph M., Jr., and Matthew C. Hulbert. *The Civil War Guerrilla: Unfolding the Black Flag in History, Memory, and Myth.* Lexington: University Press of Kentucky, 2015.

Bennett, Chet. *Resolute Rebel: General Roswell S. Ripley, Charleston's Gallant Defender.* Columbia: University of South Carolina Press, 2017.

Bennett, Michael J. *Union Jacks: Yankee Sailors in the Civil War.* Chapel Hill: University of North Carolina Press, 2004.

Berry, Stephen. *All That Makes a Man: Love and Ambition in the Civil War South.* New York: Oxford University Press, 2003.

———. *House of Abraham: Lincoln and the Todds, a Family Divided by War.* New York: Houghton Mifflin Company, 2007.

———. *Weirding the War: Stories from the Civil War's Ragged Edges*. Athens: University of Georgia Press, 2011.

Blair, William. *Virginia's Private War: Feeding Body and Soul in the Confederacy, 1861–1865*. New York: Oxford University Press, 1998.

———. *With Malice toward Some: Treason and Loyalty in the Civil War Era*. Chapel Hill: University of North Carolina Press, 2014.

Blatt, Martin H., Thomas J. Brown, and Donald Yacovone, eds. *Hope and Glory: Essays on the Legacy of the Fifty-Fourth Massachusetts Regiment*. Amherst: University of Massachusetts Press, 2001.

Bledsoe, Andrew S. *Citizen-Officers: The Union and Confederate Volunteer Junior Officer Corps in the American Civil War*. Baton Rouge: Louisiana State University Press, 2015.

Bledsoe, Andrew S., and Andrew F. Lang. *Upon the Fields of Battle: Essays on the Military History of America's Civil War*. Baton Rouge: Louisiana State University Press, 2018.

Bradley, Mark. *This Astounding Close: The Road to Bennett Place*. Chapel Hill: University of North Carolina Press, 2000.

Brady, Lisa M. *War upon the Land: Military Strategy and the Transformation of the Southern Landscapes during the American Civil War*. Athens: University of Georgia Press, 2012.

Brasher, Glenn David. *The Peninsula Campaign and the Necessity of Emancipation: African Americans and the Fight for Freedom*. Chapel Hill: University of North Carolina Press, 2012.

Broadwater, Robert P. *The Battle of Olustee, 1864: The Final Union Attempt to Seize Florida*. Jefferson, N.C.: McFarland and Company, 2006.

Broomall, James J. *Private Confederacies: The Emotional Worlds of Southern Men as Citizens and Soldiers*. Chapel Hill: University of North Carolina Press, 2019.

Browning, Judkin. *Shifting Loyalties: The Union Occupation of Eastern North Carolina*. Chapel Hill: University of North Carolina Press, 2011.

Browning, Robert M., Jr. *Success Is All That Was Expected: The South Atlantic Blockading Squadron during the Civil War*. Washington, D.C.: Brassey's, 2002.

Bruce, Dickson D., Jr. *Violence and Culture in the Antebellum South*. Austin: University of Texas Press, 1979.

Bruce, Susannah Ural. *The Harp and the Eagle: Irish-American Volunteers and the Union Army, 1861–1865*. New York: New York University Press, 2006.

Brundage, Fitzhugh. "Reconstruction in the South." *Journal of the Civil War Era*. Accessed May 15, 2020. https://www.journalofthecivilwarera.org/forum-the-future-of-reconstruction-studies/reconstruction-in-the-south/.

Buell, Thomas B. *The Warrior Generals: Combat Leadership in the Civil War*. New York: Three Rivers Press, 1997.

Burkhardt, George S. *Confederate Rage, Yankee Wrath: No Quarter in the Civil War*. Carbondale: Southern Illinois University Press, 2007.

Burton, E. Milby. *The Siege of Charleston, 1861–1865*. Columbia: University of South Carolina Press, 1970.

Bushman, Richard L. *The Refinement of America: Persons, Houses, Cities*. New York: Vintage Books, 1993.

Bynum, Victoria E. *Unruly Women: The Politics of Social and Sexual Control in the Old South*. Chapel Hill: University of North Carolina Press, 1992.

Camp, Stephanie M. H. *Closer to Freedom: Enslaved Women and Everyday Resistance in the Plantation South*. Chapel Hill: University of North Carolina Press, 2004.

Campbell, Jacqueline Glass. *When Sherman Marched North from the Sea: Resistance on the Confederate Home Front*. Chapel Hill: University of North Carolina Press, 2003.

Campbell, John. "The Seminoles, the 'Bloodhound War,' and Abolitionism, 1796–1865." *Journal of Southern History* 72, no. 2 (May 2006): 259–302.

Carmichael, Peter S. *The Last Generation: Young Virginians in Peace, War, and Reunion*. Chapel Hill: University of North Carolina Press, 2005.

———. *The War for the Common Soldier: How Men Thought, Fought, and Survived in Civil War Armies*. Chapel Hill: University of North Carolina Press, 2018.

Carnahan, Burrus M. *Lincoln on Trial: Southern Civilians and the Law of War*. Lexington: University Press of Kentucky, 2010.

Carney, Charity R. *Ministers and Masters: Methodism, Manhood, and Honor in the Old South*. Baton Rouge: Louisiana State University Press, 2011.

Cashin, Joan E. *War Stuff: The Struggle for Human and Environmental Resources in the American Civil War*. Cambridge: Cambridge University Press, 2018.

———, ed. *The War Was You and Me: Civilians in the American Civil War*. Princeton: Princeton University Press, 2002.

Cauthen, Charles Edward. *South Carolina Goes to War, 1860–1865*. Chapel Hill: University of North Carolina Press, 1950.

Cimprich, John. *Fort Pillow, a Civil War Massacre, and Public Memory*. Baton Rouge: Louisiana State University Press, 2005.

Clarke, Frances M. *War Stories: Suffering and Sacrifice in the Civil War North*. Chicago: University of Chicago Press, 2011.

Clinton, Catherine. *Harriet Tubman: The Road to Freedom*. New York: Little, Brown, 2004.

Clinton, Catherine, and Nina Silber, eds. *Battle Scars: Gender and Sexuality in the American Civil War*. New York: Oxford University Press, 2006.

Cloyd, Benjamin G. *Haunted by Atrocity: Civil War Prisons in American Memory*. Baton Rouge: Louisiana State University Press, 2010.

Cobb, James C. *Away Down South: A History of Southern Identity*. New York: Oxford University Press, 2005.

Coffman, Edward M. *The Old Army: A Portrait of the American Army in Peacetime, 1784–1898*. New York: Oxford University Press, 1986.

Coles, David James. "Far from the Fields of Glory: Military Operations in Florida during the Civil War, 1864–1865." Ph.D. diss., Florida State University, 1996.

———. "Shooting Niggers Sir: Confederate Mistreatment of Union Black Soldiers at the Battle of Olustee." In *Black Flag over Dixie: Racial Atrocities and Reprisals in the Civil War*, edited by Gregory J. W. Urwin, 65–88. Carbondale: Southern Illinois University Press, 2004.

Confer, Clarissa W. *The Cherokee Nation in the Civil War*. Norman: University of Oklahoma Press, 2007.

Connell, R. W. *Masculinities*. Berkeley: University of California Press, 1995.

Cooper, William J., Jr. *Jefferson Davis, American*. New York: Alfred A. Knopf, 2000.

Corey, David D., and J. Daryl Charles. *The Just War Tradition: An Introduction*. Wilmington, Del.: ISI Books, 2012.

Cornish, Dudley Taylor. *The Sable Arm: Negro Troops in the Union Army, 1861–1865*. New York: Norton Library, 1966.

Cowdrey, H. E. J. "The Peace and Truce of God in the Eleventh Century." *Past and Present* 46 (February 1970): 42–67.

Cox, Caroline. *A Proper Sense of Honor: Service and Sacrifice in George Washington's Army*. Chapel Hill: University of North Carolina Press, 2004.

Cozzens, Peter. *General John Pope: A Life for the Nation*. Urbana: University of Illinois Press, 2000.

Crackel, Theodore J. *Mr. Jefferson's Army: Political and Social Reform of the Military Establishment, 1801–1809*. New York: New York University Press, 1987.

Cunliffe, Marcus. *Soldiers and Civilians: The Martial Spirit in America, 1775–1865*. Boston: Little, Brown, 1968.

Davis, Nora M. *Military and Naval Operations in South Carolina, 1860–1865: A Chronological List*. Columbia: South Carolina Archives Department, 1959.

Davis, Robert S. "Escape from Andersonville: A Study in Isolation and Imprisonment." *Journal of Military History* 67, no. 4 (2003): 1065–81.

Davis, William C. *Lincoln's Men: How President Lincoln Became Father to an Army and a Nation*. New York: Simon and Schuster, 2000.

———. *Look Away! A History of the Confederate States of America*. New York: Free Press, 2002.

De Falaise, Louis. "Gen. Stephen Burbridge's Command in Kentucky." *Register of the Kentucky Historical Society* 69, no. 2 (April 1971): 101–27.

DeMello, Margo. *Animals and Society: An Introduction to Human-Animal Studies*. New York: Columbia University Press, 2012.

Dew, Charles B. *Apostles of Disunion: Southern Secession Commissioners and the Causes of the Civil War*. Charlottesville: University of Virginia Press, 2016.

Dilbeck, D. H. *A More Civil War: How the Union Waged a Just War*. Chapel Hill: University of North Carolina Press, 2016.

Dobak, William A. *Freedom by the Sword: The U.S. Colored Troops, 1862–1867*. Washington, D.C.: Center of Military History, United States Army, 2011.

Downs, Jim. *Sick from Freedom: African-American Illness and Suffering during the Civil War and Reconstruction*. New York: Oxford University Press, 2012.

Edgar, Walter. *South Carolina: A History*. Columbia: University of South Carolina Press, 1998.

Egerton, Douglas R. *Thunder at the Gates: The Black Civil War Regiments That Redeemed America*. New York: Basic Books, 2016.

Eicher, John H., and David Eicher. *Civil War High Commands*. Stanford: Stanford University Press, 2001.

Elder, Robert. *The Sacred Mirror: Evangelicalism, Honor, and Identity in the Deep South, 1790–1860*. Chapel Hill: University of North Carolina Press, 2016.

Escott, Paul D. *After Secession: Jefferson Davis and the Failure of Confederate Nationalism*. Baton Rouge: Louisiana State University Press, 1978.

Fabian, Ann. *The Unvarnished Truth: Personal Narratives in Nineteenth-Century America*. Berkeley: University of California Press, 2000.

Fahs, Alice. *The Imagined Civil War: Popular Literature of the North and South, 1861–1865*. Chapel Hill: University of North Carolina Press, 2001.

Faust, Drew Gilpin. "Christian Soldiers: The Meaning of Revivalism in the Confederate Army." *Journal of Southern History* 53 (1987): 63–90.

———. *The Creation of Confederate Nationalism: Ideology and Identity in the Civil War South*. Baton Rouge: Louisiana State University Press, 1988.

———. *This Republic of Suffering: Death and the American Civil War*. New York: Alfred A. Knopf, 2008.

Fellman, Michael. *Inside War: The Guerrilla Conflict in Missouri during the American Civil War*. New York: Oxford University Press, 1989.

Ferrell, Daniel. "'The Nation Cannot Now Be Entrusted to Hands Reeking with the Blood of Loyal Victims': Prison Propaganda, Hard War, and the Politics of Criminalization." In *Useful Captives: The Role of POWs in American Military Conflicts*, edited by Daniel Krebs and Lorien Foote, 225–53. Lawrence: University Press of Kansas, 2021.

Fisher, Noel C. *War at Every Door: Partisan Politics and Guerrilla Violence in East Tennessee, 1860–1869*. Chapel Hill: University of North Carolina Press, 1997.

Foner, Eric. *The Fiery Trial: Abraham Lincoln and American Slavery*. New York: Norton, 2010.

Foote, Lorien. *The Gentlemen and the Roughs: Manhood, Honor, and Violence in the Union Army*. New York: New York University Press, 2010.

———. "Rich Man's War, Rich Man's Fight: Class, Ideology, and Discipline in the Union Army." *Civil War History* 51 (September 2005): 269–87.

———. *Seeking the One Great Remedy: Francis George Shaw and Nineteenth-Century Reform*. Athens: Ohio University Press, 2003.

———. "The Sternest Feature of War: Prisoners of War and the Practice of Retaliation." In *Crossing the Deadlines: Civil War Prisons Reconsidered*, edited by Michael P. Gray, 81–100. Kent, Ohio: Kent State University Press, 2018.

———. *The Yankee Plague: Escaped Union Prisoners and the Collapse of the Confederacy*. Chapel Hill: University of North Carolina Press, 2016.

Förster, Stig, and Jörg Nagler. *On the Road to Total War: The American Civil War and the German Wars of Unification, 1861–1871*. Cambridge: Cambridge University Press, 1997.

Forth, Christopher E. *Masculinity in the Modern West: Gender, Civilization, and the Body*. New York: Palgrave Macmillan, 2008.

Fountain, Daniel L. *Slavery, Civil War, and Salvation: African American Slaves and Christianity, 1830–1870*. Baton Rouge: Louisiana State University Press, 2010.

Frank, Lisa Tendrich. *The Civilian War: Confederate Women and Union Soldiers during Sherman's March*. Baton Rouge: Louisiana State University Press, 2015.

Frederickson, George M. *The Inner Civil War: Northern Intellectuals and the Crisis of the Union*. New York: Harper and Row, 1965.

Friend, Craig Thompson, and Lorri Glover, eds. *Southern Manhood: Perspectives on Masculinity in the Old South*. Athens: University of Georgia Press, 2004.

Frisby, Derek W. "'Remember Fort Pillow!': Politics, Atrocity Propaganda, and the Evolution of Hard War." In *Black Flag over Dixie: Racial Atrocities and Reprisals in the Civil War*, edited by Gregory J. W. Urwin, 104–31. Carbondale: Southern Illinois University Press, 2004.

Futch, Ovid L. *History of Andersonville Prison*. Rev. ed. with introduction by Michael P. Gray. Gainesville: University Press of Florida, 2011.

Gallagher, Gary W. *The Confederate War*. Cambridge, Mass.: Harvard University Press, 1997.

———. *The Union War*. Cambridge, Mass.: Harvard University Press, 2011.

Gillispie, James M. *Andersonvilles of the North: The Myths and Realities of Northern*

*Treatment of Civil War Confederate Prisoners*. Denton: University of North Texas Press, 2008.
Glatthaar, Joseph. *Forged in Battle: The Civil War Alliance of Black Soldiers and White Officers*. New York: Free Press, 1990.
———. *The March to the Sea and Beyond: Sherman's Troops in the Savannah and Carolinas Campaigns*. New York: New York University Press, 1985.
Gorn, Elliott J. "'Gouge and Bite, Pull Hair and Scratch': The Social Significance of Fighting in the Southern Backcountry." *American Historical Review* 90 (February 1985): 18–43.
———. *The Manly Art: Bare-Knuckle Prize Fighting in America*. Ithaca, N.Y.: Cornell University Press, 1986.
Goss, Thomas J. *The War within the Union High Command: Politics and Generalship during the Civil War*. Lawrence: University Press of Kansas, 2003.
Gray, Michael P. *The Business of Captivity: Elmira and Its Civil War Prison*. Kent, Ohio: Kent State University Press, 2001.
———, ed. *Crossing the Deadlines: Civil War Prisons Reconsidered*. Kent, Ohio: Kent State University Press, 2018.
Green, Jennifer. *Military Education and the Emerging Middle Class in the Old South*. New York: Cambridge University Press, 2008.
Greenberg, Amy S. *Manifest Manhood and the Antebellum American Empire*. New York: Cambridge University Press, 2005.
Greenberg, Kenneth S. *Honor and Slavery*. Princeton, N.J.: Princeton University Press, 1996.
Grenier, John. *The First Way of War: American War Making on the Frontier, 1607–1814*. New York: Cambridge University Press, 2005.
Grimsley, Mark. *The Hard Hand of War: Union Military Policy toward Southern Civilians, 1861–1865*. Cambridge: Cambridge University Press, 1995.
Grimsley, Mark, and Brooks D. Simpson, eds. *The Collapse of the Confederacy*. Lincoln: University of Nebraska Press, 2001.
Guelzo, Allan C. *Lincoln's Emancipation Proclamation: The End of Slavery in America*. New York: Simon and Schuster, 2004.
Halttunen, Karen. *Confidence Men and Painted Women: A Study of Middle-Class Culture in America, 1830–1870*. New Haven, Conn.: Yale University Press, 1982.
Harlow, Luke E. "Forum: The Future of Reconstruction Studies." *Journal of the Civil War Era*. Accessed May 15, 2020. https://www.journalofthecivilwarera.org/forum-the-future-of-reconstruction-studies//.
Harrington, Fred Harvey. *Fighting Politician: Major General N. P. Banks*. Philadelphia: University of Pennsylvania Press, 1948.
Hauptman, Laurence M. *Between Two Fires: American Indians in the Civil War*. New York: Free Press, 1995.
Hearn, Chester G. *When the Devil Came Down to Dixie: Ben Butler in New Orleans*. Baton Rouge: Louisiana State University Press, 1997.
Hennessy, John J. *Return to Bull Run: The Campaign and Battle of Second Manassas*. New York: Simon and Schuster, 1993.
Hess, Earl J. *Field Armies and Fortifications in the Civil War: The Eastern Campaigns, 1861–1864*. Chapel Hill: University of North Carolina Press, 2005.
———. *Liberty, Virtue, and Progress: Northerners and Their War for the Union*. New York: New York University Press, 1988.

———. *The Union Soldier in Battle: Enduring the Ordeal of Combat*. Lawrence: University Press of Kansas, 1997.

Hesseltine, William Best. *Civil War Prisons: A Study in War Psychology*. New York: Frederick Ungar Publishing, 1964.

Higginbotham, Don. *George Washington and the American Military Tradition*. Athens: University of Georgia Press, 1985.

———. *The War of American Independence: Military Attitudes, Policies and Practice, 1763–1789*. New York: Macmillan, 1971.

Hijiya, James A. *J. W. De Forest and the Rise of American Gentility*. Hanover, N.H.: University Press of New England, 1988.

Hoganson, Kristin L. *Fighting for American Manhood: How Gender Politics Provoked the Spanish-American and Philippine-American Wars*. New Haven, Conn.: Yale University Press, 1998.

Hollandsworth, James G., Jr. "The Execution of White Officers from Black Units by Confederate Forces during the Civil War." In *Black Flag over Dixie: Racial Atrocities and Reprisals in the Civil War*, edited by Gregory J. W. Urwin, 52–64. Carbondale: Southern Illinois University Press, 2004.

———. *The Louisiana Native Guards: The Black Military Experience during the Civil War*. Baton Rouge: Louisiana State University Press, 1995.

Howard, Michael, George J. Andreopoulos, and Mark R. Shulman. *The Laws of War: Constraints on Warfare in the Western World*. New Haven, Conn.: Yale University Press, 1994.

Hsish, Wayne Wei-siang. *West Pointers and the Civil War: The Old Army in War and Peace*. Chapel Hill: University of North Carolina Press, 2009.

Hubbs, G. Ward. *Guarding Greensboro: A Confederate Company in the Making of a Southern Community*. Athens: University of Georgia Press, 2003.

Hunt, Robert. *The Good Men Who Won the War: Army of the Cumberland Veterans and Emancipation Memory*. Tuscaloosa: University of Alabama Press, 2010.

Jimerson, Randall C. *The Private Civil War: Popular Thought during the Sectional Conflict*. Baton Rouge: Louisiana State University Press, 1988.

Jones, Howard. *Blue and Gray Diplomacy: A History of Union and Confederate Foreign Relations*. Chapel Hill: University of North Carolina Press, 2010.

Josephy, Alvin M., Jr. *The Civil War in the American West*. New York: Knopf, 1991.

Joslyn, Mauriel P. *Immortal Captives: The Story of 600 Confederate Officers and the United States Prisoner of War Policy*. Gretna, La.: Pelican Publishing, 2008.

Kann, Mark E. *A Republic of Men: The American Founders, Gendered Language, and Patriarchal Politics*. New York: New York University Press, 1998.

Karsten, Peter. *Law, Soldiers, and Combat*. Westport, Conn.: Greenwood Press, 1978.

Kasson, John F. *Rudeness and Civility: Manners in Nineteenth-Century Urban America*. New York: Hill and Wang, 1990.

Kelman, Ari. *A Misplaced Massacre: Struggling over the Memory of Sand Creek*. Cambridge, Mass.: Harvard University Press, 2013.

Kennett, Lee. *Sherman: A Soldier's Life*. New York: HarperCollins, 2001.

Kinsella, Helen M. *The Image before the Weapon: A Critical History of the Distinction between Combatant and Civilian*. Ithaca, N.Y.: Cornell University Press, 2011.

Kohn, Richard H. *Eagle and Sword: The Federalists and the Creation of the Military Establishment in America, 1783–1802*. New York: Free Press, 1975.

Krebs, Daniel. "Useful Enemies: The Treatment of German Prisoners of War during the American War of Independence." *Journal of Military History* 77 (January 2013): 9–39.
Krebs, Daniel, and Lorien Foote, eds. *Useful Captives: The Role of POWs in American Military Conflicts*. Lawrence: University Press of Kansas, 2021.
Krick, Robert R. *Stonewall Jackson at Cedar Mountain*. Chapel Hill: University of North Carolina Press, 1990.
Kutzler, Evan A. *Living by Inches: The Smells, Sounds, Tastes, and Feeling of Captivity in Civil War Prisons*. Chapel Hill: University of North Carolina Press, 2019.
Lang, Andrew F. *In the Wake of War: Military Occupation, Emancipation, and Civil War America*. Baton Rouge: Louisiana State University Press, 2017.
Lawson, Melinda. *Patriot Fires: Forging a New American Nationalism in the Civil War North*. Lawrence: University Press of Kansas, 2002.
Leader, Jonathan M. *Walking the Deadline: The Florence Stockade Revisited*. Florence, S.C.: Florence Historical Society, 1997.
Lee, Wayne E. *Barbarians and Brothers: Anglo-American Warfare, 1500–1865*. New York: Oxford University Press, 2011.
Leonard, Elizabeth D. *Lincoln's Avengers: Justice, Revenge, and Reunion after the Civil War*. New York: W. W. Norton, 2004.
Levine, Bruce. *Confederate Emancipation: Southern Plans to Free and Arm Slaves during the Civil War*. New York: Oxford University Press, 2007.
Lewis, Kay Wright. *A Curse upon the Nation: Race, Freedom, and Extermination in America and the Atlantic World*. Athens: University of Georgia Press, 2017.
Linderman, Gerald F. *Embattled Courage: The Experience of Combat in the American Civil War*. New York: Free Press, 1987.
Linn, Brian McAllister. *The Philippine War, 1899–1902*. Lawrence: University Press of Kansas, 2000.
Logue, Larry M. *To Appomattox and Beyond: The Civil War Soldier in War and Peace*. Chicago: Ivan R. Dee, 1996.
Lucas, Marion Brunson. *Sherman and the Burning of Columbia*. College Station: Texas A&M University Press, 1976.
Lynn, John A. *Battle: A History of Combat and Culture*. New York: Basic Books, 2004.
Mack, Charles R., and Henry H. Lesesne, eds. *Francis Lieber and the Culture of the Mind*. Columbia: University of South Carolina Press, 2005.
Mackey, Robert R. *The Uncivil War: Irregular Warfare in the Upper South, 1861–1865*. Norman: University of Oklahoma Press, 2004.
Manning, Chandra. *Troubled Refuge: Struggling for Freedom in the Civil War*. New York: Alfred A. Knopf, 2016.
Marszalek, John F. *Commander of All Lincoln's Armies: A Life of General Henry W. Halleck*. Cambridge, Mass.: Belknap Press of Harvard University Press, 2004.
———. *Sherman: A Soldier's Passion for Order*. New York: Vintage, 1993.
Marvel, William. *Andersonville: The Last Depot*. Chapel Hill: University of North Carolina Press, 1994.
———. *Lincoln's Autocrat: The Life of Edwin Stanton*. Chapel Hill: University of North Carolina Press, 2015.
Mathison, Erik. *The Loyal Republic: Traitors, Slaves, and the Remaking of Citizenship in Civil War America*. Chapel Hill: University of North Carolina Press, 2018.

Matsui, John H. *The First Republican Army: The Army of Virginia and the Radicalization of the Civil War.* Charlottesville: University of Virginia Press, 2016.

Matthews, Gary Robert. *Basil Wilson Duke, CSA: The Right Man in the Right Place.* Lexington: University Press of Kentucky, 2005.

McCall, Laura, and Donald Yacovone, eds. *A Shared Experience: Men, Women, and the History of Gender.* New York: New York University Press, 1998.

McCurry, Stephanie. *Confederate Reckoning: Power and Politics in the Civil War South.* Cambridge, Mass.: Harvard University Press, 2010.

———. *Women's War: Fighting and Surviving the American Civil War.* Cambridge, Mass.: Belknap Press of Harvard University Press, 2019.

McDonough, James Lee. *William Tecumseh Sherman: In the Service of My Country; A Life.* New York: W. W. Norton, 2016.

McPherson, James M. *Battle Cry of Freedom: The Civil War Era.* New York: Oxford University Press, 1988.

———. *For Cause and Comrades: Why Men Fought in the Civil War.* New York: Oxford University Press, 1997.

———. *War on the Waters: The Union and Confederate Navies, 1861–1865.* Chapel Hill: University of North Carolina Press, 2012.

Mezurek, Kelly D. "'De Bottom Rails on Top Now': Black Union Guards and Confederate Prisoners of War." In *Crossing the Deadlines: Civil War Prisons Reconsidered,* edited by Michael P. Gray, 125–53. Kent, Ohio: Kent State University Press, 2018.

Miller, Edward A., Jr. *Lincoln's Abolitionist General: The Biography of David Hunter.* Columbia: University of South Carolina Press, 1997.

Millett, Allan Reed, Peter Maslowski, and William B. Feis. *For the Common Defense: A Military History of the United States from 1607–2013.* 3rd ed. New York: Free Press, 2013.

Mitchell, Reid. *Civil War Soldiers.* New York: Viking, 1988.

———. *The Vacant Chair: The Northern Soldier Leaves Home.* New York: Oxford University Press, 1993.

Mohr, Clarence L. *On the Threshold of Freedom: Masters and Slaves in Civil War Georgia.* Athens: University of Georgia Press, 1986.

Morrison, James L., Jr. *"The Best School in the World": West Point, the Pre–Civil War Years, 1833–1866.* Kent, Ohio: Kent State University Press, 1986.

Mountcastle, Clay. *Punitive War: Confederate Guerrillas and Union Reprisals.* Lawrence: University Press of Kansas, 2009.

Myers, Barton A. *Executing Daniel Bright: Race, Loyalty, and Guerrilla Violence in a Coastal Carolina Community, 1861–1865.* Baton Rouge: Louisiana State University Press, 2009.

Neely, Mark E., Jr. *The Civil War and the Limits of Destruction.* Cambridge, Mass.: Harvard University Press, 2007.

Neff, Stephen C. *Justice in Blue and Gray: A Legal History of the Civil War.* Cambridge, Mass.: Harvard University Press, 2010.

Nelson, Megan Kate. *Ruin Nation: Destruction and the American Civil War.* Athens: University of Georgia Press, 2012.

———. *The Three-Cornered War: The Union, the Confederacy, and Native Peoples in the Fight for the West.* New York: Scribner, 2020.

Newhall, Caroline Wood. "'Under the Rebel Lash': Black Prisoners of War in the Confederate South." Ph.D. diss., University of North Carolina at Chapel Hill, 2020.

Nisbett, Richard E., and Dov Cohen. *Culture of Honor: The Psychology of Violence in the South*. Boulder, Colo.: Westview Press, 1996.

Noe, Kenneth W. *Reluctant Rebels: The Confederates Who Joined the Army after 1861*. Chapel Hill: University of North Carolina Press, 2010.

Nulty, William H. *Confederate Florida: The Road to Olustee*. Tuscaloosa: University of Alabama Press, 1990.

Oakes, James. *Freedom National: The Destruction of Slavery in the United States, 1861–1865*. New York: W. W. Norton, 2013.

O'Connell, Robert L. *Fierce Patriot: The Tangled Lives of William Tecumseh Sherman*. New York: Random House, 2015.

Öfele, Martin W. *German-Speaking Officers in the U.S. Colored Troops, 1863–1867*. Gainesville: University Press of Florida, 2004.

Paludan, Philip. *"A People's Contest": The Union and Civil War, 1861–1865*. New York: Harper and Row, 1988.

Perry, Milton F. *Infernal Machines: The Story of Confederate Submarine and Mine Warfare*. Baton Rouge: Louisiana State University Press, 1965.

Phelps, W. Chris. *The Bombardment of Charleston, 1863–1865*. Gretna, La.: Pelican Publishing, 2002.

Phillips, Jason. *Diehard Rebels: The Confederate Culture of Invincibility*. Athens: University of Georgia Press, 2007.

———. *Looming Civil War: How Nineteenth-Century Americans Imagined the Future*. New York: Oxford University Press, 2018.

Pickenpaugh, Roger. *Camp Chase and the Evolution of Union Prison Policy*. Tuscaloosa: University of Alabama Press, 2007.

———. *Captives in Blue: The Civil War Prisons of the Confederacy*. Tuscaloosa: University of Alabama Press, 2013.

———. *Captives in Gray: The Civil War Prisons of the Union*. Tuscaloosa: University of Alabama Press, 2009.

———. *Johnson's Island: A Prison for Confederate Officers*. Kent, Ohio: Kent State University Press, 2016.

Pinheiro, Holly A., Jr. "Am I a Man: Masculinity and Black Military Service during the American Civil War." *Primavera* 94 (2019): 121–38.

Poole, W. Scott. *South Carolina's Civil War: A Narrative History*. Macon, Ga.: Mercer University Press, 2005.

Quigley, Paul. *Shifting Grounds: Nationalism and the American South, 1848–1865*. New York: Oxford University Press, 2012.

Rable, George C. *Damn Yankees! Demonization and Defiance in the Confederate South*. Baton Rouge: Louisiana State University Press, 2015.

———. *God's Almost Chosen Peoples: A Religious History of the American Civil War*. Chapel Hill: University of North Carolina Press, 2010.

Racine, Philip N. *Living a Big War in a Small Place: Spartanburg, South Carolina, during the Confederacy*. Columbia: University of South Carolina Press, 2013.

Rafuse, Ethan S. *McClellan's War: The Failure of Moderation in the Struggle for the Union*. Bloomington: Indiana University Press, 2005.

Ragan, Mark K. *Confederate Saboteurs: Building the* Hunley *and Other Secret Weapons of the Civil War*. College Station: Texas A&M University Press, 2015.

Ramold, Steven J. *Baring the Iron Hand: Discipline in the Union Army.* DeKalb: Northern Illinois University Press, 2010.

Raney, David Allen. “In the Lord’s Army: The United States Christian Commission in the Civil War.” Ph.D. diss., University of Illinois at Urbana-Champaign, 2001.

Raus, Edmund J. *Banners South: A Northern Community at War.* Kent, Ohio: Kent State University Press, 2005.

Reardon, Carol. *With a Sword in One Hand and Jomini in the Other: The Problem of Military Thought in the Civil War North.* Chapel Hill: University of North Carolina Press, 2012.

Richards, David L. *Civil War Tales from Lycoming County and North-Central Pennsylvania.* Gettysburg: Chamouni Grove Press, 2019.

Riotto, Angela M. “As Happy a Man as Ever Wore ‘Confederate Grey’: Confederate Former Prisoners of War and Their Narratives of Imprisonment, 1877–1890.” In *Useful Captives: The Role of POWs in American Military Conflicts*, edited by Daniel Krebs and Lorien Foote, 254–70. Lawrence: University Press of Kansas, 2021.

Rose, Anne C. *Victorian America and the Civil War.* New York: Cambridge University Press, 1992.

Rose, Willie Lee. *Rehearsal for Reconstruction: The Port Royal Experiment.* New York: Oxford University Press, 1964.

Rotundo, E. Anthony. *American Manhood: Transformations in Masculinity from the Revolution to the Modern Era.* New York: Basic Books, 1993.

Royster, Charles. *The Destructive War: William Tecumseh Sherman, Stonewall Jackson, and the Americans.* New York: Alfred A. Knopf, 1991.

Rubin, Anne Sarah. *A Shattered Nation: The Rise and Fall of the Confederacy, 1861–1868.* Chapel Hill: University of North Carolina Press, 2005.

———. *Through the Heart of Dixie: Sherman’s March and American Memory.* Chapel Hill: University of North Carolina Press, 2014.

Samito, Christian G. *Becoming American under Fire: Irish Americans, African Americans, and the Politics of Citizenship during the Civil War Era.* Ithaca, N.Y.: Cornell University Press, 2009.

Sanders, Charles W., Jr. *While in the Hands of the Enemy: Military Prisons of the Civil War.* Baton Rouge: Louisiana State University Press, 2005.

Schafer, Daniel L. *Thunder on the River: The Civil War in Northeast Florida.* Gainesville: University Press of Florida, 2010.

Schantz, Mark S. *Awaiting the Heavenly Country: The Civil War and America’s Culture of Death.* Ithaca, N.Y.: Cornell University Press, 2008.

Schwalm, Leslie A. *A Hard Fight for We: Women’s Transition from Slavery to Freedom in South Carolina.* Urbana: University of Illinois Press, 1997.

Sears, Stephen W. *Lincoln’s Lieutenants: The High Command of the Army of the Potomac.* New York: Houghton Mifflin Harcourt, 2017.

Sheehan-Dean, Aaron. *The Calculus of Violence: How Americans Fought the Civil War.* Cambridge, Mass.: Harvard University Press, 2018.

———. “*Lex Talionis* in the U.S. Civil War: Retaliation and the Limits of Atrocity.” In *The Civil War as a Global Conflict: Transnational Meanings of the American Civil War*, edited by David Gleeson and Simon Lewis, 172–89. Columbia: University of South Carolina Press, 2014.

———. *The View from the Ground: Experiences of Civil War Soldiers.* Lexington: University Press of Kentucky, 2007.

Shy, John. *A People Numerous and Armed: Reflections on the Military Struggle for American Independence*. Rev. ed. Ann Arbor: University of Michigan Press, 1990.

Silkenat, David. *Driven from Home: North Carolina's Civil War Refugee Crisis*. Athens: University of Georgia Press, 2016.

———. *Raising the White Flag: How Surrender Defined the American Civil War*. Chapel Hill: University of North Carolina Press, 2019.

Simpson, Brooks D. *Let Us Have Peace: Ulysses S. Grant and the Politics of War and Reconstruction, 1861–1868*. Chapel Hill: University of North Carolina Press, 1991.

Skelton, William B. *An American Profession of Arms: The Army Officer Corps, 1784–1861*. Lawrence: University Press of Kansas, 1992.

Slim, Hugo. *Killing Civilians: Method, Madness, and Morality in War*. New York: Columbia University Press, 2008.

Smith, Craig Bruce. *American Honor: The Creation of the Nation's Ideals during the Revolutionary Era*. Chapel Hill: University of North Carolina Press, 2018.

Smith, John David, ed. *Black Soldiers in Blue: African American Troops in the Civil War Era*. Chapel Hill: University of North Carolina Press, 2002.

Smith, Mark M. *The Smell of Battle, the Taste of Siege: A Sensory History of the Civil War*. New York: Oxford University Press, 2015.

Smith-Rosenberg, Carroll. *Disorderly Conduct: Visions of Gender in Victorian America*. New York: Oxford University Press, 1986.

Speer, Lonnie R. *War of Vengeance: Acts of Retaliation against Civil War POWs*. Mechanicsburg, Pa.: Stackpole Books, 2002.

Spierenburg, Pieter. *Men and Violence: Gender, Honor, and Rituals in Modern Europe and America*. Columbus: Ohio State University Press, 1998.

Springer, Paul J. *America's Captives: Treatment of POWs from the Revolutionary War to the War on Terror*. Lawrence: University Press of Kansas, 2010.

Springer, Paul J., and Glenn Robins. *Transforming Civil War Prisons: Lincoln, Lieber, and the Politics of Captivity*. New York: Routledge, 2015.

Stahr, Walter. *Seward: Lincoln's Indispensable Man*. New York: Simon and Schuster, 2012.

Steplyk, Jonathan M. *Fighting Means Killing: Civil War Soldiers and the Nature of Combat*. Lawrence: University Press of Kansas, 2018.

Sternhell, Yael A. *Routes of War: The World of Movement in the Confederate South*. Cambridge, Mass.: Harvard University Press, 2012.

Stith, Matthew M. *Extreme Civil War: Guerrilla Warfare, Environment, and Race on the Trans-Mississippi Frontier*. Baton Rouge: Louisiana State University Press, 2016.

Stoker, Donald. *The Grand Design: Strategy and the U.S. Civil War*. New York: Oxford University Press, 2012.

Stokes, Karen. *The Immortal 600: Surviving Civil War Charleston and Savannah*. Charleston, S.C.: History Press, 2013.

Stone, H. David, Jr. *Vital Rails: The Charleston and Savannah Railroad and the Civil War in Coastal South Carolina*. Columbia: University of South Carolina Press, 2008.

Stout, Harry S. *Upon the Altar of the Nation: A Moral History of the Civil War*. New York: Penguin Books, 2007.

Sutherland, Daniel E. "Abraham Lincoln, John Pope, and the Origins of Total War." *Journal of Military History* 56 (October 1992): 567–86.

———. *A Savage Conflict: The Decisive Role of Guerrillas in the American Civil War*. Chapel Hill: University of North Carolina Press, 2009.

———. *Seasons of War: The Ordeal of a Confederate Community, 1861–1865*. New York: Free Press, 1995.

Symonds, Craig L. *Lincoln and His Admirals: Abraham Lincoln, the U.S. Navy, and the Civil War*. New York: Oxford University Press, 2008.

Taaffe, Stephen R. *Commanding the Army of the Potomac*. Lawrence: University Press of Kansas, 2006.

Tap, Bruce. *The Fort Pillow Massacre: North, South, and the Status of African-Americans in the Civil War Era*. New York: Routledge, 2014.

Taylor, Amy Murrell. *The Divided Family in Civil War America*. Chapel Hill: University of North Carolina Press, 2005.

———. *Embattled Freedom: Journeys through the Civil War's Slave Refugee Camps*. Chapel Hill: University of North Carolina Press, 2018.

Thomas, Emory M. *The Confederate Nation, 1861–1865*. New York: Harper and Row, 1979.

Thomas, Keith. *Man and the Natural World: A History of the Modern Sensibility*. New York: Pantheon, 1983.

True, Marshall. "A Reluctant Warrior Advises the President: Ethan Allen Hitchcock, Abraham Lincoln and the Union Army, Spring 1862." *Vermont History* 50, no. 3 (Summer 1982): 143–50.

Urwin, Gregory J. W., ed. *Black Flag over Dixie: Racial Atrocities and Reprisals in the Civil War*. Carbondale: Southern Illinois University Press, 2004.

Utley, Robert Marshall. *Frontiersmen in Blue: The United States Army and the Indian, 1848–1865*. New York: Macmillan, 1967.

Vandiver, Frank E. *Rebel Brass: The Confederate Command System*. Baton Rouge: Louisiana State University Press, 1956.

Van Engeland, Anicée. *Civilian or Combatant? A Challenge for the 21st Century*. New York: Oxford University Press, 2011.

Varon, Elizabeth R. *Armies of Deliverance: A New History of the Civil War*. New York: Oxford University Press, 2019.

Varon, Elizabeth R., and the *Dictionary of Virginia Biography*. "Joseph T. Wilson (1837–1890)." *Encyclopedia Virginia*. Last modified May 7, 2018. https://www.encyclopediavirginia.org/Wilson_Joseph_T_1837-1890.

Ward, Andrew. *River Run Red: The Fort Pillow Massacre and the American Civil War*. New York: Viking, 2005.

Washington, Versalle F. *Eagles on Their Buttons: A Black Infantry Regiment in the Civil War*. Columbia: University of Missouri Press, 1999.

Watson, Samuel J. *Jackson's Sword: The Army Officer Corps on the American Frontier, 1810–1821*. Lawrence: University Press of Kansas, 2012.

———. *Peacekeepers and Conquerors: The Army Officer Corps on the American Frontier, 1821–1846*. Lawrence: University Press of Kansas, 2013.

Weigley, Russell F. *Towards an American Army: Military Thought from Washington to Marshall*. New York: Columbia University Press, 1962.

Weiner, Marli F. *Mistresses and Slaves: Plantation Women in South Carolina, 1830–1880*. Urbana: University of Illinois Press, 1998.

Weitz, Mark A. *The Confederacy on Trial: The Piracy and Sequestration Cases of 1861*. Lawrence: University Press of Kansas, 2005.

Westwood, Howard C. *Black Troops, White Commanders, and Freedmen during the Civil War*. Carbondale: Southern Illinois University Press, 1992.

———. "Captive Black Union Soldiers in Charleston: What to Do?" In *Black Flag over Dixie: Racial Atrocities and Reprisals in the Civil War*, edited by Gregory J. W. Urwin, 34–51. Carbondale: Southern Illinois University Press, 2004.

White, Jonathan W. *Midnight in America: Darkness, Sleep, and Dreams during the Civil War.* Chapel Hill: University of North Carolina Press, 2017.

Whites, LeeAnn, and Alicia P. Long, eds. *Occupied Women: Gender, Military Occupation, and the American Civil War.* Baton Rouge: Louisiana State University Press, 2009.

Wiley, Bell Irvin. *The Life of Billy Yank: The Common Soldier of the Union*. Baton Rouge: Louisiana State University Press, 1952.

———. *The Life of Johnny Reb: The Common Soldier of the Confederacy.* Indianapolis, Ind.: Bobbs-Merrill, 1943.

Williams, T. Harry. *P. G. T. Beauregard: Napoleon in Gray.* Baton Rouge: Louisiana State University Press, 1954.

Wills, Brian Steel. *The River Was Dyed with Blood: Nathan Bedford Forrest and Fort Pillow.* Norman: University of Oklahoma Press, 2014.

Wilson, Keith P. *Campfires of Freedom: The Camp Life of Black Soldiers during the Civil War.* Kent, Ohio: Kent State University Press, 2002.

———. "In the Shadow of John Brown: The Military Service of Colonels Thomas Higginson, James Montgomery, and Robert Shaw in the Department of the South." In *Black Soldiers in Blue: African American Troops in the Civil War Era*, edited by John David Smith, 306–35. Chapel Hill: University of North Carolina Press, 2002.

Wise, Stephen R. *Gate of Hell: Campaign for Charleston Harbor, 1863*. Columbia: University of South Carolina Press, 1994.

———. *Lifeline of the Confederacy: Blockade Running during the Civil War.* Columbia: University of South Carolina Press, 1988.

Witt, John Fabian. *Lincoln's Code: The Laws of War in American History.* New York: Simon and Schuster, 2012.

Woods, Michael E. *Emotional and Sectional Conflict in the Antebellum United States.* Cambridge: Cambridge University Press, 2014.

Woodworth, Steven E. *Jefferson Davis and His Generals: The Failure of Confederate Command in the West.* Lawrence: University Press of Kansas, 1990.

———. *While God Is Marching On: The Religious World of Civil War Soldiers.* Lawrence: University Press of Kansas, 2001.

Wooster, Robert. *The American Military Frontiers: The United States Army in the West, 1783–1900*. Albuquerque: University of New Mexico Press, 2009.

Wyatt-Brown, Bertram. *Honor and Violence in the Old South*. New York: Oxford University Press, 1986.

### *Websites*

Ancestry.com. Accessed through Texas A&M University Libraries.

Andersonville National Historic Site. https://www.nps.gov/ande/index.htm.

The Avalon Project: Documents in Law, History, and Diplomacy. https://avalon.law.yale.edu/.

Battle of Olustee. https://battleofolustee.org/.

Florida History On-Line. https://www.unf.edu/floridahistoryonline/Projects/Proj-B-P.html.

Fort Pulaski National Monument. https://www.nps.gov/fopu/learn/historyculture/the-immortal-six-hundred.htm.
Freedmen and Southern Society Project: Documents. http://www.freedmen.umd.edu/sampdocs.htm.
Lycoming County Women's History Project. https://lycoming.edu/lcwhp/fribley.html.
Soldiers and Sailors Database. National Park Service. https://www.nps.gov/civilwar/soldiers-and-sailors-database.htm.

# INDEX

*Page numbers in italics refer to illustrations and illustration captions.*


1st North Carolina Volunteers (35th USCT): Battle of Olustee, 119–26; occupation of Jacksonville, 113–14; officers and organization, 113–14; prisoners from, 126, 130, 132–34, 203–4
1st South Carolina Volunteers (33rd USCT): Confederate reaction to, 56–57; discipline, 50; enlisted men, 43; occupation of Jacksonville, 60–65; organization, 43; raids, 49, 52–56, 81; sergeants, *54*
2nd Massachusetts Infantry, 18, 38, 39, 74
2nd South Carolina Volunteers (34th USCT): action on James Island, 81; burning of Darien, Ga., 74–77; discipline, 58–59; occupation of Jacksonville, 60–61, 64; raid on Combahee River, 68–70; raid on St. Johns River, 62–63; raiding strategy, 50; siege of Fort Wagner, 100
3rd USCT, 100, 109–10
3rd Wisconsin, 179
5th South Carolina, 82
6th Connecticut Volunteers, 61, 64, 89
7th Connecticut Volunteers, 119–20, 122, 126
7th New Hampshire Volunteers, 90, 102, 119–21, 228, 236
8th Maine Volunteers, 61, 64
8th USCT, 113–22, 124, 128, 133, 237–38
10th Connecticut, 82
11th Maine, 102
13th Tennessee Cavalry, 134
21st USCT, 1, 163, 204–5
23rd Massachusetts, 75
25th South Carolina, 82
26th USCT, 151
30th Illinois, 200
32nd Georgia, 119, 164
48th New York Volunteers, 44, 89–90, 122, 124
54th Massachusetts Volunteers: attack on Fort Wagner, 87–90, 228n11, 229n21; attack on James Island 1864, 150; and Baldwin, Fla., 114–15, *115*; Battle of Olustee, 116–24, 126–27; burning of Darien, Ga., 74–77; guards of Confederate prisoners, 1–2, 163–64, 168, 209; occupation of Charleston, 254n58; occupation of Jacksonville, 113–14, 130; pay issue, 157–58; picket fight on James and Sol Legare Islands, 81–82, *83*; prisoners from, 15, 83–85, 91–98, 100, 110–11, 126, 131–34, 153–57, 160, 167–68, 181, 202–4, 253n56, 254n58; sent to Department of South, 68; and Sherman's invasion of South Carolina, 184, 190; and siege of Fort Wagner, 100, 109
55th Massachusetts, 116, 130, 155, *205*, 232n44, 235n7
64th Georgia, 119
157th New York, 152–53, 168, 170, 172, 188

Anderson, Robert, 143, 205
Andersonville Prison (Camp Sumter), 15, *131*, 131–33, 141, 155–57, 159, 161–62, 185, 203–4, 238n25, 244n43, 254n58
Andrew, John A., 24, 68, 95, 157

animals: Confederate army use of dogs, 70; contrast with human nature, 5, 15–16, 40, 61, 158, 164, 214n9; killing of dogs by Sherman's army, 180, 184, 249n16; prison turning men into, 158–60, 162–65, 169, 173, 183, 185, 207, 212; and slaves as, 44, 59; and Sherman's army confiscation of, 201; and sliding scale of civilization, 5, 146, 210
Appleton, John W. M., *76*; and 1st North Carolina, 119; and 54th Massachusetts, 111, 114, 115, 119, 143, 157; and Blacks as soldiers, 82, 158; and emancipation of slaves, 115; fate of, 150–51; and Fort Wagner siege, 88, 89; and Schimmelfennig, 147; sketches of, *83*, *90*; and slavery, 75
atrocities, 9–10, 14, 32–33, 64, 72, 123–25, 129, 134–36, 202, 208, 214n5, 217n21, 237n22, 251n38

Banks, Nathaniel, 38, 39
barbarians/barbarism: and enslavement of prisoners, 95; fear of, 5, 136; on sliding scale of civilization, 61, 215n9; and treatment of women, 61, 182; view of Black people, 15, 18, 57, 123–24, 163–64, 209–10; and view of Indigenous people, 123–24; and warfare, 78, 93, 135, 146, 171, 177, 227n63
Bates, Edward, 137
Battery Wagner. *See* Fort Wagner
Battle of Antietam, 42, 134
Battle of Cedar Mountain, 34, 38–39
Battle of the Crater, 138
Battle of Gettysburg, 146
Battle of Olustee, 116, 119–25, 155, 203, 236nn13–14
Battle of Wilmington, 203
Beard, Oliver T., 44
Beauregard, P. G. T., *79*; and 54th Massachusetts, 84, 95; and Battle of Olustee, 124, 126; and Black prisoners of war, 84, 96, 99, 110, 126; on Blacks as savage, 15; and burning of Columbia, S.C., 210; and burning of Darien, Ga., 78, 80, 197; and carnage around Fort Wagner, 91; and Charleston, S.C., 104, *105*; and civilized war, 93; and Combahee raid, 70, 80; as commander of Department of South Carolina, Georgia, and Florida, 64–65, 79, 143; and conduct of war in South Carolina and Georgia, 78, 194, 197; and customs of war, 78, 79, 92, 103, 106, 197; and Jefferson Davis, 78; and destruction of property, 78; education of, 78; and execution of Black prisoners, 98; and Fort Sumter, 145–46; and Forts Sumter and Wagner, 106, 109; and Greek fire, 141; and international opinion, 106; letter to Gillmore of, 78, 80, 92, 197, 233n54; and removal of noncombatants, 104, 106, 147; and retaliation, 79, 99, 102, 103, 104, 106, 199; and retaliation correspondence, 153; and South Carolina, 191; and states' trying all officers, 57; and treatment of prisoners, 91–92; and troops from South Carolina and Georgia, 119; and using prisoners as human shields, 145–46; and War Department, 45
black flag, 130, 136, 138, 151
*Black Phalanx, The* (Wilson), 208–9
Black troops: atrocities against, 125, 134, 138, 222n16, 229n24, 234n63; and civilized war, 44, 50, 69, 72, 75, 80, 101, 138–39; Confederate retaliation against, 4, 43, 57–58, 65, 97, 117, 166, 221n69, 229n24, 243n30; and postwar symbolism, 208–10; treatment of in Department of the South, 109–10; U.S. recruitment of, 3, 15, 65, 68; U.S. retaliation to protect, 47, 65, 92, 94–95, 110, 136, 222n16. *See also specific units*
Blair, Frank P., Jr.: 17th Corps of, 177, 189–90, 201; background of, 177; and discipline of army, 191; and executions, 200; and foraging, 201; and land mines, 183; and orders against stealing, 190
Blair, Montgomery, 137
bombardment of Charleston, 103–7, *105*, 109, 112, 141–47, 153, 170, 173, 212, 233n48
Bonham, Milledge, 96, 98–99, 104, 110, 134, 155, 156. *See also* South Carolina
Brayton, Charles Ray, 142–43
Brooks, T. B., 101–2

Brown, Philip P., Jr., 170–71, 172, 187–88
Brown, John, 49, 58, 205, 225n39
Brown, John (South Carolina freedman), 34, 36
Brown, Orin H., 95, 167, 230–31n30, 246n51
Burnside, Ambrose, 66–67, 224n37
Butler, Benjamin, 34, 216n18, 221n69

Campbell, John A., 132, 134; and free Blacks as soldiers, 96–97
Camp Oglethorpe (military prison), 132, 145, 152, 159
Camp Sumter. *See* Andersonville Prison
Charleston campaign: blockade, 19; bombardment of city, 87, 102–4, 107, 141–43, 145, 153, 167, 170; effect on noncombatants, 15, 104, 141–42, 205; human shields in, 145–46, 148, *149*, 151, 159, 165, *166*, 245n50; symbolic importance of, 18, 63, 103; Union operations against, 24, 64, 68, 80–84, 100–102, 108–9, 144, 150, 184, 190, 204, *205*, 242n20
Charleston Jail, 15, 57, 92, 95–96, 134, 153, 155, 160, 164, 167–68, 242n27, 246n51
Chase, Salmon P., 20, 29, 40, 137, 235n5
civilization: and American civilization, 50, 123–24, 158–59, 169, 173, 207; American views on, 4–5, 44, 61, 208, 210, 214–15n9; and Anglo-Saxons, 49; and black flag, 136; and Christian civilization, 27, 146, 166, 169, 171, 186, 215n12; and civilized war, 5–6, 16, 21, 27, 44, 50, 61, 78, 173, 180, 212; Confederate fears about, 56–57, 85, 123; and Confederate soldiers, 209; and correspondence with enemy, 9–10; crisis of, 16, 85, 136, 138, 158, 169, 173, 178, 180; and customs of war, 171; and gender and race, 210; and General Orders No. 100, 70–71, 138; Higginson's views on, 49, 50; and honor, 72; and House report on war practices, 208; and Indigenous people, 123, 124, 182; and international law, 208; and international opinion, 93; meaning of, 5, 15; and military prison, 158; place of Black people in, 21, 44, 50, 57, 81, 124, 139; and prisoners of war, 164, 165, 173, 185–86; during Reconstruction, 210–11, 254–55n6; and retaliation, 197, 207; and "savages," 5, 14, 50, 59, 61, 116, 123, 146, 207, 208, 215n9; and Southern civilization, 15, 57, 61, 72, 116, 139, 182, 206, 207; and treatment of prisoners of war, 14, 15–16, 95, 146, 160, 173, 208; and treatment of women, 61, 173, 182; and Union bombardment of Charleston, S.C., 142; and use of Black troops, 57, 75–76, 81, 157; and white Americans' identities, 18; as worldview, 4–5, 214–15n9
Cobb, Howell, 181
Colquitt, Alfred Holt, 119, 120, 121, 122, 126
Combahee River Raid, 69–70, *69*, 80
Confederacy: and international legitimacy, 9, 85, 97–98, 107; oaths of allegiance to, 167; and race war, 138; and racial categories, 113, 126; and requiring oaths, 41; secessionist arguments of, 56; and state laws, 80, 84; and state trials, 136; and war crimes, 199; and white Southern womanhood, 116, 182, 199; and white supremacy, 206
Confederate army: abandoned equipment of, 115; atrocities committed by, 123, 124–25, 129; and battlefield executions, 157; and Black prisoners, 15, 43, 45, 95, 125, 126, 128–35, 141; and burning of dwellings, 179; and burning of property, 191; and captured officers, 39, 40, 41–42, 58; cavalry of, 114, 117, 119, 177, 195, 197–98; and civilized war, 125, 135, 191, 212; and enslavement of Black soldiers, 157; and execution of prisoners of war, 181, 191; and Florida beef, 114; in Georgia, 177; and human shields, 145, 148; and land mines, 180, 189; and laws of war, 122; and Lincoln's policies, 30; and massacre at Fort Pillow, 134–35; and massacre of wounded men, 15, 124–25, 134; and military labor, 157; and murder of looters, 196; and murders of foragers, 189, 194–95, 197, 199–200, 202; and poisoned food, 7; and Pope's officers as felons, 41; and prisoners of war, 1, 33, 83, 84, 91, 125, 128, 180; and rape, 116; resurgence in Virginia

Confederate army (*continued*)
of, 29; and retaliation, 190, 207; savagery of, 178; scouts and spies of, 116; and slave labor, 145; and treatment of prisoners, 117; and use of Blacks as slaves, 204; and war crimes, 198; weapons used by, 88. *See also* Jones, Samuel; Lee, Robert E.; prisoners of war; *and individual unit designations, campaigns, and battles*
Confederate Congress: debates over retaliation, 10, 56–58; and guerrillas, 3; resolution on retaliation, 58, 72, 84, 85, 96, 98–99, 133, 156–57, 181, 187, 202, 230n24, 232n40, 239n40, 243n30
Confederate War Department: debates within, 15, 67, 96–99, 222n14; and exchange of prisoners, 152; official policy of ignored locally, 117, 133–34, 155; and prisoners from 54th Massachusetts, 83, 96–99, 132–34, 156–57; response to General Orders No. 100, 71–72; retaliation orders, 32–33, 38–39, 156–57, 167; views of Union policy, 31, 45, 65, 96
Counsel, George, 98, 228n5

Dahlgren, John A.: and cannon design, 85; as commander of South Atlantic Blockading Squadron, 85; and exchange of Black sailors, 246n51; and Forts Sumter and Wagner, 102; naval experience of, 85; and relations with Gillmore, 108; and Union blockade, 149
Darien, Ga., burning of, 74–78, 197, 207, 226n53, 226n61
Davis, Jefferson: and 1st South Carolina regiment, 57; and Beauregard, 78; and Blacks as inferior, 56; and Black soldiers, 45, 47, 57, 208, 239n40; and burning of Marietta courthouse, 179; and captured free Blacks, 98; and capture of Lee's son, 67; and citizens' letters, 10–11; and civilized war, 18; as Confederate president, 1, 18, 27, 31, 31–32, 33, 39, 41, 42, 43, 45, 47, 55, 56–57, 85, 94, 99, 179, 181; and Department of South Carolina, Georgia, and Florida, 191; and enlisted soldiers, 33; and execution of Blacks, 47, 137; and Fort Pillow massacre, 137; and guerrilla warfare, 214n6; and Hampton, 195; and Hunter's actions in South Carolina, 27, 32; and Hunter's retaliation letter, 65–66; and international laws of war, 57; and international opinion, 98; and land mines, 181; and Lincoln administration, 31–32; military career of, 32; and military events in Maryland, 42; and officers' guilt, 9, 217n21; orders of, 181; and Pope in Virginia, 31, 32; and Pope's officers as felons, 41, 47; pressure from slaveholders on, 133; and prisoners of war, 155; and proposal for Union prisoners, 145; response to Emancipation Proclamation of, 56–57; and retaliation, 2–3, 9, 18, 19, 32, 33, 43, 47, 57, 65–66, 67, 70, 94, 224n37; retaliation proclamation of, 18, 19, 43, 57; and servile insurrection, 57; and Sherman's discipline of soldiers, 179; and staff of 14th Corps, 179; and states' laws, 45, 47; and states trying all officers, 57; and treatment of prisoners, 42, 45, 47
Department of South Carolina, Georgia, and Florida, 64, 79, 143, 168, 191
Department of the South: and 2nd South Carolina, 58, 60, 68–70; and 8th USCT, 113; and 54th Massachusetts, 68, 113; and black flag, 138; and Black prisoners of war, 99–100, 130; Black troops in, 94, 109, 144; and civilized war, 44, 117; and Confederate officers, 186, 187; and conflict with War and Naval Departments, 63–64; and Davis administration, 43; destruction of resources of, 44, 50; and Gillmore, 78, 81, 87; Hunter as commander of, 17, 87; and Jacksonville, 60, 113; and Key West, 58; and laws of war, 73; and meaning of civilization, 15, 50; and Montgomery, 58, 60; officers brought to, 16; and order emancipating enslaved people, 21–22; plantations and people of, 27; and prisoners of war, 167–68, 186–88, 202–3; and protection of free Northern-born prisoners, 96, 202; and racial categories,

114; and retaliation, 3–4, 50, 66, 68, 70, 80, 84, 85, 87, 146, 169, 172–73, 203; and South Carolina, 190; spy network of, 68; states of, 21, 60, 175; and treatment of noncombatants, 3; and Union bombardment of Charleston, S.C., 143; Union troops in, 36, 50, 53, 54–55, 60, 72, 87, 113–23, 144; and use of Black troops, 3, 21, 36, 38, 50, 54–55; violence in, 124, 180. *See also* Florida; Foster, John G.; Georgia; South Carolina
Dix-Hill cartel, 31–32, 73, 156
Douglass, Frederick, 68, 138
Dow, Neil, 99, 243n30
DuPont, Samuel, 18–19, 24, 63–64

emancipation: Confederate response to, 47, 56–57, 133; and retaliation, 42, 47, 57; and Union policy and strategy, 17, 24, 28–29, 115, 234n61
Emerson, Ralph Waldo, 7, 14
Emilio, Luis F., 75, 89, 90, 93, 122–23, 158, 164, 227n4, 232n40, 254n58
Ewing, Charles, 179
executions: of Black soldiers, 45, 60, 84, 116, 124, 132, 134, 157, 229n24, 235n7; by Burnside, 66–67, 224n37; by Butler, 34, 221n69; of guerrillas, 3, 176, 211, 214n6, 252n47; as legal retaliation, 8–9, 67, 95, 199; and Pope's orders, 33; by Sherman, 16, 173, 180, 194–97, 199–200, 252n46; threat of, 38, 45, 66–67, 95, 99, 136, 202; of white Union soldiers, 181, 195, 252n49

Finegan, Joseph: and 2nd Florida Cavalry, 119; and 32nd Georgia, 119; and 64th Georgia, 119; and Battle of Olustee, 127; and Black prisoners of war, 125; and Federal forces, 119–20, 126, 223n20; limited military experience of, 60, 119; Seymour's letter to, 128; and troop postings, 65
Florence Military Prison, 167–68, 202–3
Florida: and 54th Massachusetts, 146–47; and Battle of Olustee, *116*, 134, 141; beef supply of, 114; Black Union forces in, 115–17, 126, 134; Federal campaigns against, 3, 15, 64–65, 113, 114, 117, 119, 138; Gillmore's expedition into, 112, 113, 114–15; insurrection of slaves in, 65; and Jacksonville, 60, 64–65, 113, 114, 116, 117, 128, 130; and Lake City, 117, 119, 125, 126, 130; martial law in, 21; and Olustee, 15, 116, 117, 122, 130, 132; and river raids, 17; and Union occupation of Jacksonville, 64–65, 223n20; and village of Baldwin, 114, 115, *115*, 116, 117. *See also* Department of the South
Forrest, Nathan Bedford, 134, 137
foraging: and Confederate murder of foragers, 180–81, 189, 191, 194, 222n16, 251n34; and customs of war, 40, 177, 194, 227n63; and raids, 62, 69; and retaliation, 194–200, 252n46; and Sherman's army, 177, 181, 190, 197–98, 200–202, 249n13; and soldier behavior, 115
Fort Gregg, 1–2, 150, 163
Fort Pillow, Tenn., massacre, 134–38, 171, 186, 240n48
Fort Sumter, 18, 81, 100, 102, 106, 108–9, 143, 145–46, 205
Fort Pulaski, 145, 168, 170–72, 185–86, 188–89, 203, 209, 250n27
Fort Wagner: and burials of Union dead, 90–91, 230n29; and capture of Black prisoners, 91, 98, 111, 153, 155–56, 204; and Confederate prisoners under fire, 1, 163–64; and international opinion, 93, 97; and retaliation, 94; siege of, 100–102, *100*, 109; Union assault on, 87–90, *89*, *90*, 228n11
Foster, John G., *144*; background of, 143; Black troops of, 184; and bombardment of Charleston, S.C., 145, 146, 147, 150–51, 170; and civilized war, 188; and Confederate prisoners of war, 147, 148, 149–50, 152, 160, 162–63, 165, 168–70, 172–73, 180, 188–89; and Confederate treatment of prisoners, 16, 146, 169–70; and customs of war, 170; and Department of the South, 143–44, 161; departure of, 64; and exchange of prisoners, 152, 153, 161, 244nn43–44; and Fort Sumter, 143; and Jones, 162, 166; and lack of troops and equipment, 144;

Foster, John G. (*continued*)
and multipronged attack on Charleston, S.C., 150–51, 242nn19–20; and pay of Black soldiers, 158; and prisoner exchanges, 162–63; and prisoners as human shields, 148–50, 151, 247n55; and prisoners of war in Charleston, S.C., 159, 160–61, 168; and rations for Confederate prisoners, 16, 168–70, 171, 172, 173, 180, 187, 188–89, 247n62; and request to attack Charleston, S.C., 144; and retaliation, 150, 151, 153, 162, 163, 168–70, 171, 180, 186, 187, 188–89, 250n19, 250n21; and treatment of Confederate prisoners, 185, 188–89, 245n50

Fribley, Charles W., *129*; burial of, 125–26, 129; as commander of 8th USCT, 113, 120–21, 127; Confederate treatment of, 15, 125–26, 127; death of, 121; and Hilton Head, S.C., 127; and Seymour, 119, 120; widow of, 127–28

Fribley, Kate Ault, 127–28, *129*, 238n31

Gardner, William, 126, 128

Garrison, William Lloyd, 205–6

General Orders No. 100, 2, 70–74, 94, 138, 188, 211, 226n50, 226n53, 233n48, 245n47

Georgia: and Andersonville Prison, *131*, 132; and Army of Georgia, 175; and Atlanta, 163, 175, 177; and burning of Marietta courthouse, 178–79; Camp Oglethorpe in, 132, 152; and Camp Sumter, 131–32, 152; and capital Milledgeville, 177; and civilized war, 184; and Confederate troops, 119, 151; Federal campaigns against, 3, 15, 176, 177, 178, 180, 181, 182–84, 190; and Fort Pulaski, 168; and Kingston, 177; land mines in, 182; martial law in, 21; and prisoners of war, 152, 161, 163, 167, 168, 173, 183; and river raids, 17; Sea Islands of, 35; and Sherman's march to Savannah, 176, 181–84; and Sherman's orders for foragers, 177; and shooting of stragglers, 179; and St. Simon's Island, 34, 36; and Union prisoners of war, 152, 161; Union soldiers in, 181. *See also* Department of the South; Hardee, William J.

Gillmore, Quincy A., *86*, *180*; and 1st South Carolina, 81; and 2nd South Carolina, 87, 100–101; and 54th Massachusetts, 80, 81, 86, 87, 92, 93, 94, 110; and attack on Charleston, S.C., 15, 86, 87, 102–3, *105*, 106, 107, 108–9, 112; and Battle of Olustee report, 127; and Beauregard's letter, 80, 92; and Black prisoners, 86, 92–94, 95, 110, 134; on Blacks as soldiers, 112; and burial of dead soldiers, 91; and Charleston Harbor, 80, 81; and civilized war, 92, 103, 106–7; and Department of the South, 3, 78, 81, 112, 188; and fighting Lee's army, 143; Florida expedition of, 112, 235n5; and Fort Sumter, 102, 106; and Fort Wagner, 87, 88, 89, 100, 102, 106, 109; and Hilton Head, S.C., 117; and hostages, 93; and importance of Charleston, S.C., 103; and James Island, 87; and Morris Island, S.C., 81, 84–85, 87, 92, 100, 101, 102, 104, 106, 109; and prisoners of war, 188; and private property, 114; and removal of noncombatants, 107, 147; replacement of, 143; and retaliation, 86, 92, 93, 94, 102, 103, 104, 106–7; and retaliation correspondence, 153, 233n54; and science of war, 85, 101, 109; and Sol Legare Island, 84–85; and Swamp Angel, 102–3; and treatment of Black soldiers, 130; and use of Black troops, 87, 93–94, 100–102, 109–10, 112, 234n61

Gooding, Corp. James, 15, 76–77, 81, 93, 107, 123, 128, 133, 157, 254n3

Gordon, George H., 38–39

Gould, Edward, 34, 36

Grant, Ulysses S.: and Black prisoners from Battle of Milliken's Bend, 230n24; and civilized warfare, 10; and command of Union armies, 135, 163, 170, 176; and Department of the South, 144, 184; and Fort Pillow massacre, 138; and prisoner exchanges, 135, 163, 167, 244n44, 246n52; and retaliation, 135, 138, 252n52; retaliation correspondence of, 9–10, 230n24, 252n52; in Virginia, 176

Greek fire, 102–3, 107, 141

guerrillas: and retaliation, 3, 28, 30, 70,

143, 176, 211, 214, 221n3, 222n16, 223n16, 252n47; skirmishes with Black troops, 34

Hagood, Johnson, 84, 91, 92, 233n54
Hale, Stephen F., 56
Halleck, Henry W.: and bombardment of Charleston, S.C., 147, 170; and capture of Lee's son, 67; and corporate guilt, 9; and customs of war, 34, 70, 169, 189; and Department of the South, 144, 169; as general-in-chief of Union armies, 6, 33–34, 94; and imprisonment with hard labor, 94; and international law, 7, 33, 41, 70; and Francis Lieber, 34, 70, 94, 135, 215n18, 230n27, 249n15; and massacre, 9; and military theory, 33; orders of, 41, 149, 150, 221n69, 244n44; and prisoners of war in Charleston, S.C., 160–61; and retaliation, 13, 34, 41, 169, 230n27; and Sherman, 184; and torture, 9; and treatment of prisoners, 13, 148–49, 150, 152, 161, 169; and Union retaliation correspondence, 34, 41; on value of Black soldiers, 112
Hallowell, Edward Needles, 111, 122, 123, 158
Hampton, Wade, *196*; and burning of Columbia, S.C., 210; and election of 1868, 254n5; and feud with Sherman, 209–10; and home defense, 198–99, 210; and laws of war, 196, 197; and murder of foragers, 197, 198, 199; and retaliation, 195, 198, 198–99, 202; on savagery of Union soldiers, 199, 210; and South Carolina, 195, 209; Southern values of, 195, 210
Hardee, William J., 168, 170, 184, 191
Harrison, George P., 187
Harrison, William Henry (54th Massachusetts), 98, 168, 228n5
Hawkins, Isaac, 132
Hawks, Esther Hill, 150, 235n7
Hawley, Joseph, 120, 236n13
Hawthorne, Sophia Peabody, 13–14, 171
Heichhold, Alex P., 122, 130, 237n18
Higginson, Thomas Wentworth: and 1st South Carolina Volunteers, 49, 50, 52, 54, 55, 57, 59, 62; and civilized war, 60, 61, 221n3; and Combahee raid, 69; and command of Black regiments, 15, 49, 50, 52, 55–56, 61–62, 64, 65; and destruction of property, 55, 60, 62; discipline of, 73–74; and Hilton Head, S.C., 63; and hostages, 60–61; and military as school for Blacks, 59; and Montgomery, 58, 75, 226n61; and oaths of allegiance to U.S., 60; and protection of women of Jacksonville, 61–62, 223n20; and views of Black people, 49
Hilton Head, S.C., 17, 18, 22, 26, 61, 73, 84, 93, 153, 168, 170, 185–89, *187*, 250n27
history: use of historical precedent in retaliation, 6, 11, 13, 26, 47, 78, 97, 104, 194, 197, 215n13, 246n52, 254n3; as judge of actions, 13, 107, 169, 207, 212; and laws of war, 70; and worldview of civilization, 5, 21, 78, 208, 210
Hitchcock, Henry: and burning of Marietta courthouse, 178–79; and civilized war, 175, 176, 183; and crisis of civilization, 180; and destruction of property, 176; and discipline of army, 178, 179; and Hampton, 210; and land mines, 183; and laws of war, 179, 183; and march to Savannah, 178, 183; and pillaging soldiers, 181; and retaliation, 183; and ride with left wing, 177; as Sherman's military secretary, 175, 176, 177; and soldiers' discipline, 176–77, 248n8; and stragglers, 179
Hitchcock, Ethan Allen, *12*; and hostages, 96; and laws of war, 11, 70; and McClellan, 28; nephew of, 175; and prisoner exchanges, 7, 11, 12, 67, 96, 162, 163, 166; and retaliation, 11–15, 67, 96, 169, 171, 186, 197, 212, 234n63, 240n50; and treatment of prisoners, 11, 13–14, 110–11
Hoar, Ebenezer R., 13–14
Holmes, Emma, 84, 107
Holt, Joseph, 67, 70, 94
honor: and Black troops, 64, 76, 81, 87, 101, 130, 137, 157; and civilized war, 6, 72, 176, 211; and court of world opinion, 10, 74, 85, 93, 103, 106, 169, 185, 207, 227n61; and gentlemanly behavior, 39, 78, 91, 164, 182; and public shaming, 39, 85, 91, 93, 125; and retaliation correspondence, 9, 14, 103

Howard, Oliver O., *180*; as commander of right wing, 177, 189, 201; and discipline of army, 191, 248n8; and foraging, 194, 201–2; and killing dogs, 249n16; and orders against stealing, 190
Hunter, David, *19*; as an abolitionist, 17, 87; and actions in South Carolina, 27, 28, 32, 63; and Blacks as soldiers, 20–23, 26, 28–29, 36, 38, 65–66, 69, 92; and burning of Darien, Ga., 226n61; and civilized war, 19, 26, 69; and Department of the South, 3, 17, 24, 87; and family separation, 23; as felon, 34; and forceful conscription of Blacks, 22–23, 26–27, 43; and General Orders No. 100, 72–73; and hostages, 66, 73, 93; and laws of war, 73; and military as school for Blacks, 59; and Montgomery's behavior, 70; and officers of as felons, 33; and operations against Charleston, S.C., 24, 64; and order emancipating enslaved people, 21–22, 24; outlawing of, 18, *19*, 38; removal from command of, 77–78; and retaliation, 18, 19, 66, 73; and shaping of policy, 29; strategy of, 17, 18, 26, 68, 80, 87, 225n39; and use of Black troops, 15, 17, 19, 26, 34, 66, 68, 87; and withdrawal from James Island, 25

Indian Rebellion of 1857–59, 11, 39, *108*, 216, 254n3
Indigenous Americans: in Confederate army, 73; treatment in Union warfare, 14, 124, 182, 211, 237n22; viewed as savages, 5, 124, 182, 199, 222n11, 237n22

James Island, S.C., 24–25, 81–84, 109, 150
Jackson, Stonewall, 31, 34, 38, 119
Jacksonville, Fla.: burning of, 63–64, 78; Union occupation of, 60–65, 117, 127–28, 130, 223n20; Union operations against, 24, 113–14
Jennings, William Henry, 133
Johnson, Edward, 204
Johnson, Hannah, 94, 230n25
Johnson, Robert, 155, 242n27
Johnson, William H., 95, 167, 230–31n30, 246n51
Jones, John B., 31, 45, 67, 96, 231n32
Jones, Samuel, *144*; background of, 143–44; and Confederate prisoners of war, 147; and customs of war, 147; demotion of, 168; and exchange of prisoners, 152, 153, 163, 244n44; and Foster, 166; and lack of troops, 167; and laws of war, 153; and prisoners as human shields, 15, 146, 148, 149, 151–52, 173; and prisoners of war in Charleston, S.C., 151–52, 159–60; and problems with troops and equipment, 144–45; and retaliation, 151, 153, 160; and slave labor, 145; telegrams of, 151; and treatment of prisoners, 148, 153, 245n50; and Seymour, 145; and Union prisoners, 145, 148

Kean, Robert Garlick Hill, 72, 97, 99, 222n14, 231n34
Kilpatrick, Judson, *193*; and burning of property, 194; and civilized war, 194; and Georgia, 181; and pillaging soldiers, 199; and retaliation, 192, 194, 194–95, 252n46
Kirk, Henry, 98

Lake City, Fla., 117, 119, 125–26, 128–30
land mines, 173, 181–83
laws of war: and bombardment of cities, 233; and burning of buildings, 55, 63, 78, 179; and declarations of outlawry, 38; development of, 215; and emancipating and arming slaves, 57–58, 71, 94–95, 132, 221n68; and General Orders No. 100, 70–71, 94; interpretation of through retaliation, 2, 4–8, 14, 216n19; and land mines, 183; and military commissions, 211; and oaths of allegiance, 41; and Philippine War, 211; and prisoners of war labor on fortifications, 216n18; and public enemies, 57; and treaties, 211; and treatment of property, 62, 78, 179
Lee, Robert E.: and Battle of Antietam, 42; and Black prisoners, 246n52, 253n53; capture of son of, 67, 234n37; and civilized war, 10, 32; and command

of Army of Northern Virginia, 29; correspondence of, 10, 31, 32; and Jefferson Davis, 32, 33; and fighting in Virginia, 143, 167, 181; and Hampton, 196; and Hunter's actions in South Carolina, 32; and Pope in Virginia, 31, 32, 41; and prisoner exchanges, 167; retaliation letters of, 32–33, 246n52; and Richmond, 168; and servile war, 32; and Sherman, 184; and surrenders, 8; and threats of retaliation, 41
Letcher, John, 41
Libby Prison, 39, 42
Lieber, Francis: as author, 70, 71, 94; and code governing retaliation, 2, 94, 230n27; and customs of war, 189, 216n18; on executions, 8, 67; and Fort Pillow massacre, 135; and General Orders No. 100, 138, 188; and international law, 2, 34, 70; and laws of war, 70, 71, 94, 138, 249n15; and retaliation, 186
Lincoln, Abraham: and abolition of slavery, 23, 29; and arresting citizens, 42; and Black prisoners of war, 96, 111, 130, 134, 136, 229n24; and bombardment of cities, 103; cabinet of, 169; and civilized war, 30, 97, 216n14; and Confederate prisoners of war, 147; and controversy with McClellan and War Department, 33; and creation of new army, 27; emancipation proclamation of, 29, 42, 47, 65, 133; and events in Virginia, 27, 42, 137; and Florida, 235n5; and Fort Pillow massacre, 135, 136–38, 240n48; and hostages, 99, 137, 224n37; Hunter's letter to, 66; and importance of Charleston, S.C., 63; and laws of war, 137, 214n5; and letter about Pope's army, 40; and McClellan, 28, 33; and military events in Maryland, 42; and military policies, 30; and oaths of allegiance, 42; and Pope's officers in Libby Prison, 42; and prisoner exchanges, 161; and reading of newspapers, 65; and retaliation, 2–3, 6, 9, 66, 85, 94, 95, 96, 99, 110, 112, 134, 135, 136, 138; and review of death sentences, 179; and threats of executions, 66–68; and treatment of prisoners, 157, 185; and use of Black troops, 4, 26, 47, 65, 68, 135, 234n61
Ludlow, William H., 73, 221n69, 237n69

Mann, Mary Peabody, 13, 14
massacre: and the American civil war, 123–24, 138–39; in Atlantic World, 222n11; and Battle of Olustee, 124–25; and Fort Pillow, 134–37, 186; and Indigenous people, 124, 182, 211, 237n22; and retaliation, 7, 9, 134–38
Mattocks, Frank, 132, 204, 239n38
McClellan, George B.: and Army of the Potomac, 27, 28, 41; and beliefs about war, 27, 29; and bombardment of cities, 103; and controversy between Lincoln and War Department, 33; and disagreement with War Department, 27; and feelings about Stanton, 27–28; and Pope, 33, 41; and operations in Virginia, 28, 29, 41; and private property, 33; and view of Lincoln, 27
Meredith, Sullivan, 99, 232n41
Montgomery, James: and 1st North Carolina, 119; and 2nd South Carolina, 50, 58, 59, 60, 62–63, 68–69, 74, 100, *101*; and 3rd USCT, 100, *101*; and 54th Massachusetts, 74, 100, *101*, 119; and Battle of Olustee, 122, 123; and Blacks as savages, 58–59; and captured prisoners, 73; and civilized war, 58, 74, 221n3; and Combahee raid, 70, 73, 225n40; and command of Black regiments, 15, 50, 59–60; and Darien, Ga., expedition, 74, 75, 226n61, 227n61; and departmental orders, 77; and General Orders No. 100, 72–73; harsh discipline of, 59–60; and Hilton Head, S.C., 63; and problems with pillaging, 75; as a religious zealot, 58, 59; and treatment of persons and property, 59, 62–63, 115
Morris, George, 204
Morris Island, S.C.: Confederate prisoners under fire on, 1–2, 148–50, 153, 163–65, 168, 209, 247n55; Union operations on, 81, 84–92, 100–102, 108–9, 143, 150–51

Newell, Robert, 150, 158
newspapers: as forum for retaliation, 107; impact on policy, 29, 31, 65, 161, 210; and names of slaves, 134; and shaping public opinion, 135, 161
noncombatants: and civilized war, 5, 27, 29, 73, 215; killed in Union bombardment, 241n14; removal from Charleston, 103, 147, 233n48; Union treatment of, 3, 124
Norton, Oliver Willcox, 120–21, 128, 236n14, 238n31

O'Connor, Michael P., 148, *149*, 152
Olustee, Fla., 15, 116, 117, 120, 125, 129, 134, 135. *See also* Battle of Olustee
Ould, Robert, 43, 73, 99, 221n69
outlawry proclamations, 1, 18, 38, 74, 130, 136–37, 139, 208, 248n8

Persons, Alexander W., 131
Pierce, Edward L., 20, 22–23
pillage: and civilized war, 30, 40, 69, 75, 177, 197; military orders regarding, 40, 114, 190, 197, 201, 248n8; and retaliation, 41, 181, *196*; and Sherman's army, 178, 180–82, 189–92, 197, 199, 201
Pope, John: and Army of Virginia, 28, 29, 30, 32, 40, 42; and Battle of Cedar Mountain, 34, 38, 39; and Battle of Second Manassas, 41; and Blacks as laborers, 29; Confederate orders against, 38, 39, 47, 220n60; and execution of citizens, 33; and guards over private property, 30; and guerrilla attacks, 30; and holding rebel civilians responsible, 30; and meetings with Stanton, 28; officers of as felons, 33, 34, 40, 41; orders of, 30, 31, 32, 40, 42, 43, 219–20n52, 220n53; and prisoners of war, 33, 92; and release of captured officers of, 43; and restraint of troops, 30, 31, 220n53; and soldiers' plundering, 40
Port Royal, S.C., 18–22, 27, 163, 189
Prichard, William, 190–91
prisoners of war: from 54th Massachusetts, 92–94, 98, 100, 104, 110–11, 134, 139, 153, 155, 156, 167–68, 181, 203, 204, 247n55, 253n56, 254n58; and American Civil War, 3, 15–16, 33, 161, 167–73; and American crisis of civilization, 16; and Andersonville Prison, 157, 159, 161, 162, 167, 203, 204; and black flag, 136, 138; and Black prisoners of war, 80, 84–85, 91–96, 97, 98–99, 100, 110–11, 125, 126, 128–35, 136, 153, 155, 156, 161, 202, 203, 208, 221n68, 223n16, 229n17, 229n24, 231n34, 238n25, 239n40, 240n49, 246nn51–52, 253n57; and bombardment of Charleston, S.C., 161; and boundary between human and animal, 158–59, 160, 162, 163, 164, 165, 169, 185, 212; British treatment of, 107–8; and Camp Lawton, 203; and Camp Oglethorpe, 159; and Camp Sumter, 204; and Charleston, S.C., 145, 149, 156, 159, 160, 161, 162, 163, 165, 167, 168–69, 185; and Charleston Jail, 92, 95, 100, 134, 153, 155, 156, 160, 167, 168, 242n27; and civilized war, 100, 202; in Columbia, S.C., 170; and Confederate officers, 137, 160, 163, 164–65, 166, 168–69, 186–87, 188, 203, 209; and Confederate prison conditions, 136, 160, 183, 185, 202–3, 203; and Confederate prisoners of war, 1–2, 8, 13, 38, 39, 58, 84, 91–93, 98–99, 110–11, 125, 130, 134, 135, 146, 147, 150, 151, 152, 158, 161–62, 163, 164, 165, 166, 168–70, 171–73, 176, 180, 183, 185, 186, 186–87, 194, 196, 199, 200, 245n47, 250n27; Confederate treatment of, 3, 11, 13, 15, 16, 84, 91–92, 95, 110, 125, 128–35, 159, 160, 208, 229n24; and Confederate trials, 99, 111; in Department of the South, 110–11, 130, 161, 172–73, 202–3; and Dix-Hill cartel, 31–32, 156; enslavement of, 132, 208, 253n57; exchanges of, 7, 11, 12, 31, 92–93, 99, 135, 152, 153, 159, 161, 162–63, 166–67, 172, 202, 203–4, 244n43; execution of, 6, 7, 9, 14, 16, 66, 84, 95, 96, 98, 99, 107–8, 130, 132, 136, 138, 155, 173, 180, 181, 191, 196–97, 199, 200, 202, 214n6, 248n10, 252n42, 252n46; and Florence, 167–68, 202, 203, 204; and food rations, 16, 91, 92, 95, 150, 151, 152, 155–56, 159, 160, 161–62, 164–65, 168–73, 185, 186–87, 188, 203, 247n62, 250n19, 250n27; and Fort Gregg, 150, 163; and Fort Strong, 163; and

Fort Wagner, 91, 163, 164; and free-born Northern Blacks, 98, 99, 134, 203, 253n53, 253n55; and Hilton Head, S.C., 186–87, 188, 189, 203, 209; and hostages, 176, 199; as human shields, 15, 139, 145–51, 173, 245n50; and jurisdiction for trials, 98–99, 134; labor of, 94, 95, 98, 132, 133, 134, 155, 167, 169, 204, 216n18; and land mines, 183; and laws of war, 132; and Lincoln's policies, 163; malnourishment of, 185, 186–87, 188, 189, 190; and Morris Island, S.C., 145, 148, 150, 153, 163, 164–65, 168, 209; murder of, 134, 173, 180, 181, 183, 189, 208; and Olustee, 135; and Pope's officers, 41, 92; in Pulaski, 170, 171–72, 185, 186–87, 188, 189, 203; and retaliation, 94–95, 99, 110, 134, 150, 161–62, 163, 168–73, 176, 180, 192, 196–97, 203, 217n27; retaliation against, 2, 8, 11, 13–14, 58, 95, 158, 160, 161, 173, 186, 188–89, 192, 194, 196–97, 202, 224n37, 252n42, 252nn46–47; Senate resolutions about, 185–86; and slaves of Southerners, 167; and Sol Legare Island, 204; and states' laws, 57, 96; state trials for, 133, 134, 155, 157, 168; treatment of, 8, 11, 13–14, 15, 16, 84, 91–92, 94–95, 110–11, 130, 132–33, 145–46, 148, 149–50, 152, 153, 155–56, 159, 161, 162, 164–65, 167–68, 169–70, 171–73, 185, 186, 187, 188, 190, 207, 208, 211, 244n44; of Union, 2, 3, 8, 11, 13, 15, 16, 92–93, 130, 139, 145, 148, 150, 151, 151–52, 153, 156, 158, 159, 161, 162, 163, 165–66, 167, 168–69, 170, 176, 181, 183, 185, 186, 188, 197, 199, 202–3, 204, 207

property: confiscation of by U.S. government, 20, 32, 41, 47; destruction of by Union troops, 50, 59, 62, *69*, 69–70, 145, 190, 221n3, 249n13; and customs of war, 78, 147, 176, 220n52; plundering of by soldiers, 11, 52, 64, 74, 115, 191; protection of in Union army orders, 27–30, 33, 40, 62, 114, 201; slaves as, 133, 204, 221n68, 229n17, 239n40, 240n49; view of Black soldiers, 77

raids: Combahee River, 68–70; Darien, Ga., 74–77; on Georgia-Florida coast, 44; to kidnap freed people, 36, 45; St. Johns River, 62–63; on South Carolina coast, 81, 184, 197; St. Mary's River, 52; as Union strategy, 15, 17, 50, 69, 80, 144, 227n61

Randolph, George W., 7, 41

rations: amount and quality of given to prisoners, 152, 160, 164–65, 168–72, 188, 203, 247n62; congressional resolutions and debate on, 185–86; and symbolism of savagery, 164–65, 169; Union retaliation regarding, 11–14, 146, 150, 161, 168–72, 185–86, 188

Reed, William Nikolaus, 113–14, 123

retaliation: and 54th Massachusetts, 110–11; and American Civil War, 1–16, 18, 72, 73, 85, 94–95, 112, 136–37, 138, 158, 163, 196–98, 211–12; and Black captured soldiers, 94, 110, 111, 112, 130, 134, 136–37, 167, 229n24, 246n52; and Blacks as soldiers, 157, 181, 209; and British reaction to Sepoy Mutiny, 11, 108; and burning of corn, houses, and bridges, 182–83; and Charleston, S.C., 104, 147–48, 161; and Christian views, 14, 171, 216n14; civilians as subjects of, 8; and civilized war, 2, 6–7, 14, 15, 18, 173, 197, 207; and Confederate officials, 2, 42–43, 58, 85, 95, 117, 170, 186–89; Confederate proclamations of, 18, 38, 43, 66, 72–73, 80, 90; and Confederate War Department, 39, 46; congressional proposal on, 185–86; and customs of war, 95, 197, 207, 216n18; and Jefferson Davis, 18, 19, 33, 43, 47, 57, 65–66, 70, 94; and deaths of foragers, 194, 195; in Department of the South, 3–4, 6, 15, 16, 70, 84–85, 87, 102, 110, 146, 169; and enslavement, 71, 94, 95; and exchange of officers, 47; and exchange of prisoners, 152, 231n34; and executions, 9, 65, 66–67, 94, 95, 136, 137, 180, 194–95, 196, 198, 211, 252n42, 252nn46–47, 252n49; and field commanders, 3, 10; and food rations, 180, 209, 250n19, 250n21; and Fort Pillow massacre, 135, 136–37, 138; and Fort Pulaski, 209; and freeborn Black soldiers, 146; and General Orders No. 100, 2, 70, 71, 72–73, 94; and guerrillas,

retaliation (*continued*)
3, 214n6, 232n16; and hostages, 93, 137, 156, 224n37, 226n50; and human shields, 146; and *Law of Nations* (Vattel), 104; and laws of war, 4, 5, 7, 8, 13, 14, 94, 95, 180, 216n19; and Lee's retaliation letter, 32–33, 34; limits of, 7–8, 230n27; and Lincoln's policies, 47, 67–68, 94, 96, 110, 112, 136, 137–38, 161, 162, 185, 240n48; and maintaining honor, 9–10, 14, 85, 103–4, 207; and military campaigns, 4, 211; and Morris Island, S.C., 150; and murder, 10, 94, 200; national debate on, 185–86; and New Orleans incident, 47; officers as targets for, 8, 9, 40, 41–42, 216n21; and pillage of homes, 207; and poisoned food, 7–8; and policy implementation, 3, 15, 95, 185, 196–97, 202, 243n31; and Pope in Virginia, 31, 40; and prisoners of war, 2, 7–9, 11, 13–14, 58, 66–67, 84–85, 94–95, 110, 148–49, 150, 151, 160, 162, 163, 165, 168–73, 176, 180, 185, 186, 192, 202, 203; proportional response of, 8, 10, 148; public opinion of, 10–11, 14, 185; and punishment for plundering, 41; and rations for prisoners, 11, 13–14, 150, 162, 168–73; and retaliation correspondence, 9–10, 32–33, 34, 41, 42, 65–66, 86, 92, 102, 103, 104, 106–7, 147–48, 149, 150, 153, 167, 169–70, 192, 196, 197, 198–99; rituals of, 2, 3, 4, 6, 7, 8, 9, 10, 12, 14, 41, 47, 50, 67, 73, 79, 80, 85, 86, 87, 94, 99, 103, 112, 139, 146, 147, 150, 153, 157, 162, 170, 176, 189, 192, 194, 195, 196, 197, 199, 202, 207, 211, 214n5, 217n28, 220n53; and slaves, 11; and soldiers' behavior, 3, 197, 199; as sternest feature of war, 2, 16; threats of, 41, 43, 75, 94, 99, 136; and torture, 14; and treatment of prisoners, 8, 11, 13–14, 15, 16, 85, 94, 146, 188; and unauthorized acts, 7, 14; and Union officials, 2, 7, 8, 43, 95; and Union prisoners of war, 168–69; and use of Black troops, 4, 43, 56, 57, 85, 94, 95; and U.S. War Department, 2, 33, 34, 94, 95, 168–69; and violence, 4, 180, 192, 199
Ripley, Roswell S., 148
Rivers, Prince, 15, 51, 52, 55
Rogers, Seth, 50, 52, 55–56, 58, 62, 226n61
Russell, Henry Sturgis, 39, 40, 41–42, 43

savage warfare: accusations of, 5, 16, 31–32, 136, 169, 182, 199, 207–9, 249n13; contrasted with civilized, 2, 5, 14, 50, 72, 208, 215n12, 216n13, 237n22; and escalation of violence, 124; historical verdict of, 212; in laws of war, 7, 9, 169, 188, 227n63, 231n34; and Reconstruction, 207–10; in retaliation correspondence, 197, 199; and sliding scale of human progress, 146, 158, 208; threat of, 5, 15, 50, 56, 58–59, 72, 75, 116, 123, 173, 178, 180, 190, 222n11; and women, 61, 116, 182, 199
Saxton, Rufus: and 2nd South Carolina, 58; and command of Black regiments, 36, 43, 44–45, 52; and Department of the South, 27, 36; and Jacksonville as a base, 60; and military as school for Blacks, 59; and occupation of Sea Islands, 36; and St. Mary's River raid, 52, 56
Schimmelfennig, Alexander, 146–47, 150
Scott, Winfield, 103
Sea Islands: and free labor communities, 19–20; skirmish on St. Catherine's, 45; skirmish on St. Helena's, 44; skirmish on St. Simon's, 34, 36; Union defense of, 34, 36, 54; Union army recruitment in, 21–23, 43
Seddon, James A.: and execution of Black prisoners, 45, 46, 98; and General Orders No. 100, 71–72; health of, 45; and military courts, 157; and prisoners of war, 99, 133–34, 156, 157, 230n24, 246n52; and proposal for Union prisoners, 145, 223n16; and retaliation, 6, 7, 46; as secretary of war, 6, 7, 15, 45, 46, 96, 97, 133, 145, 156, 244n44
Serrell, Edward W., 87, 102
servile insurrection: Confederate policy regarding, 57–58, 84, 202, 204; Confederate views of, 15, 45, 50, 56–57, 71, 207; prosecution for, 96, 98–99, 223n16; retaliation for, 47; Union views of, 21, 225n39
Sepoy Mutiny. *See* Indian Rebellion of 1857–59

Seward, William Henry, 137
Seymour, Truman, *118*; and 7th New Hampshire, 120; and 8th USCT, 120–21; and 54th Massachusetts, 126; and Battle of Olustee, 120, 122, 123, 126–27, 236n14; bizarre behavior of, 117; and Confederate cavalry, 114; and Confederate prisoners' rations, 161–62; and exchange of prisoners, 153; and execution of Black soldiers, 116, 235n7; and fighting Lee's army, 143; and Florida expedition, 117, 119, 120, 134; and Fort Wagner, 117, 120, 127; and Lake City, Fla., 119; and letter to Finegan, 128; as prisoner of war, 145; and private property, 114, 115; and retaliation, 162; and treatment of Black soldiers, 129–30, 134; and treatment of prisoners, 152–53, 161–62; and village of Baldwin, 117; war experience of, 117
Shaw, Francis George: 20, 94, 97, 207–8
Shaw, Robert Gould: and 2nd Massachusetts Infantry, 18, 39, 74; and 54th Massachusetts, 1, 50, 73, 88, 97–98, 163; background of, 17–18; burial of, 1, 15, 91, 93, 97, 125, 127, 128, 164; and civilized war, 19, 29, 73, 74, 221n3; and command of Black regiments, 15, 68, 81; Confederate order against, 38; and Darien, Ga., expedition, 74–75, 226n61; death of, 80, 88–89, 90, 93, 229n21; as felon and outlaw, 1, 18, *19*, 33; and Fort Wagner, 88, 93, 97, 117, 228n9, 228n11; and guards over private property, 29–30; international opinion of, 97–98; and Montgomery, 58, 74, 77, 87, 226n61; and Pope in Virginia, 73; and retaliation, 3, 18, 19, 85; and Henry Sturgis Russell, 38, 39, 42, 43; strict discipline of, 73–74; and use of Black troops, 19, 75
Shaw, Sarah Blake, 97, 207–8
Sherman, William Tecumseh: appointment of as superintendent of contrabands, 20; and Atlanta's capture, 163; and Black labor on plantations, 21; and burning of property, 179, 189, 191, 198, 201; cavalry of, 181; and civilized war, 175, 191; and command of Union armies, 184, 187, 188, 191, 199; and conduct in South Carolina, 184, 209; and customs of war, 199, 248n5; and Department of the South, 3, 163, 175; and discipline of army, 179, 198; and executions, 16, 173, 176, 180, 196–98, 199, 252n46; and foraging, 177, 194–95, 197–98, 201; and feud with Hampton, 209–10; Georgia campaign of, 176, 177, 178, 183–84; and guerrillas, 176; and Hitchcock, 175; and hostages, 176; inconsistency of, 178, 248n2; and invasion of South Carolina, 189–91; and land mines, 183; and march to Savannah, 183–84, 203; and murder of foragers, 196–98, 199, 200; in North Carolina, 200–201; and pillaging soldiers, 181, 189, 190, 194, 197, 198, 199, 201; and prisoners of war, 183, 187, 199; and question of destruction, 177, 190–91; and retaliation, 135, 138, 176, *178*, 180, 181, 182, 183, 194–95, 195, 196–98, 202; and retaliation correspondence, 199; and soldiers' behavior, 200, 249n13; and staff of, *180*; and treatment of persons and property, 176, 197–98, 199, 199–200, 212; Union troops under, 19, 173, 175, 176, *178*, 197–98; and use of Black troops, 26
Sigel, Franz, 30
slavery: and Black prisoners of war, 98, 99, 132, 133, 204; and Blacks as "savages," 59, 116, 222n11; and Civil War, 17, 26, 47, 56–57, 60, 68, 77, 124, 204; and Confederacy, 47, 56–57, 96; destruction of, 87; and emancipation of slaves, 24, 29, 42, 56, 57; family separation as feature of, 23; and freed Blacks as laborers, 29; as labor system, 206; and laws of war, 71; and Lincoln's abolition policy, 23, 29; Montgomery's war against, 58; and Northern Republicans, 56; and pay of Black soldiers, 157; and prisoners of war, 155; and protection of white women, 61; punishments of, 49, 74; and retaliation, 71, 94; selling of Americans into, 66, 95, 234n63; and slaveholding Confederate women, 176; and slaves on Union steamers, 69; and South Carolina law, 96; and treatment of runaway slaves, 84; and

slavery (*continued*)
use of dogs, 184; and use of freed slaves as troops, 26, 36, 47, 49, 60
Slocum, Henry W., 177, 179, *180*, 189, 201, 248n8
Smalls, Robert, 24
Smythe, Augustine Thomas, 141–44, 148, 240n2
Sol Legare Island, S.C.: 54th Massachusetts picket fight, 82–85, *83*; Black prisoners captured on, 84, 98, 134, *154*, 204
South Carolina: and 1st South Carolina Volunteers, 43–44, 52; and 54th Massachusetts, 96, 110, 111, 254n58; and Andersonville Prison, 155, 156, 157, 161; and Black prisoners of war, 85, 96, 110, 111, 134, 156, 203, 253n56; and Bonham, 96, 98–99, 110, 134, 155, 167, 168; and Charleston, S.C., 1, 2, 3, 15, 18, 19, 24, 63–64, 68, 78, 80, 84, 86, 87, 91, 92, 93, 95, 100, 102–3, 104, 106, 109, 110, 112, 139, 141, *142*, 144, 145, 146, 150, 152, 153, 155, 156, 159, 161, *166*, 167, 172, 173, 184, 204–5, 212; and Charleston Harbor, 80, 84, 109, 153, 161; and Charleston Jail, 96, 134, 153, 155, 167; and Confederate troops, 119, 184, 198; and execution of prisoners of war, 16, 180, 252n49; Federal campaigns against, 3, 15, 60, 63–64, 85–91, 102–7, 108–9, 112, 139, 150, 180; and Fort Gregg, 1, 2; and Fort Strong, 1, 2; and Fort Sumter, 81, 100, 205; and Fort Wagner, 1, 15, 87, 88–91, *89*, 94, 98, 111; free-born Black prisoners in, 96, 98–99; and Hilton Head, S.C., 17, 73, 84, 93, 109, 168, 170, 173, 185, *187*; and hostages, 96, 112, 202; Hunter's actions in, 27, 28, 93; and importance of Charleston, S.C., 147; and James Island, 24–25, *24*, 81–82, 87, 96; and killing of Union foragers, 180, 199–200; martial law in, 21; and Morris Island, S.C., 1–2, 81, 84–85, 87, 92, 96, 100, 104, 134, 143, 150–51, 152, 153, 171; and pillaging soldiers, 198, 201; prisoners of war in, 161, 169, 173, 183, 186–88, 247n62; during Reconstruction, 210; and retaliation, 95, 202; and river raids, 17, 68–70, 81; Sea Islands of, 19–20, *20*, *54*; Sherman's dislike of, 197; Sherman's invasion of, 189–91, 192, 251n31; and Sol Legare Island, 98, 134, 204; and trial of Black prisoners of war, 96, 111; and Union bombardment of Charleston, S.C., 141–43; and Union prisoners of war, 151–52, 168–69; and use of Black troops, 18, 25–26, 43–44, 47; war crimes in, 199. *See also* Department of the South
Stanton, Edwin: and Black men as soldiers, 24, 25–27, 34, 36, 38, 43, 44, 47, 69, 110; and Black prisoners, 95, 96; and Confederate prisoners' rations, 161, 169, 187–88; and creation of new army, 27; and Department of the South, 43, 44, 68, 69; and emancipation of slaves, 28, 44; and events in Virginia, 27; and Hunter's retaliation letter, *66*; and investigation of Fort Pillow massacre, 135; and laws of war, 95; and McClellan, 27–28; and prisoners of war, 161, 163, 169; and retaliation, 9, 14, 47, 67, 94–95, 137, 162, 169; as secretary of war, 11, 24, 25–26, 27, 28, 56, 64, 94–95, 158, 161, 175, 187, 188; and treatment of Union prisoners, 13, 14, 94–95, 217n27
States, Daniel, 15, 91, 204
Stephens, George E., 130
Strong, George C., 87–90, 228n9
Stuart, J. E. B., 31
Sumner, Charles, 185–86, 230n26
Sutton, Robert, 52, 55–56
Swamp Angel battery, 102–3, 104, 107

Taliaferro, William, 91
Taylor, Susie King, 36, *37*, 43
Terry's Texas Rangers (8th Texas), 181, 192, 251n34
Todd, George Rogers Clark, 156
torpedoes, 103, 108, 183
Trowbridge, Charles T., 22, 34, 36, 43, 44, 52
Truth, Sojourner, *154*, 155
Tubman, Harriet, 68–69
Turner, John W., 130

Union army: 15th Corps of, 184, 202; 17th Corps of, 177, 183, 200, 201, 202; and armies in Missouri and Mississippi, 33; and Army of Georgia, 175; and Army of the Tennessee, 175; and Army of Virginia, 30, 42; behavior of soldiers in, 31, 50, 52, 75–77, 116, 207; and burning of property, 178, 180, 190, 191, 192, 195, 204–5; casualties of, 121, 122, 123, 124–25; cavalry of, 114, 119, 134; and civilized war, 27, 50, 52, 55, 70, 72–73, 80, 123, 148, 178, 190, 212; and Confederate prisoners of war, 152–53; and confiscation of rebel resources, 30, 50, 54, 55–56, 69, 72; and court-martialing of stragglers, 179; and Department of the South, 3, 17, 50, 68–69, 113; and destruction of property, 50, 54, 64, 69, 70, 81, 178–79, 201; discipline of, 179, 200; and emancipation of slaves, 81, 115; and executions, 179, 202; foraging of, 114, 115, 177, 180, 181, 190, 194, 197–99, 201–2; former slaves in, 15, 17, 36, 62, 77, 133, 203, 204; freed Blacks in, 60; and fugitive slaves, 72; and General Orders No. 100, 70–71, 72, 73, 74; and laws of war, 55, 62, 63, 70, 73, 94, 179; manual labor of, 100, 109–10; and murder of foragers, 199–200; in North Carolina, 200–201; and officers' offenses, 32–33; and pillaging soldiers, 181, 190, 191, 192, 197–98; and prisoners of war, 98–99, 155–56; and private property, 145, 147, 191, 192, 198; and rape, 116; and retaliation, 18, 150, 198, 200, 207; savagery of, 178; and segregated regiments, 29; and straggling, 177, 178, 181, 195, 199; tactics manual of, 168; and treatment of persons and property, 11, 62, 64–65, 182; and treatment of prisoners, 152–53; and treatment of women, 182; and troops' behavior, 18, 50, 52, 61–62, 64–65; and Union prisoners of war, 2, 130; and use of Black troops, 4, 17, 18, 19, 27, 50, 54, 75, 80, 81, 100, 109–10, 130; and use of Greek fire, 102–3, *105*, 107; weapons technology of, 119; white soldiers in, 52, 55–56, 58, 61, 62, 64, 65, 75, 81, 82, 91, 100, 101–2, 110, 151. *See also* Georgia; Emilio, Luis F.; Foster, John G.; Florida; Grant, Ulysses S.; Halleck, Henry W.; Hunter, David; South Carolina; Virginia; *and individual regimental designations, campaigns, and battles*

Union navy: Black prisoners from, 95–96, 155, 166–67, 231n31, 246n51; and Charleston Harbor, 63–64, 81, 85, 100, 108; and conflict with army, 28, 64, 108; and operations in Florida, 60; and Sea Islands, 17, 19, 34

United States: oath of allegiance to, 30, 60, 130; and presidential election, 114, 135–36; Reconstruction period in, 135, 136, 207–8, 209, 210–11; spread of empire of, 211; and War for Independence, 71; and War of 1812, 71, 78, 97, 186; and western Indian wars, 182

U.S. Colored Troops. *See* Black troops; *and individual units*

U.S. Congress: and authorization to seize property, 20; and debate over ration retaliation, 185–86; and 1868 investigation of prisoner treatment, 208; and emancipation, 24, 29; and investigation of Fort Pillow massacre, 136; and prisoner exchange, 161

Usher, John P., 137

U.S. War Department: and 54th Massachusetts, 95, 110, 157; and Army of Virginia, 28; and Blacks as soldiers, 44, 65; and captured Black sailors, 95; and civilized war, 70; and Confederate Congress, 202; and Confederate prisoners of war, 168–69; and confiscation of property, 32; and constituencies' opinions on retaliation, 11; and controversy among Lincoln and McClellan, 33; and Department of the South, 27; and disagreement with McClellan, 27; and equality in pay, 112; and events in Virginia, 36, 167; and exchange of prisoners, 161, 163; and execution of Indigenous people, 211; and General Orders No. 100, 70–71,

U.S. War Department (*continued*) 94; and Hitchcock, 14–15, 163; and laws of war, 73, 94, 211; and Lee's letter, 32, 33, 34; and Lincoln's policies, 65; and occupation of Port Royal, 27; and pay of Black soldiers, 157, 158; and prisoners of war, 185; and protection of Black Federal soldiers, 73; and removal of Pope from command, 42; and retaliation, 34, 73, 117, 161; and soldiers' plundering, 42; and Union navy, 17, 63–64; and Union prisoners of war, 11; and withholding rations for Confederates, 146. *See also* Stanton, Edwin

Vattel, Emer de: *Law of Nations*, 78, 104, 107, 197, 227n63
violence: and Black soldiers, 44, 95, 124, 138; in civilized war, 5; dynamics of in Civil War, 4, 202, 214n7, 217n28; escalation of, 10, 117, 124, 136–38, 146, 192, 198; protection of noncombatants from, 6; restraint of in warfare, 5–6, 8, 14, 29, 73, 100, 136, 176, 180, 192, 215n12, 250n21
Virginia: and 2nd Massachusetts Infantry, 18; and Army of Virginia, 28, 30–31; and Battle of the Crater, 138; and Battle of the Wilderness, 145; and Beauregard, 78; and bombardment of Fredericksburg, 103; and Confederate veterans, 119; escaped slaves from, 113, 231n38; fighting in, 137, 163, 176; and Grant, 176; and guerrillas, 214n6, 252n47; and Hampton, 195, 196; and Lee's army, 143; and John Letcher, 41; and McClellan, 27, 28, 29; Pope's officers in, 92; population of, 30; and prisoners of war, 166, 167; and Richmond, 13, 28, 29, 39, 41, 84, 96, 99, 106, 109, 134, 144, 162, 167; and siege of Petersburg, 8; and trial of Union officers, 41, 234n63; Union forces in, 28, 29, 36, 40, 42, 143; and use of Blacks as slaves, 133, 239n40

Wade, Benjamin, 136
Welles, Gideon, 28, 63–64, 96, 137
Wheeler, Joseph: and capture of stragglers, 181; cavalry of, 177, 181; and killing of Union foragers, 181, 248n10, 251n34, 252n49; Kilpatrick's letter to, 192, 194; and retaliation ritual, 192, 194
Wilkins, Harry, 54
Wilkins, James A., 123
Wilkins, William D., 42
Wilson, James D., 82, 83, 227n4
Wilson, Joseph T., 208–9, 254n3
Wilson, William, 95, 167, 230n30, 231n30, 246n51
women: and bombardment of Charleston, 104–6, 145–46, 148; in General Orders No. 100, 70; as measure of civilization, 61, 116, 182; protection of in civilized war, 6, 61, 127–28, 182, 189, 199; and rape, 61, 116, 126, 182, 235n7, 249n13; and removal from Charleston, 104, 233n48; and resistance to Hunter's conscription, 23; and treatment by Union army, 55, 61–65, 124, 143, 176, 182, 190, 195, 207, 211–12, 214n6, 223n20, 235n7
Worthington, Henry, 98, 168, 228n5, 231n38